EMPLOYMENT LAW AT THE
EUROPEAN COURT OF JUSTICE

Despite the fact that the case-law of the European Court of Justice on employment related issues has become increasingly erratic of late, there is no denying the centrality of the Court's role in the development of EC employment law. Though concentration on the work of the Court of Justice may no longer be in vogue, this book examines its contribution in the employment law field in its political and economic context, as well as with reference to the juridical structures within which the Community's judicial arm is obliged to operate.

The objective is not simply to critique the employment jurisprudence of the Court but also to examine the procedural, operational and structural context in which the Court of Justice is obliged to work and to reflect on how this context may affect the jurisprudential outcome. The book focuses, in particular, on the shortcomings of the preliminary reference procedure. When the Court of Justice hands down decisions in the employment law field, Article 234 EC dictates a particular type of judicial dialogue between it and the national referring courts. It is contended that the dual dispute resolution/public interest nature of the Court's role in the preliminary reference procedure goes some way to explaining why its answers are often regarded as unsatisfactory from the perspective of the referring court and 'users' of EC law generally. The book further outlines the developing Community policy on employment and reflects on the effect which this nascent policy may have on the balancing exercises which the Court is inevitably called upon to perform in a variety of social policy contexts. Finally, part two of the book examines specific substantive areas of EC employment law. The policy considerations at play in the case-law of the Court are discussed in detail, as is the coherence of this case-law with the Community's political stance on employment.

Employment Law at the
European Court of Justice

Judicial Structures, Policies and Processes

SIOFRA O'LEARY

·H A R T·
PUBLISHING
OXFORD – PORTLAND OREGON
2002

Hart Publishing
Oxford and Portland, Oregon

Published in North America (US and Canada) by
Hart Publishing c/o
International Specialized Book Services
5804 NE Hassalo Street
Portland, Oregon
97213-3644
USA

Hart Publishing is a specialist legal publisher based in Oxford, England.
To order further copies of this book or to request a list of other
publications please write to:

Hart Publishing, Salter's Boatyard, Folly Bridge,
Abingdon Road, Oxford OX1 4LB
Telephone: +44 (0)1865 245533 or Fax: +44 (0)1865 794882
e-mail: mail@hartpub.co.uk
WEBSITE: http//www.hartpub.co.uk

British Library Cataloguing in Publication Data
Data Available
ISBN 1–84113–233–0 (hardback)

Typeset by Hope Services (Abingdon) Ltd.
Printed and bound in Great Britain on acid-free paper by
Biddles Ltd, www.biddles.co.uk

Contents

Acknowledgements

T HE BODY OF work for this book was done when I was based in Frankfurt in 1999–2000 enjoying an honorary appointment as Visiting Fellow of the Faculty of Law, University College Dublin. My thanks to the members of the Faculty and, in particular, to Dean Paul O'Connor, for their support and interest during this period and indeed since the beginning of my legal education.

I would also like to thank past and present colleagues at the Court of Justice of the European Communities who in various ways helped in the gestation of this book. Particular thanks to former colleagues in the Chambers of the late Judge G.F. Mancini, especially Vittorio di Bucci, whose vast legal knowledge and skill made working with him a veritable honour. It has been with considerable sadness and regret that I have not been able, while working on the book, to call on the advice and no doubt pointed criticism which Judge Mancini himself would have generously provided. The book, inspired partly by his contagious commitment to and interest in EC labour law and social policy, would undoubtedly have benefitted from his legal skill and wisdom.

My thanks go to Dr. José María Fernández Martín, Vittorio di Bucci, Marie Demetriou, Leo Flynn and Ulf Öberg, all of whom generously took time to contribute comments and criticisms on various chapters of the book at different stages in its development. Particular thanks, however, go to Dr. Bernard Ryan of the University of Kent, who uncomplainingly pored over the whole manuscript, provided insightful criticism and suggestions that have been invaluable, and responded to numerous e-mails. The errors and weaknesses that remain are, it goes without saying, of my own making and the views expressed are purely personal.

Finally, I would like to thank all those whose warmth and support during the course of preparation of the book—in which time I changed job, country (twice), house (three times) and became a mother—have made a period of frenetic change and activity both memorable and moving. Thanks, in particular, to Alison, for her unswerving long distance support and friendship, Cristina, Franca, Juliet, Una, Uli, Maxi and, of course, the very special O'Learys.

This book is for Camilo and Pepe—they know.

Síofra O'Leary
Luxembourg
June 2002

Introduction

IT IS COMMONPLACE in analyses of the work and operation of the Court of Justice of the European Communities to mention, even in passing, Professor Eric Stein's mythical characterisation of the Court—its fairytale location in the Duchy of Luxembourg and the benign neglect with which it was originally treated by the powers that be and the mass media.[1] The role played by the Court of Justice in the advancement of European integration is regarded, even by the Court's critics, as something of an orthodoxy.[2] However, more recent assessments of its contribution to the development of EC law rarely overlook the changed atmosphere of academic debate and comment on the Court's work since Stein first penned his oft-quoted characterisation. In political circles too, the Court's previously unchallenged ascendancy has come under attack. One of the prices, for example, of inclusion of a reference to the European Community's commitment to fundamental rights and the establishment of titles devoted to a common foreign and security policy and justice and home affairs was precisely the exclusion in the Maastricht Treaty of the possibility of judicial review by the Court of Justice. Successive intergovernmental conferences have also heard calls for the Court's wings to be clipped, as some Member States became increasingly riled at what they perceived as the Court's interference in areas of Member State sovereignty. At least some of this pressure has been the result of decisions of the Court in the labour law field, not least *Barber* or *Bötel*.[3]

---

[1] E. Stein, 'Lawyers, Judges and the Making of a Transnational Constitution' (1981) 75 *American Journal of International Law* 1–27, 1. According to Weiler, what this 'house that Eric built' achieved was to assert that a constitutional framework had come into being long before the Court was willing to use that vocabulary or, arguably, even think in those terms (J.H.H. Weiler, 'The Reform of European Constitutionalism' (1997) 35 *Journal of Common Market Studies* 97–131, 101).

Note that although the correct name for the Court is the Court of Justice of the European Communities, it is referred to throughout this work, for the sake of simplicity, as the Court, Court of Justice or European Court of Justice.

[2] See, *inter alia*, S. Weatherill, 'The common market: mission accomplished?' in V. Heiskanen and K. Kulovesi (eds.), *Function and Future of European Law* (Helsinki, Publications of the University of Helsinki, 1999) pp.33–57; A. Easson, 'Legal Approaches to European Integration: The Role of Court and Legislator in the Completion of the European Common Market' (1989) XII *Revue d'Intégration européenne/Journal of European Integration* 100–119; and H. Schepel and R. Wesseling, 'The Legal Community: Judges, Lawyers, Officials and Clerks in the Writing of Europe' (1997) 3 *European Law Journal* 165–88, 166.

[3] Cases C–262/88 *Douglas Harvey Barber v Guardian Royal Exchange Assurance Group* [1990] ECR I–1889 and C–360/90 *Arbeiterwohlfahrt der Stadt Berlin e.V. v Monika Bötel* [1992] ECR I–3589.

Mattli and Slaughter observe that:

judicial decisions that consistently and sharply contradict majority policy preferences are likely to undermine perceptions of judicial legitimacy and can result in legislative efforts to restrict or even curtail judicial jurisdiction . . . . An astute judge will anticipate these reactions and seek to avoid them.[4]

Whether the Court has acted astutely or not in recent years, it is clearly no longer the benignly neglected judicial institution of yore. The honeymoon is said to be over, with the Community's judicial institution becoming the subject of increasing comment and criticism.[5] Indeed, since the lack of critical comment on the Court's work was first remarked upon and debated,[6] the circle seems to have come full circle. Some commentators now question what they perceive as 'a stifling and defensive intellectual environment characterised by self-identification with the project of integration perceived somehow as precarious and fragile'[7] and complain of the too central role attributed to the Court in European legal studies.[8] Others describe a general 'sense of waning faith in the Court's institutional legitimacy.'[9] In the specific context of labour law, Simitis has observed that

---

[4] See W. Mattli and A.-M. Slaughter, *Constructing the EC Legal System from the Ground up: The Role of Individual Litigants and National Courts*, EUI WP RSC No.96/56, p.29.

[5] See Schepels and Wesseling, above n 2, 185. See also G. De Búrca, 'The Principle of Subsidiarity and the Court of Justice as an Institutional Actor' (1998) 36 *Journal of Common Market Studies* 217–35, 220: 'the Court seems to have been the focus of a more overt and sustained level of critical attention from the political sphere than that which even its bolder rulings in earlier years had attracted.' and the Editorial Comment, 'Quis custodiet the European Court of Justice?' (1993) 30 *Common Market Law Review* 899–903.

[6] See, for example, J.H.H. Weiler, 'Journey to an Unknown Destination: A Retrospective and Prospective of the European Court of Justice in the Arena of Political Integration' (1993) 31 *Journal of Common Market Studies* 417–46, who refers to the 'benign neglect' which the Court enjoyed for some time and the absence of any challenge to its legitimacy.

[7] See Schepel and Wesseling, above n 2, 169. See also Weiler (1993), *ibid*, 431–32; Mattli and Slaughter, above n 4, p 41: 'the era of respectful and unquestioning adulation of the Court is over.' D. Chalmers, 'Judicial Preferences and the Community Legal Order' (1997) 60 *Modern Law Review* 164–99, 172: 'while [specialist practitioners and academics] have the capacity to exercise a restraining influence upon the Court, it has been argued elsewhere that for a considerable period of time they formed an epistemic community, united not simply by their knowledge but by their deference to the Court of Justice'. J. Shaw, 'European Union Legal Studies in Crisis? Towards a New Dynamic' (1996) 16 *Oxford Journal of Legal Studies* 231–53; and M. Poiares Maduro, W*e, the Court. The European Court of Justice and the European Economic Constitution* (Oxford, Hart Publishing, 1998) p 22.

[8] See, for example, C. Kilpatrick, 'Community or Communities of Courts in European Integration? Sex Equality Dialogues Between UK Courts and the ECJ' (1998) 4 *European Law Journal* 121–47, 123; and the Introduction by J. Shaw in J. Shaw and G. More (eds), *New Legal Dynamics of European Union* (Oxford, Clarendon Press, 1995) pp 1–14, p 7.

[9] See T. Friedbacher, 'Motive Unmasked: The European Court of Justice, the Free Movement of Goods and the Search for Legitimacy' (1996) 2 *European Law Journal* 226–50, 226; A. Arnull, 'Judicial architecture or judicial folly? The challenge facing the European Union' (1999) 24 *European Law Review*. 516–24, 516; Editorial comment (1993) in *Common Market Law Review*, above n 5; P. Demaret, 'Le juge et le jugement dans l'Europe d'aujourd'hui: la Cour de justice des Communautés européennes' in R. Jacob (ed), *Le juge et le jugement dans les traditions juridiques européennes: Études d'histoire comparée* (Paris, L.G.D.J., 1996) pp 303–77, p 375, for a discussion

the large number of decisions on more or less routine conflicts, potentially repeatable in almost every employment relationship, is forcing the Court of Justice to abandon the Luxembourg idyll and to face growing publicity.[10]

Regardless of the fact that the national media are still unable to differentiate between the Court and its human rights counterpart in Strasbourg, or to grasp the distinction between an Advocate General's Opinion and a Court ruling, the fact remains that its decisions have become the subject of heightened political and popular scrutiny and its employment case-law has contributed in no small part to the greater publicity it now enjoys.

Given this prevailing critical legal *zeitgeist* amongst European Court watchers, it is probably advisable to commence any work whose focus is the Court and its contribution to a specific field of substantive EC law with some sort of apologia. Although the examination of the Court's work may no longer be in vogue and its contribution to the field of EC employment law, amongst others, has become increasingly erratic, there is no denying its centrality in this, as in other areas, of substantive EC law.[11] This is not the place to enter into the ongoing debate on whether or not the Court has indulged in unwanted or illegitimate judicial activism.[12] In certain areas, not least in the employment field, the Court has undoubtedly adopted ground-breaking decisions which could be said to have influenced the Community's political institutions when they came to adopt EC legislation. The protection of pregnant workers and those on maternity leave is one such example. Referring to the shifting nature of the Court's pregnancy and maternity rulings,[13] Davies has questioned the wisdom of the Court

of the increasing criticism of the Court by Member State governments and national courts; and generally P. Davies, 'The European Court of Justice, National Courts, and the Member States' in P. Davies *et al* (eds), *European Community Labour Law: Principles and Perspectives. Liber Amicorum Lord Wedderburn of Charlton* (Oxford, Clarendon Press, 1996) pp 95–138, for discussion of the need for acceptance of the Court's decisions by national courts and Member State governments.

[10] See S. Simitis, 'Dismantling or Strengthening Labour Law: The Case of the European Court of Justice' (1996) 2 *European Law Journal* 156–76, 160; and generally Friedbacher, *ibid*, 248, who points out that, as the most visible protector of the Community's core values, the Court is an obvious target for resentment.

[11] See also S. Leibfried and P. Pierson, 'Social Policy' in H. Wallace and W. Wallace (eds), *Policy-making in the European Union* (Oxford, OUP, 1996) pp 185–207, p.204, who comment on the unusually court-driven nature of EC social policy: 'It is as much a series of rulings from the ECJ as the process of Commission and Council initiative that has been the source of new social policy. While the Council and Commission are prone to stasis, the ECJ's institutional design fosters activism. Once confronted with litigation, the ECJ cannot escape making what are essentially policy decisions as a matter of routine.'

[12] For the latest outbreak of hostilities in the ongoing debate on judicial activism at the Court of Justice see, *inter alia*, T. Hartley, 'The European Court, Judicial Objectivity and the Constitution of the European Union' (1996) *Law Quarterly Review* 95–109; T. Tridimas, 'The Court of Justice and Judicial Activism' (1996) 21 *European Law Review* 199–210; P. Neill, *The European Court of Justice: A Case Study in Judicial Activism* (London, European Policy Forum, 1995); and D. Keeling, 'In Praise of Judicial Activism. But What Does it Mean? And has the European Court of Justice Ever Practised it?' in *Scritti in onore di Giuseppe Federico Mancini*, Vol. II, Diritto dell'Unione Europea (Milano, Giuffrè, 1998) pp 505–36.

[13] See below ch 5.

seeking to 'hew out of the rock of discrimination law a specialized pregnancy and maternity regime' but he recognised nevertheless that, in terms of *realpolitik*, the Court's rulings spurred the Member States to giving serious consideration to the Commission's proposals on maternity rights.[14] Nevertheless, doubts persist about whether courts generally and the Court of Justice in particular are the correct fora for the resolution of social policy questions. Fredman, for example, has asked whether the Court's process of decision-making, its decision-makers and its method of gathering information are up to the task.[15] Although the preliminary reference procedure avoids the disadvantages of a bipolar dispute, since the Commission and Member States are entitled to intervene and the Advocate General is on hand with an independent opinion, judicial policy can only develop on an incremental case-by-case basis and is dependent on the random arrival of questions from national courts. It is difficult in these circumstances, as Fredman points out, to produce 'a comprehensive set of principles, and frequently equally difficult to prevent anomalies'. The Court's pregnancy case-law, discussed in chapter five, also provides testimony to this.

However, the Court has not always adopted an 'activist' mantle willingly; quite often this role has been thrust upon it due to inadequate or badly drafted legislation, usually the result of protracted political wrangling between Member States.[16] Indeed, the only way in which the Community's political institutions could have totally eliminated the need for the Court to resort to judicial discretion and policy reasoning would have been by drafting laws in wholly unambiguous ways, leaving no possible contingency uncovered.[17] Regardless of the wisdom of such an approach to legislative drafting, the EC's decision-making process makes the adoption of such legislation well nigh impossible. The case-

---

[14] See P. Davies, 'The European Court of Justice, National Courts, and the Member States' in Davies *et al*, above n 9, pp 127–29. He argues that a case-by-case approach to the resolution of major social problems does not yield a coherent set of rules, pointing not only to the Court's pregnancy case-law but also to the judicial saga involving pensions which followed Case C–262/88 *Barber*. On the importance of interaction between the Court and other institutions and the effect which the Court's rulings may have on the balance of power in the policy-making process see D. Wincott, 'The Court of Justice and the European policy process' in J.J. Richardson (ed), *European Union. Power and Policy-making* (London and New York, Routledge, 1996) pp 170–84, p 183.

[15] S. Fredman, 'Social Law in the European Union: The impact of the lawmaking process' in P. Craig and C. Harlow (eds), *Lawmaking in the European Union* (London, Kluwer Law International, 1998) pp 386–411, pp 402–05.

[16] See also I. Canor, *The Limits of Judicial Discretion in the European Court of Justice* (Baden Baden, Nomos, 1998) p 57: 'It is . . . inevitable that during the decision-making process the legal quality of a text is reduced. Important quality factor[s], such as proper terminology, clearly defined concepts, consistency between objectives and means, potential overlapping with other rules, tend to be reduced by the peculiarities of the Community's legislative process where differences in political attitudes and interests are usually greater than at the national level'; and P. Eeckhout, 'The European Court of Justice and the Legislature' (1998) 18 *Yearbook of European Law* 1–28, 17: 'The Court is increasingly asked to interpret relatively young Community legislation . . . . The interpretation of such legislation puts new demands on the Court, not only in terms of workload, but also, and perhaps more importantly, in terms of the nature of the Court's task.'

[17] See in this respect Canor, *ibid*, p 26.

law of the Court on acquired rights casts ample light on the difficulties which inadequately drafted or highly compromising legislation can throw up. Directive 77/187 was adopted with the objective of protecting employees in the context of increased industrial restructuring in the EEC.[18] Nevertheless, the Directive's provisions were minimalist to say the least, with central concepts such as what constitutes a transfer of an undertaking left undefined, despite the substantial differences at Member State level as regards what such concepts entail. The Court was thus given little choice but to provide the national courts requesting guidance with a clearer idea of what exactly the Community legislature had intended when it adopted the 1977 Directive. As Simitis points out, faced with inadequate legislative provisions the Court has been forced

> to compensate for the failure to act of the legislator and assume a responsibility which is not only foreign to the judiciary but in fact detrimental to it.[19]

Numerous references followed concerning, *inter alia*, whether insolvency or related proceedings, contracting out, tripartite business and complicated lease arrangements came within the scope of application of the Directive. Over twenty years later, with the adoption of Directives 98/50 and 2001/23, which were intended to clarify the state of the law on acquired rights, the Community legislature and Member States, who had expressed dissatisfaction with aspects of the Court's case-law during the amendment procedure, could agree to do nothing better than to incorporate whole tracts of that case-law—lock, stock and barrel—into the amended text of the Directive.

THE OBJECTIVE AND REMIT OF THE BOOK

A brief overview of the normative framework within which the Court operates in the employment field is provided as part of this Introduction. Nevertheless, the reader would do well to remember that this book is not intended as a comprehensive analysis of EC employment legislation or the role of the various EC political institutions in the development of this law.[20] Neither does it cover all

---

[18] See below ch 6 and generally P. Davies, 'Transfers of Undertakings' in S. Sciarra (ed), *Labour Law in the Courts: National Courts and the European Court of Justice* (Oxford, Hart Publishing, 2001) pp 131–44.

[19] Simitis, above n 10, 164, 168 and 171: 'The strengthening of a political Union presupposes . . . the willingness of both the Council and the Commission to assume their responsibilities and therefore to stick, despite all difficulties, to policies and regulations that steadfastly put the Union's objectives into effect, instead of cumulating compromises and refining strategies of elusion. The better [this] condition is complied with, the more the European Court of Justice will be compelled to adopt a strictly case-oriented reasoning and to resist the ever present temptation to take on legislative functions.'

[20] Other authors have thankfully done such trojan work already. See, in particular, C. Barnard, *EC Employment Law*, 2nd edn (Oxford, OUP, 2000); B. Bercusson, *European Labour Law* (London, Butterworths, 1996); R. Nielsen and E. Szyszczak, *The Social Dimension of the European Union*, 3rd ed (Copenhagen, Handelshøjskolens Forlag, 1997); T. Hervey, *European Social Law and Policy* (Harlow, Longman, 1998); J. Shaw (ed), *Social Law and Policy in an Evolving European Union* (Oxford, Hart Publishing, 2001).

areas of EC employment law and social policy—from the free movement of workers and freedom of establishment to the intricacies of the European Social Fund or the applicability of national social security legislation to migrant workers pursuant to Regulation 1408/71. The aim of the book is more modest, namely to examine the contribution of the Court of Justice to the field of employment law, to appraise that case-law in the light of the procedural and structural limits within which the Court must work and to consider some of the policy considerations at play in its employment jurisprudence. A number of specific subject areas have been chosen in order to illustrate the type of policy issues with which the Court deals in the employment field and the constraints on its so-called dialogue with national courts pursuant to Article 234 EC. Although the choice of substantive subjects naturally reflects the particular preferences of the author, an effort has been made throughout to choose substantive areas which best illustrate the central arguments in the book and, obviously, those areas of EC employment law which have given rise to considerable case-law.

A quick perusal of academic journals, collections of essays and EC law monographs reveals the extent to which EC employment law and policy generally and specific issues such as indirect sex discrimination or employment protection have preoccupied certain academic circles for the past two decades. Barnard, Ellis, Hervey, Kilpatrick, McGlynn and Szyszczak have published numerous excellent works focusing on different aspects of EC sex discrimination law and examining the performance of the Court in this field.[21] While others, such as Hunt, have focused on acquired rights and judicial and legislative interaction in the shaping of EC law in that context.[22] The contextualists—Deakin, Shaw, Bercusson, and to a certain extent More and Barnard—have examined the legal, political and, in the case of Deakin in particular, economic context in which the EC's legislation and case-law must be placed.[23] At the same time, Davies, Simitis or Ryan, amongst others, have turned the critical eye of the labour law specialist on the performance of the Court of Justice and Community legislature in the employment field.[24]

---

[21] See variously, Barnard (2000), *ibid*; Kilpatrick (1998), above n 8; and C. McGlynn, 'Ideologies of Motherhood in EC Sex Equality Law' (2000) 6 *European Law Journal* 29–44.

[22] See, for example, J. Hunt, 'The Court of Justice as a Policy Actor: the case of the acquired rights directive' (1998) *Legal Studies* 336–59.

[23] See S. Deakin, 'Labour Law as Market Regulation: the economic foundations of European social policy' in Davies *et al* (eds), above n 9, pp 63–93.

[24] See, for example, Davies (1996), above n 9; Simitis, above n 10; and B. Ryan, 'Pay, trade union rights and European Community law' (1997) *International Journal of Comparative Labour Law and Industrial Relations* 305–25. As Weiler (1993), above n 6, 443, points out, the awakening of the interest of labour law or environmental law specialists has the advantage of importing far more critical apparatus to the treatment of EC law and its Court: 'the Community law importation will be judged against pre-existing substantive standards and also because these national fields have often developed their own critical tradition and the practitioners do not bring to the study of the EC and its court the exuberance of the first generation of Community lawyers.'

Note that only critics who have published in the English language are mentioned in this paragraph. This is not to detract from the work and contribution of leading EC and labour lawyers who have written in other languages, *inter alia*, Blanpain, Lyon-Caen, Vogel-Polsky, Rodríguez Piñeiro, Treu, Scarpone.

As for the wisdom of attempting to add to the aforementioned impressive body of work on EC employment law and policy, the thrust of this book and the hypotheses that it seeks to explore are distinct in at least two important respects. On the one hand, although, as in other studies, the case-law of the Court is central to the analysis, the objective here is to examine the procedural and structural context in which the Court of Justice is obliged to operate, specifically in the context of preliminary reference procedures, when handing down decisions in the employment law field. Article 234 EC dictates a particular type of judicial dialogue between the Court of Justice and national courts. Does the nature of this dialogue influence the manner and content of the Court's responses to national courts? How do internal Court procedures and working methods affect the outcome of cases? It is submitted that critiques of the Court's work—and this of course is not unique to the field of employment—often overlook these procedural or structural factors which determine the context in which the Court operates.[25]

On the other hand, the book outlines the developing EC policy on employment under Title VIII of the EC Treaty and reflects on the effect that this nascent policy may have on the balancing exercises which the Court is inevitably called upon to perform in a variety of social policy contexts.[26] The Court does not operate in an insulated judicial cocoon. In the employment field it, like the EC's other institutions, is conscious of one of society's most pressing problems, summarised by Simitis as follows: 'how can existing jobs be guaranteed while also creating new employment opportunities and without endangering the high standard of labour conditions already reached?'[27] Unsurprisingly, this highly problematic question is not answered in this book, but echoes of it surface throughout as a reflection of the political and economic context in which the Court is called upon to operate in the employment field. As regards the book's treatment of employment related issues, it should perhaps be specified that aspects of the law relating to the employment relationship (see, for example, chapter six on the Transfer of Undertakings Directive) and issues of employment policy (job creation, flexibility etc.) are both discussed. The latter is the

---

[25] See, for example, De Búrca (1998), above n 5, 232: 'The institutional constraints (its mode of appointment and lack of representativeness), textual constraints (such as are imposed by the Treaty) and practical constraints (the limits of the adjudicative forum) require the ECJ to adhere to a mode of reasoning and a set of considerations which differ from that which is open to the Community legislature when it explains why one particular policy choice is to be preferred over another.'

[26] Of the leading English language commentators on the Court's work in the employment field one in particular has focused on this question in the specific context of acquired rights: see the excellent article by G. More, 'The Acquired Rights Directive: frustrating or facilitating labour market flexibility?' in Shaw and More (eds), above n 8, pp 129–45. See also Barnard (2000), above n 20, p 27: 'the development of the Community's "social" policy is constrained—perhaps fatally—by the need to operate both within an economic and social framework [. . . .] this leads, on the one hand, to some inconsistent decisions by the Court concerning the interface between Community law on market integration and national law and, on the other, to a patchwork of Community social legislation aimed at both harmonization and minimum standards.'

[27] Simitis, above n 10, 162.

particular focus of chapter three, where the objective is to review the Court's case-law on diverse employment and indeed social policy issues over the years, before embarking on an analysis of the Employment Title. The former is the particular subject of chapter six, but clearly arises in chapters four and five as well, when indirect sex discrimination and pregnancy, maternity and childcare issues are discussed.[28]

One of the central aims of the book is thus a desire to flesh out some of the policy considerations which either surface in the decisions of the Court or which lie, sometimes barely hidden, within its rulings.[29] Contextual themes surface throughout the book—the interplay between the EU's political institutions and Member States on the one hand and its judicial institution on the other, or the tension between social and economic policy objectives which hovers throughout the Court's employment case-law. However, this is essentially a legal text, written by a lawyer. The work of the Court is thus central to the analysis of EC employment law herein, but its contribution is examined against the backdrop of the political and economic context, as well as the juridical structures within the context of which it must operate.[30]

THE PROBLEM WITH DECONSTRUCTION

The problem, of course, with deconstructing the case-law of a court which permits no dissenting opinions is that far simpler and even mundane reasons will sometimes lie behind the choice of a particular turn of phrase, far removed from the supposed policy considerations attributed to the Court by commentators. When a Court is obliged to deliberate a very large and growing number of cases on a weekly basis at both Chamber and plenary level, the risk that unfortunate turns of phrase or ambiguous terminology inadvertently, albeit clumsily, survive the deliberation process is clearly a real one. Furthermore, ambiguity may sometimes be the undesired but inevitable result of the collegiate nature of the Court's deliberations. There seems to be at least some truth in the observation that the Court's jurisprudence is not (always) the product of a fully worked out doctrine or agenda gradually developed but may owe more to serendipity or 'learning by doing'.[31] The fact that the Court does not exercise any form of docket control in the real sense and cannot determine the type or order of cases

---

[28] The terms 'labour' and 'employment' are used interchangeably in this context, regardless of the individual/collective rights connotations they may have for labour law specialists.

[29] Canor, above n 16, p 26, defines policy reasoning as the weighing and balancing of behavioural outcomes and their juridical implications.

[30] See the introduction by Shaw in Shaw and More (eds), above n 8, p 9, where she observes that political scientists' work on the Court of Justice rarely engages with a body of work on substantive EC policy areas which sometimes provides a less positive and more sanguine overall assessment of the contribution of the Court and which exhibits a strong sense of context—political and economic.

[31] See Wincott, above n 14, p 182.

being sent to it by national courts is also of importance. In addition, little attention has been paid in the past to the effect which the Court's adherence to one internal working language (which, by virtue of the history of European integration, is French), may have on the reasoning, expression and substantive content of its judgments. Any language imposes, whether by accident or intent, a certain intellectual mindset on its users. In the case of French, an unduly formalistic approach to the statement of the law may be the price being paid for the luxury of a single working language in the judicial institution which has to serve the multilingual EU.

One author has commented, in the context of the Court's free movement of goods case-law, that: [T]he possibility of distilling the Court's motive carries distinct appeal; the danger of motive analysis, however, lies precisely in this appeal . . . . "motivations" are appealing because they purport to discover the "deeper truth" by delving between the lines—a truth which, as the fruit of an essentially non-doctrinal analysis, cannot be "scientifically" (ie empirically) refuted, but then again also cannot be "scientifically" proven.[32] Nevertheless, the same author explains that the benefit of motive analysis is twofold. In the first place, it helps to locate the Court in the larger political landscape, offering some insight into how the Court as an institution affects that landscape and, conversely, how that landscape affects the institution. Secondly, motive analysis helps to supplement the technical analysis of a case or doctrine in order to better predict the direction the Court will take in future. If we are honest, policy, as distinct from political considerations, are part and parcel of the Court's adjudicative function pursuant to the Treaties,[33] although the Court rarely chooses to articulate those considerations clearly, if at all. One of the reasons why the Court's decisions inevitably involve the balancing of policy considerations is the general all-encompassing nature of its adjudicative function. Pursuant to Article 220 EC, the Court is charged with the fairly broad task of ensuring that in the interpretation and application of this Treaty the law is observed. In addition, EC Treaty principles such as discrimination, public policy, proportionality or solidarity are vague and do not stipulate on what considerations they are based. It is thus left to the Court of Justice, more often than not in the context of preliminary reference proceedings, to sort out, by a process of weighing and balancing different possible interpretations, what EC law actually requires. Finally, although the nature of the Court's adjudicative function pursuant to Article 234 EC combines elements of both dispute resolution and public interest litigation,[34] the purpose of this provision, which is to ensure the uniform interpretation of EC law, is itself very much policy-orientated.

---

[32] Friedbacher, above n 9, 235.

[33] For a convincing explanation why see Canor, above n 16; and C. Harlow, *Citizens Access to Political Power in the European Union*, EUI WP RSC No 99/2, p 45.

[34] See the discussion below in ch 2.

Fascinating suppositions may also be made about the consequences which development of EC law on an almost case-by-case basis may have (the Court having no recourse to the type of *certiorari* instrument used by the US Supreme Court to filter cases). In the context of its employment case-law, a good example is provided by a series of references received by the Court on the application of EC sex equality law to the employment rights of transsexuals, homosexuals and same-sex couples. In *P. v S. and Cornwall County Council*,[35] the Court was confronted with the plight of a transsexual applicant who had been fired from her teaching job as a result of a sex change operation. She relied, when claiming unfair dismissal, on Article 141 EC and the Sex Equality Directives adopted in the 1970s,[36] and won. In the words of Advocate General Tesauro, what was at stake in that case was 'a fundamental value, indelibly etched in modern legal traditions and in the constitutions of the more advanced countries: the irrelevance of a person's sex with regard to the rules regulating relations in society.'[37]

In the *Grant* case,[38] in contrast, which was a case clearly brought as a consequence of the Court's ruling in *P. v S.*, at issue was a travel allowance worth little more than £1000 per annum which the applicant's employer provided for employees' opposite sex partners but refused to same-sex partners. Grant's case failed, the Court choosing to confine its decision to a strict legal interpretation of the Equal Treatment Directive, to limit, therefore, the remit of its judgment in *P.* and to leave to the Community legislature the task of protecting same sex partners from sexual orientation discrimination. One can only speculate, however, what might have happened had the Court first been confronted with the dismissal of a certain Mr. Perkins before having to deal with the equal pay issue raised by *Grant*. As in *P.*, the applicant in the *Perkins* case had lost his job, this time as a direct consequence of his being homosexual—a ban on gays in the military existing at the time in the United Kingdom. After the decision in *Grant*, the national referring court, following an inquiry from the Court of Justice about whether it wished to maintain its questions, withdrew them. Had the Court been confronted first with this clearly more dramatic and costly case of hardship, would it have been more forthcoming on the scope and application of EC sex equality law than it had been when faced with what could be dismissed as the comparatively minor equal pay issue which arose in *Grant*?

An answer to this question may perhaps emerge in *KB v National Health Service Pensions Agency and another*, a reference from the English Court of Appeal.[39] The case involves a transgendered man, R, in an unmarried relationship with a woman, K. The latter works for the NHS and has requested that, in

---

[35] Case C–13/94 *P. v S. and Cornwall County Council* [1996] ECR I–2143.

[36] Specifically Council Directive 76/207/EEC of 9 February 1976 on the implementation of the principle of equal treatment for men and women as regards access to employment, vocational training and promotion and working conditions, OJ 1976 L39/40.

[37] Opinion of Advocate General Tesauro in Case C–13/94 *P. v S.*, para 24.

[38] Case C–249/96 *Lisa Jacqueline Grant v South-West Trains Ltd.* [1998] ECR I–621.

[39] Case C–117/01, OJ 2001 C150/13.

the event of her death, her pension be paid to R. The NHS pensions agency refused her application on the grounds that the assignment could only be made to those in a heterosexual relationship. As the Court of Appeal pointed out, however, although the respective conclusions in *P. v S.* and *Grant* are clear, the principle which distinguishes them is not. The national court reasoned that if the principle was that sex, as a ground of discrimination, included sexual identity and not sexual orientation, then given that the restriction in the present case was based directly on sex, the NHS refusal to give R pension rights amounted to discrimination. If the Court were to follow *P. v S.* in *KB*, one might be left with the impression that somewhere in *Grant* is a determination to avoid the financial implications which an inclusion of sexual identity within the Treaty prohibition would have for Member State social security and pension schemes. Whereas transgendered complainants are likely to be few and far between, an avalanche of claims could be expected from the gay community seeking to redress years of unequal treatment of their partners and unequal consideration of their own household responsibilities. Because, as Fredman has argued, it is national courts (and, in the background, determined litigants, trade unions and pressure groups) which determine the random arrival of questions at the Court of Justice, these cases also show how difficult it is for the Court, on the basis of Article 234 EC, to develop incrementally sound, coherent and principled judicial policy.

THE INDIVIDUAL CHAPTERS

Throughout the discussion of policy considerations in the book, the reader will come across two recurring themes. One is the suitability (and success) of the Article 234 EC reference procedure for the resolution of EC employment law disputes. The bulk of the cases which have come before the Court in the substantive areas chosen have arrived in Luxembourg by virtue of the reference procedure, rather than as a result of direct action by the Commission pursuant to Article 226 EC. Chapters one and two critically assess how the Court functions at present and examines the operation of the Article 234 EC reference procedure in practice.

Chapter one examines in considerable detail how the Court of Justice disposes of cases, preliminary references in particular. This involves analysis of the Treaty provisions on its membership and jurisdiction, the Statute of the Court, its Rules of Procedure and other documents in the public domain. This chapter is not only useful in the context of the ongoing debate on changes to the Community's judicial architecture, but it is also essential, it is submitted, to an understanding of how and why some of the Court's decisions disappoint. To understand how a case proceeds through the Court is to understand some of the constraints subject to which its members must operate: the oft-criticised time it takes the Court to resolve a case, the manner in which the Court drafts its decisions and even how the reasoning contained in those decisions is formulated. This chapter is not intended as an apology for the more ignominious examples of the Court's jurisprudence, but to criticise that jurisprudence without an understanding of these constraints is arguably to give an incomplete picture. Furthermore, if we are to exhort the Court to improve the quality of the justice (or just the law) that it is delivering, it is surely essential to identify the structural and procedural factors which may be influencing the sometimes unsatisfactory jurisprudence being handed down at present.

Chapter two also explains the constraints subject to which the Court must work, but this time in the specific context of the preliminary reference procedure. An examination of the latter could explain why the Court's answers to requests for preliminary rulings are sometimes regarded as unsatisfactory from the perspective of the referring court and 'users' of EC law generally. Chapter two specifically explores the dual dispute resolution and public interest nature of the Court's role in preliminary reference procedures. On the one hand, in increasingly detailed and complicated references involving ever more detailed questions from national courts, the Court of Justice has often been inexorably drawn closer to actual application of the relevant provisions of EC law to the facts of the case and, therefore, resolution of the dispute in hand. This happens despite the fact that its role pursuant to Article 234 EC is, in terms of EC law orthodoxy at least, confined to providing the referring court with interpretative guidance to assist in that court's resolution of the case. At the same time, as one commentator remarks 'the Court deals with questions which bear heavy implications on public interests, lays down principles, determines policy-lines, makes value choices, and formulates ideology which goes far beyond the parties of the case.'[40] This latter function seems inherent in the reference procedure, which is to ensure the uniform interpretation of EC law throughout the Community. In chapter two and subsequent chapters devoted to specific substantive areas of EC employment law, the book questions whether the Court is managing successfully to respond to the needs of national courts and whether the unresolved tension between the dispute resolution and public interest nature of its role in the preliminary reference procedure is not proving detrimental to the quality of the judicial product being delivered.

Calls for changes to the EC's judicial structures are not simply the product of the latest round of intergovernmental conferences. Over a decade ago, Weiler and Jacqué wrote of the need to give the Community's judicial architecture a major overhaul if its successful functioning was not to be jeopardised.[41] It is not the specific aim of this book to present proposals for the alteration of that

[40] See Canor, above n 16, p 16; and T. Koopmans, 'Judicial Decision-Making' in A.I.L. Campbell and M. Voyatzi (eds), *Legal Reasoning and Judicial Interpretation of European Law. Essays in Honour of Lord Mackenzie-Stuart* (London, Trenton Publishing, 1996) pp 93–104, p 98, where he refers to the tension between the propensity for deciding only what is indispensable for the case at hand and the view that the court is also the overseer of jurisprudential developments.

[41] See J.H.H. Weiler and J.P. Jacqué, 'On the Road to European Union—A New Judicial Architecture: An Agenda for the Intergovernmental Conference' (1990) 27 *Common Market Law Review*. 187–207, 199.

architecture; proposals which were to the forefront of the intergovernmental conference which concluded in December 2000 in Nice and which, mandated by enlargement, will no doubt resurface in future. If anything, chapters one and two are likely to throw up more problems than they solve in this respect, since they aim to examine how the Court operates and to highlight problems in its operations prior to the more focused analysis elsewhere in the book of the reference procedure under Article 234 EC, the role of this procedure in the development of EC employment law and the policy considerations which surface in the Court's jurisprudence in this field.

The other recurring theme is the nature of the EU's employment policy following the introduction of an employment title by the Treaty of Amsterdam and the interaction between the aims and objectives professed by the Union's political institutions and Member States and the case-law of the Court in the employment field. Chapter three first assesses the Court's perspective on employment and indeed social policy related issues in a variety of fields covered by the EC Treaty and secondary legislation. It looks at the coherence of the Court's line on employment prior to the introduction of a specific Treaty title addressing employment in the Amsterdam Treaty. An outline of this new title and the political initiatives and so-called 'soft law' which it has spawned is then provided. What are the EC's political actors and Member States required to do pursuant to this new Title and what has been achieved so far? Are the objectives of the EC's new employment policy consistent with the approach of the Court in employment cases to date or consistent with the body of EC social policy and employment legislation which the Court is regularly called upon to interpret and enforce, and vice versa? Essentially this chapter, perhaps the most difficult to integrate into the structure of the book, outlines the contours of the ongoing labour market flexibility debate which partly underpins the new Employment Title and examines the symbiosis between the case-law of the Court to date and the principal elements of this new Community employment policy.

The emphasis in the second part of the book is on specific substantive areas of EC employment law, on the policy considerations at play in the case-law of the Court and on the use of the preliminary reference procedure as a means to resolve employment law disputes in these various fields. Chapter four examines the fundamental principle of non discrimination on grounds of sex and, in particular, how the Court has managed to construct and then administer a balancing of interests when it comes to indirect sex discrimination. This chapter explores how the Court has developed its various tests, burdens of proof and objective justifications in the field of indirect sex discrimination. It also discusses whether and why, over time, the balance has been tilted in favour of one or other of the groups primarily concerned, namely employees, employers and, beyond labour law, in the case of social regulation, Member States. Chapter four also examines the operation of the preliminary reference procedure in the specific context of indirect discrimination. Do the judgments of the Court in this field reflect the tension between dispute resolution and public interest models of litigation discussed in chapter two? If so, can the Court be regarded as successfully imparting guidance to national courts on the correct interpretation (and/or application) of EC law in this field?

Chapter five studies the growing number of cases concerning the rights of pregnant workers, those on maternity leave or suffering from pregnancy related illness, and cases touching on childcare. Essentially, it appraises the approach of the Court to the delicate issue of balancing the family responsibilities of the worker, the interests of the employer and the requirements of the fundamental principle of equality. The case-law of the Court has developed on the back of the numerous preliminary reference questions which it has received from different national courts with reference to very different factual circumstances, and arguably lacks coherence. This lack of coherence can partly be attributed to two distinct and even opposing philosophies which inform the Court's rulings (and indeed EC legislation) in this area, namely equal treatment versus special treatment. With the Community's political institutions increasingly seduced by the charms of labour market flexibility, this chapter is of particular interest in terms of the compatibility of the Court's approach to employment protection with the EC's evolving employment policy, based as it is on principles, *inter alia*, of adaptability and, at the same time, equal opportunities.

A Directive on transfers of undertakings has been in place since 1977 and since its entry into force has been a rich source of cases before the Court, pursuant to Articles 226 and 234 EC, seeking both enforcement and interpretations of its provisions. What this case-law reveals are the difficulties the Court has experienced, in particular in the context of preliminary reference proceedings, in interpreting a clearly incomplete measure of social policy which requires a delicate balancing of the interests of both sides of industry and this against the background of an ever-changing economic climate. The core concepts in the 1977 Acquired Rights Directive were left largely to the Court to define and subsequent legislative amendments have done little to clarify matters, despite some Member States' and the Commission's outspoken dissatisfaction with the rulings of the Court. How successful has the Court been in giving clear and unambiguous guidance to national courts on how to interpret EC law on acquired rights, thereby facilitating its application by national courts to complicated business arrangements? A proliferation of references in acquired rights cases from the early 1990s onwards may be a cause for concern. Rather than being called upon to give overall guidance on how to interpret the Directive, the Court seems at times to be asked by national courts to apply the Directive to the particular facts of the case. In addition, as the complexion and minutiae of legal transfers change, some national courts seem unable or unwilling to glean from the already-established case-law of the Court the means to comply with the requirements of EC law. Is this due to an absence of clarity on the part of the Court or to the unwillingness of some national courts to assume greater responsibility for the application of EC law once the broad principles necessary for its interpretation have already been outlined by the Court?

THE LEGISLATIVE BACKGROUND

The focus of this book is on employment related social policy and on the general look and feel of EC employment law. The jury is still out concerning what EU social policy actually constitutes or seeks to achieve. As some commentators have remarked:

> It could be a debate about the place in economic and commercial development of social equity, of the fair distribution of resources, and of rights at work; or it could be about economic efficiency, and the degree to which this can be furthered through the manipulation of social conditions; or it could be about the search for a "level playing field" in the Single Market, so that market distortions caused by what has become known as "social dumping" can be avoided; or it could be about a new Community dimension focusing on social affairs as an area deserving attention in its own right.[42]

That being said, EC employment legislation can be divided roughly into the following principal categories: the free movement of persons, equal treatment and equal opportunities, employment protection legislation specifically geared to (minimal) protection of the rights of employees in the event of the restructuring of undertakings, legislation on information, consultation and worker participation and health and safety legislation addressing employees' working environment. Other primary and secondary Community law concerning, variously, competition, State aids, or public procurement, also has a potential effect on labour law and domestic employment policies, as chapter three indicates.[43]

The EC Treaty provisions on the free movement of persons are well-known and there is no need to reproduce them or the debates which have accompanied their development—whether legislative or judicial—in detail here.[44] Essentially, Articles 39 to 48 EC provide for the free movement of employed and self-employed persons within the European Union. Freedom of movement for workers primarily entails the freedom to move and reside in another Member State with a view to engaging in an economic activity free from discrimination on grounds of nationality as regards employment, remuneration and other conditions of work and employment. The guarantees of non-discrimination and free movement in the Treaty were translated into secondary legislation during the

[42] See F. Von Prondzynski and A. Kewley, 'Social Law in the European Union: The Search for a Philosophy' (1995/96) 2 *Columbia Journal of European Law* 265–75, 266; See also Barnard (2000), above n 20, p 21, who points to the eclectic nature of EC employment related social policy; and M. Freedland, 'Employment Policy' in Davies *et al* (eds), above n 9, pp 275–309, pp 278–79.

[43] See below ch 3 and, for a synopsis of the EU's social policy agenda, the Report of the House of Lords Select Committee on the European Communities, *The EU Social Policy Agenda*, Session 1999–2000, 20th Report.

[44] See E. Guild and D. Martin, *The Free Movement of Persons in the European Union* (London, Butterworths, 1996); J. Handoll, *The Free Movement of Persons in the European Union* (Chichester, Wiley, 1995); S. O'Leary, *The Evolving Concept of Community Citizenship: From the Free Movement of Persons to Union Citizenship* (London, Kluwer, 1996); S. O'Leary, 'The Free Movement of Persons and Services' in P. Craig and G. De Búrca (eds), *The Evolution of EU Law* (Oxford, OUP, 1999) pp 377–416; and Barnard (2000), above n 20, pp 111–96.

course of the late 1960s and early 1970s. Principally this legislation addresses the free movement and residence rights of economically active EC nationals, the rights of migrant workers and their families when resident in a Member State other than their Member State of origin and the co-ordination of Member State social security rules for those EC nationals who have availed of their free movement rights.[45] The Court has played a central role in the development of EC law relating to the free movement of persons and services. However, employment policy considerations have often arguably been of secondary importance in this jurisprudence, with the Court more concerned to ensure that the EC's fundamental freedoms were permitted to operate effectively, that barriers to free movement in the internal market were abolished and even that EC nationals not be dissuaded from availing of their right to free movement, something which, at least in the context of the free movement of workers, they have generally been unwilling to do.

EC equal treatment and equal opportunities legislation is examined in the course of chapters four and five where the case-law of the Court of Justice on indirect sex discrimination, pregnancy, maternity and attempts to reconcile family responsibilities and the workplace are examined in detail. As chapter four explains, the commitment of the original EEC Treaty to social and employment matters was limited—no direct rights were conferred by the Treaty on employees or Community citizens and the Treaty provisions were underscored by an ambivalent commitment to the pursuit of both economic and social objectives. The 1972–74 Social Action Programme, the Single European Act (SEA, 1986), the Community Social Charter (1989) and the Maastricht Treaty (1992) all marked stages in the coming of age of the social dimension of EC law.[46] More recently, the Charter of Fundamental Rights of the European Union provides in Article 23 that equality between men and women must be ensured in all areas including employment, work and pay.[47] As Bernard points out, the development

---

[45] See, in particular, Council Directive 64/221/EEC of 25 February 1964 on the co-ordination of special measures concerning the movement and residence of foreign nationals which are justified on grounds of public policy, public security or public health, OJ Eng. Sp. Ed., Series–I (63–64) p 117; Regulation (EEC) No. 1612/68 of the Council of 15 October 1968 on freedom of movement for workers within the Community, OJ Eng. Sp. Ed. 1968 L275/2 (amended by Regulation (EEC) 312/76, OJ 1976 L3/2 and Council Regulation (EEC) 2434/92, OJ 1992 L25/1); Council Directive 68/360/EEC of 15 October 1968 on the abolition of restrictions on movement and residence within the Community for workers of Member States and their families, OJ Sp. Ed. 1968 L257/13; Regulation (EEC) No 1251/70 of the Commission of 29 June 1970 on the right of workers to remain in the territory of a Member State after having been employed in that State, OJ Spec. Ed. 1970 L142/24; Regulation (EEC) No 1408/71 of the Council of 14 June 1971 on the application of social security schemes to employed persons and their families moving within the Community, OJ Eng Sp. Ed., Series–I 71(II) p 416; Council Directive 73/148/EEC of 21 May 1973 on the abolition of restrictions on movement and residence within the Community for nationals of Member States with regard to establishment and the provision of services, OJ 1973 L172/14; Council Directive 75/34/EEC of 17 December 1974 concerning the right of nationals of a Member State to remain in the territory of another Member State after having pursued therein an activity in a self-employed capacity, OJ 1975 L14/10.

[46] For a clear outline of this development see Barnard (2000), above n 20, pp 1–20.

[47] Charter of Fundamental Rights of the European Union solemnly proclaimed at Nice by the European Parliament, the Council and the Commission on 7 December 2000, OJ 2000 C364/1.

of 'Social Europe' from the early to mid-1980s and the adoption of the Social Charter, in particular, at the end of that decade, were very much a reaction to the cold and abstract welfare economics discourse underlying the single market. During the 1990s, development of the social content of the Treaties became linked to the 'People's Europe' agenda.[48] In the context of equal treatment and equal opportunities, however, until the incorporation of the Social Chapter into the text of the EC Treaty and the amendment of the former Article 119 EC in the Amsterdam Treaty in 1997, developments had been confined to Community secondary legislation and the case-law of the Court of Justice. One of the most important consequences of the piecemeal approach to sex equality law was the distinction between issues of equal pay and equal treatment which survives to date and, of course, the distinction between provisions of secondary EC law which enjoy only vertical direct effect (eg Directive 76/207) and provisions of primary EC law (eg Article 141 EC) which enjoy both vertical and horizontal direct effect. The result is that only EC Treaty provisions, specifically Article 141 EC on equal pay, can be relied on in actions before national courts against employers in both the public and private sector.

In the wake of the Member States' new found commitment in the early 1970s to a Social Action Programme, the Council adopted its first three Sex Equality Directives on equal pay, equal treatment with regard to access to employment, vocational training, promotion and working conditions and equal treatment with regard to statutory social security schemes.[49] Adopted on the same legal basis as the 1970s' Directives—Articles 94 and 308 EC—further Directives were subsequently introduced concerning equal treatment in the field of occupational schemes of social security[50] and for men and women carrying out a self-employed activity.[51] Following the introduction by the SEA of a new legal basis permitting the adoption of health and safety legislation on a qualified majority basis, the Council eventually adopted a Directive covering the rights of female

[48] See N. Bernard, 'Legislating European Union Law: Is the Social Dialogue the Way Forward?' in Shaw (ed), above n 20, pp 279–301, p 292.

[49] Council Directive 75/117/EEC of 10 February 1975 on the approximation of the laws of the Member States relating to the application of the principle of equal pay for men and women, OJ 1975 L45/19; Directive 76/207; and Council Directive 79/7/EEC of 19 December 1978 on the progressive implementation of the principle of equal treatment for men and women in matters of social security, OJ 1979 L6/24. Recent proposals to amend the Equal Treatment Directive seek to include sexual harassment as discrimination based on sex, to provide judicial protection when an employment relationship is ended as a result of a discrimination complaint, to recognise Member States' rights to adopt positive action measures and to guarantee a right to return to the same work after maternity leave—OJ 2000 C334/204. See Directive 2002/73/EC of the European Parliament and of the Council of 23 September 2002, OJ 2002 L269/15.

[50] Council Directive 86/378/EEC of 24 July 1986 on the implementation of the principle of equal treatment for men and women in occupational social security schemes, OJ 1986 L225/40, which was subsequently amended, in the light of the decision in Case C–262/88 *Barber*, by Council Directive 96/97/EC, OJ 1997 L46/20.

[51] Council Directive 86/613/EEC of 11 December 1986 on the application of the principle of equal treatment between men and women engaged in an activitiy, including agriculture, in a self-employed capacity, and on the protection of self-employed women during pregnancy and motherhood, OJ 1986 L359/56.

workers who are pregnant and on maternity leave.[52] Finally, those Member States who had agreed at Maastricht to be bound by the Social Chapter adopted a number of Directives on the burden of proof in sex discrimination cases,[53] European works councils,[54] part-time work[55] and parental leave.[56] The last two Directives transposed framework agreements concluded by the social partners at European level (UNICE, CEEP and ETUC). The Amsterdam Treaty subsequently introduced amendments to the text of the former Article 119 EC. Article 141 EC now includes a legal basis for the adoption of legislation by the Council pursuant to the co-decision procedure to ensure the application of the principle of equal opportunities and equal treatment of men and women in matters of employment and occupation, including the principle of equal pay for equal work or work of equal value.[57] It also provides that, with a view to ensuring full equality in practice between men and women in working life, the principle of equal treatment shall not prevent any Member State from maintaining or adopting measures providing for specific advantages in order to make it easier for the underrepresented sex to pursue a vocational activity or to prevent or compensate for disadvantages in professional careers.[58]

Following the introduction of Article 13 EC by the Amsterdam Treaty, a number of anti-discrimination directives have been adopted on this basis.[59] Directive 2000/78 establishes a general framework for equal treatment in employment and occupation aimed at combatting discrimination on the grounds of religion or belief, disability, age or sexual orientation as regards employment and occupation.[60] The Directive applies to all persons, as regards both the public and private sectors, in relation to conditions for access to

[52] Council Directive 92/85/EEC of 19 October 1992 on the introduction of measures to encourage improvements in the safety and health at work of pregnant workers and workers who have recently given birth or are breastfeeding, OJ 1992 L348/1, discussed below ch 5.

[53] Council Directive 97/80/EC of 15 December 1997 on the burden of proof in cases of discrimination based on sex, OJ 1998 L14/6. Following the United Kingdom's acceptance of the Social Chapter, Directives which had been adopted on the basis of the Social Policy Agreement were readopted on the basis of Article 94 EC and now apply to all Member States.

[54] Council Directive 94/45/EC of 22 September 1994 on the establishment of a European Works Council or a procedure in Community-scale undertakings and Community-scale groups of undertakings for the purposes of informing and consulting employees, OJ 1994 L254/64; extended to the United Kingdom by Council Directive 97/74/EC of 15 December 1997, OJ 1997 L10/22.

[55] Council Directive 97/81/EC of 15 December 1997 concerning the Framework Agreement on part-time work concluded by UNICE, CEEP and the ETUC—Annex: Framework agreement on part-time work, OJ 1997 L14/9.

[56] Council Directive 96/34/EC of 3 June 1996 on the framework agreement on parental leave concluded by UNICE, CEEP and the ETUC, OJ 1996 L145/4, discussed below ch 5.

[57] Article 141(3) EC. In addition, Articles 2 and 3 EC now include the principle of equality between men and women as one of the tasks of the EC as well as one of its activities and Article 137 EC provides that the EC shall complement and support the activities of the Member States in the field of equality between men and women with regard to labour market opportunities and treatment at work.

[58] Article 141(4) EC.

[59] Article 13 EC provides that the Council may take appropriate action to combat discrimination based on sex, racial or ethnic origin, religion or belief, disability, age or sexual orientation.

[60] Council Directive 2000/78/EC of 27 November 2000, OJ 2000 L303/16.

employment, to self-employment or to occupation, employment and working conditions, including dismissals and pay (Article 3(1)(a) and (c)). The Directive does not apply to payments of any kind made by State schemes or similar, including State social security or social protection schemes (Article 3(3)). Directive 2000/43 has also been adopted to implement the principle of equal treatment between persons irrespective of racial or ethnic origin.[61]

The 1972–74 Social Action Programme was also the starting point for legislation designed to afford employees limited employment protection in the event of the restructuring of the undertaking which employed them. A Directive on collective redundancies was adopted in 1975 with a view to ensuring that greater protection was afforded to workers in the event of collective redundancies, while taking into account the need for balanced economic and social development within the Community.[62] The Directive also sought to promote the approximation of Member State legislation on collective redundancies while ensuring that the improvement of living and working conditions was maintained within the meaning of Article 136 EC. The limited protection afforded by the Collective Redundancies Directive was emphasised by the fact that it did not intend to interfere with employers' freedom to bring about collective redundancies. Instead, this partial harmonisation measure set minimum standards for undertakings to ensure that they consulted with workers' representatives properly when contemplating collective redundancies and notified the competent public authorities of its plans. The 1975 Directive has since been amended by Directive 92/56 and in turn consolidated by Directive 98/59.[63] Another partial harmonisation directive was adopted in 1977, providing protection for employees in the event of a change in their employer by ensuring that their rights are safeguarded.[64] The so-called Acquired Rights Directive is discussed in detail in chapter six. Finally, the third piece of employment protection legislation following the Social Action Programme was the 1980 Insolvency Directive.[65]

---

[61] Council Directive 2000/43/EC of 29 June 2000 implementing the principle of equal treatment between persons irrespective of racial or ethnic origin, OJ 2000 L180/22. See also Council Decision of 27 November 2000 establishing a Community action programme to combat discrimination (2001 to 2006), OJ 2000 L303/23; and the Commission's proposal for a Council Framework Decision on combatting racism and xenophobia, COM (2001) 664 final.

[62] Council Directive 75/129/EEC of 17 February 1975 on the approximation of the laws of the Member States relating to collective redundancies, OJ 1975 L48/29.

[63] Council Directive 92/56/EEC of 24 June 1992, OJ 1992 L245/3, consolidated by Council Directive 98/59/EC of 20 July 1998 on the approximation of the laws of the Member States relating to collective redundancies, OJ 1998 L225/16.

[64] Council Directive 77/187/EEC of 14 February 1977 on the approximation of the laws of the Member States relating to the safeguarding of employees' rights in the event of transfers of undertakings, businesses or parts of businesses, OJ 1977 L61/126, subsequently amended by Council Directive 98/50/EC of 29 June 1998, OJ 1998 L201/88 and consolidated by Council Directive 2001/23/EC of 12 March 2001, OJ 2001 L82/16.

[65] Council Directive 80/987/EEC of 20 October 1980 on the approximation of the laws of the Member States relating to the protection of employees in the event of insolvency of their employer, OJ 1980 L283/23; subsequently amended by Council Directive 87/164/EEC of 2 March 1987, OJ 1987 L66/11.

Adopted on the basis of Article 94 EC, this Directive sought to promote the approximation of the laws of the Member States relating to insolvency while improving the living and working conditions of those employees by offering them the following limited protection in the event of insolvency. The Directive required Member States to establish institutions to guarantee payment of employees' outstanding claims resulting from contracts of employment or employment relationships. It also provided that the employer's non-payment of compulsory contributions to insurance institutions under the State social security scheme must not adversely affect employees' benefit entitlements. Finally, Member States were also obliged to ensure that the rights of former employees no longer employed at the time of the employer's insolvency were protected, particularly in respect of old-age benefits, including survivors' benefits, under occupational or supplementary schemes which fall outside the national social security system.

With the adoption of the SEA the Community legislature was provided with a specific legal basis—the former Article 118a EC—for the adoption of legislation concerning the health and safety of workers. Member States were to pay particular attention to encouraging improvements, especially in the working environment, as regards the health and safety of workers and the Council was empowered, by a qualified majority, to adopt directives laying down minimum requirements for gradual implementation. Member States remained free, however, to maintain or introduce more stringent measures for the protection of working conditions. The scope of the former Article 118a EC was discussed by the Court in the legal challenge mounted by the United Kingdom to the adoption of Directive 93/104 on working time,[66] which is discussed in detail in chapter three. A whole series of directives have been adopted on the basis of the parent Directive 89/391, which contains general principles concerning the prevention of occupational risks, the protection of safety and health, the elimination of risk and accident factors as well as the informing, consultation and balanced participation of workers and their representatives.[67] Directive 89/391 contains only minimum standards for the protection of health and safety, but it is without prejudice to existing or future national and Community provisions that are more favourable to protection of safety and health of workers at work. EC health and safety legislation—particularly that which regulates aspects of work such as working time—has been the subject of considerable debate and criticism. As we shall see in chapter three, critics argue that despite the

---

[66] Council Directive 93/104/EC of 23 November 1993 concerning certain aspects of the organisation of working time, OJ 1993 L307/18. Case C–84/94 *United Kingdom v Council* [1996] ECR I–5755.

[67] See Council Directive 89/391/EEC of 12 June 1989 on the introduction of measures to encourage improvements in the safety and health of workers at work, OJ 1989 L183/1. Discussed in detail in Barnard (2000), above n 20, ch 6. A whole series of directives have been adopted on the basis of Directive 89/391, establishing rules governing health and safety in the workplace (particularly industries regarded as posing a particular risk), relating to work equipment and to exposure to chemical, physical and biological agents.

Community paying lip service to the need for a flexible labour market, this type of legislation creates a lack of flexibility and imposes a considerable burden on employers, particularly on small businesses.

Following the adoption of the Social Policy Agreement at Maastricht and its subsequent extension to the United Kingdom and revision at Amsterdam, Article 137 EC now provides for co-decision for the adoption of minimum standard directives relating to the improvement in particular of the working environment to protect workers' health and safety, working conditions, the information and consultation of workers, the integration of persons excluded from the labour market and equality between men and women with regard to labour market opportunities and treatment at work. In March 2002, the Commission published a proposal for a Directive of the European Parliament and Council on the working conditions for temporary workers based on Article 137(2) EC. The Commission had previously consulted the European social partners on the desirability of action at EC level with respect to the flexibility of working hours and job security, but they were unable to reach agreement on the subject of temporary work.[68] The preamble of the proposed Directive states that its aim is to establish a protection framework for temporary works without imposing any administrative, financial or legislative constraints which would impede the creation and development of small and medium sized undertakings. Essentially, the proposed directive provides that temporary workers should not be treated any less favorably than a worker in the user undertaking in an identical or similar job, taking into account seniority, qualifications and skills. Differences in treatment can be justified, however, by objective reasons. Coming, as it did, hot on the heels of the 2002 European Council meeting in Barcelona (one of whose principal objectives was to ensure economic and labour market reforms thought to be necessary to enhance growth and job creation), the Commission's proposal has been criticised in certain quarters as a blast from Europe's *dirigiste* past.[69] Article 137(3) EC provides for the adoption of other minimum standards directives concerning, *inter alia*, protection of workers where their employment contract is terminated, representation and collective defense of the interests of workers and employers, including co-determination as well as financial contributions for the promotion of employment and job-creation, although the latter must be adopted by unanimity.[70]

Finally, legislation governing rights to information and consultation in the workplace have been the subject of protracted and heated debate at EC level for many years. Embryonic rights to information and consultation had been

[68] COM (2002) 149 final.

[69] See *Financial Times* 21 March 2002.

[70] Note that several health and safety directives have been adopted which are geared to the needs of specific categories of workers: see, for example, Council Directive 91/383/EEC on the improvement of the health and safety of atypical workers, OJ 1991 L206/19; Council Directive 94/33/EC of 22 June 1994 on the protection of young people at work, OJ 1994 L216/12; Directive 97/81 on part-time work.

introduced in the specific context of Directives dealing with collective redundancies, transfer of undertakings and health and safety. Article 6(1) of Directive 77/187 provided, for example, that the transferor and the transferee shall be required to inform the representatives of their respective employees affected by a transfer of the reasons for the transfer, the legal, economic and social implications of the transfer for the employees and the measures envisaged in relation to the employees. The revised Directive 98/50 contains an almost identical provision and includes an obligation to inform employees of the date or proposed date of the transfer. Other pieces of Community legislation also contain provisions for the participation of the workforce in the management and decision-making processes that affect the company for which they work. Pursuant to the 1989 Merger Regulation, when determining whether a merger with a Community dimension is compatible with the common market, the Commission's appraisal may include social considerations and it is entitled to hear the views of the recognised representatives of employees.[71]

Directive 91/533 is specifically designed to provide employees with improved protection against possible infringements of their rights and to create greater transparency in the market. It establishes obligations on an employer to inform employees of the conditions applicable to their contract or employment relationship.[72] The essential information which must be provided includes the identities of the parties, the place of work, the title, grade or nature of the work, a brief specification or description of the work, the date of commencement, the expected duration of a temporary contract, the entitlement to paid leave, the length of periods of notice, the initial basic amount, the other component elements and the frequency of payment of remuneration, the length of the employee's normal working day or week and any applicable collective agreements. Member States may provide, however, that the Directive shall not apply to employees having a contract or employment relationship not exceeding one month or eight hours in a working week and, with respect to work of a casual and/or specific nature, where its non-application is justified by objective considerations.[73]

As Barnard explains, the introduction of a more general, systematic, and institutionalised right to employee participation in corporate decision-making met with concerted resistance for over a decade.[74] Commission proposals on a Statute for a European company and a complementary Directive on the involvement of employees in the European company languished before the

---

[71] Article 18(4) of Council Regulation (EEC) no 4064/89 of 21 December 1989 on the control of concentrations between undertakings, OJ 1989 L395/1, as amended.

[72] Council Directive 91/533/EEC of 14 October 1991 on an employer's obligation to inform employees of the conditions applicable to the contract or employment relationship, OJ 1991 L288/32.

[73] See Joined Cases C–253/96 and C–258/96 *Helmut Kampelmann and others v Landschaftsverband Westfalen-Lippe and others* [1997] ECR I–6907; and Case C–350/99 *Wolfgang Lange v Georg Schünemann GmbH* [2001] ECR I–1061.

[74] See Barnard (2000), above n 20, p 517.

Council for many years. When the *Societas Europea* (SE) Regulation was finally adopted, the Directive which supplemented it regarding the involvement of employees did not establish a European model for their involvement in the reorganisation of business but at least requires management to negotiate with employees' representatives on arrangements for their involvement in the SE.[75] Similarly, provisions in a proposed directive on takeovers setting out rights of consultation for employees led to fears that the bidding process would be lengthened and rendered more costly were employees to rely on those rights, and the proposals were subsequently dropped.[76] On the basis of the Social Policy Agreement (since unanimity had not been achieved to adopt a proposed directive on the basis of the former Article 100 EC), a Directive on European Works Councils was finally adopted in 1994. Application of the Directive to corporate restructuring depends on whether prescribed thresholds for the size of the workforce are passed. Finally, in March 2002, a Directive was adopted which establishes a general framework for informing and consulting employees in the European Community.[77] The Directive covers information on the recent and probable development of the company's activities and economic situation, on the situation, structure and probable development of employment within the company and on any anticipatory measures envisaged, in particular, where there is a threat to employment and on decisions likely to lead to substantial changes in work organisation or in contractual relations. This information is to be given at such time, in such fashion and with such content as are appropriate to enable, in particular, employees' representatives to conduct an appropriate study and, where necessary, prepare for consultation. Consultation shall take place in such a way as to enable employees' representatives to meet the employer and obtain a response, and the reasons for that respone, to any opinion they might formulate. The aim of consultation is to reach agreement on decisions within the scope of the employer's powers concerning changes in work organisation or contractual relations. The preamble of the Directive notes that existing legislative frameworks on the involvement of employers in the affairs of the undertaking employing them have not always prevented serious decisions affecting employees from being taken and made public without adequate procedures having been implemented beforehand to inform and consult them. Like

[75] See Council Regulation (EC) no 2157/2001 of 8 October 2001 on the Statute for a European Company (SE), OJ 2001 L294/1 and Council Directive 2001/86/EC of 8 October 2001 supplementing the Statute for a European company with regard to the involvement of employees, OJ 2001 294/22.

[76] See amended proposal for a thirteenth European Parliament and Council Directive on company law concerning takeover bids, OJ 1996 C162/15; and, specifically, the Commission's opinion pursuant to Article 251(2) EC on the European Parliament's amendments to the Council's common position, COM (2001) 77 final.

[77] Directive 2002/14/EC of the European Parliament and the Council of 11 March 2002, OJ 2002 L80/29, sometimes referred to as the Vilvoorde Directive after the infamous closure by Renault in the late 1990s, without informing or consulting its workforce, of a car manufacturing plant in the town of Vilvoorde in Belgium.

other Directives in the employment field, however, its scope of application may be subject to a qualifying threshold by Member States, namely to undertakings employing at least fifty employees in any one Member State or establishments employing at least twenty employees in any one Member State.

1

The Operation of the Court of Justice of the European Communities

INTRODUCTION

IN A BOOK devoted to the Court of Justice, to the manner in which it deals with preliminary references in the field of employment and to an analysis of the policy considerations influential in its case-law in that field, it is perhaps essential—to borrow an expression beloved of successive British governments—to get back to basics. In other words, to analyse closely the membership, structure, organisation, working methods and general operation of the Court before setting out to critique what that Court produces by way of judicial decisions.[1] Mundane though such an exercise may at first sight appear, it is surprising how little has been written or is understood about how the Court of Justice disposes of cases and the lengthy, indeed oft outmoded, internal procedures which must be followed before a decision is negotiated and produced. Parenthetically, with

---

[1] Reference to the Court of Justice should be taken to mean the Court of Justice as a judicial body, as distinct from the Court of Justice as an EC institution including the Court of First Instance. Please also note that, although it is not clear at the time of writing whether the Nice Treaty will be ratified by all Member States, as is required by Article 48 TEU, reference is made throughout to the changes which it may bring about, not only in the EC Treaty but also in measures such as the Protocol on the Statute of the Court of Justice (hereafter EC Statute) and the new numbering which will apply particularly in the EC Statute following the entry into force of the Treaty of Nice. This approach is not to deny the legitimacy of the democratic voice of one Member State which has, at the time of writing, rejected ratification of the new Treaty, but is purely for the sake of completeness.

For material on how the Court of Justice works see, *inter alia*, D.A.O. Edward, 'How the Court of Justice Works' (1995) 20 *European Law Review* 539–58; K. Basenach, 'How judgments are reached in the Court of Justice of the European Communities in Luxembourg—Legal Basis and Legal Practice' (1993) *European Food Law Review* 51–70; G.F. Mancini and D. Keeling, 'Language, Culture and Politics in the Life of the European Court of Justice' (1995) 1 *Columbia Journal of European Law* 397–413; R. Plender (ed), *European Courts: Practice and Precedents* (London, Sweet & Maxwell, 1997); P.E. Lasok, *The European Court of Justice. Practice and Procedure* (London, Butterworths, 1994); D. Freestone, 'The European Court of Justice' in J. Lodge (ed), *Institutions and Policies of the European Community* (London, Frances Pinter Publishers, 1983) pp 43–53; S. Hix, *The Political System of the European Union* (Houndmills, MacMillan, 1999) particularly 'Judicial Politics', pp 99–129, pp 104–05; S.E. Strasser, 'Evolution and Effort: Docket Control & Preliminary References in the European Court of Justice' (1995/6) 2 *Columbia Journal of European Law* 49–105; P. Demaret, 'Le juge et le jugement dans l'Europe d'aujourd'hui: la Cour de justice des Communautés européennes' in R. Jacob (ed), *Le juge et le jugement dans les traditions juridiques européennes: Études d'histoire comparée* (Paris, L.G.D.J., 1996) pp 303–77, pp 320–52; and H.G. Schermers and D. Waelbroeck, *Judicial Protection in the European Communities*, 5th edn. (Deventer, Kluwer, 1992).

proposals seeking to reform the Community's judicial architecture, as it has grandiosely come to be known, high on the agenda of successive intergovernmental conferences, it is clearly essential to understand at least some of the problems which beset the Communities' Courts before setting out to solve them.

The aim of this book is to examine the art of EC judicial decision-making generally and policy considerations in the employment case-law of the Court of Justice in particular. In order to understand the policy considerations which surface or are hidden in the Court's decisions in the employment field it thus seems advisable to examine, at the outset, the judicial structures within which those decisions are reached and to reflect on the possible effect which those structures may have on the treatment of cases, their outcome and general content. Conscious of a tendency to over-simplify trends in the Court's jurisprudence, Weatherill has observed, for example, that:

> [T]he Court today is beset by many pressures, not least the sheer size of its workload and the range of subject areas which that workload covers. Such anxieties prompt an urgent need to rethink the structure of the Community judicature, but for the time being it is important to appreciate that any attempt to present a one-dimensional account of its activity is doomed to failure.[2]

With this warning in mind, before embarking on an analysis of the Court's performance in specific substantive areas of employment law, chapters one and two seek to assess the Court's work within the context of the procedural and structural limits subject to which it is obliged to operate.

The Court sees its jurisdiction as encompassing three broad aspects: ensuring that Community institutions act lawfully, ensuring that Member States fulfil their obligations under EC law and, finally, the preliminary reference procedure, which is regarded as the key to application of EC law in national courts.[3] In line with the general focus of this book, the emphasis in this chapter is on this third aspect of the Court's jurisdiction. Although the Commission has played an essential role in bringing before the Court infringement actions against Member States who have defaulted from their obligations in the field of employment law and several important labour law decisions have resulted from such direct action, the majority[4] of cases in this field are references from national courts

---

[2] S. Weatherill, 'The Common Market: Mission Accomplished' in V. Heiskanen and K. Kulovesi (eds), *Function and Future of European Law* (Helsinki, Publications of the University of Helsinki, 1999) pp 33–57, p 49. Most of the Court's commentators and critics seem unable or unwilling to conceive of the problems which limit the Court's freedom of action. See, however, J. Shaw and T. Hervey, 'Women, Work and Care: Women's Dual Role and Double Burden in EC Sex Equality Law' (1998) 8 *Journal of European Social Policy* 43–63, 45; and J. Shaw, 'Gender and the Court of Justice' in G. De Burca and J.H.H. Weiler (eds), *The European Court of Justice* (Oxford, OUP, 2001) pp 87–142, p 106.

[3] See Court of Justice of the European Communities, *The Court of Justice and the Institutional Reform of the European Union*, April 2000, available at http://curia.eu.int/en/txts/intergov/rod.pdf.

[4] In 2001, two hundred and thirty seven new references were introduced, four hundred and eighty seven were pending and one hundred and eighty two were disposed of either by judgment or reasoned order. See the Annual Report of the Court of Justice of the European Communities, published in March 2002, available at http:/curia.eu.int/en/pei/rapan.htm. See the analysis of statistical data

concerning the compatibility of national legislation with EC law or, rather, the interpretation which should be given the latter.[5] This chapter explains the general passage of cases through the Court of Justice, from the lodging of the order for reference with the Registry through to the Court's rendering of a final decision or reasoned order. Although the overall treatment received by cases at the Court, whether they be direct actions, preliminary references or appeals, is fairly similar, attention will be focused on the procedural steps peculiar to preliminary references pursuant to Article 234 EC.

THE COURT AND ITS MEMBERS

Membership of the Court is governed by Articles 221 to 223 EC.[6] At the time of writing, the Court consists of fifteen Judges and eight Advocates General, these members being chosen from persons whose independence is beyond doubt and who possess the qualifications required for appointment to the highest judicial offices in their respective countries or who are jurisconsults of recognised competence.[7] Advocates General are charged with assisting the Court in the performance of the duties assigned to it under the Treaty by making reasoned submissions on cases brought before the Court. In the exercise of this function they must act impartially and with complete independence.[8] There is no

up until 1996 in the excellent article by T. De la Mare, 'Article 177 in Social and Political Context' in P. Craig and G. De Búrca (eds), *The Evolution of EU Law* (Oxford, OUP, 1999) pp 215–60.

[5] C. Kilpatrick, 'Community or Communities of Courts in European Integration? Sex Equality Dialogues Between UK Courts and the ECJ' (1998) 4 *European Law Journal* 121–47, 126, complains that Article 234 EC is seen as the measure of all things and that insufficient consideration is given the role and participation of national courts in European integration.

[6] See further Articles 2 to 8 EC Statute and Articles 2 to 6 of the Rules of Procedure of the Court of Justice of the European Communities (hereafter RP), produced in a codified version in OJ 2000 C 34/1. For an article focusing on the members of the Court see S. Kenney, 'The Members of the Court of Justice of the European Communities' (1998) 5 *Columbia Journal of European Law* 101–33.

[7] At the time of writing there are eight Advocates General, with the 'Big Five' (Italy, Germany, France, the United Kingdom and Spain) nominating candidates for permanent positions and the smaller Member States nominating on a rotating basis for the remaining three positions.

Changes to the number of Judges and Advocates General have, in the past, resulted from Council decisions based on successive acts of accession—described in T. Kennedy, 'Thirteen Russians! The Composition of the European Court of Justice' in A.I.Z. Campbell and M. Voyatzi (eds), *Legal Reasoning and Judicial Interpretation of European Law. Essays in honour of Lord Mackenzie-Stuart* (London, Trenton Publishing, 1996) pp 69–91.

[8] Article 222 EC (as amended), which specifies that, should the Court of Justice so request, the Council may, acting unanimously, increase the number of Advocates General. For a specific look at the role of Advocates General and their contribution to EC law see T. Tridimas, 'The role of the Advocate General in the development of Community law: some reflections' (1997) 34 *Common Market Law Review* 1349–87; F. Jacobs, 'Advocates General and Judges in the European Court of Justice: some personal reflections' in D. O'Keeffe (ed), *Liber Amicorum in Honour of Lord Slynn of Hadley. Judicial Review in European Law* (The Hague, Kluwer Law International, 2000) pp 17–28; and generally A. Arnull, *The European Union and its Court of Justice* (Oxford, OUP, 1999). The parties may not comment on the Opinion of the Advocate General, although this rule has given rise to considerable discussion in the light of the case-law of the European Court of Human Rights: see, in particular, the Order of the Court in Case C–17/98 *Emesa Sugar (Free Zone) NV v Aruba* [2000] ECR I–665.

requirement that Judges be specialists in EC law or that they be able to function easily, if at all, in French, the internal working language of the Court. Admittedly, specialist knowledge of all aspects of EC law, given how vast the subject has become, seems rather a tall order. In addition, there is much to be said for the Member States drawing candidates from national legal stock, thereby ensuring that those who serve on the European bench are not so detached from the operation of domestic law, its procedural minutiae included, that their answers in references for preliminary rulings, in particular, prove unworkable in practice. However, a lack of specialist EC law knowledge, coupled with moderate to poor ability to draft and negotiate legal decisions in French (negotiating skills being, presumably, what collegiate decisions demand), means that a steep learning curve may await newly appointed Judges. If they are replaced after having served only one six year term those skills will have to be mastered by an incoming member who may be similarly unfamiliar with the procedural and substantive aspects of the law with which the Court deals and/or with its internal working language.[9]

Both Judges and Advocates General are appointed by the common accord of the governments of the Member States for a renewable term of six years.[10] In practice, Member State governments have in the past chosen their own candidates following internal selection procedures[11] and have informed the Council

---

[9] Strasser, above n 1, 93–94, observes that 'a judge may need two or three years to gain adequate expertise in substantive and procedural Community law, adjust to the system, and achieve fluency in French. During the last year of tenure, a judge will wind down his involvement. As a result, some judges may have only two or three years of optimal efficiency.' See also the argument to the same effect put forward by P.J.G. Kapteyn and P. VerLoren van Themaat, *Introduction to the Law of the European Communities*, 3rd ed. edited and further revised by L.W. Gormley (The Hague, Kluwer Law International, 1999) p 257.

[10] The Judges at the Court of First Instance are also appointed in this way, although the Treaty specifies in Article 225 EC (Article 224 EC as amended) that members of the Court of First Instance must simply be chosen from persons whose independence is beyond doubt and who possess the ability required for appointment to (high) judicial office (the amendment in brackets resulting from the Nice Treaty). Note that the six year term of office of members of the Court of Justice compares with nine years for Judges on the International Court of Justice and the European Court of Human Rights, four years for members of the WTO Appellate Body; and eight years for the members of the Executive Board of the European Central Bank, whose members retire in rotation. In contrast, members of the United States Supreme Court enjoy life tenure.

[11] Kenney remarks, above n 6, 108, that '[A]ppointment to the ECJ in some countries displays many of the same mixed features of ambassadorships in some cases, such as exile for a party luminary who is in trouble, a retirement prize for exemplary public service, the removal of a competitor within a party, or a consolation prize for a failed judicial appointment.' See also Demaret, above n 1, p 321, on the selection of candidates according to national political families.

There is evidence of growing pressure at Member State level for internal selection procedures to change or, at the very least, for them to become less political and more transparent. The Belgian government, which generally seeks to balance party, region and language when making appointments, was petitioned by a large group of lawyers opposed to the appointment as a Judge of a former Deputy Prime Minister (*European Report*, No 2068, 18 September 1995). When the British government wished to find a replacement for the 'British' Judge in the Court of First Instance in 1999 it advertised the post in the national press and conducted interviews.

of Ministers, which in turn has ratified the Member State's decision.[12] One of the results of this acceptance by Member States of other Member States' proposed candidates was the presumption of a link between the number of Judges and the number of Member States and a resulting assumption that each Member State was entitled to appoint at least one Judge. As one former President of the Court contended, however, nothing in the Treaty would have prevented the Court being composed entirely of Russians.[13]

In its 1995 Report on the application of the TEU, the Court spoke of the positive effects of this nationality rule in terms of the representativeness and legitimacy of the Court and the primordial need for it to understand and be fully acquainted with the different legal cultures on which EC law is based and from which it draws inspiration.[14] It has been suggested, however, that the Court's understanding of the Member States' different legal cultures would not be untowardly threatened as long as the main legal families—Common, Germanic, Romanistic and Scandinavian—were represented in some way in the make-up of the Court.[15] In addition, carving out a greater role for the already existing division of the Court devoted to the research and documentation of national law and its interface with EC law would go some way to compensating for any expertise lost due to the periodic absence of Judges of any one nationality.[16] In a document entitled *The EC Court of Justice and the Institutional Reform of the EU*, published in April 2000, the Court seemed, with the prospect of enlargement and with a substantial increase in its membership looming large, to have undergone a change of heart. It pointed out, without taking a position on what

---

[12] Although there are some reported cases of disputes over appointments. See, for example, the dispute between Italy and Spain over the appointment of the Court's additional Judge in 1988, discussed in N.L. Brown and T. Kennedy, *Brown & Jacobs The Court of Justice of the European Communities*, 4th edn (London, Sweet & Maxwell, 1994) p 44. According to Schermers and Waelbroeck, above n 1, p 451: '[Before Member States select their candidates] informal consultation will have taken place with the result that the other Member States occasionally persuade a Member State to propose another candidate during the course of these consultations.'

[13] In his contribution to the *Festschrift for Lord Mackenzie Stuart*, above n 7, Kennedy examines how the number of members of the Court has increased with successive accessions and discusses the delicate issue of nationality and membership of the Court and the changes which should be made to this unwritten rule of one Member State one Judge when the EU becomes so large that such a link is untenable.

[14] *Report of the Court of Justice on Certain Aspects of the Application of the Treaty on European Union*, May 1995 (hereinafter referred to as the 1995 Report, available at http://europa.eu.int/en/agenda/igc-home/eu-doc/justice/cj_rep.html). See also Demaret, above n 1, p 321. Note, however, that parties cannot seek a change in the composition of the Court or one of its Chambers on the ground of the nationality of a Judge or due to the absence from the formation of a Judge with the same nationality as the party: Article 18 EC Statute (as amended).

[15] See W. Van Gerven, 'The role and structure of the European judiciary now and in the future' (1996) 21 *European Law Review* 211–23, 219. He advocates that the rule that every Member State must have a Judge at the Court should be altered so that every Member State is entitled to have a Judge *or* an Advocate General.

[16] See also Kennedy, above n 7, p 81; and de la Mare in Craig and De Búrca (1999), above n 4, p 249, who suggests that in high-level EC cases the Court should aim to construct a more complete EC *Brandeis* brief, *inter alia*, by relying on 'comparative research assembled by the Court's research and documentation centre, which should be made readily and publicly available in advance.'

is clearly a delicate political problem, that further increases in membership could entail the Court being transformed from a judicial collegiate body to something like a deliberative assembly. Furthermore, the majority of cases in a larger court would have to be decided by smaller Chambers of Judges, thus jeopardising the coherence of the case law.[17] In any event, in the Treaty amending the TEU and EC Treaty, signed in Nice in February 2001, the Member States amended Article 221 EC to the effect that 'The Court of Justice shall consist of one judge per Member State.'

Another consequence of the appointment system dictated by the EC Treaty has been ongoing criticism and concern about whether the appointment of members can be said to be truly in line with principles of democracy, transparency and the rule of law, all fundamental tenets of EU law by virtue of the preamble and Articles 1 and 6 TEU. The European Parliament has called for several years, for example, for proposed judicial candidates to undergo some sort of parliamentary scrutiny, albeit not along the lines of the hearings which are standard procedure in the United States for proposed appointees to the Supreme Court.[18] In its 1995 Report, the Court was clearly not enamoured with such proposals.[19] One of the Court's main concerns seems to be that public hearings might lead members to publicly prejudge positions they might have to adopt in the exercise of their judicial function. Bringing this rather weak argument to its logical conclusion, however, sitting members of the Court should be prevented from publishing their views on case-law in academic articles or making public speeches on the Court's decisions, and Advocates General, whose views on particular topics of EC law have been clearly broadcast in their previous Opinions, should be barred from subsequently becoming Judges. A quick look, however, at academic literature and the EC conference circuit reveals to what extent the Court's members engage in publishing and public-speaking activities[20] and a number of former Advocates General have subsequently

---

[17] See below for further discussion of the use of Chambers and the issue of the coherence of the Court's judgments.

[18] See, for example, the European Parliament's Resolution of 17 May 1995 on the functioning of the TEU, OJ 1995 C151/56, point 23(ii) and the Resolution of 14 April 2000 containing the European Parliament's proposals for the Intergovernmental Conference which culminated in Nice, available at http://www.europarl.eu.int/igc2000. As to why some of the original Member States, which were themselves familiar with the appointment of constitutional judges by a constitutional authority, did not insist on greater democratic involvement at EC level see C. Pennera, 'The Beginnings of the Court of Justice and its Role as a Driving Force in European Integration' (1995) 1 *Journal of European Integration History* 111–27, 115; and for a discussion of the European public's general lack of interest to date in the nomination of members of the Court see Demaret, above n 1, p 321.

[19] 1995 Report, above n 14: '[A] reform involving a hearing of each nominee by a parliamentary committee would be unacceptable. Prospective appointees would be unable to adequately answer the questions put to them without betraying the discretion incumbent upon persons whose independence must, in the words of the Treaties, be beyond doubt and without prejudging positions they might have to adopt with regard to contentious issues which they would have to decide in the exercise of their judicial function.' See Kenney (1998), above n 6, n 122, who suggests that some members are against this and some in favour.

[20] See H. Schepels and R. Wesseling, 'The Legal Community: Judges, Lawyers, Officials and Clerks in the Writing of Europe' (1997) 3 *European Law Journal* 165–88.

served as Judges. Past experience also suggests that at least some of today's most prolific commentators on the Court's case-law may tomorrow become members of the Court—yet should they refrain from expressing their opinions on the content and drift of the Court's jurisprudence? Furthermore, members of the Commission's Legal Service and of the Community affairs divisions of Member State Foreign Affairs' ministries have subsequently been appointed as members of the Court of Justice. No-one has ever suggested that their previous activities prejudged the stance they would take as Members of the Court.[21] As Kapteyn and Verloren van Themaat, both former members of the Court, point out, the present system means that: '[V]ery great confidence indeed is [. . .] placed both in the disinterestedness of the governments with respect to their appointment and in the moral qualities of the persons appointed'.[22] In lieu of confirmation hearings, the establishment of a judicial appointments board consisting of senior members of national judiciaries has also been mooted, whose task it would be to assist in the appointment of the members of the Court of Justice.[23]

Criticism has also sometimes been voiced as regards the professional background of the different members of the Court. The qualifications stipulated in the Treaty mean that not only those who qualify for judicial office at national level are eligible but also a variety of others considered learned in the law. As a result, the Court has always counted amongst its ranks former academics, politicians and high-ranking civil servants, as well as national judges and high-ranking practising lawyers eligible at national level to serve on the judiciary.[24] This heterogenous makeup has not always endeared the Court's bench to critics hailing from Member States where time-honoured tradition has meant that appointment to judicial office is the culmination of long, distinguished service at the national bar. For many years, the lack of a female presence at the Court was an additional bone of contention. Indeed those who have witnessed hearings in,

---

[21] Article 18 EC Statute (as amended) provides of course that no Judge or Advocate General may take part in the disposal of any case in which he has previously taken part as agent or adviser or has acted for one of the parties, or in which he has been called upon to pronounce as a member of a court or tribunal, of a commission of inquiry or in any other capacity. Judges and Advocates General may also inform the President that they do not consider that they should take part in the judgment or examination of a particular case and the President may, where he considers there are special reasons, deem that a Judge or Advocate General should not sit or make submissions in a particular case.

[22] See Kapteyn and VerLoren van Themaat, above n 9, p 251; and A. Arnull, 'Judicial architecture or judicial folly? The challenge facing the European Union' (1999) 24 *European Law Review* 516–24, 522 remarks on the lack of transparency which also surrounds the appointment of staff of the members' chambers.

[23] See, for example, the discussion in the Report on the 1996 IGC prepared by the House of Lords Select Committee on the European Communities, Session 1994–1995, 21st Report, para 260; J.H.H. Weiler, 'The European Union Belongs to its Citizens: three modest proposals' (1997) 22 *European Law Review* 150–56; the Report compiled by the British Institute for International and Comparative Law, *The Role and Future of the European Court of Justice* (London, BIICL, 1996) p 124; and Van Gerven, above n 15, 221.

[24] Demaret, above n 1, p 321, suggests that the diversity in the Court's makeup is undoubtedly due to the diversity of the subject matter with which the Court deals, but the prestige of the Court as well as the attractive judicial salaries on offer mean that candidates are attracted from beyond the narrower circle of professional judges and magistrates.

say, major discrimination cases before the full Court may have been struck by the homogeneity of the bench in terms of age, sex and ethnicity. Fortunately, the winds of change began blowing in national government circles in 1999, with the appointment of the first female Judge at the Court of Justice, followed by further female appointments to the posts of Judge and Advocate General in 2000.

INTERNAL STRUCTURE: ADMINISTRATIVE AND JUDICIAL

The chambers of Judges and Advocates General are but the tip of the iceberg when it comes to the internal structure and organisation of the Court of Justice. The Court is assisted by a Registrar and Registry, which is the first port of call for cases lodged at the Court and which serves as the point of reference for national courts, lawyers, litigants, Member State governments and EC institutions.[25] It is the Registry that notifies the opening of proceedings and all other procedural steps to the parties, the Member States, the Commission and other Community institutions concerned. When it comes to references for preliminary rulings from national courts, this means notifying the order for reference to all Member States in their own official language.[26] The Court also houses a Research and Documentation Division whose task it is to prepare comparative studies on specific questions of national or EC law which have been raised in a case before the Court. It is usually the Judge who has been appointed as Rapporteur or the designated Advocate General[27] who request such research notes, since they are the members most acquainted with the case at this early stage. In addition, on reaching the Court, all preliminary references are the subject of an initial examination by a member of the Research and Documentation Division. They examine, *inter alia*, whether the referring body is a court or tribunal of a Member State as required by Article 234 EC, whether the subject matter of the reference comes within the Court's jurisdiction, whether the reference arises out of a real dispute and whether the questions are relevant.[28] The Research and Documentation Division also indicates similar or connected issues which have already arisen and includes in its report a brief analysis of the case and questions referred. Details of this preliminary examination are then passed to the designated Judge-Rapporteur and Advocate General.

Those who have attended oral hearings at the Court will have seen some of its small army of interpreters at work and may have seen members of its

---

[25] See Articles 224 EC (Article 223 EC as amended) and 12–19 RP. Article 17(1) RP provides that the Registrar shall be responsible, under the authority of the President, for the acceptance, transmission and custody of documents and for effecting service as provided by these RP. Article 16 RP provides that the Registry shall keep all pleadings and supporting documents.

[26] Article 104(1) RP. For a discussion of how long it takes to translate the order into the various working languages of the Court see Strasser, above n 1, 63–64.

[27] See below for an explanation of the assignment of cases.

[28] See further D. O'Keeffe, 'Is the Spirit of Article 177 under Attack? Preliminary References and Admissibility' (1998) 23 *European Law Review* 509–36, 531.

Information Division liasing with the European correspondents of the various national media. Those who have read decisions of the Court or Opinions of Advocates General in any language other than French will have benefited from the fruits of the labour of the large, but strained, lawyer-linguist translation division, whose task it is to translate the many thousands of pages of documents with which the Court deals and the many thousands of pages of judicial text which it produces into and out of French.[29] The Court also employs a number of *lecteurs d'arrêts*, whose task it is to ensure consistency in the French terminology used by the Court. For lawyers, the most visible points of reference at the Court are the members and their chambers, each containing three legal secretaries, who are involved in the preparation of the cases for which their member is responsible.[30] Although the decisions of the Court are collegiate, allowing no dissenting opinions, the designated Judge-Rapporteur signs the Report for the Hearing and is clearly recorded in each decision as the Rapporteur.[31] Article 36 EC Statute (as amended) states that decisions must contain the name of the Judges that participated in the deliberations and this information, as we shall see, is sometimes used by assiduous Court-watchers to chart divergence and disagreement between different formations. Designation as a Judge-Rapporteur means that it is that Judge's responsibility to steer the case through the various procedural stages, both written and oral, until a decision is reached.

The Court sits in plenary session either as the full court or as a small plenary. The Court may also form Chambers, each consisting of three, five or seven Judges. At present the Court houses two large Chambers, each consisting of seven Judges, five of whom will be assigned to sit in any given case. The Court also has four small Chambers consisting of four or three Judges, respectively, of whom three will sit in a case.[32] With the entry into force of the Treaty of Nice, the Court may sit in a Grand Chamber which shall consist of eleven Judges, with the President of the Court presiding.[33] Presumably the intention is to refer to the Grand Chamber the large number of cases for which the Court presently sits in

---

[29] For a detailed look at the Court's linguistic régime see L. Sevón, 'Languages in the Court of Justice of the European Communities' in *Scritti in onore di Giuseppe Federico Mancini. Diritto dell'Unione europea*, vol. II (Milan, Giuffrè Editore, 1998) pp 933–50; as well as the report on translation posted on the Court's internet site.

[30] On the role of legal secretaries at the Court see S. Kenney, 'Beyond Principals and Agents. Seeing Courts as Organisations by Comparing *Référendaires* at the European Court of Justice and Law Clerks at the U.S. Supreme Court' (2000) 33 *Comparative Political Studies* 593–625.

[31] Schermers and Waelbroeck, above n 1, p 461, state that the Court does not like to stress the influence of the Judge-Rapporteur on the case and ceased publishing his name in the 1970s when one of the European law journals started publishing the cases under the name of the Judge-Rapporteur involved. This practice was later discontinued. Although it is true that the outcome of a case tells the reader nothing about the position of the Judge-Rapporteur, at present the designation (rapporteur) follows the name of the Judge who has steered the case through the Court.

[32] See Article 15 EC Statute for present quora and Article 17 EC Statute (as amended) for future quora. For a challenge to the chamber system and the lack of transparency regarding the assignment of Judges to a particular formation see Case C–7/94 *Landesamt für Ausbildungsförderung Nordrhein-Westfalen v Lubor Gaal* [1995] ECR I–1031, paras 10–15.

[33] Articles 221 EC and 16 EC Statute (as amended).

plenary formation (fifty nine cases in 2001 alone) and the introduction of such a Chamber is to ensure that, with growing membership, and with the one Member State one Judge rule also enshrined in the Nice Treaty, deliberation of the most controversial or novel cases does not become too unwieldy.[34]

The decision to assign a case to a Chamber and, if so, which Chamber, is taken at the end of the written procedure, when all parties have made their submissions, the Judge-Rapporteur has prepared his preliminary report on the case, highlighting the legal issues and difficulties which it raises, the Advocate General has been heard and the preliminary report has been distributed, along with a draft Report for the Hearing, to all members of the Court.[35] Assignment to a Chamber indicates that 'the difficulty or importance of the case or the particular circumstances are not such as to require that the Court decide in plenary session.'[36] During the course of the written procedure, the chambers of the Judge-Rapporteur will have made contact with that of the designated Advocate General and any particular difficulties which the case may present may be discussed. Preliminary reports are distributed well in advance of the general administrative meeting of the Court in order to give all members a chance to familiarise themselves with the case.[37] Article 9(3) of the Court's Rules of Procedure provide that the Court shall lay down criteria by which, as a rule, cases are to be assigned to Chambers, but no such rules have been publicly articulated by the Court. In the past, a Member State or EC institution could request that a case be heard by the plenary.[38] The amendment of Articles 221 EC and 16 EC Statute following the Nice Treaty may mean that they simply request recourse to a Grand Chamber, the full court being used only for a very limited number of cases. The decision to assign to the full Court, a Chamber or, in the future, a Grand Chamber, is essentially based on the difficulty or novelty of the legal questions involved and, no doubt, on their political content and potential for controversy. Where a Chamber is initially assigned to deal with a case it may subsequently, at any stage, refer a case back to the Court.[39]

The Court emphasised in its 1995 Report that the ample use it makes of Chambers, coupled with the fact that resort to the plenary is no longer automatic in certain cases, has helped to speed up the time it takes to dispose of certain cases. In recent years, for example, routine Article 226 EC infringement proceedings, particularly those which are uncontested by the Member State concerned, seem to be decided by Chambers of three Judges when in the past

---

[34] Recourse to the plenary will be limited, in the revised EC Treaty, to cases of dismissal or misconduct by the Ombudsman and members of the Commission and Court of Auditors. The Court may still decide, however, where it considers that a case is of exceptional importance, to refer the case to the full Court.

[35] Article 95(2) RP.

[36] Article 95(1) RP. See further Rodney in Plender (ed), above n 1, at pp 657–61, on what kind of cases can be expected to be assigned to Chambers.

[37] See Articles 44 RP on general administrative meetings and what preliminary reports contain.

[38] Articles 221 EC and 95(2) RP, although this does not apply to staff cases.

[39] Article 95(3) RP.

they were decided by larger formations. As we have seen, cases may be referred back from a Chamber to the plenary and, in future, the Grand Chamber, if more difficult questions emerge as the case is being examined and prepared by the Judge-Rapporteur, after the oral hearing, or even at the end of the oral phase when the Advocate General has already presented his Opinion.[40] With the increasing assignment of cases to five Judge Chambers, the latter are regarded as one of the main motors of the court: 'Numerous landmark judgments have been handed down by a five-judge chamber. It consists of sufficient judges to command authority yet is small enough to be conducive to the devising of homogeneous collegiate judgments.'[41] Rodney puts his finger on what must be one of the greatest advantages of a case being assigned to a Chamber of five Judges, namely the greater cohesion which can be achieved in a judgment deliberated by five rather than between eleven and fifteen Members. It has been argued, however, that greater use of Chambers might give rise to inconsistencies in the case-law of the Court.[42] Whether this is true, and certainly there are examples of Chambers being overridden by the plenary, the plenary taking a different position to a Chamber, or divergence between different Chambers,[43] it is also true that the plenary itself has at times been the source of inconsistencies and incoherence.[44] Furthermore, as Ellis remarks, in a review of the sex equality case-law of the Court at the end of the last decade:

> it is noteworthy that most of [the Court's] more comprehensible and forward-looking decisions on sex equality have been those of its Chambers, rather than the full Court.

[40] Which was the case in Joined Cases C–267 and 268/91 *Keck and Mithouard* [1993] ECR I–6097, the Advocate General having presented his Opinion to the assigned Chamber before the case was referred back to the plenary.

[41] Rodney in Plender (ed), above n 1, p 659.

[42] See the Court of Justice's April 2000 document; and G. De Búrca, 'The Principle of Subsidiarity and the Court of Justice as an Institutional Actor' (1998) 36 *Journal of Common Market Studies* 217–35, 221, who refers to the 'bigger and less cohesive Court sitting more frequently in chambers.' Advocate General Jacobs has also expressed concern about whether the use of three-Judge Chambers leads to consistent practice in M. Andenas (ed), *Article 177 References to the European Court—Policy and Practice* (London, Butterworths, 1994) pp 111–12.

[43] See below ch 4 for a comparison of Cases C–360/90 *Arbeiterwohlfahrt der Stadt Berlin e.V. v Monika Bötel* [1992] ECR I–3589 and C–278/93 *Edith Freers and Hannelore Speckmann v Deutsche Bundespost* [1996] ECR I–1165, or ch 5 for a discussion of the plenary decision in Case C–394/6 *Mary Brown v Rentokil Ltd* [1998] ECR I–4185, which overruled a five-Judge Chamber in Case C–400/95 *Handels- og Kontorfunktionaerernes Forbund I Danmark (Elisabeth Larsson) v Dansk Handel Service* [1997] ECR I–2757. A fascinating area of research would be a comparison in a specific substantive area, such as, for example, social policy, of the outcome of cases assigned to the two large Chambers. Since the latter were reorganised in 1999, with Judges who had previously sat in the Fifth Chamber moving to the Sixth, and vice versa, the research, to be meaningful, would have to be limited to a specific timeframe.

[44] Compare, for example, the decision of the Court in Case C–450/93 *Eckhard Kalanke v Freie Hansestadt Bremen* [1995] ECR I–3051 and the decision handed down just over a year later in Case C–409/95 *Hellmut Marschall v Land Nordrhein Westfalen* [1997] ECR I–6363. On the general subject of precedent see A. Arnull, ' Owning up to fallability: precedent and the Court of Justice' (1993) 30 *Common Market Law Review* 247–66, 264, who suggests that the Court's general reluctance to confront inconsistencies in its case law may be due in part to the collegiate nature of its decisions, which often embody a number of compromises.

If it is true that the Court has now become too large for effective decision-making, then perhaps it ought to give further consideration to permitting Chambers to determine a wider range of cases . . . .[45]

CASE MANAGEMENT

It is the job of the President of the Court, who is elected by the college of Judges for a renewable period of three years, to oversee the distribution, management and progress of the Court's cases.[46] Article 8 of the Court's Rules of Procedure specifically states that the President shall direct the judicial business and administration of the Court and shall preside at hearings and deliberations.[47] This latter provision applies to hearings and deliberations of the plenary, since each Chamber appoints its own President at the beginning of the judicial year for the duration of that year.[48] The President does not act as a Judge-Rapporteur in cases before the Court, but he enjoys considerable power when summing up and presiding over deliberations in the plenary.[49] It is the President of the Court who assigns the Judge-Rapporteur.[50]

There seem to be no rules on the attribution of cases to Judge-Rapporteurs and those that have developed have never been made public. By examining the Court Reports one can see that long-serving Judges may, over the years, develop specialisation in a particular field and this 'specialisation' may be inherited by the member nominated for appointment by that Judge's Member State government. However, the Court has never openly allowed particular Chambers to specialise in any one field.[51]

Charged with the management of the Court's cases, the President is ultimately responsible for ensuring as speedy a resolution as possible. A preoccupation with the effectiveness of the judicial protection offered by the Court and with the increasing demands placed on the Court by an ever-growing workload, a backlog of cases and continued budgetary restraints (which have been of particular importance as regards the resources available for translation), has

---

[45] See E. Ellis, 'The Recent Jurisprudence of the Court of Justice in the Field of Sex Equality Law' (2000) 37 *Common Market Law Review* 1403–26, 1426.

[46] Articles 223 EC and 7 RP. The election is by secret ballot and takes place after each three year partial replacement. Only Judges may vote, although the Court has recommended that Advocates General, as equal members of the Court, should be allowed to participate in the election. Donner, a former President of the Court, described the process of electing the President as 'triennial periods of embarassment and secrecy', cited in Kenney, above n 6, 108, n 29.

[47] For a more complete list of the President's duties and powers see Schermers and Waelbroeck, above n 1, p 458.

[48] Article 10 RP. In the event that the Treaty of Nice comes into force, Article 16 EC Statute (as amended) will provide that Presidents of Chambers of five Judges shall also be elected for three years.

[49] See R. D'Sa and P. Duffy, 'Presidency of the Court and Constitution of Chambers' in Plender (ed), above n 1, pp 169–91, p 172.

[50] Article 9(2) RP.

[51] Van Gerven, above n 15, 222, calls for the practice of informal specialisation to be extended and rendered transparent by the official creation of specialised Chambers.

consistently come across in recent years in the President's foreword to the annual reports of the Court.[52] The Rules of Procedure provide that he shall fix a deadline for presentation by the Judge-Rapporteur of his preliminary report on cases for which he is responsible.[53] In practice, instructions exist within the Court which establish the time limits which Judge-Rapporteurs must meet at the various stages of the written and oral procedure and it is the task of the President's chamber to ensure that those time limits are met. From the moment a case is assigned, the Judge-Rapporteur is responsible for the preliminary inquiries in the case and the preparation of the preliminary report and Report for the Hearing. However, the full court remains formally seised of the case and it is only after the general administrative meeting of Judges and Advocates General that the case is assigned to the full court or to one of its Chambers.

Prior to the introduction of amendments in 2000 and 2001, in one of the few provisions granting the Court power to respond quickly in cases of urgency, Article 55(2) of the Court's Rules of Procedure gives the President power to give priority to a case in special circumstances.[54] Normally the order by which cases are dealt with is determined by when the preparatory inquiries in them have been completed.[55] Plender remarks, correctly, on the various practical constraints which undermine just how effective giving priority to a case can actually be, given the way in which the Court does and, to a certain extent, must, operate.[56] Before a case reaches the oral stage of procedure the written submissions will, in any case, have to be translated (unless the language of the case is French), the Judge-Rapporteur will have had to prepare his preliminary report and Report for the Hearing (which will subsequently be translated from French into the language of the case) and the administrative meeting will have taken place at which the case is examined for the first time by other members of the Court and assigned to a particular formation. In general a period of six weeks

[52] See, for example, the reference to the steady build up of cases in the 1998 Annual Report of the Court of Justice of the European Communities (Luxembourg, 1999) and the considerable detail in the 1997 Annual Report on the Court's quest for greater efficiency, accompanied by the explanation of the various procedural stages through which a case must pass.

[53] Article 44(1) RP. See also the Court's attempt at a delicate remonstrance with the Court of First Instance over the untoward delay in a case before the latter—Case C–185/95 P *Baustahlgewebe GmbH v Commission* [1998] ECR I–8417. Although the Court upheld the applicant's complaint, it underlined the unique difficulties experienced by the Court of First Instance (at para 43: 'Account must also be taken of the constraints inherent in proceedings before the Community judicature, associated in particular with the use of languages . . ., and of the obligation . . . to publish judgments in the languages referred to in Article 1 of Regulation No 1 of the Council of 15 April 1958 determining the languages to be used by the E.E.C.'), clearly aware of the awkwardness of its own position given the length of time it often takes itself to deliver its rulings—a case perhaps of the pot calling the kettle black!

[54] D. Wyatt, 'Procedure and Principles' in M. Andenas (ed), *Article 177 References to the European Court—Policy and Practice* (London, Butterworths, 1994), pp 77–81, p 78, criticises the lack of transparency surrounding requests for priority, with litigants sometimes simply being informed that cases must await their turn.

[55] Article 55(1) RP.

[56] See R. Plender, 'Oral Procedure' in Plender (ed), above n 1, pp 427–55, p 437. See also D. Vaughan, 'The Advocate's View' in Andenas (ed), above n 54, pp 55–62.

will elapse before the oral hearing takes place after the general administrative meeting, the intervening time being devoted to translation of the Report for the Hearing and its notification to the parties and those entitled to present submissions in the case. In addition, the Registry will have to try to fix a date for the hearing and the latter will not always be agreeable to all the lawyers concerned. Indeed difficulties surrounding the actual fixing of a date for a hearing can delay the oral hearing for anything from a week to several months. Finally, a further 6 weeks or more will elapse before the Advocate General's Opinion is delivered and it is impossible at the outset to predict how long the Court's deliberations may take thereafter. Cases generally move more quickly through Chambers than the full Court, but priority is generally most pressing and most frequently requested by national courts in respect of complex or at the very least controversial cases whose natural destination is the plenary. In any case, the provision for priority pursuant to Article 55(2) RP is limited to the oral stage of procedure.

It is rare these days to come across a commentary which does not mention the Court's growing workload and its increasing, untenable backlog of cases.[57] Indeed concern about the speed of Community justice, as distinct from the quality of that justice, dominated the 1999–2000 IGC discussions on reform of the Community's judicial architecture. At present, the Court has no formalised power to control its own docket. Of particular interest as regards the development of informal methods of controlling its caseload has been the development in recent years of a growing body of case-law on the (in)admissibility of references from national courts for preliminary rulings. This issue will be discussed in detail in chapter two, since it is contended that its development, and the controversy that surrounds it, underscore problems with the preliminary reference procedure. Those who comment on the Court's caseload generally accept that it is overworked and that it will be unable, in the near future, to reduce its present backlog of cases.[58] This ever increasing backlog and the considerable time it takes the Court to hand down its decisions pose a clear threat to the Court's commitment to effective judicial protection.[59] Litigants and national courts may

---

[57]   See, for example, Weatherill, above n 2, p 49; Sevón, above n 29; and Andenas, above n 54.

[58]   See, for example, L. Sadat Wexler, 'The Role of the European Court of Justice on the Way to European Union' in P.M. Lützeler (ed), *Europe After Maastricht. American and European Perspectives* (Providence/Oxford, Bergahn Books, 1994) pp 159–75, pp 168–69.

[59]   On the subject of delay, the Court is clearly a target for criticism, given that the average time it took to dispose of a preliminary reference in 2001 was 22.7 months. It is also true, however, that the Court is sometimes criticised for delays for which it is not responsible. In Case C–167/97 *R v Secretary of State for Employment, ex parte Nicole Seymour-Smith and Laura Perez* [1999] ECR I–623, a case for which priority was presumably requested by the House of Lords given the number of similar cases pending at national level, the Judicial Committee of the House of Lords decided to make a reference in December 1996, the formal Order for Reference was dated 13 March 1997, but the case was only lodged in Luxembourg on 2 May 1997. See also G. Bebr, 'The Preliminary Proceedings of Article 177 EEC—Problems and Suggestions for Improvement' in H.G. Schermers *et al* (eds), *Article 177 EEC: Problems and Experiences* (Amsterdam, North Holland, 1987) pp 345–65, p 359; Lester, in the same volume, pp 191–92, on the inordinate delay in forwarding the reference in Case 222/84 *Marguerite Johnston v Chief Constable of the Royal Ulster Constabulary* [1986] ECR 1651; and generally Vaughan in Andenas (ed), above n 54.

be less willing to seek a preliminary ruling if it means postponing resolution of the case for anything from one to three years and this at a time when the Court's 'political and psychological basis . . . is still very frail'.[60]

For some time the Court has suggested measures requiring amendment of the EC Treaty and its Statute and has in fact adopted others in its own Rules of Procedure with a view to reducing the backlog and avoiding a further onslaught of references. Thus, it recommended the transfer to the Court of First Instance of jurisdiction in certain cases, not least permitting the Court of First Instance to hear and determine questions referred for a preliminary ruling pursuant to Article 234 EC in certain matters to be defined by the Council.[61] Prior to the IGC which culminated with the ill-tempered signing of the Treaty of Nice, the Court also recommended the establishment of a system to filter appeals from the Court of First Instance, the establishment of a board of appeal with judicial powers to determine staff disputes, as well as tribunals, or appellate bodies of a judicial nature with jurisdiction to hear and determine disputes in matters concerning industrial and commercial property.

Article 225(1) EC, as amended by the Treaty of Nice, provides that the Court of First Instance shall have jurisdiction to hear and determine actions or proceedings referred to in Articles 230, 232, 235, 236 and 238, with the exception of those reserved in the EC Statute. Pursuant to Articles 220 and 225a EC, as amended, judicial panels may be attached to the Court of First Instance in order to exercise judicial competence in certain specific areas. Appeals lie against decisions of judicial panels to the Court of First Instance and, exceptionally, to the Court of Justice, where there is a serious risk of the unity or consistency of EC law being affected. Perhaps most significantly, Article 225(3) EC (as amended by the Treaty of Nice) now provides that 'The Court of First Instance shall have jurisdiction to hear and determine questions referred for a preliminary ruling under Article 234, in specific areas laid down by the Statute.' Preliminary rulings handed down by the Court of First Instance may also, exceptionally, be reviewed by the Court of Justice where, once again, there is a serious risk of the unity or consistency of Community law being affected. The Court of First Instance may also refer a case to the Court of Justice where it considers that the case requires a decision of principle which is likely to affect the unity or

[60] See T. Koopmans, 'The Future of the Court of Justice of the European Communities' (1991) 11 *Yearbook of European Law* 15–32, 23. On reluctance to seek a reference due to the delay involved see Sir Thomas Bingham MR, 'The National Judge's View' and Vaughan in Andenas (ed), above n 54, pp 43–48; and R. Voss, 'The National Perception of the Court of First Instance and the European Court of Justice' (1993) 30 *Common Market Law Review* 1119–34, 1124, who states that the length of the reference procedure is a particular disincentive for Employment Tribunals.

[61] See the *Contribution of the Court of Justice and the Court of First Instance to the Intergovernmental Conference* (available at http:/curia.eu.int/en/txts/intergov/cig.pdf). Decisions by the Court of First Instance by way of preliminary ruling would, however, be subject to review by the Court of Justice 'where the Court of Justice considers that such review is necessary in order to ensure the unity and coherence of Community law', a condition which gained acceptance when limited Article 234 EC jurisdiction was extended to the Court of First Instance (Article 225 EC as amended).

consistency of Community law.[62] Finally, the Treaty now authorises the Court to dispense with the Opinion of an Advocate General where the case does not require his involvement.[63] The possibility of the Court of First Instance hearing preliminary references has not gone without criticism in either academic or Court circles. Arnull observes, for example, that from a purely practical point of view, references may cut across several areas of EC law and it seems difficult to confine Court of First Instance jurisdiction to predefined categories.[64] Within the Court itself, Advocate General Ruiz Jarabo has argued that: 'there can be only one court of cassation and that the day that two different interpretations of EC law are given by the two courts the death knell will sound for the preliminary-ruling procedure.' In his view, the possibility of review of Court of First Instance decisions by the Court of Justice will not provide an adequate means of avoiding the disruptive effect of a disagreement between the two Community courts.[65]

Even prior to the changes incorporated in the Treaty of Nice, the Court has made increasing use of Chambers in recent years. A number of changes have also been made to its Rules of Procedure.[66] Most importantly, Article 104a now provides for an expedited procedure in preliminary reference cases where the circumstances establish that a ruling on the question put to the Court is a matter of exceptional urgency. The President decides, at the request of the national court and on a proposal from the Judge-Rapporteur, after hearing the Advocate General, whether to apply this accelerated procedure. Where the request is allowed, a date for the hearing may be fixed immediately and written observations must be submitted within a period prescribed by the President, which shall not be less than fifteen days. Parties may be directed to limit themselves in their written observations to the essential points of law raised.[67] In addition, Article 44 of the Rules of Procedure specifically provides that a Judge-Rapporteur

---

[62] Article 225(3) EC (as amended). In a declaration attached to the Nice Treaty the Conference stated that, in such cases, the Court of Justice should act under an emergency procedure.

[63] Article 222 EC (as amended). Article 20 EC Statute (as amended) further specifies that '[W]here it considers that the case raises no new point of law, the Court may decide, after hearing the Advocate General, that the case shall be determined without a submission from the Advocate General.' However, if, in particular, a preliminary reference involves no new point of law, one wonders why it cannot be disposed of by reasoned order with reference to existing case-law pursuant to the procedure established in Article 104(3) RP.

[64] A. Arnull, 'Judicial architecture or judicial folly? The challenge facing the European Union' (1999) 24 *European Law Review* 516–24, 520; and A. Johnston, 'Judicial Reform and the Treaty of Nice' (2001) 38 *Common Market Law Review* 499–523.

[65] Paras 70–74 of his Opinion in Case C–17/00 *François de Coster v Collège des Bourgmestres et Echevins de Watermael-Boitsfort* [2001] ECR I–9445.

[66] See, for the initial proposals by the Court of Justice and Court of First Instance, the discussion paper entitled *The Future of the Judicial System of the EU*, sent to the Council on 10 May 1999.

[67] Article 62a RP provides for an expedited procedure in direct actions 'where the particular urgency of the case requires the Court to give its ruling with the minimum of delay.' The Court has said in its Annual Report on its activities in 2001 that it intends to use these procedures with caution, where it appears properly justified in the event of particular or exceptional urgency. See, for example, Case C–189/01 *Jippe and others* [2001] ECR I–5689, a case concerning EC policy on the eradication of foot and mouth disease.

should recommend as a matter of course in his preliminary report whether or not the oral part of the procedure should be omitted as provided for in Article 44a.[68] Finally, greater provision has been made for the use of modern communication technology when communicating with the Court's Registry.[69]

It is necessary in passing to mention another issue which rarely catches the eye of commentators but which, in fact, may dominate how the Court must be managed for several months, if not an entire judicial year, every three years. Article 223 EC provides that there shall be a partial replacement of Judges and Advocates General every three years.[70] For the decisions of the full Court to be valid, however, only the Judges who were present at the oral hearing may participate in the deliberations and, in addition, a quorum must be attained for the decision to be valid.[71] With renewal, it remains uncertain, sometimes until quite soon before the commencement of the new judicial year on 7 October, whether those Judges whose mandates have expired and who wish to be renewed will in fact be successful.

To avoid problems with quora which this triennial 'Big Bang' in the Court's composition would otherwise entail, it is forced to act in a number of ways. The composition of the plenary Court and Chambers in oral hearings must be organised at a very early stage prior to the renewal in October to ensure that a sufficient number of Judges remain (essentially those whose mandates are not at an end) to see pending cases in which there has already been an oral hearing through to the end. In addition, cases which have reached a certain point in their passage through the Court, essentially those in which the oral hearing has been completed, must be delivered prior to the end of the judicial year to ensure that the Judge-Rapporteur in charge of the case whose mandate is coming to an end has completed his task of steering the case through the Court and the problem of managing a quorum from those who sat at the oral hearing is not faced. In the event that a Judge-Rapporteur does not complete a case, or a quorum is not reached, a case will have to be passed on to a new Judge-Rapporteur and, if there has been an oral phase, it will have to be reopened, increasing the time it will take the Court to dispose of the case. In order to avoid these scenarios, the workload of the Court in renewal years can be extraordinarily heavy. More cases which might otherwise go to a Chamber of five Judges are sent to the plenary to avoid the absence of the necessary quorum. The amount of time which Judges can spend on important cases is necessarily limited, given that almost all cases are priority at this stage. Yet if a case is heard before the plenary it will

---

[68] See below on the use of reasoned orders to dispose of preliminary references.

[69] Article 79(2) RP.

[70] Members of the Court of First Instance are also appointed for a six year renewable term and a similar provision on partial renewal of membership is to be found in Article 225 EC (Article 224 EC as amended).

[71] See Articles 26 and 27(2) RP and 15 EC Statute (as amended). For an explanation of how the composition of the plenary and Chambers is determined for each case see J. Pompe and R. Plender, 'The Registry' in Plender (ed), above n 1, p 236.

automatically 'consume a very considerable number of judge-hours'.[72] Plenary hearings and deliberations take up to three days of the week, compared to one day for the work of Chambers. In addition, the smaller number of Judges present in the deliberation of a case before a Chamber of five Judges means that it is inevitably easier to reach a decision agreeable to a majority, if not the whole formation. The same cannot be said for the plenary, where numerous other Judges will presumably be ready and waiting to criticise and amend whatever draft has been prepared by the Judge-Rapporteur.[73]

Of course, this state of affairs affects not only the members and their chambers, the lawyers who revise all Court judgments and the various translation services have to work flat out. On leaving the Court in 1988, Judge Mackenzie-Stuart, who had just completed his term of office as President and who therefore had been responsible for overall case management at the Court berated the failure of Member States to help solve the problems which the Court faced as a result of renewal of mandates.[74] The fact that the Court is overworked and under pressure as a result of renewal, does not of course excuse *uncommunautaire* reasoning,[75] for example, or indeed the paucity of reasoning so often criticised by commentators.[76] However, if one is to criticise a court about the length of time it takes to hand down a ruling it is essential to reflect on the factors which hinder or aid that court's ability to fulfil its functions. Studies have revealed that dips in the Court's productivity can be linked to the reappointment of potentially half of the bench every three years.[77] Clearly, there is something to be said for an extension of members' mandates, although any extension might have to be accompanied by the exclusion of a renewal of their term of office. Unfortunately, neither the length nor the question of the renewal of Members' mandates were the subject of amendment in the Treaty of Nice.

[72] Edward, above n 1, 552.

[73] The problems posed by the three year replacement rule are also recognised by Van Gerven, above n 15, 221, who proposes (along the lines of Article 40(6) ECHR) that members be allowed to continue to deal with such cases as they already have under consideration. Such a system means the Court would be provided, temporarily at least, with additional, experienced manpower and that the allocation of cases would remain efficient. Presumably, however, questions of continued remuneration would prove problematic, as would the forecasting of how long it would take to complete the case in hand.

[74] Address of Lord Mackenzie-Stuart on the occasion of his retirement from office, reproduced in Kennedy, above n 7, pp 74–75. The decisions to appoint the German and Spanish Judges were only taken on 26 and 30 September 1988, respectively, despite the fact that the new judicial year started on 7 October. For a similar complaint regarding Member States' failure to appoint replacement Judges and the resulting effect on the planning of the Court's workload, see Kapteyn and VerLoren van Themaat, above n 9, p 251, n 394. See, however, Schermers and Waelbroeck, above n 1, p 452, who suggest that replacement and the selection of new Judges have caused no problems.

[75] See L. Gormley, 'Assent and respect for judgments: uncommunautaire reasoning in the European Court of Justice' in L. Krämer *et al.* (eds), *Law and Diffuse Interests in the European Legal Order. Liber Amicorum Norbert Reich* (Baden-Baden, Nomos, 1997) pp 11–29.

[76] For a discussion of the drafting and reasoning of Court of Justice decisions see below.

[77] See further Strasser, above n 1, particularly 60.

WRITTEN PHASE OF PROCEDURE

The written phase of procedure at the Court consists of the communication to the parties and to the institutions of the Community whose decisions are in dispute, of applications, statements of case, defences and observations, and of replies, if any, as well as of all papers and documents in support or of certified copies of them.[78] 'The object of the written procedure is to delimit the dispute and to set out for the judges all the claims of the parties by informing them of the pertinent facts, the form of order sought and the pleas in law and arguments of the parties so as to enable the court to give a decision on the dispute.'[79] Demaret notes that the emphasis on the importance of written submissions at the Court is in line with the multilingual nature of the Community and reflects the tradition both of the French *Conseil d'État*, on which the Court was largely modelled, and of the six founding Member States.[80]

In cases governed by Article 234 EC, Article 20 EC Statute (Article 23 EC Statute following the Treaty of Nice) provides that the decision of the court or tribunal of a Member State which suspends its proceedings and refers a case to the Court shall be notified to the Court by the court or tribunal concerned. The decision is then notified by the Registrar to the parties, the Member States, the Commission and also to the Council, European Central Bank or Council and European Parliament jointly if the act, the validity or interpretation of which is in dispute, originates from one of them.[81] The parties have two months in which to lodge their written observations, save when the expedited procedure provided by Article 104a of the Rules of procedure applies, when they may have as little as fifteen days. Thereafter, they must wait until the oral hearing to comment on the observations and arguments of other parties and interveners, as the written procedure under Article 234 EC is not adversarial.[82] The time it takes parties to submit their observations, the length and complexity of those observations, and the workload of the translation service will all affect how quickly the documents in the case file are translated into French, ready for the

---

[78]   Article 20 EC Statute (as amended); Articles 37–44a RP.

[79]   See A. Valle Galvez, 'Stages of the Procedure' in Plender (ed), above n 1, pp 277–85, p 281, citing the Court of First Instance Notes for Guidance, point I. The purpose of written observations in preliminary reference procedures 'is to suggest the answers which the Court should give to the questions referred to it, and to set out succinctly, but completely, the reasoning on which those answers are based. It is important to bring to the attention of the Court the factual circumstances of the case before the national court and the relevant provisions of the national legislation at issue.' (See Notes for guidance to counsel in written and oral proceedings).

[80]   Demaret, above n 1, p 325.

[81]   The Registrar also notifies EEA States and the EFTA Surveillance Authority, which may also submit written observations.

[82]   Usher in Plender (ed), above n 1, p 791, notes that once the observations have been lodged in a reference, the Registry will send copies to all those who were entitled to be notified of the original reference, although there appears to be no legal rule which actually requires this. Since the written observations are submitted without knowledge of the other observations being submitted in the case, this practice should help to improve the adversarial nature of the oral hearing.

Judge-Rapporteur to begin his preliminary analysis of the file and prepare the preliminary report for the general administrative meeting and the Report for the Hearing. As Edward has pointed out, the fact that the Judge-Rapporteur, if he does not understand the language of the case, may only be in a position to examine the file once all the submissions have been translated means that a number of important questions relating to admissibility, the joining of cases[83] or a possible suspension, can only be dealt with when a considerable amount of work has already been done on the case by the translation service.[84] In practice, it may take six months after it has been lodged for a preliminary reference to be 'ripe' for treatment by the Judge-Rapporteur.

As we have seen, the first document produced by the Judge-Rapporteur will normally be the preliminary report. Accompanied by a copy of the Report for the Hearing, the preliminary report is sent to the Advocate General assigned to the case for his comments. Once the preliminary report is approved by the Advocate General, or amendments proposed by him, and accepted by the Judge-Rapporteur, have been made, the report is distributed to the other members of the Court in preparation for the weekly general meeting. The purpose of the report is to enable the members of the Court to determine to which formation the case should be sent, whether measures of inquiry are necessary[85] and whether any other preparatory steps,[86] such as questions for the parties,

---

[83] The Court may, at any time, after hearing the parties and the Advocate General, order that two or more cases concerning the same subject-matter be joined for the purposes of the written or oral procedure or of the final judgment (Article 43 RP). The procedure is usually initiated by the President, the Registry or the Judge-Rapporteur. Joinder can take place between references from different courts as long as the questions are identical or the cases have the same subject-matter. Where references are similar but one has reached procedurally a more advanced state, it may be too late and no longer convenient to join them. See A. Valle Galvez, 'Written Procedure' in Plender (ed), above n 1, pp 287–347, p 334 on the different phases of the procedure for which joinder may be used.

[84] Edward (1995), above n 1, 541. The preliminary examination of the reference carried out by the Research and Documentation Division may not have identified any problems or those that have been identified may not actually be confirmed until the written observations of the parties have been received and, if necessary, translated. Strasser, above n 1, 64, also estimates that it takes at least six months before work on the case reaches this stage.

[85] Article 60 RP provides that the Court may at any time, in accordance with Article 45(1) RP, after hearing the Advocate General, order any measure of inquiry to be taken or that a previous inquiry be repeated or expanded. The Court may direct the Chamber or the Judge-Rapporteur to carry out the measures so ordered. These measures may include personal appearance by the parties, requests for information and the production of documents, oral testimony, commissioning of an expert's report, inspection of a place or thing. Article 24 EC Statute (as amended) also concerns the supply of information and the production of documents. Measures of inquiry are used when the resolution of a particular fact is necessary to enable the Court to give judgment in the case and are most commonly ordered between the end of the written phase of procedure and the beginning of the oral phase, although they can in practice be ordered at any stage. Since, pursuant to Article 234 EC, it is not for the Court to test the veracity of the facts presented to it, or to resolve the case, but rather to concentrate on questions of law and interpretation, measures of inquiry are of limited relevance in this context. See Plender (ed), above n 1, p 359, for a discussion of the Court's under-utilisation of these instruments.

[86] For the difference between measures of inquiry and preparatory steps see Valle Galvez in Plender (ed), above n 1, p 342. Preparatory measures are identified by the Court in its Notes for Guidance (part C, pt.1(a)) as, *inter alia*, requests to examine in greater detail issues which have not been adequately canvassed, requests to concentrate pleadings on certain issues or requests to answer certain questions at the oral stage.

requests for the production of documents or the supply of further information[87] are necessary for the case to proceed. The preliminary report may also include a request for the Registry to distribute certain documents or EC legislation and a request for a research note from the Research and Documentation Division if that has been deemed necessary. The Judge-Rapporteur tries to explain to his colleagues, as succinctly as possible, the fundamental aspects of the case, its factual and legal context and the points of law, or even political sensitivities,[88] which the case raises. In the event that the Judge-Rapporteur is of the opinion that the case is inadmissible, his preliminary report will explain this to the general meeting and be accompanied by a draft order of inadmissibility which will subsequently be deliberated by the Chamber or a plenary court formation to which the case is assigned by the meeting. A Judge-Rapporteur or Advocate General will also alert the President's Chamber if, in the case of a reference for a preliminary ruling, the questions asked have been resolved by previous decisions of the Court. In such cases, the Registry may furnish the national court with a copy of these decisions and inquire whether the referring judge wishes to maintain the reference before the Court.[89] Once the case has been assigned at the general meeting to the full Court or a Chamber, and a date for a hearing (if, as is more often than not the case, a hearing is to take place) has been set, the Report for the Hearing is sent to the translation division where it is translated from French into the language of the case and then sent by the Registry to the various parties for their comments in advance of the oral hearing.[90]

Edward noted in 1995 that although in the past preliminary reports offered a fairly full analysis of the issues in the case, the increased workload of Judges means that they neither have the time to prepare, nor the time to read long reports and that Judge-Rapporteurs tend to keep their observations to a few paragraphs.[91] However, the general meeting may be the first and last occasion afforded Judges and Advocates General to examine some cases. In these circumstances, it is surely essential that a clear picture is drawn at this early stage regarding what the case entails, what questions are likely to arise in the course of its resolution and what information, perhaps lacking in the case file, is essential for a fruitful oral hearing and a well-reasoned and well-informed final decision.

---

[87] In accordance with Article 24 EC Statute (as amended), or as a measure of inquiry under Article 45(2)(b) RP. The former power is more informal than the latter since the Court need not make a formal order for a preparatory inquiry. In general the Court proceeds by way of an informal letter or request made by the administrative meeting.

[88] Edward, above n 1, 553, remarks that the Judge from the Member State in which a preliminary reference has originated may know about special features of the case about which the Judge-Rapporteur and Advocate General may not be aware and that this may prove a deciding factor in determining how the case should be dealt with.

[89] See also R. Plender, 'Oral Procedure' in Plender (ed), above n 1, pp 427–55, p 429.

[90] Where there is no hearing, the report is known as the Report of the Judge-Rapporteur and is distributed to the parties allowing them a specified time within which to comment.

[91] Edward, above n 1, 552.

ORAL PHASE OF PROCEDURE

Article 18 EC Statute provides that the oral procedure shall consist of the reading of the report presented by a Judge acting as Rapporteur (something which never actually happens in practice, the Report being taken as read), the hearing by the Court of agents, advisers and lawyers entitled to practise before a court of a Member State, the hearing of any experts or witnesses and the submissions of the Advocate General. The Judge-Rapporteur does not, in practice, read out the Report for the Hearing and the Court is now allowed to dispense with the need for an oral hearing in certain circumstances.[92] In addition, as regards references under Article 234 EC, where the answer to the referred question can be clearly deduced from existing case-law or where the answer admits of no reasonable doubt, the Court can, pursuant to Article 104(3) of its Rules of Procedure, give its decision by reasoned order in which, if appropriate, reference is made to its previous judgment or the relevant case-law.[93]

Evolving from a number of legal systems, which in turn belong to quite different legal families, procedure at the Court of Justice has obviously given rise to considerable comment. This is particularly true of the oral phase of procedure at the Court and the role and value of its oral hearings. Plender observes that the importance attached to oral hearings by the Court itself has changed over the years, in line with its increased workload and the resulting pressures on its simultaneous interpretation services.[94] In order to assist those who appear before the Court, the latter has produced Notes for Guidance of Counsel in written and oral proceedings. The Court emphasised in these Notes that the purpose of the oral hearing is to answer the questions put by the Court and to explain and expand the more complex points and those which are difficult to grasp. The oral procedure must be seen as supplementing the written procedure and should involve no repetition of what has already been said in writing. The Judges and Advocate General also meet counsel in the robing room before the hearing begins and they may, at that stage, mention points on which they would like counsel to dwell. Increasingly, the Court seems to indicate to counsel, prior

[92] See Articles 104 (4) RP (references for preliminary rulings), 120 RP (appeals against decisions of the Court of First Instance) or 44a RP, unless the relevant parties have submitted an application setting out the reasons for which they wish to be heard.

[93] See its use in the Order in Joined Cases C–405/96 and C–408/96 *Béton Express and Others v Direction Régionale des Douanes de la Réunion* [1998] ECR I–4253. The Court's original proposal to the Council was that it be given the power to respond to requests for preliminary rulings by reasoned order in clear cases. See A. Arnull, 'Judging the New Europe' (1994) 19 *European Law Review* 3–15, 11.

[94] In Joined Cases 29, 31, 36, 39–47, 50–51/63 *SA des Laminoirs Usines de la Providence v High Authority* [1965] ECR 911, for example, the Court conducted oral hearings over several days and 'either permitted, requested or engaged in seven written communications during the oral stage'. See Plender in Plender (ed), above n 1, p 438. Such a luxury would now be unthinkable with extended oral hearings being allowed, and even then sparingly, in large cases before the Court of First Instance, like those involving cartels in cartonboard and cement.

to the hearing, on which points or issues they should concentrate. From the point of view of the bench, a successful oral hearing should allow the Court to clarify points which the written observations have left unclear or even untouched and, specifically in the context of references for a preliminary ruling, provide the parties with their only opportunity to respond to the written observations of others.[95]

However, anyone who has sat in the court-rooms armed with a copy of the Report for the Hearing, which is published in the language of procedure on the day of the hearing and synopsises the parties' written submissions, is well aware that counsel appearing before the Court frequently ignore these pointers. In the words of one well-seasoned member of the Luxembourg bench 'The least useful, and certainly the most boring, form of oral pleading consists of the pleader reading from a prepared text in which he merely repeats points already made in writing and takes no account of what has been said by others. Unfortunately, this is also a common form of oral pleading before the Court.'[96] Clearly, the fact that Judges and pleaders cannot always understand each other without simultaneous interpretation and that spontaneity is lost as a result, along with some of what the pleader is trying to convey, has an important effect on, at the very least, the liveliness of the hearing.[97] Furthermore, the orthodox version of the division of competences under Article 234 EC suggests that the Court is not concerned with the resolution of the case and it is sometimes assumed, as a result, that it is unconcerned with the factual background or context in which the questions are asked.[98] The establishment of the Court of First Instance and the transfer of a number of heads of jurisdiction to that Court have certainly

---

[95] It is unclear to what extent the Court is pleased when presented with new arguments at the oral stage. In a case involving the 1977 Directive on Acquired Rights—Case C–29/91 *Dr Sophie Redmond Stichting v Hendrikus Bartol and Others* [1992] ECR I–3189—the Court remarked (para.20), that a new argument presented at the oral hearing had not been put forward in the written observations submitted to the Court and was not supported by any document in the case-file.

[96] See Edward, above n 1, 554.

[97] *Ibid.* Interpretation is normally provided from each of the languages in which any counsel or witness addresses the Court into each of the other languages used by other counsel or witnesses and from each of the languages used by counsel or witnesses to the preferred language of a Judge or Advocate General sitting in the case. In recent years, with the accession of new Member States and the increase in the combination of languages required, the Court has increasingly resorted to a 'relay' system of translation, whereby one interpreter works from the language being used in Court to another interpreter who in turn interprets into the language required by counsel or the bench.

[98] See J. Usher, 'References for Preliminary Rulings' in Plender (ed), above n 1, pp 761–809, p 779: 'The jurisdiction of the ECJ on references for preliminary rulings is at most, depending on the provision under which the reference is made, either to interpret a provision of Community law or to pronounce upon the validity of an item of Community secondary legislation, which are quintessentially matters of law'. See also Freestone, *loc. cit.*, 50; and G. Ress, 'Fact-finding at the European Court of Justice' in Lillich, R.B., *Fact-finding Before International Tribunals*, Eleventh Sokol Colloquium (Ardsley-on-Hudson, New York, Transnational Publishers Inc., 1992) pp 177–203, p 181. The Court has consistently asserted that it is for national courts to establish the facts of the case—see, for example, Case 13/61 *De Geus v Bosch* [1962] ECR 45, its first preliminary reference. For discussion of the exceptional use of preparatory inquiries by the Court to establish facts in Article 234 EC cases see S. Morris, 'Preparatory Inquiries' in Plender (ed), above n 1, pp 349–416, pp 358–59 and regarding the question of admissibility see below ch 2.

lessened the Court of Justice's overall fact-finding responsibilities. However, as its inadmissibility jurisprudence reveals, the Court increasingly relates the question of law that it is being asked to determine to the specific facts of the case. The answer it gives in a preliminary ruling may be generally applicable but there is an unavoidable element of dispute resolution in the Court's work and it clearly feels uncomfortable and unhappy when asked to determine questions of law without full knowledge of the facts.[99] Yet it is questionable whether the procedure which governs preliminary references is suitable to such a dispute resolution role. As Everling has cogently argued:

> all those taking part in the proceedings submit their arguments to the Court simultaneously without knowledge of the case put forward by the others. Comment on the written argument is possible only at the hearing which suffers as a result. The Court occasionally tries to mitigate these deficiencies by putting questions to those taking part in the proceedings who then have the opportunity to supplement their written observations. What is more, the facts underlying the case cannot be clarified satisfactorily and in particular the Court cannot hear evidence . . . Important questions therefore have to be left open and referred back to the national court for further findings to be made.[100]

Nevertheless, other factors explaining why the oral hearing can be such a dry and unhelpful affair suggest that neither the Court nor those who appear before it are getting the best out of the oral hearing at present. Mancini and Keeling remark that:

> The typical advocate in continental Europe is accustomed to put on his robe, make his submissions—would-be Cartesian in France, ornate in Italy, ponderous in Germany, entangled in the Netherlands, artful in Greece—and bid adieu. If a member of the bench dares to question, let alone interrupt him, he is at a loss, coughs, stares at the ceiling and grumbles out a usually irrelevant answer. Some go so far as to resent these judicial interferences, as they would call them, and make no effort to conceal their annoyance.[101]

Similarly, Edward states that pleaders before the Court of Justice are allowed to speak uninterrupted and remarks that '[T]his is thought odd by pleaders bred in the common law tradition, but lawyers from many other traditions find it difficult to cope with interruptions.'[102] However, if the purpose of the oral hearing is to lay solid ground for the Advocate General to deliver his Opinion and the Court to deliberate, whether or not counsel appearing before the Court are 'comfortable' or not should clearly be irrelevant. In the first place, they are either pleading in their own language or a language in which they feel perfectly

---

[99] See Ress, *ibid*, pp 194–200; and below ch 2, for a discussion of the dispute resolution and public action facets of litigation pursuant to Article 234 EC.

[100] See U. Everling, 'The Member States of the EC before their Court of Justice' (1984) 9 *European Law Review* 215–41, 223–24.

[101] See Mancini and Keeling, above n 1, 401.

[102] See Edward (1995), above n 1, 549 and 554.

comfortable.[103] Admittedly, allowances must be made for the constraints imposed by simultaneous interpretation, but it seems extraordinary that their comfort or discomfort when under judicial fire from the bench should perturb the Court. Secondly, although lawyers from civil law countries may be less used to the 'adversarial' tone of the oral hearings regarded as the norm in the common law world, this deference to the judicial context in which lawyers are used to working seems an unfortunate hangover from the early days of the Community when common law jurisdictions had not yet joined and when French or civil legal culture was predominant. Finally, perhaps the majority of counsel appearing before the Court do so on a regular basis. This is certainly true of agents for the Community institutions and Member States and is also true of many counsel for private parties who have built up, in their respective Member States, a large EC law practice.[104] It seems all the more remarkable, given the experience of these well-seasoned practitioners appearing in Luxembourg, that the Court should concern itself with whether or not they are used, at national level, to being interrupted during their speeches or subject to questioning or requests for clarification. What may be true is that when asked detailed questions regarding 'turkey tails, milk centers, animal offal, or refrigerators'[105] a lawyer may not, on the spot, be able to provide the necessary details, technical or otherwise, in reply (although national or Commission experts often accompany counsel to provide assistance). If the Court has found this to be the case it should resort as much as possible to written questions sent to the parties prior to the oral hearing or should direct counsel, prior to the oral hearing, to the issues which it wishes to hear discussed.[106]

[103] The Court may authorise the use of another Community language as the language of the case: Article 29(2)(b) and (c) RP.

[104] See also C. Barnard and E. Sharpston, 'The Changing Face of Article 177 References' (1997) 34 *Common Market Law Review* 1113–71, 1168, who refer to Article 234 EC references being the province of a small, exclusive coterie of courts serviced by a specialist Bar; de la Mare in Craig and De Búrca, above n 4, p 256, for the relative numbers of national lawyers appearing before the Court; and generally W. Mattli and A.-M. Slaughter, *Constructing the European Community Legal System from the Ground Up: The Role of Individual Litigants and National Courts*, EUI WP RSC No 96/56, p 18, who refer to the 'small size and relatively closely knit character of the legal community in each [Member State], forged by ties of education, socialization and professional mobility between the professoriate, private practice and the judiciary.'

[105] Taken from M.L.Volcansek, *Judicial Politics in Europe. An Impact Analysis* (New York, Peter Lang Publishing Inc., 1986) p 27.

[106] The Court of First Instance operates in a similar linguistic environment to the Court and is subject to identical constraints, yet it is well-known that its oral hearings involve far freer and more exacting exchanges between the bench and counsel. Non-publication of the Reports for the Hearing since 1994 makes it impossible to gauge how often the Court demands written responses from the parties, Member States and the Commission in preliminary reference cases. C.-D. Ehlermann and J. Pipkorn, 'The Role of the Commission in Preliminary Proceedings Under Article 177 EEC' in Schermers *et al* (eds), above n 1, pp 293–334, p 296, emphasise the usefulness of the Court asking questions, but suggest that the Court has considerably extended its practice of putting questions to all or some of the intervening parties. In contrast, writing about the Court's rejection of references from national courts due to inadequate factual and legal information O'Keeffe (1998), above n 28, 510, complains that, in Joined Cases C–320–322/90 *Telemarsicabruzzo SpA v Circostel* [1993] ECR I–393, 'despite being put on notice by the Commission concerning the lack of information supplied

Admittedly, certain members of the bench and certain Judge-Rapporteurs are active and persistent in their questioning. Mancini and Keeling comment on the change in the style and format of hearings which the arrival of common law Judges heralded at the Court and the fact that 'their colleagues loved their refusal to listlessly accept the kind of assistance which the lawyers were prepared to give them and started to act in similar fashion.'[107] However, members of the Court are not the only interested parties to complain about the oral phase. One practitioner has remarked that the least helpful oral procedures are those in which the Judges do not appear to have formed a provisional view of what the key issues are and pose few questions.[108] The best oral procedures from the advocate's point of view also seem to be those where the Judges have a clear focus of what they want to learn from the hearing and have a clear focus of the case, usually at the instigation of the Judge-Rapporteur.

There may, however, be a serious reason for this apparent disenchantment with oral hearings and the failure of Judges and Advocates General to capitalise on what is, effectively, their last chance to add to the information already in the case file before the Opinion is delivered and deliberation begins. Unless the Court takes the unusual step of, for example, ordering measures of inquiry,[109] once the oral hearing is over there is little possibility of further information from the parties and no further contact with national government or EC institution agents. To all intents and purposes, the Court, at this stage, is on its own, unless of course it decides to reopen the oral procedure or request further information from the national court. Reference has been made previously to the Court's heavy workload, to the unceasing arrival of new cases at the Court and its failure, despite trojan efforts, to reduce the backlog of cases. The Court, as we have seen, has no formal control over the cases it receives and the result is an ever-lengthening docket. On a day to day basis what this means for members is an endless round of general meetings, oral hearings and deliberations arranged intensively from Tuesday to Friday. A Judge-Rapporteur may be presenting a complex and controversial draft judgment in an extremely important case at the deliberation of the plenary on any Wednesday or Friday, but he will simultaneously be working on the preliminary reports and Reports for the Hearing in several cases in preparation for the general meetings on Tuesdays, will have had to attend hours of oral hearing (not all, as we have seen, useful) during the course of the week and will also be working on other draft judgments for deliberation in Chambers or the plenary. The draft before the plenary may be one of several, with several other drafts to follow. By the time the oral hearing takes

by the national court, the Court posed written questions prior to the hearing only to the Italian Government, and then only concerning two technical questions, rather than to elucidate the nature of the dispute. It is particularly striking that no questions were asked of the parties even though they had submitted observations to the Court.'

[107]   Mancini and Keeling, above n 1, 401.

[108]   See Wyatt in Andenas (ed), above n 54, p 79; see also D. Anderson, *References to the European Court* (London, Sweet & Maxwell, 1995) p 264.

[109]   Article 60 RP.

place, apart from the Judge-Rapporteur and the designated Advocate General, other Judges in the formation will likely have had little contact with the case.[110] They will have discussed briefly its passage through the general meeting and will no doubt have prepared for the approaching hearing. However, at no time will they have sat down with their colleagues to discuss at length problems that they may have spotted in the file.[111] In contrast, members of the relevant formation in cases before the Court of First Instance meet immediately before the hearing to exchange opinions on how the hearing should proceed. In addition, the chamber meets immediately after each hearing to discuss a general outline of how the case should be resolved. This mini-deliberation may mean that their preparation for the hearing which precedes it has to be more rigorous. Following a hearing before the Court of Justice, the members of the relevant formation must await the Opinion of the Advocate General and, thereafter, the first draft judgment of the Judge-Rapporteur, so that it may be many weeks, even months, before they have an opportunity to discuss the case again.

Suspicion about the little contact which Judges may have had with a case file up until and after the oral hearing, or the inadequacy of the information in the case file, are confirmed by Edward:

> The potential ramifications of the case may not become clear until the Advocate General's Opinion has been delivered. Even then, the Rapporteur, or other members of the Court, may not agree with the parties or the Advocate General as to what the real issues are, or how they should be defined. So the Court's deliberations are often devoted as much to identifying the issues as deciding how to answer them.[112]

Similarly, Rodney remarks, in the context of referral back of a case from a Chamber to the plenary: 'it is more usual that it occurs after the Advocate General's Opinion, since it is only at that stage that the Judges of the Chamber begin deliberating and consider the points raised at the oral hearing and in the opinion'[113] Finally, Weiler makes the following observation:

---

[110] See also Schermers and Waelbroeck, above n 1, p 461: 'In recent years the workload of the Court of Justice has considerably increased. It may be expected that this development strengthens the influence of the Judge-Rapporteur. When the other Judges have less time to study the case they will more easily be tempted to follow the studied opinion of the Judge-Rapporteur.'

[111] Presumably they may have discussed the case briefly and informally with colleagues but there is no requirement that they do so and no provision at all for a meeting of the formation prior to the hearing.

[112] See Edward, above n 1, 545 and 557: 'the point at issue often becomes clear only in deliberation.' This certainly seemed to be the case in Joined Cases C–267 and 268/91 *Keck and Mithouard* [1993] ECR I–6097. For other examples of celebrated cases which have been reopened after a first Opinion was delivered, see Plender, above n 1, p 451. See also D. Edward, 'Advocacy Before the Court of Justice. Hints for the Uninitiated' in G. Barling and M. Brealey (eds), *Practitioners' Handbook of EC Law* (London, Trenton Publishing, 1998) pp 27–45, p 40, where he notes that when the Judge-Rapporteur's preliminary report and Report for the Hearing are presented at the weekly general administrative meeting the Court usually accepts them without discussion.

[113] See Rodney in Plender (ed), above n 1, p 661; and Strasser, above n 1, 83. Basenach, above n 1, 57, remarks on the importance of the Advocate General's Opinion, but notes that it entails a considerable delay before the deliberations begin by which time the impressions of the hearing have already paled.

With the prompting of a former Member of the Court we tried in my Harvard seminar to construct the schedule of a judge on the ECJ. Approximate as our calculations must have been, we concluded that between meetings and deliberations and actual hearings the workload is such that judges have very little time to think deeply about many of the cases—especially those for which they are not the reporting judge—which they eventually have to decide.[114]

One possible change to the present system which might radically alter the oral hearing, the conduct of deliberations and the speed with which the Court can dispose of a case might be the presentation of the Advocate General's Opinion at the oral hearing itself or one or two weeks beforehand. It would surely be far preferable for the Court to deliberate a case shortly after the hearing with the issues still clear in their minds, and the presentation of the Opinion in this way would undoubtedly enhance the quality of the hearing and the exchange between the bench and the parties and concentrate the hearing on the essential and most difficult aspects of the case.

These comments reveal that, although the Judges are clearly familiar with the case file when they attend the oral hearing, they have, in actual fact, had very little opportunity to examine the ramifications of the case or to identify the missing elements in the file.[115] It is the task of the Judge-Rapporteur to prepare the oral hearing better and more extensively than his colleagues, but if he himself is disinclined to ask questions or probe further the submissions of counsel, his colleagues may be equally disinclined or more so. Given the pressure of other pending cases, this 'quality time' problem is not unique to the oral stage of the procedure but is no doubt an issue at the all important deliberation stage. As Weiler again points out: 'The year has so many days, the day has so many hours, the Court has so many judges, the judges have so many cases (indeed many)—time to think, to reflect, to deliberate is the most scarce resource of the institution.'[116] A related issue, and one which also has the potential to affect the legitimacy of the Court's judicial role is what Fiss describes as the bureaucratization of the judiciary—signifying the tendency for courts to surround themselves with a series of adjunct institutions—by which Fiss, writing in the US context, means special masters, hearing officers and more law clerks.[117]

---

[114] See J.H.H. Weiler, 'The Function and Future of European Law' in Heiskanen and Kulovesi, above n 2, pp 9–22, p 18.

[115] Vaughan's idea of creating a special department in the Court responsible for the preparation of Reports for the Hearing is interesting in terms of speeding up the passage of cases through the Court, but it would be a negative move from the point of the Judges' knowledge of the case file (see Vaughan in Andenas (ed), above n 54, p 58). of more use might be a limitation on the number of pages of written submissions which the parties can submit.

[116] See Weiler in Heiskanen and Kulovesi, above n 2, p 19.

[117] See O. Fiss, 'The Social and Political Foundations of Adjudication' (1982) 6 *Law and Human Behaviour* 121–28, 126. The Report on the Court of Justice compiled by the BIICL, above n 23, p 47, also notes that the increase in the caseload of the Court has in turn led to an increase in the number of legal secretaries and a change in their role: 'more work—including the preparation of early drafts of judgments and Opinions—is now delegated to legal secretaries.' Echoes of Fiss' concern, this time in the specific context of the EC's judiciary, can be found in Weiler in Heiskanen and Kulovesi,

Although his comments refer to the American judiciary, the causes which he identifies for such developments may have some pertinence for the EU, namely 'overwork, the need for specialized knowledge, or a desire of a judge to insulate himself from public criticism and scrutiny.'[118]

As part of the present drive to reduce the time it takes the Court to hand down preliminary rulings, it has been suggested that the oral hearing could be dispensed with in certain cases. In defence of the oral hearing, particularly in the context of the reference procedure, Wyatt argues that if justice for the applicant is to be done and seen to be done, maintaining the oral phase is essential. In certain types of cases, particularly judicial review, the applicant will only gain a clear view of the case against him at the oral stage. It will be at this stage that he can respond to the arguments presented by the defendant and any Member States who have weighed in on the defendant's side.[119] It is suggested that a revision of the Court's approach to the conduct of oral hearings would be preferable, with clear instructions being given to counsel prior to the hearing about what issues the Court wishes to hear discussed, more intensive questioning, the adoption of the Court of First Instance's practice of a mini-deliberation following the oral hearing so that members can thrash out at that early stage the problems they have with the case and even the presentation of the Advocate General's Opinion prior to the hearing as previously mentioned. At present, the working method of the Court, as dictated both by its Rules of Procedure and long-established practice, mean that a large amount of time lapses between the different stages of procedure (production of the preliminary report for the general meeting, the hearing, delivery of the Advocate General's Opinion, deliberation, delivery of the judgment) when the Judge-Rapporteur and his or her colleagues on the bench must deal with a case. With five hundred new cases introduced in 2001 and nine hundred and forty three cases pending at the end of that year, it seems time to reflect on whether this arrangement is conducive to a clear understanding of the legal questions involved and the efficient and rapid production of quality jurisprudence.

THE DELIBERATION

Little has been written about what is undoubtedly the most fundamental stage through which a case must pass before a decision is handed down, namely the

above n 2, pp 18–19, who remarks that questions may legitimately be raised about the role and influence of legal secretaries at the Court of Justice and comments that justice in which legal secretaries write and judges merely approve is justice denied. See also P. Craig, 'The Jurisdiction of the Community Courts Reconsidered' in De Búrca and Weiler (eds), above n 2, pp 177–226, pp 219–20. Although little has been written about the work of legal secretaries at the Court, one commentator has observed that: '[I] would be remiss as a reporter if I did not at least note the odd whisperings in the corridors of the ECJ of particular judges who delegated too much (or who lacked the ability either in law, French, intellect or motivation), or clerks who seized too much power.' (Kenney (2000), above n 30, 613).

[118] See Fiss, *ibid*, 126.
[119] Wyatt in Andenas (ed), above n 54, p 79.

deliberation or consultation stage. Clearly, the secrecy which surrounds the Court's work and the collegiate nature of its rulings renders insightful comments on how the Court reaches its decisions difficult, if not impossible. Commentators generally assume from short, dry judgments,[120] or those which are quickly overturned without an explicit reason for the overruling being provided,[121] that the Court was particularly divided on this or that issue. But the lack of discussion in its judgments of how it reaches its decisions and the lack of dissenting opinions means there is no concrete proof in support of these conjectures.

The secrecy which shrouds the Court's judicial activities is founded on a number of provisions in the EC Statute and in its Rules of Procedure.[122] All members of the Court, both Judges and Advocates General, are present at the Court's weekly general administrative meeting, in which judicial and administrative decisions are taken. However, from a judicial perspective, what is essentially being decided at such meetings are points of procedure—where a case should be assigned, whether a research note is necessary, whether written or oral questions should be posed to one or more parties. In contrast, only Judges may be present in the deliberation room during its judicial deliberations and the deliberations of the Court, according to its Statute, 'shall be and shall remain secret.'[123]

A Judge-Rapporteur will try to introduce his case into the weekly deliberations of the relevant Chamber or full Court as soon as possible after the Advocate General has delivered his Opinion. In any event, he will have indicated following the delivery of the Opinion whether or not he intends to follow the Advocate General and how he intends to proceed with the case. At this stage, a Judge-Rapporteur may decide either to discuss the case with his colleagues in the deliberation room on the basis of a draft judgment which he prepares and distributes prior to the deliberation, or he may prefer to seek the views of his colleagues from the outset on how the case should be dealt with. In such cases, which are usually the most complex and/or divisive, he will probably circulate a note prior to the deliberation explaining the fundamental aspects of the case and outlining the different approaches open to the Court.[124] Other Judges, unhappy perhaps with the Judge-Rapporteur's decision to follow or not, as the case may be, the Opinion of the Advocate General, may also, at this early stage,

---

[120] See, for example, the Court's first encounters with positive discrimination in Cases C–450/93 *Kalanke* and C–409/95 *Marschall*.

[121] See, for example, Cases C–400/95 *Larsson* and C–394/96 *Brown* discussed below in ch 5.

[122] See Articles 2 of the EC Statute (as amended) and 3 RP. Other Court officers, including legal secretaries, take a similar oath.

[123] Articles 35 EC Statute (as amended) and 27 RP.

[124] Edward, above n 1 , 555, suggests that it is expected, though it does not always happen, that a Judge who disagrees with the course proposed by the Judge-Rapporteur, or who feels that the latter or the Advocate General have overlooked an important point, will write a note explaining his position.

request that the case first be discussed on the basis of a deliberation note which they themselves have prepared. In the main, however, it is the Judge-Rapporteur who presents the first draft or deliberation note to the relevant formation. In the event that the initial deliberation is on the basis of a note or series of notes, the President of the Court or the assigned Chamber will seek consensus on how the Judge-Rapporteur should proceed in the case and the latter, when he next brings the case before the formation, will do so on the basis of a draft judgment encapsulating the consensus previously reached.

It will be up to the Judge-Rapporteur to defend his position, as reflected in any draft judgment or notes which he has distributed, before his colleagues in the deliberation. He will usually be the first invited by the President to speak on the case.[125] Since other Judges may already have expressed their opinion in writing prior to the deliberation, he may have to speak at length. Other Judges will then speak in turn. If the discussions on a draft judgment or note do not reach a consensus and a clear difference of opinion has emerged a vote will usually be taken. Whichever camp the Judge-Rapporteur finds himself in, he is obliged from then on to produce a draft judgment in accordance with the wishes and arguments of the majority. Edward observes, however, that the fact that a vote has been taken or a consensus reached does not mean that those opposed to the position of the majority, or at least less convinced by it, play no further role in the deliberation of the case. The Judge-Rapporteur will nevertheless have to produce a draft reflecting the majority position and this will be gone through painstakingly by all members of the formation to weed out unhappy turns of phrase or what may appear to them to be unnecessary dicta. Both those in favour and those against the decision will continue to participate in the formulation of the legal reasoning of the decision and in the drafting of individual paragraphs. It may take numerous drafts and untold amounts of tinkering to reach the final decision: 'This essentially, is what "collegiality" means. All members of the Court are responsible, up to the last minute, for making the judgment as good as it can be, even if they disagree with the result.'[126]

Clearly, what is of the utmost importance is the extent to which the Judges are divided over specific issues. A lack of dissenting opinions means that it is impossible to sort the Judges into clear cut constituencies when it comes to the different social, political and economic issues with which a case may confront them. However, writing about various challenges emerging to the established wisdom of constitutionalism in the EU, Weiler regards the emergence of new constituencies in the Court of Justice as one such challenge:

> There are challenges from, yes, new constituencies within the Court of Justice (We should not commit the error of imagining the Court as an homogeneous actor free

---

[125] *Ibid*, 556

[126] *Ibid*, 556. Demaret, above n 1, p 324, n82, notes that, although exceptional, it has been known for a Judge to be critical in his academic writings of jurisprudence of the Court to which he belongs but in respect of judgments in which he did not participate.

of internal factions, disagreements and internal conflicted views on many issues, including the contours of constitutionalism. The oft deep divisions on fundamental issues between Advocates General—full Members of the Court—and the Court itself surely mirror similar divisions within the College of Judges).[127]

In the absence of dissenting opinions, the existence of these different constituencies will obviously affect the content, reasoning and some would argue, the quality, of the decisions of the Court.[128] A much delayed decision, the reopening of the oral phase of procedure or posing lengthy and detailed questions to parties are all cited as possible evidence of division amongst the members and difficulty in reaching a solution acceptable to all, or at the very least to a majority.[129]

Judicial Reasoning and Language in the Decisions of the Court of Justice

Although the Judges are bound to preserve the secrecy of their deliberations, they are also, by virtue of Article 36 EC Statute (as amended by the Nice Treaty), bound to state the reasons on which a judgment is based. In addition, Article 63 of the Rules of Procedure specifies that a judgment shall contain, *inter alia*, a summary of the facts, the grounds for the decision and an operative part which includes the decision as to costs. In recent years, the Court has come under increasing criticism for the 'cryptic, Cartesian style which characterises many of its decisions,'[130] for its 'often stunted reasoning and its frequently oracular

---

[127] J.H.H. Weiler, 'The Reformation of European Constitutionalism' (1997) 35 *Journal of Common Market Studies* 95–131, 106. See also the comments of Mattli and Slaughter (1996), above n 104, pp 41–42, on revisionism at the Court, as exemplified by decisions such as *Keck*, or the slapping down of the Commission for exceeding its powers under the Treaty, which: 'have evoked howls of protest from older and more activist generation of judges such as Mancini, themselves following in the founding footsteps of Pescatore and Lecourt.' See, however, F.G. Jacobs and K.L. Karst, 'The "Federal" Legal Order: The U.S.A. and Europe Compared. A Juridical Perspective' in M. Cappelletti, M. Seccombe and J.H.H. Weiler (eds), *Integration Through Law*, vol 1 bk 1 (Berlin, de Gruyter, 1985) pp 169–243, p 191: '[The Court of Justice] is collegiate in that it operates as a relatively detached, if not cloistered, institution, enjoys a substantial *esprit de corps*, engenders a pro-Community ethos, and readily assimilates new and independent-minded members.'

[128] See De Búrca, above n 42, 232, who argues that the effect of institutional, textual and practical constraints require the Court to adhere to a particular mode of reasoning; and Demaret, above n 1, p 332, who suggests that the need to compromise might explain why 'la motivation de certains arrêts ne soit pas d'une cohérence parfaite'. In the specific context of sex discrimination, see S. Fredman, 'Affirmative Action and the Court of Justice: A Critical Analysis' in J. Shaw (ed), *Social Law and Policy in an Evolving European Union* (Oxford, Hart Publishing, 2000) pp 171–95, p 176: 'the European Court has found it difficult to generate coherent and predictable principles. This is not helped by the way in which [its] decisions are constructed: instead of permitting a lively debate in the form of majority and dissenting judgments, the appearance of unanimity is achieved at the cost of compromises which are often inscrutable.'

[129] Demaret, above n 1, p 332.

[130] Weiler in Heiskanen and Kulovesi, above n 2, p 21.

tone'[131] and for its 'sometimes maddening Delphic offerings.'[132] Rubenstein refers to what he sees as the Court's production of 'jurisprudence by word processor',[133] while De Búrca argues that:

> it is incumbent on the ECJ itself to find a way of responding to the complex problems which are being brought before it, rather than avoiding acknowledgement of the inter- pretative choices it makes and presenting its rulings as the incontrovertible readings of an uncontested text.[134]

The Court's judgments bind national courts, yet its 'extreme laconicism'[135], its failure or unwillingness to distinguish or overrule previous decisions and the ambiguous nature of some of its decisions may have the effect that national courts fail to correctly apply rulings which they do not understand or find unhelpful.[136] They may often be tempted to resort to Opinions of the Advocates General in an attempt to decipher what the Court meant. As Gormley pointed out in the aftermath of the *Keck* decision, the policy consideration behind that judgment was clearly the fact that too many litigants were making use of the forum of the Court, but there is no account taken of the fact that it was the Court itself which incited such an approach 'by being too ready to pronounce in [. . .] terms which left the national courts nothing to evaluate at all.'[137] Clearly, the fact that, pursuant to Article 234 EC, the Court should, formally at least, only interpret Community law, with the result that it should not touch questions of compatibility, only adds to the confusion. As chapter four underlines in the context of application of the proportionality and objective justification prin- ciples relevant to indirect discrimination, the Court at times engages with and at other times avoids the question of how the national court should apply those

---

[131] Mancini and Keeling, above n 1, 398. See also U. Everling, 'Reflections on the Reasoning in the Judgments of the Court of Justice of the European Communities' in *Festskrift til Ole Due* (Copenhagen, G.E.C. Gads Forlag, 1994), pp 55–74, p 56, where he refers to disquiet about the 'apo- dictic brevity' of the Court's judgments; De Búrca, above n 42, 233; Demaret's lament, above n 1, p 333, that, when compared to the literary quality of the opinions of common law judges like Justice Holmes, Learned Hand or Lord Denning, the prose of the Court of Justice appears dull or bleak; and generally, J. Bengoetxea, N. MacCormick and L.M. Soriano, 'Integration and Integrity in the Legal Reasoning of the European Court of Justice' in De Burca and Weiler (eds), above n 2, pp 43–85.

[132] See H. Schepel, 'Reconstructing Constitutionalisation: Law and Politics in the European Court of Justice' (2000) 20 *Oxford Journal of Legal Studies* 457–68, 466.

[133] See Rubenstein (1999) *Industrial Relations Law Review*, cited in S. Hardy and R.W. Painter, 'The New Acquired Rights Directive and its Implications for European Employee Relations in the Twenty-First Century' (199) 6 *Maastricht Journal of International and Comparative Law* 366–79, 369.

[134] See De Búrca, (1998), above n 42, 234.

[135] See the Report of the BIICL, above n 23, p 95.

[136] In the context of indirect sex discrimination cases see S. Prechal, 'Combatting Indirect Discrimination in Community Law' (1993) *Legal Issues of European Integration* 81–97, who remarks that the Court's rulings may sometimes leave national judges no wiser as to the correct interpretation of EC law and national judges may themselves fail to provide the Court with enough information to ensure that the preliminary ruling is in fact useful.

[137] See Gormley, above n 75, p 22.

principles to the case in hand. Worryingly, one former Member of the Court intimates that more time may be spent deliberating portions of the reasoning which are not included in the final version than on those sentences that are finally adopted.[138]

However, what is often forgotten when it comes to the work of the Court generally, and the functioning of its deliberations in particular, is that at least twelve of the fifteen Judges do not work in their mother tongue. At previous written and oral stages in the procedure help was always at hand from members of the Judge's own chamber, from other chambers, from francophone lawyers whose job it is to revise the language in draft decisions and from simultaneous interpreters present in Court during the oral hearing. No such facilities are available in the Court's deliberation room; the Judges are alone and they must defend their views and criticise those of others in a language which is not their own mother tongue.[139] Mancini and Keeling remark that 'the fact of having to speak French . . . in the deliberation room and having to draft judgments in French, puts the non-francophones at a definite disadvantage vis-à-vis their brethren from France, Belgium and Luxembourg.'[140] They go on to state that those francophone colleagues, being accomplished gentlemen, do not consciously take advantage of their colleagues' handicap but recognise that 'the full mastery of a language . . . is an irresistible weapon; and the owner of that weapon will not be likely to refrain from using it.'[141] Edward acknowledges that the use of French is criticised on the grounds that it gives an unacceptable predominance to French as the language of Community law, that it unduly favours francophones and gives precedent more generally to French or continental legal culture.[142] He, like some other former Members of the Court,[143] does not accept these criticisms and emphasises the need for the Court to be restricted to one internal working language.

The use of one working language has obvious advantages when it comes to drafting legal documents and decisions. However, the fact that decisions have to be reached in a language which is not that of all but a very small minority may be as much to blame for the Court's much criticised style as the need to compromise and accommodate the opinions and criticisms of any minority. The more informal and discursive style and content of the Opinions of Advocates General is generally welcomed when compared to the decisions of the Court,

---

[138] See Everling (1994), above n 131, p 68.

[139] French was, as Edward notes, above n 1, 546, n 36, the sole official language of the ECSC Treaty, the most convenient common language of the first members of the Court, schooled, no doubt, in what was then the language of diplomacy and it is also the host Member State's official language. See also Mancini and Keeling, above n 1, 399, who remark that the French monopoly in the deliberation room is a consequence of the hegemony which France as a political power exerted in the framing and the early application of the Treaty.

[140] Mancini and Keeling, above n 1, 398.

[141] *Ibid*, 398.

[142] Edward, above n 1, 546.

[143] See also Mancini and Keeling, above n 1, 398.

but it is too often forgotten that Advocates General are able to express themselves with total, uncompromised freedom in their own language. Hix has observed that, on the cultural side, different systems of training judges, different promotion systems, and different career paths produce different patterns of behaviour and reasoning by judges—such as formal versus pragmatic, deductive versus inductive, and abstract versus consensual.[144] It is arguable that one of the consequences of reliance on French and French alone, as the working language of the Court for administrative and judicial purposes, is that French legal reasoning sets the tone, style and forms of expression adopted.[145] Underpinning French legal tradition, as Everling points out, is the notion that the authority of the judge requires no justification. Clearly there are advantages for a Court to work through a single language, but there is surely a risk that the cultural and intellectual baggage which accompany that language may act like a straitjacket when used by non Mother tongue speakers to whom that culture and intellectual logic may be foreign. Furthermore, while one language may be essential for the drafting of the final legal text, it is less defensible if members of the relevant formation are limited to that one language when putting their views across, whether in writing or orally, during the course of the deliberation.

Dissenting Opinions

Several well-tried arguments are cited in favour of the present collegiate system of decision-making at the Court. First and foremost is the need to protect the independence of the Judges.[146] They are appointed by the common accord of Member State governments for a period of just six years and the independence of its members which any court must safeguard might be jeopardised if it was known which way they had voted.[147] The relative youth of the EU, the delicate system of checks and balances which its institutional structure represents and the ever-present democratic deficit mean that the legitimacy of the EU and its institutions remains fragile. In such circumstances, it is said that legal certainty and the likelihood that national courts, Member States and other EC institutions will follow the decisions of the Court is enhanced by the production of one single collegiate judgment rather than hesitant decisions including dissenting and concurring judgments. It is said that allowing dissenting opinions would '[raise] the spectre of a "politicised" Court, openly divided into liberals and

---

[144] See Hix, above n 1, p 119.

[145] See also Everling (1994), above n 131, p 67.

[146] See, *inter alia*, Freestone, above n 1, 44, who argued (albeit in 1983) that the integration of national interests had not yet reached the stage that the collegiate judgment could be abandoned without risk; Gormley, above n 75, p 13; Kapteyn and VerLoren van Themaat, above n 9, p 251; Schermers and Waelbroeck, above n 1, p 497.

[147] As an example, Schermers and Waelbroeck, *ibid*, suggest that the failure to re-appoint the second president of Euratom, considering that he had been generally regarded as a first class president, may have lain in his refusal to accept the views of the French government.

conservatives, or perhaps, more to the point, integrationists and sceptics, hence damaging the "mask" of formal legal rationality.'[148] In the same vein, allowing dissenting judgments may dissuade those who have dissented in the past from changing their point of view and adhering to the position of the majority in future cases. The lack of open dissent is also said to encourage compromise in the formulation of judgments and the accomodation of the different views of Judges from different legal systems. In the particular context of Article 234 EC references, a national judge who seeks guidance may be more likely to follow a single ruling handed down by the Court than one which has clearly been the product of internal division and dissent. It has also been suggested that the existence of dissenting opinions could open an avenue for possible abuse by national courts.[149] From a practical point of view, the absence of dissenting judgments may actually contribute to a speedier resolution of the case, since translation is limited at present to one text and members are not afforded the opportunity to produce sometimes lengthy dissenting or concurring opinions.

However, most of these arguments are easily countered. In the first place, as regards independence, the introduction of dissenting opinions could be accompanied by a change in the term of office of members of the Court, with a non-renewable but extended mandate replacing the present arrangement.[150] Given the time it takes for Judges to become accustomed to the Court's work and linguistic regime, a nine or even twelve-year term would seem desirable. Such a change would ensure that the stance adopted by serving members in any particular case would be free from pressure. In any case, the importance of single judgments for the safeguarding of the independence of the Court and its Judges may be overstated. The Opinions of Advocates General, who are also subject to the same system of appointment and renewal, may not always be welcome to the ears of the Member State that appointed them, but there is no evidence to suggest that they have not been renewed as a result of their stance in any particular case. In addition, if there is dissatisfaction in Member State capitals with certain decisions of the Court, there are far more fundamental and detrimental ways to encroach on the independence of the Court as an institution than by waiting for the next renewal of membership. Unhappy with the position which the Court had taken in *Barber* as regards the applicability of EC sex

---

[148]   Schepel, above n 132, 466.

[149]   See the BIICL Report, above n 23, p 121. Although, even in the absence of dissenting opinions it is always open to national courts to depart from those aspects of decisions with which they do not agree.

[150]   See also Arnull (1993), above n 44, 265; and Weiler in Heiskanen and Kulovesi, above n 2, p 21, who link the introduction of dissenting opinions to the establishment of a longer, non-renewable term of office. Weiler regards the existing system as 'an affront to the integrity of the European legal system'. Gormley, above n 75, p 13, n 9, notes, however, that, in certain Member States, the political colour of a candidate plays a notorious role in questions of nomination or renomination and the protection afforded by a single judgment should not therefore be under-estimated when it comes to ensuring that the authority of the Court is maintained. See also Strasser, above n 1, 94; Demaret, above n 1, p 323.

equality law to occupational pension schemes and specifically the unclear consequences for pension schemes and pension claimants of its inclusion in the decision of a temporal limitation, the Member States annexed the so-called *Barber* protocol to the Maastricht Treaty. The aim of the protocol was clearly to prescribe how the decision of the Court in *Barber* was to apply and, presumably, to limit, what the Member States regarded as its negative effects.[151] The actual effect of the protocol was to prejudge the outcome of a number of other pension cases pending before the Court.

It is also said that the absence of dissenting opinions bestows greater authority on the judgments of the Court and facilitates evolution in its jurisprudence, since changes of opinion are not identifiable.[152] However, although they cannot clearly be attributed to individual Judges, it is not difficult to map changes of heart in the Court's jurisprudence, not least in recent employment law decisions.[153] Past judgments are, whether black letter lawyers like it or not, indicative of a bench more or less disposed to 'communautaire' reasoning and more or less liberal when it comes to issues of social policy and, specifically, sex discrimination. In favour of dissenting opinions is the consideration that by bringing arguments out in the open a more coherent, better reasoned and even balanced majority decision may be the result.[154] Judges will not have to bear the responsibility for decisions to which they object but they will be under increased pressure to produce well-reasoned arguments with respect to those decisions with which they concur. Given the powerful criticism of the reasoning to which the present day 'compromising' Court resorts, an improvement in the reasoning used in decisions and in the coherence of its judgments is clearly a very cogent argument in favour of doing away with the present rule precluding dissent. Furthermore, like the Opinions of Advocates General, dissenting judgments may enhance the balanced development of EC law and will indicate to parties, Member States, EC institutions and national courts that their arguments have been taken seriously by the Court. As Weiler argues, 'The dissent often produces

---

[151] See T. Hartley, 'The European Court, Judicial Objectivity and the Constitution of the European Union' (1996) 112 *Law Quarterly Review* 95–109, 105; the Editorial comments in (1993) 30 *Common Market Law Review* 899–903, 902; and Demaret, above n 1, p 371. Another example is provided by the initial Commission proposal to revise Directive 77/187/EEC on the approximation of the laws of the Member States relating to the safeguarding of employees' rights in the event of transfers of undertakings (OJ 1977 L 61/27), where the Commission, under pressure from certain Member States and other interested parties, sought to moderate the Court's interpretation of the 1977 Directive, particularly as regards its application to the contracting out of services. See further below ch 6. Finally, Article 141(4) EC was a clear move in the Amsterdam Treaty to reverse or overcome what was perceived as the outright rejection by the Court in Case C–450/93 *Kalanke* of Member State affirmative action. See A. Arnull, 'Taming the Beast? The Treaty of Amsterdam and the Court of Justice' in D. O'Keeffe and P. Twomey (eds), *Legal Issues of the Amsterdam Treaty* (Oxford, Hart Publishing, 1999) pp 109–21, for other examples of the Court's capacity for creativity being limited in the Amsterdam Treaty.

[152] Demaret, above n 1, p 334.

[153] See, for example, Ellis, above, n 45.

[154] See also Weiler in Heiskanen and Kulovesi, above n 2, p 21; and the BIICL Report, above n 23, p 119.

the paradoxical effect of legitimating the majority because it becomes evident that alternative views were considered even if ultimately rejected.'[155] Separate and dissenting opinions are allowed at the International Court of Justice and the European Court of Human Rights without detriment to the binding and authoritative nature of the decisions of those courts.[156] While it is true that the introduction of dissenting opinions would add to the burden of translation, it might also shorten the amount of time spent deliberating a compromise solution which all Judges are willing to sign. Furthermore, it is questionable, even unlikely, given accession and the transfer of ever wider jurisdiction to the Court of First Instance, that the Court of Justice will remain the EU's court of cassation in all matters for much longer and radical new thinking will be needed when constructing whatever court takes its place.

[155] Weiler in Heiskanen and Kulovesi, above n 2, p 21.
[156] See, however, D. Freestone, 'The European Court of Justice' in J. Lodge (ed), *Institutions and Policies of the European Communities* (London, Frances Pinter, 1983) pp 43–53, p 44, who remarks that national judges at the International Court of Justice are seen as reluctant to vote against their own states.

2

Article 234 EC and EC Employment Law: Is the Preliminary Reference Procedure Still Working?

INTRODUCTION

JUST AS THE Court of Justice of the European Communities is regarded as having played a fundamental role in furthering European integration through law, so too Article 234 EC is considered as having been the most successful weapon in its legal arsenal in this respect. Students of EC law become rapidly familiar with the names and effects of the landmark judgments rendered by the Court of Justice in preliminary reference proceedings in the 1960s and 1970s. *Van Gend en Loos, Costa v ENEL, Simmenthal* and *Van Duyn* are but a few members of the Court's hall of fame—the ground-breaking rulings in each of these cases having been made possible by references from national courts to the Court of Justice requesting preliminary rulings.[1]

Numerous treatises and commentaries have been written about the way in which the EC's legal system was transformed through use of the reference procedure, about the role the Court played in this transformation and about national courts' reasons for having recourse to the reference procedure in the first place and their acceptance, in the main, of the decisions handed down by the Court of Justice.[2] The purpose of this chapter is not to retrace these

---

[1] Case 26/62 NV *Algemene Transport- en Expeditie Onderneming van Gend en Loos v Dutch Fiscal Administration* [1963] ECR 3; Case 6/64 *Flaminio Costa v E.N.E.L.* [1964] ECR 1141; Case 106/77 *Amministrazione delle finanze dello Stato v Simmenthal* [1978] ECR 629; Case 41/74 *Yvonne van Duyn v Home Office* [1974] ECR 1337. Kilpatrick bemoans this box of 'constitutional moments' repeatedly set before the reader for his or her delectation (C. Kilpatrick, 'Community or Communities of Courts in European Integration? Sex Equality Dialogues Between UK Courts and the ECJ' (1998) 4 *European Law Journal* 121–147, 126). Nevertheless, an analysis of the functioning and evolution of Article 234 EC would be incomplete without reference to them.

[2] See variously H.G. Schermers *et al.* (eds), *Article 177 EEC: Experiences and Problems* (Amsterdam, North Holland, 1987); A. Arnull, 'References to the European Court' (1990) 15 *European Law Review* 375–391; D. Anderson, *References to the European Court* (London, Sweet & Maxwell, 1995); M. Andenas (ed), *Article 177 References to the European Court—Policy and Practice* (London, Butterworths, 1994). For an analysis of the acceptance by national courts of the preliminary rulings handed down by the Court of Justice see, *inter alia*, A.-M. Slaughter, A. Stone Sweet and J.H.H. Weiler (eds), *The European Court and National Courts—Doctrine and Jurisprudence. Legal Change in its Social Context* (Oxford, Hart Publishing, 1998); M.L. Volcansek, *Judicial Politics in Europe: An Impact Analysis* (Frankfurt-am-Main, Peter Lang,

well-trodden paths. The intention instead is to examine whether the way in which Article 234 EC operates and the relationship which it imposes between the Court of Justice and national courts has an effect on the answers given by the Court in preliminary references, specifically preliminary references in the field of EC employment law. A quick perusal of the relevant academic literature reveals that few commentators now question whether something inherent in Article 234 EC, or in the underlying theory on which it is based—essentially that EC law can be stated by the Court of Justice *in abstracto*—is a potential source of problems.[3] Tracing the use of this key Treaty provision since it was first styled at the conference tables of Paris and Rome in the 1950s, this chapter questions whether, at least in the specific context of EC employment law, Article 234 EC can be said to be working, providing national courts with sufficiently clear guidelines on the interpretation of EC law and its underlying principles, thereby allowing them to resolve the disputes of which they are seised.

AN OVERVIEW OF THE ESSENTIAL FEATURES OF ARTICLE 234 EC

Although Article 234 EC is familiar, even wearisome, territory for many readers, what follows is a brief, incomplete account of its essential features. The Treaty provision establishing the celebrated preliminary reference procedure provides as follows:

> The Court of Justice shall have jurisdiction to give preliminary rulings concerning:
> (1) the interpretation of the Treaty;
> (2) the validity and interpretation of acts of the institution of the Community and of the ECB;
> (3) the interpretation of the statute of bodies established by an act of the Council, where those statutes so provide.
> Where such a question is raised before any court or tribunal of a Member State, that court or tribunal may, if it considers that a decision on the question is necessary to enable it to give judgment, request the Court of Justice to give a ruling thereon.

1986); W. Mattli and A.-M. Slaughter, *Constructing the European Community Legal System from the Ground Up: The Role of Individual Litigants and National Courts*, EUI WP RSC No 96/56; J.H.H. Weiler, 'Journey to an Unknown Destination: A Retrospective and Prospective of the European Court of Justice in the Area of Political Integration' (1993) 31 *Journal of Common Market Studies* 417–46; K.J. Alter and J. Vargas, 'Explaining Variations in the Use of European Litigation Strategies. European Community Law and British Gender Equality Policy' (2000) 33 *Comparative Political Studies* 452–82; S. Hix, *The Political System of the European Union* (London, MacMillan Press Ltd., 1999), especially ch 4; and in the specifix context of labour law S. Sciarra (ed), *Labour Law in the Courts: National Judges and the European Court of Justice* (Oxford, Hart Publishing, 2001). For a note of caution on the issue of acceptance by national courts see Kilpatrick (1998), above n 1, 128.

[3] See, exceptionally, D. Edward, 'The Problem of Fact-finding in Preliminary Proceedings under Article 177 EEC' in Schermers *et al.* (eds), above n 2, pp 216–20, p 216; and, for an early commentary which touched on this issue A. Pepy, 'La rôle de la Cour de justice des Communautés européennes dans l'application de l'article 177 du traité de Rome' (1966) *Cahiers de droit européen* 459–89, 464 *et seq*.

Where any such question is raised in a case pending before a court or tribunal of a Member State, against whose decision there is no judicial remedy under national law, that court or tribunal shall bring the matter before the Court of Justice.'

As chapter one explained, in the event that the Treaty of Nice comes into force, the Court of First Instance may in future have jurisdiction to hear and determine questions referred for a preliminary ruling in specific areas laid down by the EC Statute. Its decisions may exceptionally be subject to review by the Court of Justice where there is a serious risk of the unity or consistency of Community law being affected.[4]

The purpose of the preliminary reference procedure is essentially threefold. It provides for judicial review of Community acts, ensures uniformity in the interpretation of EC law and facilitates the application of EC law by national courts.[5] As regards its scope, the EC treaty specifies the four issues with respect to which preliminary rulings may be requested: interpretation of the Treaties, interpretation of acts of the institutions, validity of acts of the institutions, and interpretation of the statutes of bodies established by an act of the Council, where those statutes so provide. The Court regards a preliminary ruling as binding on the national court as to the interpretation of the Community provisions and acts in question.[6] Given that the principal purpose of the reference procedure is to ensure the uniform interpretation of EC law, it is not surprising that the Court also regards its preliminary rulings, particularly those concerning the validity of acts of the institutions, as being of general application.[7] In *Simmenthal*, for example, the Court emphasised that a preliminary ruling on the interpretation of a rule of Community law 'clarifies and defines where necessary the meaning and scope of that rule as it must be or ought to have been understood and applied from the time of its coming into force.' However, the Court has never explicitly defined the extent of the binding effect on other national courts of one of its rulings on the interpretation of a Treaty or Community act.[8] Although the Court was, for some time, loath to admit it, its Article 234 rulings may also serve as precedents in future cases involving the same EC law provisions.[9]

---

[4] Article 225 EC (as amended).

[5] See, for example, Case 166/73 *Rheinmühlen v Einfuhr- und Vorratsstelle für Getreide* [1974] ECR 33, para 2.

[6] See Case 29/68 *Milch-, Fett- und Eier Kontor GmbH v Hauptzollamt Saarbrücken* [1969] ECR 180, para 3; Case 61/79 *Denkavit* [1980] ECR 1205, 1223; and, on the meaning of 'binding' Case 52/76 *Benedetti v Munari Flli s.a.s* [1977] ECR 163.

[7] Case 66/80 *International Chemical Corporation v Ammistrazione delle finanze dello Stato* [1981] ECR 1191, 1215.

[8] For an account of the long-running debate on this issue see Anderson, above n 2, pp 303 *et seq.*; and the discussion in Pepy, above n 3, 484 *et seq.*

[9] On the subject of precedent see A. Arnull, 'Owning up to fallability: precedent and the Court of Justice' (1993) 30 *Common Market Law Review* 247–66. The disposal of preliminary references by means of reasoned orders pursuant to Article 104(3) of the Court's Rules of Procedure makes this more explicit.

Qualification as a Court or Tribunal of a Member State

The question whether the referring court qualifies as a court or tribunal of a Member State within the meaning of Article 234 EC is a question of Community law for the Court of Justice to decide. The Court looks at a number of factors in order to determine whether the national body is eligible to refer questions for a preliminary ruling: whether it is established by law, whether it is permanent, whether its jurisdiction is compulsory, whether its procedure is *inter partes*, whether it applies rules of law, and whether it is independent. These factors are considered as a whole in order to determine whether the body seeking to refer questions for a preliminary ruling performs a judicial function.[10] The Court has also interpreted the condition 'of a Member State' flexibly so that, for the purposes of EC law, courts and tribunals in a number of far-flung and not so far-flung overseas territories are considered eligible to refer questions.[11]

Obligation or Discretion to Refer

A related issue concerns whether the referring court or tribunal enjoys discretion to refer or is obliged to do so by virtue of being a body 'against whose decisions there is no judicial remedy under national law'.[12] Lower courts have a discretion to refer questions of interpretation to the Court of Justice when such a reference is necessary to enable them to give judgment, but they, like higher courts, remain obliged to request a preliminary ruling before they may rule that a Community

[10] See, *inter alia*, Case 102/81 *Nordsee v Reederei Mond* [1982] ECR 1095 (arbitration tribunals); Case C–393/92 *Municipality of Almelo v Energiebedrijf Ijsselmij NV* [1994] ECR I–1477 (national court deciding on an appeal against an arbitration award); Case C–111/94 *Job Centre Coop. Arl.* [1995] ECR I–3361 (body seised of an appeal brought against a decision in non-contentious proceedings); Case C–54/96 *Dorsch Consult Ingenieurgesellschaft v Bundesbaugesellschaft Berlin mbH* [1997] ECR I–4961 (Federal Supervisory Board in public procurement matters); Case C–337/95 *Parfums Christian Dior v Evora BV* [1997] ECR I–6013 (Court of Justice of the Benelux); Case C–134/97 *Victoria Film A/S* [1998] ECR I–7023 (Swedish Revenue Board); and Case C–416/96 *Nour Eddline El-Yassini v Secretary of State for the Home Department* [1999] ECR I–1209 (Immigration Adjudicator). See also criticism of this case-law in the Opinion of Advocate General Colomer in Case C–17/00 *François de Coster v Collège de Bourgmestres et Echevins de Watermael-Boitsfort* [2001] ECR I–9445.

[11] See, for example, Joined Cases C–100/89 and C–101/89 *Kaefer and Procacci v France* [1990] ECR I–4647 (Tribunal administratif of Papeete in French Polynesia) or Case C–260/90 *Bernard Leplat v Territory of French Polynesia* [1992] ECR I–643; Case C–355/89 *Department of Health and Social Security v Christopher Stewart Barr and Montrose Holdings Limited* [1991] ECR I–3479 (Deputy High Bailiff, Douglas, Isle of Man); or Case C–171/96 *Rui Alberto Pereira Roque v His Excellency the Lieutenant Governor of Jersey* [1998] ECR I–4607 (judicial body of Bailiwick of Jersey).

[12] See generally Schermers *et al.* (eds), above n 2; and B.H. Ter Kuile, 'To Refer or not to Refer: About the Last Paragraph of Article 177 of the EC Treaty' in D. Curtin and T. Heukels (eds), *Essays in Honour of H.G. Schermers* (Dordrecht, Martinus Nijhoff, 1994) pp 381–89.

act is invalid.[13] As regards courts that are obliged to refer, abstract and concrete theories have developed on exactly which Member State courts are so bound.[14] The former suggests that only the highest courts are constrained by Article 234 EC to refer questions. In accordance with the concrete theory, in contrast, courts judging in final instance, whatever that may mean in each individual Member State in each individual case, constitute the highest court for the purposes of Article 234 EC. The Court of Justice seemed to prefer the concrete approach in *Costa v ENEL* when, in a reference from the lowest Italian court it held that: '[U]nder Article [234] national courts against whose decisions, as in the present case, there is no judicial remedy, must refer the matter to the Court of Justice so that a preliminary ruling may be given upon the "interpretation of the Treaty" whenever a question of interpretation is raised before them.'[15]

Over the years, the Court has introduced nuances to the rules governing the obligation to refer of courts against whose decisions there is no judicial remedy. In the *Da Costa* case, it signalled to national courts that the authority of a preliminary ruling already given by the Court might deprive the obligation to refer of its purpose. This was the case, said the Court, especially when the question raised is materially identical to a question that has already been the subject of a preliminary ruling in a similar case.[16] Some years later, the Court established what is known as the *acte clair* doctrine. Essentially, a national court may take upon itself the responsibility of resolving a question of Community law when it is 'so obvious as to leave no scope for any reasonable doubt as to the manner in which the question raised is to be resolved.'[17]

As a result of a series of amendments to the EC Treaty, the obligation on courts of last resort to refer questions to the Court of Justice is no longer uniform, however. References pursuant to the 1968 Brussels Convention on jurisdiction and the enforcement of judgments in civil and commercial matters are restricted to appellate courts,[18] as are references on matters of jurisdiction

---

[13] Case 314/85 *Firma Foto-Frost v Hauptzollamt Lübeck-Ost* [1987] ECR 4199, 4230: 'divergence between courts in the Member States as to the validity of Community acts would be liable to place into jeopardy the very unity of the Community legal order and detract from the fundamental requirement of legal certainty.'

[14] See further the Opinion of 21 February 2002 of Advocate General Tizzano in Case C–99/00 Criminal Proceedings against Kenny Roland Lyckeskog, paras 32 *et seq*, nyr. ECR.

[15] Case 6/64 *Costa v ENEL.*

[16] Joined Cases 28/62–30/62 *Da Costa en Schaake NV and others v Nederlandse Belastingadministratie* [1963] ECR 31. This is sometimes referred to as the *acte éclairé* doctrine.

[17] See Case 283/81 *CILFIT v Ministre de la Santé* [1982] ECR 3415, paras 16–21. The decision by the national court to resolve the case itself must be assessed in the light of the specific characteristics of Community law, the particular difficulties to which its interpretation gives rise and the risk of divergences in judicial decisions within the Community; a requirement with which it seems impossible, in practice, to comply. See further, H. Rasmussen, 'The European Court's Acte Clair Strategy in *C.I.L.F.I.T.*' (1984) 9 *European Law Review* 242–59; and G.F. Mancini and D. Keeling, 'From CILFIT to ERT: the constitutional challenge facing the European Court' (1991) 11 *Yearbook of European Law* 1–13.

[18] Pursuant to the Protocol of 3 June 1971, on the interpretation of the Court of Justice of the Convention of 27 September 1968 on jurisdiction and the enforcement of judgments in civil and commercial matters, OJ 1983 C97/11.

concerning the Agreement relating to Community Patents.[19] Similarly, the Amsterdam Treaty introduced several new permutations in terms of the courts eligible to refer questions on issues falling within both the first (Title IV EC— visas, asylum, immigration and other policies related to the free movement of persons) and third (Title VI TEU—provisions on police and judicial cooperation in criminal matters) pillars.[20] In recent years, one of the proposed solutions to the structural imbalance between the volume of incoming cases and the Court's ability to dispose of them has actually been to reserve the power to make references to supreme courts alone or to exclude courts of first instance from the preliminary reference procedure. The idea is to leave it to national legal systems to filter the cases which make it to the higher courts and from there to the Court of Justice. In its Report on the Future of the Judicial System of the European Union and its 1995 Report to the intergovernmental conference which concluded in Amsterdam,[21] the Court argued against such changes to the Article 234 procedure. In its view, the need to ensure the uniform interpretation of EC law meant that all national courts and tribunals should retain the right to refer questions.

The Division of Functions Between the Court of Justice and National Referring Courts

In accordance with what was referred to in chapter one as the orthodox position on the division of functions between the Court of Justice and the national referring court, it is considered the task of the former to interpret the law and that of the latter to apply it.[22] The Court has confirmed this version of the division of

---

[19]   OJ 1989 L401/1. See also the First Protocol on the interpretation of the Rome convention on the law applicable to contractual obligations, which permits preliminary references only to be made by courts of the contracting states acting as appeal courts, OJ 1989 L48/11.

[20]   For further discussion see A. Arnull, 'Taming the Beast? The Treaty of Amsterdam and the Court of Justice' in D. O'Keeffe and P. Twomey (eds), *Legal Issues of the Amsterdam Treaty* (Oxford, Hart Publishing, 1999) pp 109–21.

[21]   Both available on http:/www.curia.eu.int/cj/en/txts/intergov

[22]   See, for example, Case C–231/89 *Gmurzynska-Bscher v Oberfinanzdirektion Köln* [1990] ECR I–4003, para 21: 'Since the purpose of the Court's jurisdiction under Article 177 of the Treaty is to ensure the uniform interpretation of Community law in all the Member States, the Court confines itself to inferring from their wording and spirit the meaning of the Community rules at issue. It is then for the national courts alone to apply the provisions of Community law so interpreted, taking into account the circumstances of fact and law in the case which has come before it.' See also Case 28/70 *Otto Witt KG* [1970] ECR 1021: 'The Court may not apply the Treaty to a specific case.' The slippery distinction between interpretation and application had been at issue, however, from the very first preliminary reference—see Case 13/61 *De Geus v Bosch* [1962] ECR 45, 50–51; and further G. Bebr, 'The Possible Implications of *Foglia v Novello II*' (1982) 19 *Common Market Law Review* 421–41. P. Craig and G. De Búrca, *EC Law. Texts, Cases & Materials* (Oxford, Clarendon Press, 1995) p 400, suggest that this orthodox vision of the relationship between the two levels of jurisdiction was no doubt over-idealised and not readily sustainable. See also K. Lenaerts, 'Form and Substance of the Preliminary Rulings Procedure' in D. Curtin and T. Heukels (eds), *Institutional Dynamics of European Integration. Essays in Honour of Henry G. Schermers*, Vol II (Dordrecht, Martinus Nijhoff Publishers, 1994) pp 355–80. This axiom is reproduced here, however, as representative of what the Court of Justice has repeatedly stated its relationship with national courts to be.

functions between the two jurisdictions on numerous occasions, stipulating that it: 'is entitled to pronounce on the interpretation of the Treaty and of acts of the institutions but cannot apply them to the case in question since such application falls within the jurisdiction of the national court.'[23] This vision of judicial cooperation means that the national court and the Court of Justice, both keeping within their respective jurisdiction, make direct and complementary contributions to the working out of a decision.[24] It is not considered up to the Court to determine the compatibility of national legislation with EC law in the context of a preliminary reference.[25] One of the direct consequences of this approach and one which, at least initially, the Court was keen to endorse, is that the national court alone is concerned with the factual circumstances of the case.[26] The Court has also insisted that it is wholly for the national court to determine the need for and appropriateness of a reference.[27] In subsequent sections, however, when discussing the nature of the Court's adjudicative role pursuant to Article 234 EC and the issue of the admissibility of preliminary references, the value of some of these judicial pronouncements will be called into question.

---

[23] Case 35/76 *Simmenthal SpA v Ministero delle Finanze* [1976] ECR 1871; Case 222/78 *ICAP v Beneventi* [1979] ECR 1163, 1177; and the Order in Case C–286/88 *Falciola v Comune di Pavia* [1990] ECR I–191, 195.

[24] See Case 16/65 *Schwarze v Einfuhr- und Vorratstelle Getreide* [1965] ECR 877.

[25] See, for example, Case C–15/96 *Schöning-Kougebetopoulou v Freie und Hansestadt Hamburg* [1998] ECR I–47, paras 9–14, where the Court reformulated the question referred by the national court in order to give the impression that it was not carrying out such a determination; and Case 111/76 *Officier van Justitie v Van den Hazel* [1977] ECR 901. This supposed division of functions has frequently been challenged by commentators. See, for example, P. Demaret, 'Le juge et le jugement dans l'Europe d'aujourd'hui: la Cour de Justice des Communautés Européennes' in R. Jacob (ed), *Le juge et le jugement dans les traditions juridiques européennes. Études d'histoire comparée* (Paris, L.G.D.J., 1996) pp 303–77, p 312: 'Mais ce rappel est devenu de pure forme et ne trompe personne. Lorsqu'une question préjudicielle est posée à l'occasion d'un conflit entre droit national et droit communautaire, la réponse de la Cour équivaut dans la grande majorité des cas à une déclaration de compatibilité ou d'incompatibilité de la norme nationale avec le droit communautaire. Le juge européen est en effet de plus en plus souvent amené à interpréter le droit communautaire à la lumière d'un contexte factuel précis, celui du litige pendant devant le juge national. D'une interprétation ainsi particularisée se déduit presque automatiquement la portée admissible de la norme nationale en cause. Simultanément, les réponses de la Cour de Justice ne laissent normalement guère de liberté au juge national en ce qui concerne l'application du droit communautaire au litige dont il est saisi.'

[26] See, for example, Joined Cases C–399/92, C–409/92, C–425/92, C–34/93, C–50/93 and C–78/93 *Stadt Lengerich v Angelika Helmig and others* [1994] ECR I–5727, para 8; Case 5/77 *Tedeschi v Denkavit* [1977] ECR 1555, 1574; Case 83/78 *Pigs Marketing Board v Redmond* [1978] ECR 2347, 2368; Case C–435/97 *World Wildlife Fund (WWF) and others v Autonome Provinz Bozen and others* [1999] ECR I–5613, paras 31–32; Case C–235/95 *AGS Assedic Pas-de-Calais v Dumonet Froment* [1998] ECR I–4531, paras 25–26; and the discussion of Common Customs Tariff (CCT) classification cases in the Opinion of Advocate General Jacobs in Case C–338/95 *Wiener S.I. GmbH v Hauptzollamt Emmerich* [1997] ECR I–6495. See also above ch 1 for a discussion of the fact-finding mechanisms open to the Court and their use in the preliminary reference procedure.

[27] See, for example, Case 10/69 *S.A. Portelange v S.A. Corona Marchant International* [1969] ECR 309, para 7: 'When a court or tribunal requests the interpretation of a Community provision or of a legal concept connected with it, it must be assumed that that court considers such interpretation necessary to the solution of the dispute before it.' See also Joined Cases C–399/92, C–409/92, C–425/92, C–34/93, C–50/93 and C–78/93 *Helmig*, paras 8–9.

Clearly the European Court's concern at the outset was to develop a relationship of co-operation rather than one of hierarchy with national courts and to encourage them to make use of the reference procedure.[28] This encouragement can clearly be seen in cases like *Da Costa* and *Costa v ENEL* where the Court indicated that it was willing to answer questions which had already been asked in similar cases and that it was also willing to extract from imperfectly formulated references those questions which relate to the interpretation of EC law.[29] This relationship, often said to be essential to 'the spirit of Article [234]'[30], is reflected in the dialogue which has built up over the years between national courts and the Court of Justice on both a formal and informal basis. The Court, for example, has rejected requests by parties that it answer additional questions, stressing that it is for the national court and not the parties to seek a preliminary ruling and determine the contents of the reference.[31] The underlying rationale is that the preliminary reference procedure—at least in theory—reflects a dialogue between judicial equals concerning the abstract interpretation of EC law rather than the involvement of the Court of Justice *qua* superior court in the resolution of the case before the national referring court. The Court has also held that it is up to the national court to assess whether the Court's preliminary ruling has clarified matters for them sufficiently or whether a further reference is necessary.[32] On an informal basis, it has long been the Court's practice to inquire of a national referring court whether it wishes to maintain a reference if a ruling is handed down in the meantime in a similar case. The language of co-operation is regarded as 'very real recognition of the particular and distinct skills and functions that national courts and EC courts bring to EC litigation, the obvious suitability of one or other of such forums to perform certain functions, such as fact finding by a specialist national tribunal'.[33]

However, it is arguable that the horizontal relationship between the Court of Justice and national courts on which this orthodoxy relies has, as changes in the Court's jurisprudence testify, become more vertical in nature. The Court increasingly observes that although it is not for it to rule on the compatibility of

---

[28] See also C. Barnard and E. Sharpston, 'The Changing Face of Article 177 References' (1997) 34 *Common Market Law Review* 1113–71.

[29] See, for example, Case 66/77 *Kuyken v Rijksdienst voor Arbeidsvoorziening* [1977] ECR 2311, paras 10–12. See, however, Case C–235/95 *AGS Assedic Pas-de-Calais*, para 26: 'to alter the substance of questions referred for a preliminary ruling would be incompatible with the Court's function under Article [234]'.

[30] See, for example, the Opinion of Advocate General Mancini in Case 14/86 *Pretore di Salò v Persons unknown* [1987] ECR 2545, 2557. In Case C–83/91 *Weinand Meilicke v ADV/ORGA.F.A. Meyer* [1992] ECR I–4871, para 25, the Court referred to the 'spirit of cooperation' which must prevail in the preliminary reference procedure.

[31] See, for example, Case C–412/96 *Kainuun Liikenne Oy and Oy Pohjalan Liikenne Ab* [1998] ECR I–5141, paras 22–24.

[32] See, for example, the Order in Case 40/70 *Sirena Srl v Eda Srl* [1979] ECR 3169.

[33] See T. de la Mare 'Article 177 in Social and Political Context' in P. Craig and G. De Búrca (eds), *The Evolution of EU Law* (Oxford, OUP, 1999) pp 215–60.

a national law with EC law, it does have the jurisdiction to provide the national court with all the elements of interpretation under EC law to enable it to assess questions of compatibility for the purpose of deciding the case before it. Anderson observes that, '[t]hough the Court remains punctilious in its refusal to rule under Article 234 EC on the validity of national laws, the disclaimer of jurisdiction is increasingly one of form rather than substance.'[34] This change in attitude is also evident in the Court's revised approach to both the relevance of the factual background and the general issue of the admissibility of preliminary references. The following sections examine some of the fault lines in the division of functions between national courts and the Court of Justice pursuant to Article 234 EC.

THE CHANGING NATURE OF THE RELATIONSHIP BETWEEN NATIONAL COURTS AND THE COURT OF JUSTICE (I): THE ADJUDICATIVE ROLE PURSUANT TO ARTICLE 234 EC[35]

It is widely accepted that, when adjudicating, a court is involved in the pursuit of what might be termed public and private purposes. The latter consist in the achievement of procedural and substantive justice for the parties to the litigation. In contrast, public purposes focus, *inter alia*, on the clarification, development and uniform interpretation of the law, the maintenance of public faith in the legal system, the assurance of correct procedure and the elimination of abuse, the protection of general public interests which may be affected by the outcome of a case and the maintenance of a balance between the interests of the State on the one hand, and those of the private sector or of individuals, on the other.[36] Although any attempt to compare adjudication at the Court of Justice with that carried out by the US Supreme Court must carry the usual waiver,[37] it is submitted that the American constitutional debate on the distinction between the dispute resolution and public action models of litigation is useful when it comes to understanding what is an inherent tension in the task with which the Court of Justice is charged pursuant to Article 234 EC.

---

[34] See Anderson, above n 2, p 69.

[35] Some of this section draws on G.F. Mancini, 'The role of the supreme courts at the national and international level: a case study of the Court of Justice of the European Communities' in P. Yessiou-Faltsi (ed), *The Role of the Supreme Courts at the National and International Level* (Thessaloniki, Sakkoulas, 1998) pp 421–52, which the present author helped to prepare.

[36] See further J.A. Jolowicz, 'The Role of the Supreme Court at the National and International level' in Yessiou-Faltsi (ed), *ibid*, pp 37–63.

[37] See in this respect D.A.O. Edward, 'What Kind of Law Does Europe Need? The Role of Law, Lawyers and Judges in Contemporary European Integration' (1998/99) 5 *Columbia Journal of European Law* 1–14, 3, citing James Bryce's *The American Commonwealth*: 'The reader [. . .] must not expect the problems America has solved, or those which still perplex her, to reappear in Europe in the same forms [. . .] Nothing can be more instructive than the American experience if it be discreetly used, nothing will be more misleading to one who tries to apply it without allowing for the differences in economic and social environment.'

The dispute resolution model of adjudication refers to the traditional judicial role of the courts as the authorities endowed with the power to determine particular, ongoing disputes between identified litigants and as the settlers of conflicts. Dispute resolution has been characterised as being bipolar, defined by the parties to the case, about an identified set of completed events and involving an independent right or remedy. Furthermore, the impact of the judgment is confined to the parties to the case.[38] In contrast, the public action model of litigation treats courts as institutions 'with a distinctive capacity to declare and explicate public values—norms that transcend individual controversies and that are concerned with the conditions of social and political life'.[39] As Chayes explains, the characteristics of what he calls public action litigation contrast sharply with those displayed by dispute resolution: the party structure is amorphous, the traditional adversary relationship no longer applies and the judge is the dominant figure in organising and guiding the case and draws support not only from the parties and their counsel but from a wide range of external sources. In addition, the judge is said to become the creator and manager of complex forms of ongoing relief which have widespread effects on persons not before the court and which require his ongoing involvement in administration and implementation.[40] What echoes of these models can be detected in the way in which the Court of Justice deals with references from national courts seeking preliminary rulings?

Aspects of the public action model seem to flow logically from the very purpose, scope and consequences of the procedure established by Article 234 EC. The duty of the Court of Justice thereunder is to provide a preliminary ruling which interprets Community law in order to aid the national court in its application of the law to the facts of the particular case. As Weiler has stated: '[O]ne of the main tasks of the European Court is not so much the administration of

---

[38] See A. Chayes 'The Role of the Judge in Public Law Litigation' (1976) 89 *Harvard Law Review* 1281–316, 1282–83.

[39] See P.M. Bator, D.J. Meltzer, P.J. Mishkin and D.L. Shapiro, *Hart and Wechsler's Federal Courts and Federal System*, 3rd ed., (Westbury/New York, Foundation Press, 1988) pp 79 *et seq*; O.M. Fiss, 'The Social and Political Foundations of Adjudication' (1982) 6 *Law and Human Behaviour* 121–28, 124: '[S]tructural litigation identifies a set of values. These values transcend the private ends implied by the dispute resolution model and inform and limit the function of our government. They stand as the core of a public morality and serve as the substantive foundations of structural litigation. The social function of contemporary litigation is not to resolve disputes, but rather to give concrete meaning to that morality within the context of the bureaucratic state.' Or A. Stone Sweet, *Governing with Judges. Constitutional Politics in Europe* (Oxford, OUP, 2000), p 140: 'in activating constitutional review litigants delegate to constitutional judges policy issues that could have been dealt with in other, non-constitutional, forums.'

[40] See Chayes, above n 38, 1284, who specifically identifies employment discrimination cases as avatars of this public action (what he calls public law) litigation; and L.L. Fuller, 'The Forms and Limits of Adjudication' (1978) 92 *Harvard Law Review* 353–409, 357, who contrasts the customary way of thinking of adjudication as a means of settling disputes or controversies with adjudication as a form of social ordering. See also, in the context of the Court of Justice, A. Barav, 'Le juge et le justiciable' in *Scritti in onore di Giuseppe Federico Mancini* (Milan, Giuffrè, 1998) pp 1–74, p 2.

justice in individual cases, but the function of overseeing the development of Community law in important principled cases.'[41] Any meddling on the Court's part with the circumstances preceding or proceeding the reference is excluded. In *Costa v ENEL*, the Court thus emphasised that Article 234 EC 'is based on a clear separation of functions between national courts and the Court of Justice' and that it does not have the power to 'investigate the facts of the case or to criticise the grounds and purpose of the request for interpretation.'[42] In *Van Gend en Loos*, the Court was requested to interpret the notion of customs duties existing before the coming into force of the Treaty, which it did, its interpretation being subsequently applied to resolve the dispute pending before the national court on the reimbursement of duties imposed by the Dutch authorities. Yet few students of EC law remember or are concerned with the actual outcome of the case when it returned to the Netherlands. Rather, they remember *Van Gend en Loos* for the principle which, in accordance with the aforementioned definition of the public action model, transcended the individual controversy and was concerned with the direct effect of Treaty rules, namely with a public value of supreme importance for the constitutional architecture of the EC.

Similarly, the three *Defrenne* cases arose out of a specific employment dispute between a Belgian air hostess and her employer, Sabena airlines.[43] But those cases reached the Court of Justice partly due to the persistence of a redoubtable Belgian lawyer who had taken up Ms. Defrenne's cause and undoubtedly the reason why she did so was because that cause presented the Court with a fine opportunity to proclaim general principles concerning the applicability of Article 141 EC and the nature of the principle of equal pay thereunder. As chapter four reveals, the decisions of the Court in the *Defrenne* trilogy went far beyond the narrow confines of the employment dispute in question. As regards equality law disputes generally, which could in one light be regarded simply as cases of individual grievance, Fitzpatrick observes that 'an act of discrimination is, by definition, collective, being either directly or indirectly on the basis of a person's sex and, in cases of mere institutional discrimination, the collective nature of the discrimination, and hence some form of "public interest" in its correction, is even more apparent.'[44]

The theory behind Article 234 EC thus suggests that the Court is not involved in contentious proceedings designed to settle a dispute but instead is taking part in a special procedure whose aim is to ensure the uniform interpretation of EC

---

[41] See, for example, J.H.H. Weiler, 'The European Court, National Courts and References for Preliminary Rulings—The Paradox of Success: A Revisionist View of Article 177 EEC' in Schermers *et al.* (eds), above n 2, pp 366–78, p 368.

[42] Case 6/64 *Costa v ENEL*, 593.

[43] Cases 43/75 *Defrenne* [1976] ECR 455; 149/77 *Defrenne v Société anonyme belge de navigation aérienne (Sabena)* [1978] ECR 1365; and 80/70 *Defrenne v Belgian State* [1971] ECR 445.

[44] See B. Fitzpatrick, 'Towards Strategic Litigation? Innovations in Sex Equality Litigation Procedures in the Member States of the European Community' (1992) 8 *International Journal of Comparative Labour Law and Industrial Relations* 208–31, 211.

law by co-operation between the Court of Justice and national courts.[45] This theory further suggests that the Court should not be seeking to give the referring court the 'correct' answer specific to a given case, but to give it a ruling of general significance which can be applied to the facts of the case.[46] As Edward observes: 'the Community judge is increasingly called upon to operate, not an on/off switch which produces the 'right' answer, so that one party wins and the other loses, but a synthesizer which adjusts the relative strength of conflicting normative claims and produces an acceptable balance between them.'[47] The Court itself characterises the preliminary reference procedure as a 'non-contentious procedure excluding any initiative of the parties, who are merely invited to be heard in the course of the procedure.'[48] In accordance with the characteristics of the public action model outlined above, Article 234 EC cases, at least before the Court of Justice, are not bipolar and the Court relies on submissions provided not simply by the parties and their counsel, but also on those presented by Member States and, invariably, the Commission.[49] This possibility of intervention by Member States and the Commission is seen as proof of the quality of Article 234 EC as a general procedure with 'a variable content of judicial policy-making'.[50]

---

[45] See the Order of the President of the Court in Case C–181/95 *Biogen v Smithkline Beecham* [1996] ECR I–717, para 5: 'Article [234] does not envisage contentious proceedings designed to settle a dispute but prescribes a special procedure whose aim is to ensure a uniform interpretation of Community law by cooperation between the Court of Justice and the national courts and which enables the latter to seek the interpretation of Community provisions which they have to apply in disputes brought before them.' See, however, G. De Búrca, 'The Principle of Subsidiarity and the Court of Justice as an Institutional Actor' (1998) 36 *Journal of Common Market Studies* 217–35, 231. She recognises that judicial rulings are often not simply individual decisions on a point relevant to particular litigants only, but can have broader policy implications, but regards preliminary rulings as rulings on a point confined to the facts of a particular dispute.

[46] See Advocate General Jacobs in Case C–338/95 *Wiener*, para 50; and, in the context of the Court's pregnancy case-law, where the coherence of the series of decisions delivered by the Court is often questioned, C. Boch, 'Official: During Pregnancy, Females are Pregnant' (1998) 23 *European Law Review* 488–94, 494.

[47] See Edward (1998/99), above n 37, 12.

[48] See Case 44/65 *Hessische Knappschaft v Maison Singer and sons* [1965] ECR 965, 971; and Case 28–30/62 *Da Costa*, where, having identified the need to ensure the uniformity of EC law as being the function of the Court under Article 234 EC, it held: 'This aspect of the activity of the Court within the framework of Article [234] is confirmed by the absence of parties, in the proper sense of the word, which is characteristic of this procedure.'

[49] See C.-D. Ehlermann and J. Pipkorn, 'The Role of the Commission in Preliminary Proceedings Under Article 177 EEC' in Schermers *et al.* (eds), above n 2, pp 293–334. R. Dehousse points out that, although the observations of the EC institutions and intervening governments are often cast in the rigid mould of legal argument, it is not difficult to make out very specific political interests in the background, 'Integration Through Law Revisited: Some Thoughts on the Jurisdiction of the European Political Process' in F. Snyder (ed), *The Europeanisation of Law: the Legal Effects of European Integration* (Oxford, Hart Publishing, 2000) pp 15–29, p 25.

[50] See de la Mare in Craig and De Búrca (eds), above n 33, p 240. See also Demaret in Jacob (ed), above n 25, p 328: 'Les renvois préjudiciels ont un intérêt qui va au-déla du litige particulier qui les a provoqués comme l'atteste la possibilité offerte par le statut de la Cour de Justice aux États membres, à la Commission et, dans une certaine circonstance, au Conseil de déposer des observations écrites'. On the issue of intervention generally and reasons why Member States intervene see Anderson, above n 2, pp 231–34.

Perhaps a good example in the employment field of the Court being drawn inexorably to balancing conflicting normative claims and consideration of the public interest is when it has to deal with the issue of remedies for breach of the fundamental Treaty principle of non-discrimination on grounds of sex. Dispute resolution, as we saw, concerns a closed set of events. Yet, a review of the Court's remedies cases in the employment field—*Defrenne II*,[51] *Marshall*,[52] *Sutton*,[53] *Emmott*[54] or *Levez*[55]—all reveal a concern with the balancing of the interests of the parties, the Member States and indeed EC law as a whole, given that protection of the fundamental principle of equality and large amounts of public funds were at stake.[56] As Chayes explains, with reference to the public action role of courts in litigation, the courts may seek to fashion an arrangement which is capable of safeguarding, at least partially, the interests of both parties, and perhaps even of others as well.[57] In balancing the need for Member States to respect the fundamental principle of sex equality with the interests of legal certainty and the need to protect the financial equilibrium of Member State social security, pension and other schemes, this is precisely what the Court of Justice has sought to do. Public interest considerations also emerge in other areas of the Court's employment and sex equality jurisprudence. In *Hill and Stapleton*,[58] for example, the Court was confronted with the question whether the treatment of job-sharers in the Irish civil service amounted to indirect discrimination. It looked at the reasons behind the choice of job-sharing by public sector workers, namely their desire to combine work and family responsibilities and held that the protection of women and men within family life and in the course of their professional activities is a principle which is widely recognised in the legal systems of the Member States as being the natural corollary of the equality between men and women recognised by EC law.[59] The Court's public action role is not, of course, limited to the preliminary reference procedure. The very language of Article 220 EC, to the effect that the Court must see that 'in the interpretation and application of the Treaty the law is observed', implies that the Court's concern with public

---

[51] Case 43/75 *Defrenne II*.

[52] Cases 152/84 *Helen Marshall v Southampton and South-West Hampshire Health Authority* [1986] ECR 723; and C–271/91 *Helen Marshall v Southampton and South-West Hampshire Health Authority* [1993] ECR I–4367.

[53] Case C–66/95 *R v Secretary of State for Social Security, ex parte Eunice Sutton* [1997] ECR I–2163.

[54] Case C–208/90 *Theresa Emmott v Minister for Social Welfare and the Attorney General* [1991] ECR I–4269.

[55] Case C–326/96 *B.S. Levez v T.H. Jennings (Harlow Pools) Ltd.* [1998] ECR I–7835.

[56] See, however, Fitzpatrick, above n 44, 211, who remarks that the tendency of national employment law is to compensate the 'victim' rather than to challenge the source of the discrimination.

[57] Chayes, above n 38, 1293.

[58] Case C–243/95 *Hill and Stapleton v Revenue Commissioners and Department of Finance* [1998] ECR I–3739.

[59] See Case C–243/95 *Hill and Stapleton*, para 42, discussed further in chs 4 and 5.

purposes—the clarification, development and uniform enforcement of EC law—is intended by the Treaty to be paramount.[60]

Clearly, the dispute resolution and public action models of adjudication may intertwine and this seems to be precisely what they have done in the context of the preliminary reference procedure.[61] De la Mare categorises the type of discourse which Article 234 EC fosters as follows: supremacy or constitutional discourse in which high level values are posited against and located within EC law (eg the creation of fundamental human rights' jurisprudence); public law discourse (eg the nature of the principle of proportionality or the principles governing public liability); and discourse which develops specific notions within particular branches of EC law (eg the notion of 'confusion' in EC trade mark law). Yet these three categories could be said to veer from public action litigation *par excellence* to litigation which approaches dispute resolution. Although it is charged by Article 234 EC with the task of interpreting EC law and not with applying it to the facts of individual cases, in recent years the Court has vigorously insisted on a detailed presentation by the national court of such facts, with the obvious consequence of getting objectively closer to participating in dispute resolution.[62] In the *Djabali* case, for example, when refusing to answer the referring court, the Court of Justice emphasised that '[T]he justification for a preliminary reference is not that it enables advisory opinions on general or hypothetical questions to be delivered but rather that it is necessary for the effective resolution of a dispute.'[63] Thus the preliminary reference procedure seeks not only to safeguard the uniformity of EC law but also, on a more mundane level, to assist the national judge in resolving a concrete case. Simitis argues that the growth in preliminary rulings illustrates and confirms the advancing instrumentalism of the European Court of Justice for the resolution of national

---

[60] See also G. Ress, 'Fact-finding at the European Court of Justice' in R.B. Lillich, *Fact-finding Before International Tribunals* (Ardsley-on-Hudson/New York, Transnational Publishers Inc., 1992) pp 177–203, p 184: 'Article 164 requires that the Court ensures the observation of the law of or derived from the treaties. This calls for a more inquisitorial character of the proceedings, along with the fact that usually matters of public and not just private interest are at stake before the Court.' And I. Canor, *The Limits of Judicial Discretion in the European Court of Justice* (Baden Baden, Nomos, 1998) p 16: 'the Court deals with questions which bear heavy implications on public interests, lay down principles, determines policy-lines, makes value choices, and formulates ideology which goes far beyond the parties of the case.'

[61] See also S. Simitis, 'Dismantling or Strengthening Labour Law: The Case of the European Court of Justice' (1996) 2 *European Law Journal* 156–76, 171, who describes the Court's dual role as the deliberate combination of the traditional judicial function with a clearly consultative role.

[62] In Joined Cases C–320/90, C–321/90 and C–322/90 *Telemarsicabruzzo S.p.A v Circostel and Ministero delle Poste e Telecomunicazioni and Ministero della Difesa* [1993] ECR I–393, for example, the Court considered this practice as a code of conduct which referring courts would do well to follow if their references are to be deemed admissible, para 6: 'the need [it held] to provide an interpretation of Community law which will be of use to the national court makes it necessary that the national court define the factual and legislative context of the questions it is asking or, at the very least, explain the factual circumstances on which those questions are based.'

[63] Case C–314/96 *Ourdia Djabali v Caisse d'Allocations Familiales de l'Essonne* [1998] ECR I–1149, para 19.

disputes.[64] The jurisprudence of the Court now teems with judgments drawing heavily on the facts of the case, with the result that the interpretation of Community law which the Court provides may in the end be intimately linked to the factual background of the cases referred. One of the remedies cases mentioned earlier—*Levez*—provides an excellent example. The applicant had been a victim of pay discrimination by her employer. He had paid her less than a male colleague for performing the same work but had repeatedly misled her as to the male colleague's earnings with the result that when she finally discovered the truth and lodged a claim for the arrears due to her, her claim was barred by a provision of national law which limited arrears of pay in equal pay claims to a period of two years prior to the commencement of proceedings. Rather than straightforwardly indicating to the national court that such a rule could be regarded as unlawful if it were found to be more restrictive than equivalent national procedural rules or capable of hindering the application of the fundamental principle of equal pay,[65] the Court specifically linked its answer to the facts of the *Levez* case. In other words, it held that the application of a rigid two year limit on arrears was contrary to EC law where, as here, the delay in claiming was due to the employer's misrepresentation.[66] It took another preliminary reference in *Preston and Fletcher*[67] to provide the national court with a more general and less factually specific ruling on the lawfulness of national procedural limitations of this type.

One explanation for this shift in the approach of the Court is provided by Edward. Essentially he suggests that, pursuant to Article 234 EC, the Court was being asked to operate in a sort of factless vacuum, which may have been possible at an early stage when the broad principles of EC law were still undecided. That stage soon passed, however, with the result that the great majority of Article 234 EC references raise questions which are almost meaningless without reference to their factual context.[68] However, with the Court more clearly and frequently engaged in dispute resolution, it becomes increasingly difficult to

---

[64] Simitis, above n 61, 173; see also Demaret in Jacob (ed) above n 25, p 312, on the greater factual emphasis in Article 234 EC cases.

[65] An approach adopted in Case C–246/96 *Mary Teresa Magorrian and Irene Patricia Cunningham v Eastern Health and Social Services Board and Department of Health and Social Services* [1997] ECR I–7153.

[66] Lester's criticism of the Court's answers to questions posed by United Kingdom courts in early sex equality cases suggest that this tendency to narrow the scope of application of the Court's preliminary rulings has always been present (See A. Lester, 'The Uncertain Trumpet. References to the Court of Justice from the United Kingdom: Equal Pay and Equal Treatment without Sex Discrimination' in Schermers *et al.* (eds), above n 2, pp 164–94, pp 170–71, for his discussion of Case 129/79 *MacCarthys Ltd v Wendy Smith* [1980] ECR 1275. Mrs. Smith's case was regarded as a famous victory but he argues that it went no further than the narrow and particular facts of her case.

[67] Case C–78/98 *Shirley Preston and others v Wolverhampton Healthcare NHS Trust and others* and *Dorothy Fletcher v Midland Bank* [2000] ECR I–3201.

[68] See D. Edward, 'The Problem of Fact-finding in Preliminary Proceedings Under Article 177 EEC' in Schermers *et al.* (eds), above n 2, pp 216–20, p 217; and G. Bebr, 'The Preliminary Rulings of Article 177 EEC—Problems and Suggestions for Improvement' in Schermers *et al.* (eds), above n 2, p 346.

maintain the chimera that its judicial pronouncements under Article 234 EC are unconcerned with the factual circumstances of the individual case, involve no application of EC law and no determination of the compatibility of national law with EC law. The fact that the Court finds itself ever more concerned with the facts of the cases referred must also raise concerns about whether the guarantees normally accorded to parties at national level with regard to judicial fact-finding are provided at the level of the Court of Justice in preliminary reference proceedings. It is generally accepted that this procedure is not well-adapted to the process of fact-finding. Presumably because of the interpretation/application division of functions on which it is based, there are no rules of evidence, the parties exchange a single set of observations and have an opportunity to comment on the observations of others in the course of a relatively short oral hearing during which the Court may, but often does not, pose any questions.[69] Another cause for concern is the effect which an increased dispute resolution role will have on the Court's already considerable case-load.

In *R. v Secretary of State for Employment, ex parte Nicole Seymour-Smith and Laura Perez*,[70] the Court was asked to resolve a series of highly complex and detailed questions by the national court concerning, *inter alia*, the statistical evidence required to establish indirect discrimination. Any answer it gave was likely to provoke dissent from some quarter or other, given the number of cases depending on its interpretation in the United Kingdom and the hopes pinned on the Court in that Member State, where it was often seen as the only venue in which the continued erosion of national employment protection legislation could be curbed. In the *Seymour-Smith* decision one sees a tool frequently used by the Court to divert attention away from the fact that its answer to the national referring court actually does provide a clear ruling on the compatibility of the national legislation at issue, In the words of one commentator:

> to the extent that the national rules in issue are described in the order of reference, the Court will name them in its grounds of judgment and interpret the relevant provisions of Community law in a manner tailored to the content of those rules, solve the compatibility question directly and then express the terms of that solution in a (not always very) neutral form in the operative part of its judgment.[71]

In the event, the Court's statement to the effect that the statistics submitted at national level did not appear to show that a considerably smaller percentage of women than men was able to fulfil the criterion imposed by the disputed rule was the subject of sharp criticism in academic literature. Ellis has remarked, for

---

[69] See Anderson, above n 2, pp 75–77 and R.A.A. Duk, 'Some Remarks of a Dutch Advocate on the Preliminary Reference Procedure of Article 177 EEC' in Schermers *et al.* (eds), above n 2, pp 204–09, p 208.

[70] Case C–167/97 [1999] ECR I–623.

[71] See Lenaerts in Curtin and Heukels (eds), above n 12, p 364; and W. Van Gerven, 'The Role and Structure of the European Judiciary now and in the future' (1996) 21 *European Law Review* 211–23, 219–20. An example in the field of sex discrimination might be Case C–180/95 *Nils Draehmpaehl v Urania Immobilienservice OHG* [1997] ECR I–2195.

example, that the Court sailed perilously close in this case to the jurisdictional dividing line between itself and the national court.[72] However, had the Court not referred to the statistical evidence presented to it in the order for reference there was a risk that its decision would simply have contained a series of references to its pronouncements in previous decisions on indirect sex discrimination, with little more. How useful are such general restatements of the law to a national referring court which is presumably armed with a set of court reports already and which is clearly in two minds about how to apply such established jurisprudence to the facts of the case before it?

The conclusion must be that the relationship between national courts and the Court of Justice—although still central to the success and operation of the reference procedure and the uniform application of EC law—has changed over the years. Indeed, introduction of the principles of direct effect and supremacy made such change inevitable. Although it is in the Court's interest to preserve the semblance of an equal and co-operative relationship with national courts,[73] it is clear that, as regards the interpretation and validity of EC law, it is in a hierarchically superior position.[74] Clinging, as the Court and many Court-watchers do,[75] to the idea that the spirit of co-operation which imbued Article 234 EC is its essential aim and raison d'être is unhelpful. Uniformity in the interpretation and application of EC law is essentially the aim of Article 234 EC, co-operation was the means initially chosen to promote that objective. What is arguably more worrying than the Court's insistence on more information from referring courts for it to accept references is the lack of clarity regarding the real role it is intended to play in the context of the preliminary reference procedure. This lack

---

[72] See E. Ellis, 'The Recent Jurisprudence of the Court of Justice in the Field of Sex Equality' (2000) 37 *Common Market Law Review* 1403–26, 1409.

[73] See in this respect, Lord Mackenzie Stuart, 'Suggestions of the Court of Justice for the Role of the Representatives of the Governments, the Commission and the Council' in Schermers *et al.* (eds), above n 2, pp 335–37, p 337, who insists that the relationship is that of a dialogue between collaborators: 'by introducing the concept of lower court/appellate court into the relationship between the national judge and the Court of Justice of the European Communities there is a real danger of damaging the mutual trust and confidence which has been painstakingly established over three decades.' This arguments tallies with de la Mare's suggestion in Craig and De Búrca (eds), above n 33, p 228 that, by insisting that the relationship with national courts is non-hierarchical, the Court's intention is to sweeten or conceal the bitter pill of supremacy. See also I. Maher, 'National Courts as European Community Courts' (1994) 14 *Legal Studies* 226–43, 227, who argues that 'the system of split judicial functions and dependency on national courts will survive the tension inherent in it as long as the European Court continues to cultivate the goodwill and cooperation of national courts.'

[74] See de la Mare in Craig and De Búrca (eds), above n 33, p 227: 'in genuine questions of Treaty or EC legislative interpretation the reference procedure becomes, on the federalist view, a simple control mechanism that provides for definitive, hierarchical question answering.'

[75] See, for example, Case C–83/91 *Meilicke*; and D. O'Keeffe, 'Is the Spirit of Article 177 Under Attack?' (1998) 23 *European Law Review* 509–36, 516–20. Barnard and Sharpston, above n 28, 1114, also rely on what they regard as the basic principles governing the operation of Article 234 EC which, until recently, were fairly clear. They cite, in support of this statement, the excellent collection of papers by Schermers *et al.* (eds), above n 2. What is remarkable about the latter is how perspicacious the editors of and contributors to that work were in terms of their awareness of the fundamental flaws in the reference procedure and the gap which already existed in 1987 between theory and practice when it came to its operation.

of clarity, it is submitted, may have a deleterious effect on the precise values which the procedure was intended to safeguard, specifically the uniform application of EC law. Weiler identifies this lack of clarity as 'a tension between the capacity of a supreme court to act as an unchecked last resort appeal instance in the normal administration of individual justice and its capacity to "oversee" the judicial development of a system and have the appropriate impact on such developments.'[76] In one case the Court may adopt a hands-off approach to questions, say of justification or proportionality in indirect sex discrimination cases, whereas in another it may actually wade in and provide the national court with such detailed instructions as to effectively resolve the dispute at national level. Mutual, fruitful, co-operative dialogue between the Court of Justice and national courts (the ultimate enforcers of EC law[77]) is clearly essential to the effective operation, interpretation and application of EC law. It could be argued that sensitive recognition of changes which have occurred in this mythical judicial relationship over the years is now called for. At present, as de la Mare points out, the Court regularly reverts to its favoured technique, reiterating, in response to a national court's questions, compendious principles of law and directing the national court to apply that law. However, '[S]uch a restatement may often contain no *answer* to the question in a form expected by an ECJ-illiterate national court; and yet that is deliberate, either because the ECJ considers the answer already exists in the case law or because it feels the question is a request actually to apply the case law to the facts, a job usually reserved for the national court.'[78]

In the specific context of equal pay and equal treatment, Lord Lester, who was involved in numerous pioneering cases in this field, has expressed his dissatisfaction with the lack of clarity and coherence in some of the Court's decisions and has underlined the difficulties which national courts have experienced in applying the Court's rulings.[79] In the field of indirect discrimination, for example, where the facts of the case (specifically whether the impugned legislation or practice affects a far greater proportion of female or male workers) have not yet been established, the Court generally indicates what facts have to be decided for the national court to fill in the blanks in the Court's preliminary ruling. However, this kind of reference back does not guarantee the uniform application of EC law and may leave a national court, which has suspended a

---

[76] J.H.H. Weiler, 'The European Court, National Courts and References for Preliminary Rulings. The Paradox of Success: A Revisionist View of Article 177 EEC' in Schermers *et al.* (eds), above n 2, pp 366–78, p 369.

[77] See also J.H.H. Weiler, 'The Function and Future of European Law' in V. Heiskanen and K. Kulovesi (eds), *Function and Future of European Law* (Helsinki, Publications of the Faculty of Law University of Helsinki, 1999) pp 9–22, pp 19–20: 'The European Court can pronounce on the supremacy of Community law, or on the *Francovich* principle of Member State liability all it wants, so to speak. These doctrines become effective only when accepted and practised by national courts under the guidance of the highest courts in each Member State.'

[78] See de la Mare in Craig and De Búrca (eds), above n 33, p 222.

[79] Lester in Schermers *et al.* (eds), above n 2, pp 164–94.

case, explained it to the Court and awaited its answer, in the expectation that it will be conclusive of the case, extremely dissatisfied.[80] Yet if national courts are unhappy or confused by the answers they are receiving from the Court there is a risk that they will a) refrain from posing questions in future,[81] b) apply the Court's response to the facts of the case in an unsatisfactory or inconsistent manner,[82] or c) make further references to the Court seeking clarification.[83] The first two scenarios may mean that the uniform application of EC law risks serious disruption,[84] while the last poses further problems for the Court in terms of its growing workload.

THE CHANGING NATURE OF THE RELATIONSHIP BETWEEN NATIONAL COURTS AND THE COURT OF JUSTICE (II): THE THORNY QUESTION OF (IN)ADMISSIBILITY

Cases like *Da Costa* and *Schwarze* are usually taken as the starting point for discussion by those who criticise the Court's present jurisprudence on the (in)admissibility of Article 234 EC references. In *Da Costa*, the Commission had urged the Court to dismiss the reference for lack of substance, as the questions on which an interpretation was requested had already been decided in *Van Gend en Loos*. The Court replied that:

> Article [234] always allows a national court, if it considers it desirable, to refer questions of interpretation to the Court again. This follows from Article 20 of the Statute of the Court of Justice, under which [prior to the renumbering introduced by the Nice Treaty], the procedure laid down for the settlement of preliminary questions is automatically set in motion as soon as such a question is referred by a national court. The Court must, therefore, give a judgment on the present application.[85]

This expansive approach towards references from national courts re-emerged in *Schwarze*. Where it appears that the real object of a reference is a review of the validity of Community acts rather than their interpretation, the Court held that it must nevertheless decide the questions, instead of holding the referring

---

[80] See Lenaerts in Curtin and Heukels (eds), above n 12, p 367.

[81] See Lester in Schermers *et al.* (eds), above n 2.

[82] The co-operative dialogue between the Court and the referring court seems to have broken down entirely in Case 96/80 *J. P. Jenkins v Kingsgate (Clothing Productions) Ltd.* [1981] ECR 911. See further Lester in Schermers *et al.* (eds), above n 2, pp 177–83, and the discussion of the *Jenkins* case below ch 4.

[83] See also Barnard and Sharpston, above n 28, 1121; and with respect to scenario a), O'Keeffe (1998), above n 75, 532.

[84] See also C.W.A. Timmermans, 'Judicial Protection Against the Member States: Articles 169 and 177 Revisited' in Curtin and Heukels (eds), above n 12, pp 391–407, p 404: 'Open questions, normally, can only get open answers. These are of little use, and may even be damaging, for the purposes of the uniform application of Community law for which Article [234 EC] is designed.'

[85] Cases 28–30/62 *Da Costa*.

court to a strict adherence to form which would only serve to prolong the Article 234 EC procedure and be incompatible with its true nature. The Court added that:

> strict adherence to formal requirements may be defended in the case of litigation between two parties whose mutual rights must be subject to strict rules, it would be inappropriate to the special field of judicial cooperation under Article [234], which requires the national court and the Court of Justice . . . to make direct and complementary contributions to the working out of a decision.[86]

The Court has, as we have seen, also been happy to extract from imperfectly formulated questions those questions pertaining to the interpretation of the Treaty and has refused to criticise the grounds and purpose of requests for a preliminary ruling. As far as it is concerned: 'Article [234] is based on a distinct separation of functions between national courts and tribunals on the one hand and the Court of Justice on the other hand and it does not give the Court jurisdiction to take cognisance of the facts of the case, or to criticise the reasons for the reference.'[87] The Court was clearly trying to encourage national judges to refer questions by emphasising the lack of hierarchy and formality in the reference procedure: 'Acceptance by the Member States of the Court's jurisdiction, and indeed of the Community legal order itself, depended on giving the maximum encouragement to national courts to refer questions to Luxembourg.'[88] The desired outcome of this encouragement to refer was greater uniformity in the interpretation and application of EC law.[89]

The two references in *Foglia v Novello*[90] are regarded as the harbinger of what seemed like a change of heart at the Court as regards its generous acceptance of references. The circumstances surrounding these two references are well known and will not be repeated here.[91] Essentially, the Court did not regard the dispute which had given rise to the reference by the Italian court as genuine and it declined to give a preliminary ruling:

> In order that the Court may perform its task in accordance with the Treaty it is essential for national courts to explain, when the reasons do not emerge beyond any doubt

---

[86] Case 16/65 *Schwarze*, p 886.

[87] Case 35/76 *Simmenthal SpA v Ministero delle Finanze* [1976] ECR 1871, para 4.; and Case 5/77 *Tedeschi*, para 17.

[88] See Anderson, above n 2, p 95.

[89] For a comprehensive view of this early case-law see A. Barav, 'Preliminary Censorship? The Judgment of the European Court in *Foglia v. Novello*' (1980) 5 *European Law Review* 443–68.

[90] Case 104/79 *Pasquale Foglia v Mariella Novello* (No 1) [1980] ECR 745; and Case 244/80 *Pasquale Foglia v Mariella Novello* (No 2) [1981] ECR 3045.

[91] See variously Barav (1980), above n 89; Barnard and Sharpston, above n 28, 1121–23; O'Keeffe (1998), above n 75; Craig and De Búrca, above 33, pp 431–33; A. Arnull, *The European Union and its Court of Justice* (Oxford, OUP, 1999). On the question of admissibility generally see M. O'Neill, 'Article 177 and Limits to the Right to Refer: an End to the Confusion' (1996) 2 *European Public Law* 375–91; W. Alexander, 'La recevabilité des renvois préjudiciels dans la perspective de la réforme institutionelle de 1996' (1995) *Cahiers de droit européen* 561–76; and T. Kennedy, 'First Steps Towards European *Certiorari*?' (1993) 18 *European Law Review* 121–29.

from the file, why they consider that a reply to their question is necessary to enable them to give judgment. . . . [t]he duty assigned to the Court by Article [234] is not that of delivering advisory opinions on general or hypothetical questions but of assisting in the administration of justice in the Member States.[92]

The Court also stressed that the national court must allow it to be in a position to make any assessment inherent in the performance of its own duties, in particular in order to check whether it has jurisdiction.[93]

The number of references declared inadmissible by the Court rose considerably in the early 1990s,[94] revealing that, although the circumstances of *Foglia* might have been unusual, the Court was increasingly willing, some would say even eager, to vet the references being sent to it by national courts. In some cases it has simply denied that it has jurisdiction under the EC Treaty over the questions the Court has been asked to consider. In others it has demonstrated its determination to control more strictly whether the conditions for a reference established in Article 234 EC are satisfied. Thus, it is prepared to examine whether a genuine dispute is pending and continues to examine whether the referring body enjoys the power to refer. In addition, the Court is now prepared to inquire whether the issue is a hypothetical one,[95] whether the questions being asked have an actual connection with the dispute the national court must resolve,[96] or whether adequate information has been referred by the national court or tribunal.[97] In the *Meilicke* case, for example, it reiterated its original

---

[92] Case 244/80 *Foglia v Novello (No 2)*, paras 17–18. As Barav notes, however, above n 89, p 33, no other reference has since been rejected by the Court on the same basis. Case C–105/94 *Ditta Angelo Celestini v Saar-Sektkellerei Faber GmbH and Co.* [1997] ECR I–2971, which resembled *Foglia* on the facts but where nothing in the case file indicated a fabricated dispute, was not rejected as inadmissible and Advocate General Fennelly, para 24 of his Opinion, counselled utmost caution in the application of the *Foglia* precedent.

[93] Case 244/80 *Foglia v Novello (No 2)*, para 19.

[94] See Barav, above n 89, 33; and Barnard and Sharpston, above n 28, 1113. Note, however, the Court's decision in Case 52/76 *Benedetti*, where it stated that it could not answer the referred questions effectively owing to a lack of precision in the Order for Reference; or Case 222/78 *ICAP v Beneventi* [1979] ECR 1163, 1178, where the Court, confronted by a question of too general a nature to allow a useful reply, preferred to abstain from doing so.

[95] Order in Case C–361/97 *Rauhollah Nour v Bergenländische Gebietskrankenkasse* [1998] ECR I–3101, paras 12–13.

[96] Case C–375/96 *Galileo Zaninotto v Ispettorato Centrale Repressione Frodi and others* [1998] ECR I–6629, paras 79–80.

[97] See, for example, Order in Joined Cases C–128/97 and C–137/97 *Criminal Proceedings against Italia Testa and Mario Modesti* [1998] ECR I–2181, paras 5–6, 12–15; and Order in Case C–326/95 *Banco de Fomento e Exterior v Pechim e.a.* [1996] ECR I–1385, paras 6–12. On this last point, Barav compares the new approach of the Court to factual and legislative information, discussed in the text immediately following this note, with early cases such as Case 77/72 *Capolongo* [1973] ECR 611 or Joined Cases 98, 162 and 258/85 *Michele Bertini and Giuseppe Bisignani v Regione Lazio and Unità sanitarie locali* [1986] ECR 1885, where the Court was willing to excuse the referring court's lack of precision regarding the facts of the case, the reason for the reference and the relevance/utility of the questions being referred for the resolution of the case at national level, and proceeded to give preliminary rulings. See also Barnard and Sharpston, above n 28, 1127–41; and O'Keeffe (1998) above n 75, 514.

position on the co-operative nature of the reference procedure and the distinctive roles of the Court of Justice and national courts thereunder. It then added:

> The Court has already made it clear that the need to provide an interpretation of Community law which will be of use to the national court makes it essential to define the legal context in which the interpretation requested should be placed and that, in that respect, it may be convenient, in certain circumstances, for the facts of the case to be established and for questions of purely national law to be settled at the time the reference is made to the court, so as to enable the latter to take cognisance of all the features of fact and of law which may be relevant to the interpretation of Community law which it is called upon to give. Without such information the Court may find it impossible to give a useful interpretation.[98]

In *Telemarsicabruzzo* the Court also repeated the need for the national court to define the factual and legislative context of the questions it is asking and stressed that such information is particularly important in areas of law characterised by complex legal and factual situations.[99] The Court also seems keener to learn from the national court why it considers a preliminary ruling is necessary to enable the national court to give judgment.[100]

Barnard and Sharpston argue that, in imposing these conditions—the issue to be tried must be real and not hypothetical, adequate information must be provided, and the questions asked must be relevant to the dispute before the national court—the Court has departed from the wording of Article 234 EC and from its previous jurisprudence. Although the shift in its jurisprudence is difficult to deny, it is more questionable whether Article 234 EC demands slavish acceptance by the Court of references from national courts.[101] It is also far from clear why the Court should be constrained to accept references in cases where the factual and legal circumstances framing the national court's questions is unclear or not even provided. It remains for the national court to determine the factual context in which it and the Court of Justice must work, or to provide the Court with a clear hypothesis on the basis of which the latter must work. However, as questions from national courts become more and more complex, it seems inevitable that the Court will require a clear account of the circumstances

---

[98] Case C–83/91 *Meilicke* para 26.

[99] Joined Cases C–320–322/90 *Telemarsicabruzzo*. See also the Order of the Court in Case C–157/92 *Banchero (No 1)* [1993] ECR I–1086 and the decision in Case C–387/93 *Banchero (No 2)* [1995] ECR I–4663; Case C–458/93 *Criminal Proceedings against Mustafa Saddik* [1995] ECR I–511; Case C–257/95 *Gérard Bresle v Préfet de la Région Auvergne and Préfet du Puy-de-Dôme* [1996] ECR I–235; Order in Case C–2/96 *Criminal Proceedings against Sunino and Data* [1996] ECR I–1545; Case C–101/96 *Criminal Proceedings against Italia Testa* [1996] ECR I–3081; Case C–191/96 *Criminal Proceedings against Mario Modesti* [1996] ECR I–3939; and Case C–196/96 *Criminal Proceedings against Hassan Lahlou* [1996] ECR I–3947.

[100] See, for example, Case C–343/90 *Manuel José Lourenço Dias v Director da Alfândego do Porto* [1992] ECR I–4673, para 19.

[101] See also D. Wyatt, 'Following up *Foglia*: why the Court is right to stick to its guns' (1981) 6 *European Law Review* 447–51, 447: 'the proposition that national courts have been granted the unequivocal *right* to demand judgment under Article [234] on any legal question, however hypothetical or without purpose [cannot] be readily accepted.'

of the case in order to enable it to give a ruling which is meaningful both for the referring court and for other courts which, in similar circumstances, may have to apply the essence of the Court's ruling. Admittedly, in such circumstances, the Court moves ever closer to performing a dispute resolution function. Furthermore, as the Advocate General explained in *Telemarsicabruzzo*: 'it is unsatisfactory both on principle and in practical terms for the Court to have to extract from the parties' observations in the main proceedings the information which it requires on the factual and legal background to the questions in a reference. Such work may not merely be very demanding in terms of resources but may also carry a risk of errors.'[102] As regards research on the legal background to the case, the Judge-Rapporteur and Advocate General may be assisted by their legal secretaries and by the small Research and Documentation Division, but the Court may remain dangerously blind to the factual background against which the questions have been framed.[103] At best it will be able to give a ruling based on a range of different possible factual scenarios which it will stress it is for the national court to determine, as it often does in the context of indirect sex discrimination cases,[104] at worst it will give an embarrassingly erroneous judgment, useless to the national court in its resolution of the case in hand.[105] Furthermore, as the Court has repeatedly pointed out, it is on the basis of the Order for Reference lodged at the Court, translated into the Community's working languages and communicated by the Registry, that Member State governments and other interested parties decide whether or not to submit observations to the Court pursuant to Article 20 EC Statute. The more complete the Order for Reference is the better for all concerned.

Some of the criticism of the Court's (in)admissibility case law is understandable. The message sent to national courts has been quite unclear with the Court, for example, resorting to the case file in some instances to supplement the information in the order for reference, while refusing to go beyond the order in other cases, with the result that they are rejected as inadmissible. In addition, there are also charges, which seem justified, that the Court is quite happy to

---

[102] Joined Cases C–320–322/90 *Telemarsicabruzzo*, Opinion of Advocate General Gulmann, at para 20. In Case 19/81 *Arthur Burton v British Railways Board* [1982] ECR 555, it seems that the Court's statement of facts did indeed contain an error. See also the Opinion of Advocate General La Pergola in Case C–35/98 *Staatssecretaris van Financiën v B.G.M. Verkooijen* [2000] ECR I–4071. See Lester in Schermers *et al.* (eds), above n 2, pp 185–87. He identifies the source of the problem as the Court's assuming the facts to be otherwise than as had been agreed for the purposes of the reference. In Case C–415/93 *Union Royale Belge des Sociétés de Football Association v Bosman* [1995] ECR I–4921, Advocate General Lenz, para 75 of his Opinion, pressed for a more benevolent approach to the requirement of adequate information: 'rejection of a reference for a preliminary ruling on the ground of an inadequate account of the factual and legal context should therefore be restricted to exceptional cases.'

[103] Albeit Article 104(5) RP now specifically empowers it to ask the national court for further clarification. On the need for the Court to be in greater contact with national referring courts see, variously, Ehlermann and Pipkorn in Schermers *et al.* (eds), above n 2, p 297; O'Keeffe (1998), above n 75, 726; Barnard and Sharpston, above n 28, 1145–53.

[104] See below ch 4.

[105] A risk which the Court seemed aware of in Case 77/72 *Capolongo*, para 8.

accept a reference as admissible when the question referred is interesting and of significant constitutional/principled importance, when it might have rejected it had the questions been less interesting.[106] In these circumstances, national courts, particularly those unaccustomed to using the preliminary reference procedure may feel unwilling, when their reference is rejected, to refer further questions to the Court in future. In addition, though a case may have been rejected as inadmissible, it may have taken the Court several months, if not years (at least in part due to the procedural and operational constraints outlined in chapter one), to make this ruling, thereby adding to the cost and delay experienced by parties to the case at national level.[107]

However, the Court's evolving stance on the admissibility of references from national courts highlights not simply what the Order for Reference should contain or whether the Court should be expected to piece together the information contained in the Order, the case file and the written observations submitted to it in order to form an overall view of the questions it is being asked to answer.[108] Rather, the issue of (in)admissibility goes to the heart of some of the problems inherent in the preliminary reference procedure, specifically whether the Court's public interest or dispute resolution function is paramount thereunder, whether it is possible, or ever was, to develop coherent legal principles more or less *in abstracto* and, most importantly, whether national courts are still receiving rulings conducive to the correct and efficient resolution of disputes. Is the Court being asked in reference cases to do the impossible—to give answers to complex questions without fully understanding the factual and legal background to those questions; to produce fine, broad statements on the principles of EC law and yet give sufficiently precise and useful answers to allow national judges to apply its preliminary rulings to the cases in hand?[109] Caught between a rock and a hard place, the Court is being asked, with four hundred and eighty seven references pending as of the end of 2001, to perform both dispute resolution and public action adjudicative functions in the context of Article 234 EC references. O'Keeffe may be right to counsel against recourse to a judicially-created

---

[106] See, in this respect, the persuasive reasoning deployed by the Court in Case C–415/93 *Bosman* on the question of admissibility and, generally, O'Keeffe (1998), above n 75, 522–23.

[107] See O'Keeffe (1998), above n 75, 511 and 515, describing the time it took the Court to dispose of Case C–428/93 *Monin Automobiles v Maison de Deux Roues* [1994] ECR I–1707; and Case C–66/97 *Banco de Fomento e Exterior SA v Amândio Maurício Martins Pechim e.a.* [1997] ECR I–3757; and Anderson, above n 2, p 111, commenting on the twenty seven months which it took the plenary court to reject the reference in Case C–320 to C–322/90 *Telemarsicabruzzo* as inadmissible: 'The ultimate decision to refuse jurisdiction [. . .] clearly represents a policy decision and not simply a case of questions which were manifestly impossible to answer.'

[108] See Barnard and Sharpston, above n 28, 1151. As regards the inconsistency in the Court's present approach compare, however, the Order in Case C–326/95 *Banco de Fomento e Exterior*, para 11 (where the information in the order for reference was considered inadequate) with the Court's approach in Case C–316/93 *Nicole Vaneetveld v Le Foyer SA* [1994] ECR I–763; Case C–18/93 *Corsica Ferries Italia Srl v Corpo dei Piloti del Porto di Genova* [1994] ECR I–1783; or Case C–17/94 *Criminal proceedings against Denis Gervais and Others* [1995] ECR I–4353, para 21.

[109] See also Weiler in Schermers *et al.* (eds), above n 2, p 369 (quoted above, text at n 78).

doctrine of admissibility for references as 'a disguised palliative for an absence of other methods to limit the Court's case-load',[110] but repeated Intergovernmental Conferences have failed to come up with a means to improve how the Court deals with its present, untenably full docket and it remains to be seen whether recent tinkering with the Court's working methods will prove effective. Extension of the jurisdiction of the Court of First Instance to give preliminary rulings could actually make matters worse in terms of the time it will take to hand down decisions, the risk posed to the coherence of the Court's case-law and, consequently, the respect for that case-law afforded by national courts. Furthermore, given that the Court of First Instance has been involved principally, if not exclusively, in dispute resolution, there may be an even greater tendency in future to narrow the scope of rulings to the particular facts of the case to the detriment of the public action/public interest role which Article 234 rulings should arguably perform.

THE QUALITY OF THE COURT'S PRELIMINARY RULINGS UNDER ATTACK

As chapter one revealed, there is growing discontent with the quality and content of the preliminary rulings delivered by the Court in reference cases. It was suggested in that chapter that at least some of this unhappiness might be quieted if the Court opted for a less formal, homogenised form of drafting. As Weiler and others have argued, the present, cryptic, Cartesian style 'with its pretence of logical legal reasoning and inevitability of results is not conducive to a good conversation with national courts.'[111] In addition, although it does not befit an English speaker to question the hegemony which the French language enjoys at the Court, it would be wrong to overlook the effect which the Court's internal working language may have on the form and context of legal texts and its own judicial style. The admission of dissenting opinions was proposed as a further means to respond to justified criticism of the Courts' often-parsimonious judicial reasoning.

Yet it is arguable that discontent with the quality and content of the Court's judgments goes beyond the problems posed by the multi-lingual conditions under which it must work, the form of its judgments or the lack of provision for explicit dissent. What many commentators regret is the Court's failure or inability to provide referring courts with workable, clear answers. In the context of sex equality, for example, Kilpatrick remarks on the unhelpful nature of the Court's ruling in the *Jenkins* case:

> The ECJ did not give the referring court an answer which allowed it to deal with the issue before it. In an extremely confused judgment, it at times seemed to indicate that

---

[110] O'Keeffe (1998), above n 75, 530.
[111] See Weiler (1999) in Heiskanen and Kulovesi (eds), above n 77, pp 9–22, p 21.

paying a female-dominated part-time group less would infringe Article [141] only if it was a pretext for the employer's covert intention to pay women less. At other times, the employer's intention did not seem to be relevant.[112]

Lester is even more scathing of the Court's equivocal statements in *Jenkins* on the crucial issues of the relevance of intention and the nature of the employer's justification:

> The Court's apparent inability to reach a consensus and therefore to give a clear judgment on these questions has created great uncertainty about Community law. It has engendered further costly and protracted litigation. It has dampened enthusiasm for references under Article [234]. And it may well have damaged the Court's prestige among judges remarkable not for their insularity but for their sense of responsibility for protecting enforceable Community rights.[113]

In the event, the referring court in *Jenkins* found itself left in considerable doubt as to the effect of Article 141 in relation to unintentional indirect discrimination.[114] Similarly, on the question of objective justification of indirect sex discrimination in *Seymour-Smith*, the Court vacillated between the more demanding level of scrutiny which it had previously applied to measures taken by employers and Member State legislation generally and the less onerous level it had devised with reference to national social security legislation in particular. It is submitted that some of the Court's difficulties stem from the dual role which it is expected to perform under Article 234 EC. If it maintains too much distance from the factual and legal circumstances of the case which the national judge is trying to resolve, it risks providing a ruling of little utility.[115] Repetition of broad principles of EC law may not be sufficient to enable a national court to determine the correct outcome, from the point of view of EC law, of a novel case which has developed on the basis of particular circumstances.[116]

In an early Sunday trading case, *Torfaen BC v B & Q plc*.[117] the Court outlined the principles of EC law relating to the applicability of the Community rules on the free movement of goods and the possibility of justifying equal burden rules. However, such rules, in order to be justified, also had to comply with the requirements of the principle of proportionality, and the Court left this determination to the national courts. The result, now famous, was that some national courts found that the rules which restricted Sunday Trading were com-

---

[112] See Kilpatrick, above n 1, 140.

[113] See Lester in Schermers *et al.* (eds), above n 2, pp 182–83.

[114] See the decision of the Employment Appeal Tribunal in [1981] ICR 715.

[115] See Chayes, above n 38, 1297, on the complex and continuous interplay between fact evaluation and legal consequence.

[116] See also Demaret in Jacob (ed), above n 25, p 313: 'une interprétation trop abstraite au vu des faits de l'espèce, c'est-à-dire une réponse peu précise de la Cour de Justice, ne serait pas très utile au juge national. Surtout, elle ne contribuerait pas à assurer une application uniforme du droit communautaire à travers les États membres.'

[117] Case 145/88 [1989] ECR 385.

patible with Article 28 EC, while others found that they were not. On other occasions, the Court chose to apply, more or less, the principle of proportionality itself, with not altogether happy results. The Court's sex discrimination jurisprudence provides further examples of the Court sometimes directing the referring court to perform the necessary proportionality test and at other times assuming that responsibility itself. In the *Sirdar* case,[118] for example, the Court was asked whether the exclusion of female soldiers from the Royal Marines was incompatible with the Equal Treatment Directive.[119] Having accepted that decisions taken by Member States in regard to access to employment, vocational training and working conditions in the armed forces for the purposes of ensuring combat effectiveness do not fall altogether outside the scope of EC law, the Court turned to the question whether the Marines' discriminatory exclusion rule could be justified. The applicant was a cook and the exclusion of female soldiers such as the applicant from the Royal Marines was due, explained the Court, to the interoperability rule established by the Marines for combat effectiveness according to which all members of the corps are engaged and trained with the possibility of front line combat in mind. In such circumstances, concluded the Court:

> the competent authorities were entitled, in the exercise of their discretion as to whether to maintain the exclusion in question in the light of social developments, *and without abusing the principle of proportionality*, to come to the view that the specific conditions for deployment of the assault units of which the Royal Marines are composed, and in particular the rule of interoperability to which they are subject, justified their composition remaining exclusively male.[120]

The Court thus determined the issue of the proportionality of the exclusionary rule itself, despite the fact that, as the Report for the Hearing stated, the applicant had submitted evidence to the effect that hugely overweight male cooks were being employed by the Royal Marines who had never been involved in combat in their military lives!

REVISING THE ROLE OF NATIONAL COURTS IN THE REFERENCE PROCEDURE

So far, chapters one and two have concentrated on some of the problems besetting the reference procedure—*inter alia*, the length of time it takes the Court to dispose of a case, the ever-increasing number of references, the procedural and linguistic constraints under which the Court must operate when it comes to

---

[118] Case C–273/97 *Angela Maria Sirdar v The Army Board, Secretary of State for Defence* [1999] ECR I–7403.

[119] Directive 76/207/EEC of 9 February 1976 on the implementation of the principle of equal treatment for men and women as regards access to employment, vocational training and promotion, and working conditions, OJ 1976 L39/40.

[120] Case C–273/97, para 31 (emphasis added).

disposing of cases,[121] the ambivalent function of the reference procedure and of the Court's adjudicative role thereunder, the confused signals conveyed to national courts by the Court's developing (in)admissibility doctrine and the regular and increasing criticism to which the Court is subject in terms of the quality and content of its rulings. Given these problems, Weiler's comment in 1987 to the effect that the paradox of the innovative reference procedure was that it was likely to become a victim of its own success, seems prescient. The system, as it is operating at present, is not conducive to quality preliminary rulings being handed down to national courts. This state of affairs has inevitable consequences for the uniform interpretation and application of EC law, for the respect afforded the judicial pronouncements of the Court of Justice generally and for the fruitfulness of future dialogue between the Community Court and what must often be confused and frustrated national courts.[122]

Since the close of the Intergovernmental Conference which culminated in the Amsterdam Treaty, and indeed before, proposals for the reform of the EC's judicial architecture and its judicial procedures have abounded. These proposals concentrated on methods to reduce the backlog of cases at the Court and measures to ensure the continued efficacy of the Court as an institution with the accession of new Member States.[123] They ranged from: proposals to encourage national courts to decide more questions of EC law without references to the Court; improvement of the quality of orders for reference and the information provided therein; the possibility for the national court to suggest answers to the questions posed; the possibility for the Court of Justice to seek further clarification from national courts concerning the questions referred; elimination of the oral procedure or shortening of the written procedure; introduction of a fast track for certain cases; introduction of some form of docket control or filtering procedure; involvement of decentralised bodies responsible for dealing with references from courts within a particular area of territorial jurisdiction and limiting those national courts empowered to make a reference. In the event, the Nice Treaty focused on reforms aimed at the handling of cases on the Kirchberg—limited involvement of the Court of First Instance in the reference procedure with the possibility of appeal to the Court (Article 225(3) EC as amended); the possibility of dispensing with the need for the Advocate General's

---

[121] See also Bebr in Schermers *et al.* (eds), above n 2, p 358, who suggests that the Court's Rules of Procedure were drafted with contentious proceedings, not the reference procedure, in mind. In his view, the particular features of the preliminary procedure and its special problems were probably not realised at the time.

[122] See M.L. Volcansek, *Judicial Politics in Europe. An Impact Analysis* (New York, Peter Lang Publishing Inc., 1986) p 270: 'if the judicial mandate is clear and communicated, if the environment is favorable to the ultimate policy, and if the body creating norms can achieve and maintain legitimacy as a symbol among interpreting and implementing publics, acceptance of legal norms can be expected.'

[123] See the report of the BIICL, *The Role and Future of the European Court of Justice* (London, BIICL, 1996) and A. Arnull, 'Judicial architecture or judicial folly? The challenge facing the EU' (1999) 24 *European Law Review* 516–24.

Opinion where his involvement is not required (Articles 222 EC and 20 EC Statute as amended); the creation of judicial panels to hear certain classes of action (Article 225a EC as amended); and reorganisation of Chambers and the creation of a Grand Chamber, with the result that recourse to the full Court will be extremely limited (Articles 221 and 16 EC Statute as amended). The purpose of this section is not to assess those reforms, which seem to have concentrated on the speed with which justice can be delivered rather than the quality of that justice. Rather, this section concentrates on one particular aspect which it is suggested would go some way to resolving present difficulties with Article 234 EC references, namely reviewing the role of national courts, or perhaps even their perception of their role under Article 234 EC and their relationship with the Court of Justice. This inevitably entails a re-examination of the respective roles of the Court in interpreting EC law and of national courts in applying that law to the facts of the cases. As Simitis has argued: 'the conditions under which [national courts] can consult the Court have to be revised. The Court must remain the authentic interpreter of Community law, though not at the price of an almost arbitrary instrumentalisation for national controversies.'[124]

While pursuing unrelentingly what is deemed to be the fundamental objective of the preliminary reference procedure, namely uniformity in the interpretation and application of EC law, it seems that the Court has for too long sought to achieve the impossible and provide principled yet increasingly detailed answers to the hundreds of references which are lodged by national courts annually. Signs of how thin the line is between dispute resolution and public action in adjudication litter the Court's preliminary rulings. While it may take the Court just over twenty two and a half months, on average, to hand down a preliminary ruling, the Judges (and perhaps to a lesser extent Advocates General) are, as chapter one points out, afforded surprisingly little time to reflect on and deliberate each case. Despite its enormous workload and its very circumscribed ability to influence that workload through use of the nascent inadmissibility doctrine and other devices described in chapter one, the Court still clings in its rulings to the notion that it is for it to interpret EC law and for national courts to apply it. Edward, writing in a personal capacity, states that:

> [A]s Community law develops, the ground rules become more clearly established and the work-load of the Court increases, national courts will necessarily assume the primary responsibility of applying Community law. Judgments are written in such a way as to provide the national judge with a "programme" for solving the case—setting out the points to be considered, the order in which they should be addressed and the elements of fact that are likely to be of relevance at each stage.[125]

---

[124] Simitis, above n 61, 174.

[125] D. Edward, 'Views from the European Courts' in G. Barling and M. Brealey (eds), *Practitioners' Handbook of EC Law* (London, Trenton Publishing, 1998) pp 27–45, p 34. For the United Kingdom debate on whether or not a court should refer see Anderson, above n 2, p 123, who compares the restraint counselled by Lord Denning in *Bulmer v Bollinger* [1974] Ch 401 with the active encouragement of Sir Thomas Bingham MR in *R v International Stock Exchange, ex parte*

He cites judgments such as *Faccini Dori*, *Brasserie du Pêcheur*, *Peterbroek* and *Van Schijndel* as evidence of this trend.[126] Yet the case-law of the Court in the field of indirect sex discrimination or acquired rights does not always, it seems, bear out his conviction.

In his Opinion in *Wiener SI GmbH v Hauptzollamt Emmerich*,[127] Advocate General Jacobs tackled some of these difficult issues. The decision of the Court in that case (a decision more famous for the article of clothing discussed than for the weighty matters of legal principle which the Court tackled when interpreting the relevant provisions of EC law), resulted in a ruling by the Court's First Chamber. One can only imagine the fun which this all-male Chamber had drafting a judgment that tried to determine the correct definition, for the purposes of the CCT, of a night-dress.[128] Advocate General Jacob's mind was clearly on more serious matters, however—namely the appropriate division of tasks, at this stage of European integration, between the Court of Justice and national courts. The question referred by the *Bundesfinanzhof* was admissible and the order for reference, according to the Advocate General, set out the relevant facts and legal issues in an exemplary fashion. However, Advocate General Jacobs observed that the Court's present approach to preliminary rulings had the drawback of attracting a virtually infinite number of questions of interpretation: 'Every national court confronted with a dispute turning on the application of Community law can refer a question which, if more or less properly phrased, this Court is bound to answer after the entire proceedings have taken their course.'[129] Writing prior to the introduction of Article 104(3) of the Court's rules of procedure, the Advocate General saw the danger of the Court ending up answering references where similar questions had already been answered and where there was little doubt, given existing case law, as to the correct interpretation of EC law. Even specific rulings handed back to national courts did not always obviate the need for further references.[130]

According to the Advocate General, the solution to this constant flow of cases, many of which concerned the application of fairly clear principles of EC

Else (1982) Ltd. [1993] CMLR p 715. Anderson suggests that the expectation was in any case that as national judges became more familiar with EC law the number of cases which they were able to tackle themselves with complete confidence was expected to grow.

[126] See also M. Lagrange, 'The Theory of *Acte Clair*: A Bone of Contention or a Source of Unity?' (1971) 8 *Common Market Law Review* 314–24, 317–18, who urges national courts not to slavishly refer but to weigh up the seriousness of their doubts and examine the relevance of the question; and Demaret in Jacob (ed), above n 25, p 332.

[127] Case C–338/95 [1997] ECR I–6495.

[128] Case C–338/95 *Wiener* was not of course the first case in which the Court's honourable members were forced to grapple with the intricacies of women's undergarments for the purposes of customs classifications—see also Case C–395/93 *Neckermann Versand v Hauptzollamt Frankfurt-am-Main* [1994] ECR I–4027.

[129] Case C–338/95 *Wiener*, para 14 of the Advocate General's Opinion. Academic commentators have been eager, in the past, to encourage national courts to do just that. See, for example, Schermers and Waelbroeck, above n 2, p 409: '[T]here is no doubt that an immediate preliminary ruling on every question of direct effect is highly desirable, even if not obligatory.'

[130] As Cases C–338/95 *Wiener* and C–395/93 *Neckermann* demonstrate.

law, rather than its interpretation, was not to impose more stringent admissibility criteria but instead a greater measure of self-restraint on the part of both national courts and the Court of Justice. Specifically, national courts should be encouraged to reflect on the appropriateness of referring a case to the Court:

> A reference will be most appropriate where the question is one of general importance and where the ruling is likely to promote the uniform application of the law throughout the European Union. A reference will be least appropriate where there is an established body of case-law which could readily be transposed to the facts of the instant case; or where the question turns on a narrow point considered in the light of a very specific set of facts and the ruling is unlikely to have any application beyond the instant case.[131]

For its part, in areas where there is an already established body of case-law,[132] the Court could simply recall the principles and rules of interpretation developed by this case-law and leave it to the national court to apply these principles to the particular issue with which it is confronted. A means could be found to allow the Court to provide such general, non-specific answers very speedily. In general, Advocate General Jacobs argued that the purpose of Article 234 EC would be best served when there is a genuine need for uniform application of the law throughout the EU because the question is one of general interest and that detailed answers to very specific questions will not always promote uniform application. He concluded that:

> Excessive resort to preliminary rulings seems therefore increasingly likely to prejudice the quality, the coherence, and even the accessibility, of the case-law, and may therefore be counter-productive to the ultimate aim of ensuring the uniform application of the law throughout the European Union. If only cases raising a point of some general importance are referred to the Court, then a more balanced case-law—and a more balanced development of the case-law—is likely to result.[133]

Although Advocate General Jacobs clearly accepted the need to tailor the Court's answer to the circumstances of the individual reference, arguably what he was urging was a greater 'public action' content in the references being sent

---

[131] Case C–338/95 *Wiener*, para 19 of the Advocate General's Opinion.

[132] The customs classification of goods, the classification of goods as waste for the purpose of Community legislation on waste, the meaning of transfer of undertakings pursuant to Directive 77/187/EEC of 14 February 1977 on the approximation of the laws of the Member States relating to the safeguarding of employees' rights in the event of transfers of undertakings, businesses or parts of business (OJ 1977 L61/26), and the meaning of taxable amount in the area of Value Added Tax, were cited by the Advocate General as examples of areas with respect to which this new spirit of self-restraint would be particularly apposite. A word of caution is voiced by Weiler when it comes to any revision of the reference procedure and the relationship between the Court of Justice and national courts thereunder—see Weiler in Schermers *et al.* (eds), above 2, p 371. In his view, one must distinguish between the courts which are repeat players in the system—fiscal and commercial courts called upon to apply EC law as a matter of growing routine—and one-shot players faced with the need to interpret and apply EC law possibly for the first, and only, time in their judicial careers.

[133] Case C–338/95 *Wiener*, paras 50, 60 and 62 of the Advocate General's Opinion.

to the Court—a return to general issues of interpretation and lesser involvement in dispute resolution.[134]

It seems that, within the Court, and amongst academic commentators, some regard new-found approaches to admissibility and evolutionary proposals such as those advocated by Advocate General Jacobs as either heretical or too risky to contemplate. In Barnard and Sharpston's opinion, 'the occasional "super-fluous" reference is a small price to pay for preserving the uniformity of Community law—which is the whole *raison d'être* of the Article [234] proced-ure.'[135] O'Keeffe also chastises the Court for its betrayal of the 'spirit' of Article 234 EC. These critics are undoubtedly correct in their assessment of the import-ance of uniformity, but they do not, nor do most critics of the Court's admit-tedly haphazard admissibility case-law, address the Advocate General's cogent arguments about the risks to that very uniformity and indeed to effective judic-ial protection which the present functioning of the preliminary reference procedure poses. With over two hundred new preliminary references lodged each year we are not talking about one or two superfluous cases. That the Court's initial stance on its obligation to answer questions referred by national courts was expansive cannot be denied; that this expansive approach was directly mandated by Article 234 EC remains open to question. In *Hoffman-La Roche,* for example, the Court stated that:

> [I]n the context of Article 177, whose purpose is to ensure that Community law is interpreted and applied in a uniform manner in all the Member States, the particular objective of the third paragraph is to prevent *a body of national case-law* not in accord with the rules of Community law from coming into existence in any Member State.[136]

A body of national law in accord with EC law can be ensured if superior courts are complying with their EC law obligations. Support for this vision of a more targeted or refined purpose for the reference procedure can be gleaned from the work of one of the Communities' most eminent jurists, Pescatore. Opting for the organic theory of what constitutes a court or tribunal against whose deci-sion there is no judicial remedy, the former Judge Pescatore stated:

---

[134] See also Simitis, above n 61, 174. As Lord Lester has maintained (see Lester in Schermers *et al.* (eds), above n 2, p 194): 'the reference procedure will not work properly unless the Court of Justice is able to decide questions referred under Article 177 in a manner which enables the Community law to develop on the basis of intelligible and rational principles. Only then will the vital partnership between the Court of Justice and national courts work efficiently; only then will the parties have suf-ficient confidence to invoke Community law and to seek references.' Increasingly limiting its answers in preliminary rulings to the specific factual context outlined by the national court may help that court to resolve the particular dispute before it, but it will not necessarily lead to the principled development and interpretation of EC law and may ensure that the Court's caseload remains alarm-ingly heavy as bewildered national courts seek to determine whether the *ratio* (if one is decipherable) of the Court's previous rulings can be transposed to the facts of the case before them.

[135] Barnard and Sharpston, above n 28, 1171.

[136] Case 107/76 *Hoffmann-La Roche AG v Centrafarm Vertiebsgesellschaft Pharmazeutischer Erzeugnisse mbH* [1977] ECR 957, para 5 (emphasis added), cited by Advocate General Jacobs in his Opinion in Case C–338/95 *Wiener*, para 55.

By using that expression the Treaty is referring to supreme courts whose jurisdiction extends throughout the territory of a given Member State. It is they that ultimately lay down the case law applicable to all matters which fall within their jurisdiction. It is necessary to ensure—and this is the thinking which inspires the system provided for in Article 177—that, in matters of Community law, *case law does not develop in the supreme courts which differs as between the various Member States*.[137]

The wording of Article 225 EC, as amended by the Treaty of Nice, is also interesting in this respect. It provides that the Court of First Instance will refer a case to the Court of Justice where it considers that the case requires 'a decision of principle likely to affect the unity or consistency of Community law'. The implication is, of course, that not all references concern questions of principle and/or are likely to affect the unity or consistency of EC law.

Has the time not come for national courts, which are, after all, 'Community courts of general jurisdiction'[138], to take greater charge of their Community law obligations and reflect before they refer questions of interpretation to the Court which they may, by applying already established case-law, be in a position to answer themselves?[139] Van Gerven has called for close monitoring of references when they first reach the Court in order to determine into which category they fall. It should be established whether the questions should never have been asked, whether they can be answered with reference to previous decisions or whether further in-depth examination of the questions is required. In the first two cases Van Gerven proposes a variety of different ways in which national courts could liase with the Court and some of its specific departments or according to which the Court could deliver its decision in an expedited manner.[140] Clearly, recent changes in the Court's Rules of Procedure will go some way to limiting the need for the Court to repeat, in the form of a full-blown judgment, what it has already stated in its answers to national courts in previous cases.[141] The Court also seems to be more actively questioning national courts about whether, in the light of a decision handed down in a separate case, those courts wish to maintain their references for a preliminary ruling. However, even such

---

[137] P. Pescatore, *References for Preliminary Rulings Under Article 177 of the EEC Treaty and Co-operation Between the Court and National Courts* (Luxembourg, 1985) p 19. See also Weiler in Schermers *et al.* (eds), above 2, p 375: 'a mature system can tolerate a certain level of non-uniformity.'

[138] See Case T–51/89 *Tetra Pak Rausing SA v Commission* [1990] ECR II–309.

[139] See Weiler in Schermers *et al.* (eds), above n 2, p 373; de la Mare in Craig and De Búrca (eds), above n 33, p 247: 'The objective must be to encourage and trust national courts to answer more of the routine questions themselves, so as only to use the Article 177 reference procedure to refer questions raising wider issues that go beyond the simple resolution of the litigation before the Court.'; D. Wyatt, 'Practice and Procedure' in Andenas (ed), above n 2, pp 77–81, p 81: 'as the pressures on the Court of Justice suggest that European justice will only be done if the national courts rise to the task of giving Community law full force and effect in every case, whether they refer that case to Luxembourg or not.' And, in a similar vein, W. Van Gerven, 'The role and structure of the European judiciary now and in the future' (1996) 21 *European Law Review* 211–23, 220.

[140] See Van Gerven, *ibid.* 220.

[141] See the discussion of these changes in ch 1 above.

an informal filtering system will be hindered by the multilingual context within which the Court must work and its operation, to be successful, will require considerable changes in how the Court—including the Judge-Rapporteurs' chambers—handle incoming references.

There is a risk, of course, that passing on greater responsibility to national courts will have a detrimental effect on the uniform application of EC law. Assessing the extent to which national courts have complied with the preliminary rulings and interpretations of EC law already handed down by the Court of Justice, is not, as stated above, the object of the present research. However, the research carried out by others to date appears to point to a high degree of compliance.[142] Furthermore, a failure by national courts to refer questions to the Court should not be associated automatically with 'disobedience' or an unwillingness to co-operate on their part. As Kilpatrick points out: 'failure to refer may sometimes represent not the nadir of judicial co-operation but its apex—like the relationship between an old married couple who do not need to talk to each other explicitly to know what the other requires.'[143] There is evidence that most national courts have taken to EC law and the principle of supremacy and its consequences slowly but with relish, although patterns vary from one Member State to the next and the accession of new Member States will present a clear challenge in this respect.[144] Judgments of the High Court and House of Lords in cases like *Ex parte Equal Opportunities Commission*[145] and *Seymour-Smith*[146] are cited as evidence of national courts enthusiastically fulfilling their functions as Community law courts, with the House of Lords in the former case not requiring a reference to the Court of Justice in order to impugn an Act of Parliament.[147] As

---

[142] See, in particular, Slaughter, Stone Sweet and Weiler, above n 2; Barnard and Sharpston, above n 28, 1170: 'National courts have shown themselves perfectly capable of determining points of EC law themselves'; in the context of labour law generally Sciarra (ed), above n 2; and the Commission's annual reports to the European Parliament on the application of EC law.

[143] Kilpatrick, above n 1, 128. See also de la Mare in Craig and De Búrca (eds), above n 33, p 244: 'once a domestic system accepts the basic supremacy rules a low referral rate may be due to a strong domestic version of precedent, with decisions of the ECJ being loyally followed.' *Cf.* Arnull (1999), above n 123, 521, who suggests that courts of last instance are those least in need of assistance from the European Court of Justice and who questions the ability of courts at the lower end of the national judicial ladder to cope without the present, unlimited possibility of referral. In the employment field, however, it is arguable that the lower courts, labour courts and industrial tribunals in many Member States have been the engines which pulled the train of equality in their wake.

[144] See also S. Fredman, 'Labour Law in Flux: the Changing Composition of the Workforce' (1997) 26 *Industrial Law Journal* 337–52, 348, who notes that, in the two main areas in which the resolution of conflict between EC and domestic law was left to the courts—transfers of undertakings and sex discrimination—national courts, after some resistance, eventually imbibed the Court of Justice's approach and reproduced it with vigour.

[145] [1994] ICR 317.

[146] [2000] 1 All ER 857.

[147] See the discussion in D. Nicol, 'Disapplying with relish? The Industrial Tribunals and Acts of Parliament' (1996) *Public Law* 579–89; and K.J. Alter and J. Vargas, 'Explaining Variation in the Use of European Litigation Strategies. European Community Law and British Gender Equality Policy'(2000) 33 *Comparative Political Studies* 452–82, 462, who pinpoint the 1990s as the time when the House of Lords recast itself as a progressive force on European law and equality issues in order to 'regain control of domestic jurisdiction by asserting its own supreme authority to interpret EC law.'

Kilpatrick has remarked with reference to certain judgments of the House of Lords and Court of Appeal in the field of equality:

> [they] read like judgments which could have been written by the ECJ (in a teleological period) if it had been instructed to craft its judgment in the common law rather than the civilian style. The courts carefully and properly considered all of the relevant ECJ decisions, demonstrating a deep understanding of the implications of EC law and straightforwardly granted declarations that national law contravened EC law where such declarations seemed justified in the current state of EC law.[148]

---

[148] See Kilpatrick, above n 1, 114.

3

EC Social and Labour Law and Employment Policy: Judicial Perspectives and the Flexibility Debate

INTRODUCTION

T HUS FAR CHAPTERS one and two have examined the context within which references for preliminary rulings are dealt—in particular, the procedural, structural, historical and even linguistic constraints subject to which the Court must provide interpretative guidance to national referring courts. This chapter moves away from the judicial structures and processes which may influence how the Court formulates its employment law decisions to the very substance of the book—the employment law decisions themselves. Its purpose is specifically to question the interrelationship between EC social and labour law and EC employment policy, or, more to the point, the compatibility of the former with the latter. This discussion takes places against the backdrop of the ongoing debate on the need for greater flexibility in the EU labour market.[1]

The introduction of the employment title in the Treaty of Amsterdam was clearly not the first indication of the European Community's involvement in the field of employment. Employment-related issues—be it the living and working conditions of workers in the coal and steel industry, the rights and obligations of migrant workers, the rules governing the free provision of services or the principle of equal pay for male and female workers—had concerned the Community's institutions since the signing of the Treaties of Paris and Rome. For its part, the Court of Justice has been called upon for decades to decide a wide range of questions with consequences, both direct and indirect, for the employment rights of individual Community citizens and indeed for labour law and policy in the Member States themselves. The controversial compensation sums paid to workers, mainly female, who were the victims of sex discrimination; the decision by a national court that the qualifying thresholds for the

---

[1] Note that the terms 'labour' and 'employment' are used interchangeably here and little if any attention is paid to the niceties of the individual versus collective rights distinction which these terms are sometimes used to denote.

enjoyment of employment protection rights (which were a central plank of that Member State government's drive to deregulate the labour market) were incompatible with EC law; and limitations on the extent to which contracting out could cut down on employees' acquired rights are but a few of the most well-known examples of the consequences which EC law has had for national labour law.[2] With the Community's employment strategy now based on principles of entrepreneurship, employability, adaptability and equal opportunities, it remains to be seen whether the Court's appreciation of labour-related issues will somehow be affected in the future.

With a view to gaining an insight into the approach which the Court has developed in a variety of fields which have a bearing on national labour and, more generally, social law and policy and examining whether there was any coherence in its stance on employment-related issues prior to the introduction of specific EC Treaty provisions on employment policy, the following section analyses its decisions in areas ranging from the free movement of persons to public procurement and State aids. This survey is followed by a broad outline of the debate on the need for greater flexibility in the EU labour market. As chapter one observed, the Court does not operate in a judicial vacuum. Whether one likes it or not, it is unlikely that the individual members of the Court are deaf to the arguments made for or against labour market reform or, at the very least, to the passions which this debate arouses in their own Member States. Thereafter, steps taken by the Community legislature and Member States pursuant to the Employment Title inserted into the EC Treaty by the Amsterdam Treaty of 1997 are outlined. The question arises whether the Community's objectives with respect to employment and, specifically, the central pillars of its employment strategy sit comfortably with the commitment elsewhere in the Treaty, in secondary legislation and, of course, in the jurisprudence of the Court, to a minimum level of social protection and the fundamental principle of equality. It is hoped to tease out answers to these questions in subsequent chapters on the case-law of the Court in relation to specific substantive areas of EC employment law.

EC JUDICIAL PERSPECTIVES ON EC SOCIAL AND LABOUR LAW

The Free Movement of Goods

As Davies has observed, the introduction of the Community's internal market programme in the late 1980s and the increasingly sophisticated jurisprudence of the Court of Justice on the four freedoms led labour lawyers to question

---

[2] See E. Szyszczak, 'Future Divisions in European Union Social Policy' (1995) 24 *Industrial Law Journal* 19–32, 19; and M. Poiares Maduro, 'Europe's Social Self: "The Sickness Unto Death" ' in J. Shaw (ed), *Social Law and Policy in an Evolving European Union* (Oxford, Hart Publishing, 2000) pp 325–49.

whether and, if so, to what extent, Community rules could restrict Member State freedom to determine the content and scope of domestic social and labour law.[3] As regards, in the first place, the effect of EC Treaty rules on the free movement of goods on national labour law and employment protection legislation, attention has been focused on a series of cases which came before the Court in the 1980s and early 1990s concerning national restrictions on trading and opening hours.[4] In *Conforama*, for example, the Court was asked whether the Treaty prohibition of measures having an effect equivalent to quantitative restrictions on imports precluded national measures which prohibited the employment of workers on Sundays. The Court accepted that national rules governing the opening hours of retail premises reflect certain political and economic choices which are justifed with regard to EC law in so far as their purpose is to ensure that working and non-working hours are arranged so as to accord with national or regional socio-cultural characteristics. In the existing state of EC law, the Court concluded that these were matters for the Member States, but added that the restrictive effect on trade which stems from such rules did not seem disproportionate to the aim pursued.[5]

The legal tool used by the Court in order to divert clashes between integration dictated by the internal market and national socio-economic preferences, not least as regards the organisation of the labour market, is thus the category

---

[3] See P. Davies, 'Market Integration and Social Policy in the Court of Justice' (1995) 24 *Industrial Law Journal* 49–77; See also C. Barnard, *EC Employment Law* (Oxford, OUP, 2000) p 30, who questions the challenge the Court's decisions have posed to the integrity of national systems of labour law and social protection in the interests of market-creating at EU level; and K. Lenaerts and P. Foubert, 'Social Rights in the Case-law of the European Court of Justice' (2001) 28 *Legal Issues of Economic Integration* 267–96.

[4] For detailed discussion of the Sunday Trading cases see M. Poiares Maduro, *We, the Court. The European Court of Justice and the European Economic Constitution. A Critical Reading of Article 30 of the EC Treaty* (Oxford, Hart Publishing, 1998) pp 32, 43–46, 83, 92–93. See variously Case C–145/88 *Torfaen BC v B & Q plc* [1989] ECR 3851; Case C–306/88 *Rochdale BC v John Stewart Anders* [1992] ECR I–6457; Case C–304/90 *Reading BC v Payless DIY Ltd and others* [1992] ECR I–6493; Case C–169/91 *Council of the City of Stoke-on-Trent and Norwich County Council v B & Q plc* [1992] ECR I–6635; Case C–312/89 *Union départementale des syndicats CGT de l'Aisne v SIDEF Conforama and Others* [1991] ECR I–997; Case C–332/89 *Criminal proceedings against André Marchandise and others* [1991] ECR I–1027; Joined Cases C–69/93 and C–258/93 *Punto Casa SpA v Sindaco del Comune di Capena and others* [1994] ECR I–2355; Joined Cases C–418–421/93, C–460–464/93, C–9–11/94, C–14–15/94, C–23–24/94 and C–332/94 *Semeraro Casa Uno v Sindaco del comune di Erbusco and others* [1996] ECR I–2975.

[5] In Case C–145/88 *Torfaen*, paras 13–14, a decision which preceded that in Case C–312/89 *Conforama*, the Court controversially left it to the national court to determine whether the impugned Shops Act was proportionate to the legitimate aim which it pursued. The plethora of cases which followed *Torfaen*, with national courts struggling to correctly identify the purpose of the Sunday trading prohibition, balance the interests at stake and apply the principle of proportionality, famously led to the retrenchment of the Court in Joined Cases C–267 and C–268/91 *Keck and Mithouard* [1993] ECR I–6097. Following *Keck and Mithouard* see Joined Cases C–401/92 and C–402/92 *Tankstation 't Huekske vof v J.B.E. Boermans* [1994] ECR I–2227, where the Court held that the principle of the free movement of goods does not preclude the application of national legislation concerning opening hours for shops, provided that they apply to all traders operating within the national territory and that they affect in the same manner the marketing of domestic products and products from other Member States.

of public interest exceptions. The latter is taken to include the derogations from the free movement rules explicitly provided for in the EC Treaty in Articles 30, 39(3), 45 and 55, as well as the judicially created category of mandatory or imperative requirements established in the case-law of the Court. Contested rules of domestic labour or social law may be found to be (indirectly) discriminatory or restrictive of free movement, but the Court can nevertheless indicate to the national court that those rules are justifiable with reference to some overriding public interest objective provided that they comply with the requirements of the principle of proportionality.[6] In the alternative, as Davies, points out, the Court sometimes finds that the contested national rules do not exhibit any discriminatory or restrictive characteristics, so that the issue of justification does not actually arise.[7] This judicial technique enables the Court to define the scope of the relevant provisions of EC law more or less broadly or narrowly according to whether it wishes the contested national legislation to be caught and priority to be given to the Treaty's fundamental freedoms. The upshot of reliance on this approach is that the Court rarely engages in overt balancing of national rules, policies and values with the values, policies and objectives underlying EC law.[8] Even when the Court does classify a measure as discriminatory or restrictive of free movement, it will not always engage in judicial review of the proportionality of the impugned measure, leaving it to the national court, ostensibly due to the division of judicial functions dictated by Article 234 EC, to assess its necessity and appropriateness. These judicial techniques are not unique to the Court's treatment of employment-related national measures or those suspect from the perspective of discrimination on grounds of sex, but they have proved particularly useful when, as is often the case in the context of national social and employment legislation, sensitive socio-economic issues not directly the subject of EC law are at stake.

The Freedom to Provide Services

In the context of the EC Treaty rules on the freedom to provide services, the Court has been confronted with a variety of employment-related preliminary references regarding the application of the relevant EC Treaty rules to the services provided by employment agencies, the provision of services by posted workers

---

[6] Of course, this is the orthodox position as reflected in the case-law of the Court in the late 1980s and early 1990s. The prevailing state of the law concerning discriminatory, indirectly discriminatory and restrictive national measures and whether and with reference to what they can be justified is now somewhat more ambiguous than it once was. In the particular context of services see the discussion in J.M. Fernández Martín and S. O'Leary, 'Judicially-created exceptions to the free provision of services' (2000) 11 *European Business Law Review* 347–62.

[7] See Davies (1995), above n 3, 52.

[8] *Ibid*, 67. For other examples of use of this judicial technique see Case C–249/97 *Gabriele Gruber v Silhouette International Schmied GmbH* [1999] ECR I–5295, discussed below ch 5; and Case C–379/98 *PreussenElektra AG v Schleswag AG* [2001] ECR I–2099.

'imported' from the service provider's Member State of establishment and the compatibility generally with the EC Treaty provisions on the free provision of services of host Member State social and employment legislation when applied to the employees of a service provider established in another Member State. Albeit for the reasons outlined in chapter two, the Court never deals with the questions referred to it by national courts in the stark terms of compatibility.

The Court has made clear that it regards 'the provision of manpower [as] a particularly sensitive matter from the occupational and social point of view. Owing to the special nature of the employment relationships inherent in that kind of activity, pursuit of such a business directly affects both relations on the labour market and the lawful interests of the workforce concerned.'[9] Although the principal aim of the EC Treaty rules on the freedom to provide services is to enable the provider of a service to pursue his activities in the Member State where the service is given without suffering discrimination, when compared to the nationals of that Member State or without unnecessary restriction, the specific and sensitive nature of the supply of manpower means that it is permissible for Member States, and amounts to a legitimate choice of policy pursued in the public interest, to subject the provision of manpower within their borders to a system of licensing. This is in order to be able to refuse licences where there is reason to fear that such activities may harm good relations on the labour market or that the interests of the workforce affected are not adequately safeguarded. What a host Member State cannot do, however, is to duplicate unnecessarily the rules applicable to the provider of services in his Member State of establishment, since this might lead to disguised discrimination against those providers in relation to national providers of services. In *Webb* and subsequent cases the Court has sought to balance the legitimate interests of the Member States in applying provisions of national social and labour legislation with the sort of 'mutual recognition' requirement essential to the effective functioning of a common market. In *Webb*, however, unlike many of the Sunday trading cases mentioned above, an assessment of proportionality was built into the Court's interpretation of the Treaty provisions on services and its guidelines to the national referring court.

The *Rush Portuguesa* case was the first of many concerning the application of social and labour legislation to the employees of a provider of services in the

---

[9] Case 279/80 *Criminal Proceedings against Alfred Webb* [1981] ECR 3305, para 18. The case concerned staff recruitment services provided by an employment agency established in one Member State to undertakings established in another. See also the Opinion of Advocate General Slynn, p 3329: '[the] activities [of employment agencies] may have an important bearing on issues of national, regional or sectoral labour policy, on the function and operation of State employment services and on labour relations.' On the application of EC rules to the activities of public placement agencies see also Case C–41/90 *Klaus Höfner and Fritz Elser v Macrotron GmbH* [1991] ECR I–1979 (often referred to as *Macrotron*), discussed below; Case C–55/96 *Job Centre coop. arl.* [1997] ECR I–7119; and Case C–134/95 *Unità Socio-Sanitaria Locale no. 47 di Biella (USSL) v Istituto nazionale per l'assicurazione contro gli infortuni sul lavoro (INAIL)* [1997] ECR I–195, albeit in the latter two cases EC Treaty provisions on services were held to be inapplicable since the activities in question were confined within a single Member State.

construction sector established in another Member State.[10] In one sense, the Court gave priority in the *Rush Portuguesa* case to the objective of free movement over the insistence of the host Member State that its national labour legislation apply to the employees of the visiting provider of services. It held that the Treaty provisions on services preclude a Member State from prohibiting a person providing services established in another Member State from moving freely on its territory with all his staff and preclude that Member State from making the movement of staff in question subject to restrictions, such as a condition as to engagement *in situ* or an obligation to obtain a national work permit. To impose such conditions on the person providing services established in another Member State would discriminate against that person in relation to his competitors established in the host country who are able to use their own staff without restrictions, and, moreover, would affect his ability to provide the service.

On the other hand, however, the Court held that EC law does not preclude a Member State from extending its social legislation or collective labour agreements to any person who is employed, even temporarily, within their territory, regardless of the country in which the employer is established. National rules on, for example, social security contributions or minimum wages, were thus to be regarded as pursuing an aim of public interest worthy of protection. Compliance with such rules may be required, even if one of the fundamental Treaty freedoms is restricted, provided that the requirement of proportionality is respected. It seems likely, as Davies suggests, that the purpose of the inclusion of this proviso was to prevent the use of posted workers by providers of services undermining social and labour legislation, and presumably industrial equity, in the host Member State.[11] By permitting the application of national treatment as far as labour standards were concerned, the Court, while upholding the principle of the free provision of services, opted for an approach which was not destructive of national rules.[12] Recital 12 of the Posted Workers Directive subsequently took up the principle established in this and other services cases and the Directive itself lays down a core of mandatory rules for minimum social protection to be observed by employers who post workers to perform temporary work in the territory of the Member State in which the service is to be provided.[13]

---

[10] Case C–113/89 *Rush Portuguesa Lda v Office national d'immigration* [1990] ECR I–1417. The case involved the provision of services in France by a Portuguese construction company which brought its own labour force from Portugal for the duration of the works and whose workforce did not possess French work permits.

[11] For confirmation of this thesis see the reasoning of the Court in Case C–165/98 *Criminal proceedings against André Mazzoleni and Inter Surveillance Assistance SARL, as the party civilly liable, third parties: Éric Guillaume and others* [2001] ECR I–2189, para 36, discussed below.

[12] See P. Davies, 'Posted Workers: Single Market or Protection of National Labour Law Systems?' (1997) 34 *Common Market Law Review* 571–602, 590. See also Joined Cases 62/81 and 63/81 *Seco v EVI* [1982] ECR 223 and Case C–43/93 *Raymond Vander Elst v Office des migrations internationales* [1994] ECR I–3803.

[13] See, in particular, Article 3 of Directive 96/71/EC of the European Parliament and the Council, of 16 December 1996, concerning the posting of workers in the framework of the provision of services, OJ 1996 L18/1.

In a case which also involved the provision of construction services, *Guiot*, the Court was asked whether Articles 49 and 50 EC preclude a Member State from requiring undertakings established in another Member State and temporarily carrying out works in the first Member State, to pay employers' social security contributions in respect of employees assigned to those works, where that undertaking is already liable for comparable employers' contributions with respect to the same employees for the same period of work in the Member State of establishment.[14] There was no doubt that, as in *Rush Portuguesa*, such legislation was liable to restrict the freedom of the undertaking subject to the dual burden to provide the services it wished, since it put them on an unequal footing as compared to providers of services/employers established in the host Member State. The Court recognised that 'the public interest relating to the social protection of workers in the construction industry may, *because of conditions specific to that sector*, constitute an overriding requirement justifying such a restriction'.[15] It continued, however, that that is not the case where the workers in question enjoy the same protection, or essentially similar protection, by virtue of employers' contributions already paid by the employer in the Member State of establishment. This is similar to the principle underpinning *Webb*. What is of particular interest in *Guiot*, however, is that the Court was willing to contemplate that conditions specific to the construction industry might justify certain social protection measures for workers in that industry.[16] It had previously been criticised for its laconic approach to the conditions specific to a different sector—dock work—in *Merci Convenzionali Porto di Genova v Siderurgica Gabrielli*. There the Court had held that Articles 39, 82 and 86 EC precluded Italian rules from conferring on an undertaking the exclusive right to organise dock work and the obligation to hire Italian nationals for this purpose, but it disregarded social arguments in favour of the dock labour monopoly, specifically the need to combat casualisation of labour in this field.[17]

In the *Guillaume* case, the Court had to examine similar questions to those which had arisen in *Guiot,* but this time in the context of an undertaking established in a frontier region, some of whose employees were required to perform, on a part-time basis and for brief periods, a part of their services in the adjacent territory of a Member State other than that in which the undertaking was established.

---

[14] Case C–272/94 *Criminal proceedings against Michel Guiot and Climatec SA* [1996] ECR I–1905. The social security contributions at issue were in respect of bad weather and loyalty stamps well-known in the construction industry.

[15] Case C–272/94 *Guiot*, para 16 (emphasis added). Davies observes (1997), above n 12, 597, that the building industry is one where abuses, both connected and unconnected with the posting of workers, are rife.

[16] The employer's contributions at issue in Case C–272/94 *Guiot* were also for compensation to be paid to workers due to unemployment caused by bad weather and, more surprisingly, for bonuses to be paid to construction workers who had been with the employer throughout the year.

[17] Case C–179/90 *Merci Convenzionali Porto di Genova SpA v Siderurgica Gabrielli SpA* [1991] ECR I–5889. On dock work generally see also Cases C–22/98 *Criminal proceedings against Jean Claude Becu, Annie Verweire, Smeg NV and Adia Interim NV* [1999] ECR I–5665; and C–163/96 *Criminal proceedings against Silvano Raso and Others* [1998] ECR I–533.

Was the requirement to comply with the host Member State's national rules on minimum wages where the workers enjoyed comparable overall protection in the Member State of establishment (although the minimum wage itself there was lower) in line with the EC Treaty rules on the free provision of services? The Court reiterated the principle which it had already established in previous case-law— Community law does not preclude a Member State from requiring an undertaking established in another Member State which provides services in the territory of the first State to pay its workers the minimum remuneration fixed by the national rules of that State.

However, that was not the end of the matter. Before applying their minimum wage legislation to a service provider established in an adjacent region of another Member State the national authorities in the host Member State must consider whether the application of those rules was necessary and proportionate for the purpose of protecting the workers concerned. The objective pursued—namely the protection of workers—might be regarded as attained without the imposition of the host Member State's rules if all the workers concerned enjoy an equivalent position overall in relation to remuneration, taxation and social security contributions in the host Member State and the Member State of establishment. In fact, application of the host Member State rules could constitute a disproportionate administrative burden:

> including, in certain cases, the calculation, hour-by-hour, of the appropriate remuneration for each employee according to whether he has, in the course of his work, crossed the frontier of another Member State and, second, in the payment of different levels of wages to employees who are all attached to the same operational base and carry out identical work. This last factor might, in its turn, result in tension between employees and even threaten the cohesion of the collective labour agreements that are applicable in the Member State of establishment.[18]

In more recent cases the Court has stressed that national courts must determine whether the national rules at issue in the cases before them provide for the protection of posted workers or whether they actually seek to protect domestic undertakings. The social legislation at issue, whether it concerns entitlement to a minimum wage or the guarantee of paid leave, must entail a real advantage for the workers concerned which contributes *significantly* to their social protection. If one compares *Webb* and *Rush Portuguesa* on the one hand and *Guillaume* and subsequent decisions concerning the provision of services in the construction sector on the other, it is arguable that these later cases are much more dismissive of social legislation in the Member State of establishment and capable therefore of considerably more erosion of national legislation in this field. The

---

[18] Case C–165/98 *Guillaume*, para 36. See paras 37–40 of the decision for discussion of some of the relevant factors—duration of the provision of services, their predictability, whether the employees are attached to a single operational base in the Member State of establishment—which the competent authorities must evaluate when determining whether the application of national rules in the host Member State is necessary and proportionate given the aim pursued.

Court's instructions to national referring courts on application of the principle of proportionality are now considerably more detailed and rigorous.[19] They must balance the objectives pursued by the social and labour legislation in the host Member State with the administrative and financial burden which it imposed on the service provider. There must be no less restrictive means to achieve the same result. Furthermore, it must be demonstrated that application of that legislation contributes *significantly* to the social protection of posted workers for it to apply. It is not enough simply to suggest that the social protection of workers generally is the objective of the legislation; it must actually be shown that application of the legislation confers a genuine benefit on the posted workers themselves which significantly adds to their social protection.[20]

Public Procurement

The case-law of the Court of Justice on public procurement provides further examples of clashes between the demands imposed on Member States by the creation of an internal market based on an open market with free competition and the dictates of domestic socio-economic policies. The *Beentjes* case concerned the compatibility with EC public procurement rules of a domestic strategy or programme designed to combat unemployment.[21] The applicant in the case contested the rejection of his lower bid for the realisation of a public works project by the awarding authority. Amongst the considerations which had led the awarding authority to reject the applicant's bid was the fact that it was not in a position to comply with a condition set out in the contract notice to the effect that the workforce must be made up of at least 70 per cent long-term unemployed persons recruited through the regional employment office. The

---

[19] On the erosion of national social laws in the name of the demands of competition see S. Simitis and A. Lyon-Caen, 'Community Labour Law: A Critical Introduction to its History' in P. Davies *et al.* (eds), *European Community Labour Law. Principles and Perspectives. Liber Amicorum Lord Wedderburn* (Oxford, Clarendon Press, 1996) pp 1–22, p 11.

[20] See Joined Cases C–49/98, C–70/98, C–71/98, C–50/98, C–52–54/98, C–68/98 and C–69/98 *Finalarte Sociedade de Construção Civil and others v Urlaubs- und Lohnausgleichskasse der Bauwirtschaft* [2001] ECR I–7831, para 42; Joined Cases C–369 and C–376/96 *Arblade and Leloup* [1999] ECR I–8453; Case C–493/99 *Commission v Germany* [2001] ECR I–8163, where the Court held that an establishment requirement imposed on undertakings in the construction industry which wished to contract out workers to a consortium or to other undertakings in the same industry had not been shown to be necessary to achieve the aim of providing social protection for the workers in the building industry. Furthermore, a condition to the effect that more than 50 % of total staff working time must be spent by workers on construction sites for an undertaking to be regarded as belonging to the construction sector under German law complicated access to the German market and was not justified by any overriding reason of public interest. See also Case C–164/99 *Portugaia Construçoes Lda* [2002] ECR I–787.

[21] Case 31/87 *Gebroeders Beentjes BV v State of the Netherlands* [1988] ECR 4635. For an excellent analysis of the case and discussion of the use of social clauses in public procurement see J.M. Fernández Martín, *The EC Public Procurement Rules. A Critical Analysis* (Oxford, Clarendon Press, 1996) especially pp 58–64.

Court had to determine whether this condition came within the provisions of the Public Works Directive relating to candidates' technical and economic qualifications and whether such a condition was a legitimate contract award criterion within the meaning of the Public Works Directive and whether it was compatible with EC law.[22] In a judgment criticised, like so many others, for the paucity of its judicial reasoning, the Court seemed to conclude that this additional specific condition was compatible with the Directive's provisions as, in the words of one commentator, 'it was not covered or explicitly prohibited by any of them.'[23] The Court simply emphasised, however, that 'in order to be compatible with the directive such a condition must comply with all the relevant provisions of Community law, in particular the prohibitions flowing from the principles laid down in the Treaty in regard to the right of establishment and the freedom to provide services.'[24] The Court did not sanction the wisdom of including such a condition and seemed to indicate that the inclusion of social clauses in tenders can be lawful. Its concern was simply that the obligation to employ long-term unemployed persons might give rise to discrimination contrary to the prohibition of discrimination on grounds of nationality, in that tenderers from the Member State concerned might be able to satisfy it while tenderers from other Member States would find it more difficult to do so.[25] It therefore directed the national court simply to ensure that the contested condition did not give rise to direct or indirect discrimination and stipulated that such conditions must be mentioned in the contract notice so that interested undertakings could be aware of them.

The consequences of the decision of the Court in *Beentjes* were highly contested, not least due to the incomplete and unsatisfying nature of the Court's reasoning when it came to the compatibility of the employment clause in question with the Public Works Directive specifically and EC law generally. Many commentators submitted that the Court's ruling indicated that the Public Procurement Directives did not exclude secondary policies being pursued by public procurement through the insertion of additional contractual conditions. What is striking about *Beentjes* is the Court's unwillingness to tackle directly the question of the compatibility of a long-term unemployment clause with the Treaty provisions on the free provision of services and establishment, despite its apparent sympathy with what can undoubtedly be regarded as a legitimate social policy aim. As Fernández Martín observed: 'at the time the [*Beentjes*] judgment was rendered, the fight against long-term unemployment and the

---

[22] Council Directive 71/305/EEC of 26 July 1971 concerning the coordination of procedures for the award of public works contracts, OJ English Special Edition 1971 (II), p 682.

[23] See Fernández Martín, above n 21, p 59.

[24] Case 31/87 *Beentjes*, para 29.

[25] As Fernández Martín, above n 21, p 64, points out, the Court did not assess the potential discriminatory effect of the clause as regards long-term unemployed labour established in other Member States.

incorporation of young persons in the labour market had become primary objectives of the Community's social and economic cohesion policy'.[26]

The decision in *Beentjes* has since been confirmed and somewhat clarified by the Court's ruling in *Commission v France*, a case concerning the tendering procedure for a public works contract relating to the construction of a secondary school.[27] The Commission complained that criteria contained in the contract notices relating to the campaign against unemployment infringed the provisions of Directive 93/37 which specified the criteria upon which the contracting authorities shall base their award of contracts.[28] The Commission distinguished *Beentjes* by arguing that the employment-related criterion was here characterised as an award criterion in the contract notices, whereas in the former case it had simply been a condition of performance. The Court would have none of this, remarking that the contested employment criterion in the instant case had been used as the basis for rejecting a tender and constituted, contrary to the Commission's claims, a criterion for the award of the contract. The Court held that the provision of Directive 93/97 on award criteria did not preclude all possibility for contracting authorities to use as a criterion a condition linked to the campaign against unemployment, provided that that condition was consistent with all the fundamental principles of EC law. In other words, as in *Beentjes*, such a criterion must respect the principle of non-discrimination flowing from the provisions of the Treaty on the freedom of establishment and the freedom to provide services and must be expressly mentioned in the contract notice so that contractors may become aware of its existence.

The employment protection objectives underlying some EC secondary legislation may also conflict with the rationale behind EC public procurement rules, whose purpose is to facilitate European-wide competition between undertakings and eliminate practices which restrict that competition. In *Oy Likenne*, drivers dismissed by an undertaking which had lost a tender to operate local bus services were re-employed by the undertaking which had won the tender but on conditions less favourable overall than those which they had previously enjoyed when working for the first contractor.[29] When the drivers succeeded at first instance in their claim that a transfer had taken place, implying that the provisions of Directive 77/187[30] applied, the successful tenderer argued that the application of the Acquired Rights Directive to the contract of an award procedure would obstruct competition between undertakings and prejudice the aim of

---

[26] See Fernández Martín, above n 21, p 63. On the legality of social clauses in public procurement see generally C. Tobler, 'Encore: "Women's Clauses" in 'public procurement under Community law' (2000) 25 *European Law Review* 618–31.

[27] Case C–225/98 [2000] ECR I–7445.

[28] Council Directive 93/37/EEC of 14 June 1993, concerning the coordination procedures for the award of public works contracts, OJ 1993 L199/54.

[29] See Case C–172/99 *Oy Likenne Ab v Pekka Liskojärvi and Pentti Juntuner* [2001] ECR I–745.

[30] Council Directive 77/187/EEC of 14 February 1977 on the approximation of the laws of the Member States relating to the safeguarding of employees' rights in the event of transfers of undertakings, businesses or parts of businesses, OJ 1977 L 61/26, discussed below ch 6.

Directive 92/50 on the award of public service contracts.[31] The Court held that the circumstance that a transaction comes under Directive 92/50 does not of itself rule out the application of Directive 77/187. According to the Court, the Public Procurement Directives are not intended to exempt contracting authorities and service providers from laws and regulations applicable in the social sphere or that of safety. When preparing their bids, economic operators must make assessments as to whether, if their bid is accepted, it will be in their interest to take over significant assets from the existing contractor, including some or all of their staff, and indeed whether they will be obliged to do so. The Court regarded that assessment and the costs involved as part of the workings of competition.[32]

Competition Law and Public Undertakings

National rules and practices in the social and labour law field do not escape the application of the EC competition rules. In *Höfner and Elser*, the Court had to examine the question of the applicability of these rules in the context of references concerning the monopoly enjoyed by public placement agencies. It held that the fact that employment procurement activities were normally entrusted to public agencies could not affect the economic nature of the activities in question.[33] A public employment agency engaged in the business of employment procurement could be classified as an undertaking for the purpose of the application of EC competition rules. According to the Court, as an undertaking entrusted with the operation of services of general economic interest, a public agency engaged in employment procurement is, pursuant to Article 86(2) EC, subject to the prohibition contained in Article 82 EC, so long as the application of this provision on the abuse of a dominant position does not obstruct the performance of the particular task assigned to the public employment agency. The grant by a Member State of the exclusive right to carry on employment procurement is in breach of Article 86(1) EC where a situation is created in which the public agency cannot avoid abusing its dominant position. The Court held that that is the case when, *inter alia*, the exclusive right granted extends to

[31] Council Directive 92/50/EEC of 18 June 1992 relating to the coordination of procedures for the award of public service contracts, OJ 1992 L209/1.

[32] See Case C–172/99 *Oy Likenne*, paras 23–24, P. Davies, 'Amendments to the Acquired Rights Directive' (1998) 27 *Industrial Law Journal* 365–73, 370–71, on provision by Member States for the transferor to notify the transferee of all rights and obligations which will be transferred; and *Interpretative communication of the Commission on the Community law applicable to public procurement and the possibility for integrating social considerations into public procurement*, COM (2001) 566, OJ 2001 C333/27. According to the Commission, social considerations cover a wide range of issues and fields including measures to ensure compliance with fundamental rights, with the principle of equality of treatment and non-discrimination, with national legislation on social affairs, with Community directives applicable in the social field, such as the Directives on the transfer of undertakings or posted workers, as well as preferential clauses.

[33] Case C–41/90 *Höfner and Elser*, often referred to as *Macrotron*.

executive recruitment, when the agency is manifestly incapable of satisfying prevailing market demand and when the pursuit of employment procurement activities by private recruitment agencies is rendered impossible by the maintenance in force of a statutory provision under which such activities are prohibited and contracts entered into are void.[34]

What one witnesses in *Höfner and Elser* is an example of what Szyszczak refers to as the traditional role of the State to use macro-policy in order to create and defend employment being subject to the same external constraints of the (partial) regulatory machinery of the EU as private power.[35] *Höfner and Elser* suggests that there is no special exception in the competition rules which might shelter social and labour issues from the market. The Court's approach was consistent with the Community's attempts to open up whole sectors of the economy—telecommunications, energy etc—and reduce the role of traditional State monopolies.[36] The reform of public sector recruitment services and the reduction of restrictions on private sector agencies which its decision essentially called for is also in line with what has been called the New Keynesian employment policy agenda.[37] What the Court did not do in *Höfner and Elser*, however, unlike in previous cases such as *Webb*, was to refer to the delicate nature of the services provided by employment agencies and underline the reason why the provision of such services were generally the subject of statutory limitations or protective measures.

While national social and labour law do not automatically fall outside the scope of application of EC competition rules, the Court has repeatedly stated that 'Community law does not detract from the powers of the Member States to organise their social security systems'[38] the latter being an area not subject, as of yet, to Community competence. The relationship between EC competition rules and national social security legislation was specifically at issue in a series of cases where the Court had to address the compatibility with those rules of

---

[34] See also Case C–55/96 *Job Centre*, para 38; and Case C–258/98 *Criminal proceedings against Giovanni Carra and others* [2000] ECR I–4217, para 13.

[35] See E. Szyszczak, 'The New Parameters of European Labour Law' in D. O'Keeffe and P. Twomey, (eds), *Legal Issues of the Amsterdam Treaty* (Oxford, Hart Publishing, 1999) pp 141–55, p 142.

[36] Although it must be said that the Court has a chequered history when it comes to State monopolies and has not always been willing in recent years to subject the social values said to underlie such monopolies to the internal market dynamics which inform other aspects of its case-law, see, in this respect, the decisions in Case C–124/97 *Läärä* [1999] ECR I–6067 (Finnish gaming monopoly); or Case C–189/95 *Criminal proceedings against Harry Franzén* [1997] ECR I–5909 (Swedish alcohol monopoly).

[37] See further P. Teague, 'New Keynesianism and active labour market policies in Europe' in *Economic Citizenship in the European Union. Employment relations in the new Europe* (London and New York, Routledge, 1999) pp 106–35, p 116.

[38] See variously Case 238/82 *Duphar BV and others v Netherlands* [1984] ECR 523; Joined Cases C–159/91 and C–160/91 *Christian Poucet v Assurances Générales de France and Caisse Mutuelle Régionale de Languedoc-Roussillon* [1993] ECR I–637, para 6; Case C–70/95 *Sodemare SA v Anni Azzurri Holding SpA and Anni Azzurri Rezzato v Regione Lombardia* [1997] ECR I–3395, para 27; and Case C–120/95 *Nicolas Decker v Caisse de maladie des employés privés* [1998] ECR I–1831.

national collective agreements concluded in the pursuit of specific social policy objectives.[39] In *Albany*, undertakings which objected to their compulsory affiliation to a sectoral pension fund (since they had made alternative arrangements with an insurance company) argued that the fact that the fund enjoyed a legal monopoly to administer supplementary pension schemes was contrary to EC competition rules.[40] In particular, they argued that the Dutch authorities infringed those rules by making affiliation to the sectoral pension fund compulsory at the request of the social partners who created the fund, thereby granting exclusive rights to the fund. The Court emphasised that a harmonious, balanced and sustainable development of economic activities and a high level of employment and social protection figure amongst the EC's objectives in Article 2 EC. Furthermore, Articles 138 and 139 EC also encourage the development of a dialogue and the conclusion of collective agreements between management and labour at European level. With these Treaty aims and aspirations in mind the Court concluded that 'the social policy objectives pursued by [collective agreements between organizations of employers and workers] would be seriously undermined if management and labour were subject to Article [81(1)] of the Treaty when seeking jointly to adopt measures to improve conditions of work and employment'.[41] Collective agreements concluded in the pursuit of social policy objectives, by virtue of their nature and purpose, do not fall within the scope of EC competition rules, specifically Article 81(1) EC. The decision to make affiliation to a sectoral pension fund compulsory at the request of the social partners was thus acceptable.[42] Not surprisingly, the *Albany* decision has been regarded as 'a victory for the maintenance of a role for the Member States and social partners in the regulation of labour and social security law.'[43]

[39] For a more in-depth discussion of these cases than is possible in the present context see T. Hervey, 'Social Solidarity: A Buttress Against Internal Market Law?' in Shaw (ed), above n 2, pp 31–47; L. Gyselen, annotation of Case C–67/96 *Albany* (2000) 37 *Common Market Law Review* 425–48; and S. Evju, 'Collective Agreements and Competition Law. The *Albany* Puzzle, and *van der Woude*' (2001) 17 *International Journal of Comparative Labour Law and Industrial Relations* 165–84.

[40] Gyselen explains the three pillars of social protection in the field of pensions which are essential to an understanding of Case C–67/96 *Albany* and its ilk. Essentially there are three levels: statutory basic pensions which national authorities offer to the population as a whole; collective forms of pension which supplement the basic statutory pension and in which participation can be optional or mandatory, which was the level at issue in *Albany*; and supplementary pension or life insurance arrangements.

[41] Case C–67/96 *Albany*, para 59.

[42] The decision of the Court in Case C–67/96 *Albany* has since been confirmed with respect to health care insurance in Case C–222/98 *Hendrik van der Woude v Stichting Beatrixoord* [2000] ECR I–7111, paras 24–27; and with respect to a supplementary pension scheme that had not been set up within the context of a collective agreement in Joined Cases C–180/98 and C–184/98 *Pavel Pavlov v Stichting Pensioenfonds Medische Specialisten* [2000] ECR I–6451. Note, however, that a pension fund charged with the management of a supplementary pension scheme set up by a collective agreement is not, following *Albany*, exempt from the application of EC competition rules. It must still be established that there is no abuse of a dominant position contrary to Article 82 EC.

[43] See S. Vousden, '*Albany*, Market Law and Social Exclusion' (2000) 29 *Industrial Law Journal* 181–91, 187–88.

State Aids

Article 87(1) EC provides that 'any aid granted by a Member State or through State resources in any form whatsoever which distorts or threatens to distort competition by favouring certain undertakings or the production of certain goods shall, insofar as it affects trade between Member States, be incompatible with the common market.'[44] The Court has consistently held that the partial reduction of social charges devolving upon undertakings in a particular sector of industry constitutes an aid within the meaning of Article 87(1) EC if such a measure is intended partially to exempt those undertakings from the financial burden arising from the normal application of the general system of compulsory social security and insurance contributions imposed by law.[45] However, it has been reluctant in some cases to subject national labour law provisions to the full force of EC Treaty rules on State aids.

In *Sloman Neptun* the Court was asked whether a national rule which exempted certain employment contracts from national labour regulations could be regarded as a form of State aid.[46] The Court held, on the one hand, that the impugned shipping register system did not seek, through its object and general structure, to create an advantage which would constitute an additional burden for the State or public or private bodies designated or established by the State. On the other, the benefits which accrued to the German shipping undertakings were not paid for by the State.[47] The contested measure only sought to alter in

---

[44] Note that Articles 87(2) and (3) EC provide a list of exceptions of aid which will be deemed automatically to be compatible with the common market and a further list of types of cases where the aid may be deemed to be compatible. Article 88 EC provides that the Council may, in exceptional circumstances, declare an aid compatible with the common market.

[45] See Case 173/73 *Italy v Commission* [1974] ECR 709. The Court held that the partial reduction of public charges devolving upon undertakings in a particular sector of industry constituted a state aid within the meaning of Article 87 EC and that the alleged social aim of a measure does not suffice to shield it from the application of the Treaty rules on State aids. See also Case 203/82 *Commission v Italy* [1983] ECR 2525; and Case C–75/97 *Belgium v Commission* [1999] ECR I–3671, where the Court held that a system under which certain undertakings in a particular industrial sector are accorded the advantage of increased reductions in social security contributions relieved them of some of their costs and conferred on them advantages which improved their competitive position. The social character of such measures did not exclude them outright from classification as aid for the purposes of Article 87 EC (para 25).

[46] Joined Cases C–72/91 and C–73/91 *Sloman Neptun Schiffahrts AG v Seebetriebsrat Bodo Ziesemer der Sloman Neptun Schiffahrts AG* [1993] ECR I–887. At issue in the case was German legislation which enabled merchant vessels entered in its shipping register to employ seafarers who were nationals of non-EU States and had no permanent abode or residence in Germany to be subjected to working conditions and rates of pay which were not covered by German law and were considerably less favourable than those applicable to German seafarers.

[47] As regards whether measures which do not represent a charge on public funds should, in any case, qualify as State aid see M. Slotboom, 'State Aid in Community Law: A Broad or Narrow Definition?' (1995) 20 *European Law Review* 289–301. In Joined Cases C–52/97, C–53/97 and C–54/97 *Epifanio Viscido, Mauro Terragnolo and Others v Ente Poste Italiane* [1998] ECR I–2629, point 14, also a case in the field of social protection, the Court only referred to the absence of a transfer from State resources.

favour of shipping undertakings the framework within which contractual relations are formed between those undertakings and their employees.[48] The Court continued: 'The consequences arising from this, in so far as they relate to the difference in the basis for the calculation of social security contributions and to the potential loss of tax revenue because of the low rates of pay, referred to by the Commission, are inherent in the system and are not a means of granting a particular advantage to the undertakings concerned.'[49]

The referring court in the *Kirsammer-Hack* case also sought to determine whether national legislation which excluded small businesses from a national system of protection from unfair dismissal was compatible with the Treaty prohibition on State aids.[50] German legislation on unfair dismissal did not apply to undertakings which employed no more than five employees, account only being taken of those employees whose normal period of work exceeded ten hours per week or forty five hours per month. The applicant's employer employed only two workers on a full-time basis and four of those employed on a part-time basis worked less than the statutory minimum prescribed by the legislation. The applicant argued that small businesses, since they were not obliged to pay compensation in the event of socially unjustified dismissals or to bear the legal expenses incurred in proceedings concerning the dismissal of workers, thus seemed to enjoy a significant competitive advantage over other undertakings. The Court of Justice was unconvinced, however. As in *Sloman Neptun*, it was satisfied that there was no intention to favour particular undertakings and that there had been no transfer of State resources. It pointed out that only advantages granted directly or indirectly through State resources are to be considered as State aid within the meaning of Article 87(1) EC. The exclusion of a category of businesses from the protection system in question did not entail, in its view, any direct or indirect transfer of State resources to those businesses 'but derives solely from the legislature's intention to provide a specific legislative framework for working relationships between employers and employees in small businesses and to avoid imposing on those businesses financial constraints which might hinder their development.'[51]

More recent case-law of the Court suggests a more expansive approach to the Treaty's State aid rules when it comes to national measures or agreements in the social and labour law field governing, variously, unemployment, poverty and social exclusion. Joint financing by a Member State through a public fund of measures accompanying a social plan drawn up by undertakings experiencing employment problems was regarded as illegal State aid in *France v Commission*.[52]

---

[48] Of relevance to the Court's conclusion may have been the submissions by the German government emphasising the decline of the German shipping industry (see Joined Cases C–72/91 and C–73/91 *Sloman Neptun*, para 9).

[49] Joined Cases C–72/91 and C–73/91 *Sloman Neptun*, para 21.

[50] Case C–189/91 *Petra Kirsammer-Hack v Nurhan Sidal* [1993] ECR I–6185.

[51] *Ibid*, paras 16–17.

[52] Case C–241/94 [1996] ECR I–4551.

The French government's argument, to the effect that general measures of this type designed to combat unemployment fall outside the scope of application of the EC Treaty rules, failed. Similarly, measures intended by the Italian government to enable it to take effective action in areas of training and job promotion for the benefit of young persons experiencing difficulties in the labour market were not, simply due to their social character, to be excluded outright from being categorised as aid.[53] Thus, although cases like *Sloman Neptun* and *Albany* indicate a certain sensitivity on the part of the Court to social and labour law issues, national legislation or collective agreements in this field will fall foul of Treaty rules unless they comply with the fundamental principles underpinning the internal market and free competition.[54]

Health and Safety Legislation

EC Treaty provisions and secondary legislation relating to the single market have not been the only source of social and/or labour law jurisprudence at the Court of Justice. In more recent years, positive legislation such as that adopted on the basis of the health and safety provisions of the former Article 118a EC have been the subject of decisions of the Court. Unhappy with the adoption of the Working Time Directive, which laid down minimum health and safety requirements, on the basis of this Treaty provision, the United Kingdom sought to have the Directive annulled.[55]

The Directive provides, *inter alia* that Member States are to take the necessary measures to ensure that every worker is entitled to a minimum daily rest period of eleven consecutive hours per twenty four hour period, to a rest break where the working day is longer than six hours, to a minimum uninterrupted rest period of twenty-four hours in each seven-day period and finally to four weeks' paid annual leave. Article 6 of Directive 93/104 requires Member States to take the measures necessary to ensure that, in keeping with the need to

---

[53] Case C–310/99 *Italy v Commission* [2002] ECR I–2889. The Italian measures in question sought to promote youth employment and the conversion of fixed term contracts into open ones by means of a reduction in social security contributions. The Court held that this constituted illegal State aid. See also the Commission's guidelines concerning aid to employment, OJ 1995 C334/4.

[54] See also Cases C–251/97 *France v Commission* [1996] ECR I–4551; and C–75/97 *Belgium v Commission*.

[55] Case C–84/94 *United Kingdom v Council* [1996] ECR I–5755. See the annotation by L. Waddington, 'Towards a Healthier and More Secure European Social Policy?' (1997) 4 *Maastricht Journal of European and Comparative Law* 83–100. Council Directive 93/104/EC of 23 November 1993 concerning certain aspects of the organisation of working time, OJ 1993 L307/18. In accordance with the framework Directive in this field—Council Directive 89/391/EEC of 12 June 1989 on the introduction of measures to encourage improvements in the safety and health of workers at work, OJ 1989 L183/1—Directive 93/104 applies to all sectors of activity in the public and private sectors, with the exception of air, rail, road, sea, inland waterway and lake transport, sea fishing, other work at sea and the activities of doctors in training. On the exclusion of certain sectors from the scope of application of the Working Time Directive see Case C–133/00 *J.R. Bowden, J.L. Chapman and J.J. Doyle v Tuffnells Parcels Express Ltd* [2001] ECR I–7031.

protect the health and safety of workers, the period of weekly working time is determined by the two sides of industry or by national legislation, provided that the average working time for each seven-day period, including overtime, does not exceed forty-eight hours. Article 17 provides for a whole series of derogations, some of which take account of the specific characteristics of the activity concerned, others which are permitted on condition that the worker receives compensatory rest periods or other appropriate protection, and others still which may be concluded by means of collective agreement or agreements between the two sides of industry.

The United Kingdom's annulment action focused on infringement of the principle of proportionality and the legitimacy of the chosen health and safety legal basis. It argued that there was no established link between working time and health and safety and that the Directive should therefore have been adopted on the basis of Articles 94 or 308 EC, with the result that a unanimous vote would have been required in Council. Clearly the United Kingdom action was an attempt to annul not simply the Working Time Directive but also to stymie use of the health and safety provisions of the EC Treaty as a legal basis for the adoption of further labour market regulatory measures to which it was opposed.[56] The Court did not agree with the United Kingdom's narrow interpretation of the legal basis provided by the former Article 118a EC. It held that it was the appropriate legal basis for the adoption of Community measures whose principal aim is the protection of the health and safety of workers, notwithstanding the ancillary effects which such measures may have on the establishment and functioning of the internal market.[57] It insisted that the scope for Community legislative action regarding the health and safety of workers provided by the former Article 118a EC must be widely interpreted. Community action designed to provide such protection could comprise measures which are of general application and not merely measures specific to certain categories of workers. In addition, the Court held that Directives adopted on the basis of the old Article 118a EC have to be in the nature of minimum requirements only in the sense that Member States remain at liberty to adopt more protective measures.

What is particularly interesting from the point of view of the Court's involvement in employment policy issues is precisely the care it took in this case to give them a wide berth.[58] The United Kingdom government argued, as regards the

---

[56] See also R. Dehousse, 'Integration Through Law Revisited: Some Thoughts on the Juridication of the European Political Process' in F. Snyder (ed), *The Europeanisation of Law: The Legal Effects of European Integration* (Oxford, Hart Publishing, 2000) pp 15–29, p 18.

[57] Case C–84/94 *United Kingdom v Council*, para 22. Note that Article 137 EC, as amended by the Amsterdam Treaty, now provides that the Community shall support and complement the activities of the Member States as regards both improvement of the working environment to protection workers' health and safety, as well as in the field of working conditions.

[58] See also S. Sciarra, 'Building on European Social Values: an Analysis of the Multiple Sources of European Social Law' in F. Snyder (ed), *Constitutional Dimensions of European Economic Integration* (London, Kluwer Law International, 1996) pp 175–206, p 188, who remarks on the Community legislature's avoidance in Directive 93/104 of reference to the regulation of working time as a means to combat unemployment through the regulation or redistribution of working hours.

aim of Directive 93/104, that it represented a continuation of the Community's earlier thinking and of a series of earlier initiatives at Community level concerned with the organization of working time in the interests of job creation and reduced unemployment. In its view, the Directive was, in reality, a measure concerned with the overall improvement of the living and working conditions of employees and with their general protection, and was so broad in scope and coverage as to be capable of classification as a social policy measure. The Court recognised, as the Directive itself did in its preamble, that the legislation constitutes a practical contribution towards creating the social dimension of the internal market. However, simply because the Directive fell within the scope of the Community's social policy did not mean that the former Article 118a EC was an inappropriate legal basis. The Court pointed out that the organisation of working time is not necessarily conceived as an instrument of employment policy, that if indeed it were viewed as a means to combat unemployment a number of economic factors would have to be taken into account and that the Directive itself had urged in the preamble that the improvement of workers' safety, hygiene and health is a Community objective which should not be subordinated to purely economic considerations. The Court concluded that while it could not be excluded that the Directive might affect employment, that was clearly not its essential objective.[59] The Court's arguments reflected those of the Advocate General, who had pointed to the potential of measures designed to reorganise working time not simply for job creation and redistribution but also as means to improve health and safety, to improve productivity, service to consumers and competitiveness.[60]

BECTU was another positive statement of the Court's willingness to ensure the effective application of the provisions of the Directive.[61] United Kingdom regulations implementing the Directive provided that workers could accrue rights to paid annual leave only after completion of a qualifying period of thirteen weeks continuous employment with the same employer. The purpose of

---

[59] Case C–84/94 *United Kingdom v Council*, para 30.

[60] See the Opinion of Advocate General Léger in Case C–84/94 *United Kingdom v Council*, paras 85–89. For information on the implementation of Directive 93/104 see Commission Report, *State of Implementation of Directive 93/104/EC of 23 November 1993 concerning certain aspects of the organisation of working time*, COM (2000) 787. Directive 2000/34/EC of the European Parliament and of the Council of 22 June 2000 amending Directive 93/104/EC, OJ 2000 L195/41 now extends the Directive to all sectors of activity, both public and private, subject to a series of limited exceptions. On the scope and application of the working time Directive see Case C–133/00 *Bowden*; Case C–303/98 *Sindicato de Médicos de Asistencia Pública (SIMAP) v Consellería de Sanidad y Consumo de la Generalidad Valenciana* [2000] ECR I–7963 (application of the Directive to the on-call activities of medical emergency personnel); annotation by J. Fairhurst, 'SIMAP—Interpreting the Working Time Directive' (2001) 30 *Industrial Law Journal* 236–43; Order of the Court of 3 July 2001 in Case C–241/99 *Confederación Intersindical Galega (CIG) v Servicio Galego de Saúde (Sergas)*, applying the decision in *SIMAP* on the basis of Article 104(3) of the Court's Rules of Procedure; Case C–386/98 *Commission v Italy* [2000] ECR I–1277 (non-transposition); and Case C–46/99 *Commission v France* (non-transposition) [2000] ECR I–4379.

[61] Case C–173/99 *R v Secretary of State for Trade and Industry, ex parte Broadcasting, Entertainment, Cinematographic and Theatre Union (BECTU)* [2001] ECR I–4881.

such a restriction was presumably to balance the exigencies of employment protection with concerns for the competitiveness of undertakings, particularly small and medium sized entrerprises who were to be subject to new burdens in terms of cost and workforce inflexibility as a result of the adoption of the Directive.[62] Its effect, however, was to limit the scope of application of the Directive, particularly as regards workers engaged on short-term contracts.

The Court held that a national rule such as that at issue in *BECTU* violated Article 7 of the Working Time Directive.[63] It regarded the right to paid annual leave as a particularly important principle of Community social law from which there can be no derogations[64] and observed that the Working Time Directive did not distinguish between workers on fixed-term contracts and those on contracts of indefinite duration. Indeed the Court noted that rules such as those applied in the United Kingdom could actually give rise to abuse, since employers might be tempted to evade the obligation to grant paid annual leave to which every worker is entitled by more frequent resort to short-term employment relationships.[65] The Court added that workers on short-term contracts often find themselves in a more precarious situation than those employed under longer term contracts, so that it is all the more important to ensure that their health and safety are protected in a manner consonant with the purpose of Directive 93/104. As regards the United Kingdom's arguments based on the reference in Article 7 to the implementation of the right to paid leave 'in accordance with the conditions for entitlement to, and granting of, such leave laid down by national legislation and/or practice', the Court specified that this concerned the conditions of exercise of the right not the conditions of entitlement to that right. Finally, the Court held that the need to avoid imposing excessive burdens on SMEs could not be relied on to limit the exercise of a right to annual paid leave at national level. The health and safety of workers should not be subordinated to purely economic considerations and the Directive, which was adopted on the basis of the former Article 118a EC, had already taken into consideration the effects which the organisation of working time may have for small and medium-sized undertakings, since this is one of the conditions to which measures based on this provision are subject.

[62] See in this respect G. Ricci, 'BECTU: an unlimited right to annual paid leave' (2001) 30 *Industrial Law Journal* 401–08, 402. Case C–173/99 *BECTU*.

[63] Article 7(1) provides that Member States shall take the measures necessary to ensure that every worker is entitled to paid annual leave of at least four weeks in accordance with the conditions for entitlement to, and granting of, such leave laid down by national legislation and/or practice.

[64] The Court seems to have been slightly more measured in its choice of terminology than Advocate General Tizzano, who regarded the right to paid annual leave as a fundamental social right. He referred to the Charter of Fundamental Rights of the European Union, OJ 2000 C 364/1, and the declaration in Article 31(2) that every worker has the right to limitation of maximum working hours, to daily and weekly rest periods and to an annual period of paid leave, although he recognised that it was not, formally, binding. Significantly, the Charter was not cited by the Court.

[65] Case C–173/99 *BECTU*, para 46. For similar reasoning see also Case C–109/00 *Tele Danmark A/S v Handels- og Kontorfunktionaerernes Forbund i Danmark (HK)* [2001] ECR I–6993, discussed below ch 5.

Apart from the breadth of the Court's case-law and the extent of the EC's involvement, whether direct or indirect, in the social and labour law sphere, what this overview of its case-law essentially demonstrates is the lack of any coherent vision when it comes to this area of the law. The Court's critics, particularly those in Member States which call for reduced or minimal EC involvement in the social field, point to the regulatory zeal with which the Court has tackled references. In reality, the case-law suggests that the Court has simply balanced the need, on the one hand, to defend national labour laws, social policy and industrial equity with, on the other, the effective functioning of the internal market. Thus, for example, the application of national social and labour law to posted workers is legitimate only to the extent that it is necessary and effective and adds to the protection already enjoyed by those workers pursuant to the legislation of their employer's Member State of establishment. Similarly, it is clear that Member States may pursue objectives of employment policy such as the maintenance of high employment or the maintenance of a particular industrial sector.[66] However, the means chosen to attain those objectives must be compatible with EC Treaty rules—hence the 'erosion' spoken of by labour lawyers. While the Court of Justice has not explicitly engaged in the flexibility debate it has clearly been alive to its existence and to the EU's burgeoning employment difficulties.[67]

THE CONTESTED CONSEQUENCES OF LABOUR MARKET REGULATION

The performance of the Court in cases touching on social and labour law issues must thus be considered against the backdrop of this ongoing debate on the need for greater flexibility in the EU labour market and on the interaction between labour market regulation, specifically employment protection measures, and economic competitiveness, or indeed the detrimental effect which the former is said by some to have on the latter. Although unemployment rates in the EU are decreasing, they nevertheless remain much higher than those in the United States or, within the EU, the United Kingdom—the Member State whose deregulated labour market most resembles that in the United States.[68] Indeed the United Kingdom's refusal at Maastricht to be bound by the Social chapter was

---

[66] See, for example, Case C–75/97 *Belgium v Commission*, para 37.

[67] In Case C–75/97 *Commission v Belgium*, para 37, the Court remarked that Member States had been urged by the Commission in its Guidelines on aid in employment (OJ 1995 C334/4) to reduce labour costs.

[68] An unemployment rate of 8.4% was recorded for the eurozone area in February 2002, dropping to 7.7% in the EU as a whole (see Eurostat monthly statistics available at http://europa. eu.int/comm/eurostat). See P. Lourtie, *Solving Europe's Unemployment Problem. The Demystification of Flexibility*, College of Europe, WP No 10 (Brussels, European Interuniversity Press, 1995) ch 1, for an account of the rise in employment in the EC from the 1970s onwards and a comparison with the US; Teague, above n 37, pp 107 *et seq*; and A. Martin, *Social Pacts, Unemployment and EMU Macroeconomic Policy*, EUI WP RSC No 2000/32.

founded on the then Conservative government's conviction that labour market regulation meant decreased competitiveness.[69] This conviction even survived the change to a Labour government in the United Kingdom in 1997.[70]

The meaning of labour market flexibility depends, it would seem, like beauty, on the eye of the beholder! It can, as Fredman observes, denote numerical flexibility, involving the adjustment of labour inputs to meet fluctuations in the employers' needs (usually by using part-time, temporary or casual work contracts or altering working time patterns). In contrast, it can also denote formal flexibility, which relates to changes in the tasks of workers rather than their numbers and consists in the ability of employers to require employees to adjust their skills to match the demands of changes in workload, technology or production methods.[71] As we will see, it is sometimes unclear to which of these different aspects of flexibility measures adopted pursuant to the EC Treaty's Employment Title aspire.

The possible effect of labour market regulation on the employment rates, efficiency and general competitiveness of labour markets have long been debated. The ability of the US to create employment and maintain low unemployment figures is usually associated with the greater flexibility of its economy generally

---

[69] On business opposition to increased EC competence in the social field based on its equation of social protection with uncompetiveness see S. Mazey and J. Richardson, 'Agenda Setting, Lobbying and the 1996 IGC' in G. Edwards and A. Pijpers (eds), *The Politics of European Treaty Reform* (London, Pinter, 1997) pp 226–48, pp 237–43. See also A. Moravcsik and K. Nicolaïdis, 'Explaining the Treaty of Amsterdam: Interests, Influence and Institutions' (1999) 37 *Journal of Common Market Studies* 59–85, 63.

[70] A telling anecdote is recounted in this respect of a conversation between Jacques Chirac and Tony Blair prior to the 1997 British General Election: 'The French President had found consolation in the thought that the defeat of the Tories (sister party to his neo-Gaullist RPR) would at least result in a more Euro-friendly British government sending its representatives to the Council of Ministers. Tony Blair gave him a polite warning. He should not assume that Labour would fully implement the whole Social Chapter in the Maastricht Treaty. The New Labour government would not risk the loss of efficiency at home and sales abroad which would naturally follow inflexible labour markets. The President responded that his economists believed that the costs of the social chapter—ranging from paternity leave to job-loss compensation—were low on the list of industrial detriments. Indeed they probably paid for themselves by stimulating the efficiency which follows commitment. Tony Blair disagreed. His economists had no doubt about the need for labour market flexibility. The argument went on until Chirac tapped Blair on the knee and asked him, "Am I right in thinking that you are the leader of the British left and that I lead the French right, or is it the other way round?" ' See R. Hattersley, 'In Search of the Third Way' (2000) 71 *Granta* 231–55, 241. On the position of New Labour on EC employment issues see C. Tucker, 'The Luxembourg Process: the UK View' (2000) 16 *International Journal of Comparative Labour Law and Industrial Relations* 71–83. For a concrete example of Labour's ambivalent approach to EC social policy see the account by Ricci, above n 62, 406, of its 'soft' compliance with the Working Time Directive.

[71] See the excellent article by S. Fredman, 'Labour Law in Flux: the Changing Composition of the Workforce' (2000) 26 *Industrial Law Journal* 337–52, 338. See also S. Sciarra, *How 'Global' is Labour Law? The Perspective of Social Rights in the European Union*, EUI WP LAW No 96/6, p 4: S. Deakin and H. Reed, 'The Contested Meaning of Labour Market Flexibility: Economic Theory and the Discourse of European Integration' in Shaw (ed), above n 2, pp 71–99, pp 73–75; C. Barnard, 'Flexibility and Social Policy' in G. De Búrca and J. Scott (eds), *Constitutional Change in the European Union. From Uniformity to Flexibility?* (Oxford, Hart Publishing, 2000) pp 197–217; and S. Deakin and G. Morris, *Labour Law* (London, Butterworths, 1998) p 39 *et seq.*

and its labour market in particular; flexibility being taken to denote the absence of labour market regulation and what are regarded as the 'rigidities' which regulation entails. In the run up to the introduction of Euro coins and banknotes in January 2002, the chairman of the US Federal Reserve was confident that, regardless of the introduction of the Euro, US economic performance would remain superior to that of the EU and attract greater investment. The main reason for this was said to be Europe's relatively rigid labour markets; in particular, the fact that it is easier and cheaper to hire and fire workers in the US.[72] Similarly, in an OECD report on labour market flexibility in the 1980s, possible causes for Europe's high unemployment levels were identified as including too restrictive employment protection legislation (which discourages recruitment and inhibits dismissals[73]), high non-wage labour costs (particularly employer tax and social security contributions[74]), high wage costs and (high) statutory minimum wages in some States.[75]

Labour market regulations seek to protect workers from unfair labour market developments in two distinct ways. In the first place, employment protection legislation concerns security of income and/or employment. Workers' employment situation is protected by making it more costly or more difficult for employers to dismiss them without cause. Examples of such legislation in the EC context is the so-called Acquired Rights Directive discussed in chapter six. Essentially, this Directive seeks to ensure that, in the event of corporate restructuring, the obligations of the original employer vis-à-vis his employees are transferred to the new employer following the restructuring and that

---

[72] *Financial Times*, 1 December 2001. Regulations regarding hiring are taken to mean rules favouring disadvantaged groups, conditions for using temporary or fixed-contracts and training requirements. Regulations concerning firing cover redundancy procedures, mandatory notice periods, severance payments and special requirements for collective dismissals and short-time work schemes (See ECB, *Labour Market Mismatches in Euro Area Countries*, March 2002). Employment protection of this type can, according to the ECB, be provided by the private market, labour legislation, collective bargaining agreements and court interpretations of legislative and contractual provisions.

[73] See further Teague, above n 37, p 114, where he suggests that institutional rules governing the labour market may encourage both employers and employees to be more selective about offering and accepting jobs, thereby causing tensions between the demand and supply sides of the labour market. Employers subject to stringent hiring and firing rules may adopt stiffer recruitment criteria to attract highly motivated workers and high levels of benefits may encourage the unemployed to wait longer for a job which more closely meets their expectations in terms of pay and working conditions. See also Lourtie, above n 68, pp 50–53.

[74] See also R. Blanpain, 'The European Union, Employment, Social Policy and the Law' in R. Blanpain *et al.* (eds), *Institutional Changes and European Social Policies after the Treaty of Amsterdam* (The Hague, Kluwer Law International, 1998) pp 1–65, pp 8–9. The Commission's 1993 White paper on *Growth, Competitiveness and Employment*, Bull. EC. Supp. 6/93, COM (93) 700, discussed below, estimated that about 35–40% of total labour costs in the European economy consist of non-wage commitments such as employer social security contributions. Eurostat statistics reveal that, in 1999, one quarter of the average EU hourly wage went on social security contributions. See also the report of the ECB, *Labour Market Mismatches in Euro Area Countries*, March 2002.

[75] OECD, *Labour market flexibility*, 1986.

employees cannot simply be dismissed as a result of the transfer.[76] Examples of national employment protection surfaced in cases like *Kowalska, Kirsammer-Hack* and *Seymour-Smith*, which involved national collective agreements or legislation on severance grants following the termination of employment, the exclusion of small businesses from the scope of application of national unfair dismissal legislation and the imposition of a qualifying period for the enjoyment of national unfair dismissal protection.[77] Secondly, labour market regulations seek to limit the extent to which wages may fluctuate over time or differ between workers performing similar duties. Minimum wage legislation, equal pay rules for male and female workers who perform equal work or work of equal value and provisions governing collective bargaining and the role of social partners are examples of this type of labour market regulation.[78] The essential purpose of employment protection legislation is to reduce uncertainty by enhancing job and/or income security. This involves a number of advantages both for employees and employers in terms of greater job satisfaction, attachment to the job, arguably greater productivity and also internal flexibility.[79] Employment protection has its costs, however. It may increase labour and administrative costs in a number of ways—by obliging employers to provide wages above a certain minimum, to provide compensation in the event of redundancy, to make perhaps considerable and complicated social insurance contributions on the part of his employees and to comply with various other regulatory requirements. Furthermore, although it may enhance the working environment of those in employment, particularly those with indefinite employment contracts, it may also work to the disadvantage of the unemployed or temporary workers on the margins of the labour market and may contribute to worsened social exclusion.

Despite the prevailing assumption that certain Member States' continuing commitment to labour market regulation is at the root of the EU's higher unemployment rates, conclusive arguments to this effect have yet to be produced. Economists and labour market analysts continue to trade expert articles and theses detailing why their theories supporting or opposing this assumption are

[76] The employment protection afforded by the Acquired Rights Directive is clearly limited since it provides that the employees of a transferred undertaking can be dismissed for economic, technical or organisational reasons entailing changes in the workforce. See below ch 6 for a detailed discussion of the Acquired Rights Directives. For a comprehensive comparison of employment protection regulations see T. van Peijpe, 'Employment Protection in Industrialised Market Economies' in R. Blanpain (ed), *Employment Protection under Strain*, Bulletin of Comparative Labour Relations 33–1998, pp 33–65.

[77] See Cases C–33/89 *Maria Kowalska v Freie und Hansestadt Hamburg* [1990] ECR I–2591; C–189/91 *Kirsammer-Hack*; and C–167/97 *R v Secretary of State for Employment, ex parte Nicole Seymour-Smith and Laura Perez* [1999] ECR I–623.

[78] See G. Bertola, *Labour Markets in the European Union*, EUI Working Papers, RSC No 99/24, pp 4–5. Compare Teague, above n 37, pp 139–64, pp 141–42, who classifies the Equality Directives as employment protection legislation and the Collective Redundancies, Transfer of Undertakings and Insolvency Directives as measures concerning workers' rights.

[79] See OECD, 'Employment Protection and Labour Market Performance' in *Employment Outlook*, 1999, OECD, p 68.

correct.[80] In recent years, many commentators' assumptions that the EU's poor job market performance is due to high and rigid wage costs have come under attack. Even a recent OECD report has suggested that there appears to be little or no association between the strictness of national employment protection legislation and overall unemployment.[81] Interestingly, what the 1999 OECD report does identify is that the strictness of employment protection legislation has a negative effect on overall employment/population ratio and that this is particularly the case for youths and prime-age women: 'it reverses for prime-age men, consistent with the hypothesis that EPL [employment protection legislation] protects the jobs of prime-age men (who are mainly insiders) at the cost of reducing employment for prime-age women and youths (who are mainly outsiders).'[82] The level and fluctuation of exchange rates and interest rates is arguably of as much if not greater relevance to economic performance and competitiveness than merely labour costs.[83] This seems to be borne out by the negative effect that the United Kingdom's decision not to adopt the Euro has had for British industry, with several car manufacturers in particular shutting up shop or reducing their activities in the United Kingdom. Although centralised collective bargaining comes in for criticism in the OECD report, the social partnerships which it has produced have been of fundamental importance in some Member States—not least Ireland, where the average annual employment growth rate in 1997–2000 was 6.9 per cent—in improving economic and job performance in the last decade.[84] Investment in infrastructure and worker

[80] See, *inter alia*, H. Sarfati, 'Negotiating Trade-offs Between Jobs and Labour Market Flexibility in the European Union' (1998) *International Journal of Comparative Labour Law and Industrial Relations* 307–23, who explains the challenges from economists to the linkage between European job performance and rigid wage structure and rejects evidence of a causal link between labour market flexibility and drops in unemployment; OECD, 'Employment Protection and Labour Market Performance' in *Employment Outlook*, 1999, OECD, pp 69 *et seq.* and 120 *et seq.* for a summary of the findings of several economic theorists assessing how employment protection regulation affects labour market performance; S. Deakin and F. Wilkinson, 'Rights vs Efficiency? The Economic Case for Transnational Labour Standards' (1994) 23 *Industrial Law Journal* 289–310, 292 *et seq.* for an account of the economic critique of labour standards; F. Wilkinson, 'Equality, efficiency and economic progress: The case for universally applied equitable standards for wages and conditions of work' in W. Sengenberger and D. Campbell (eds), *Creating Economic Opportunities. The Role of Labour Standards in Industrial Restructuring* (Geneva, International Institute for Labour Studies) pp 61–86; and G. Bertola, T. Boeri and S. Caves, 'La protection de l'emploi dans les pays industrialisés: repenser les indicateurs' (2000) 139 *Revue internationale du Travail* 61–78.

[81] OECD, 'Employment Protection and Labour Market Performance' in *Employment Outlook*, 1999, OECD, ch 2.

[82] OECD, 'Employment Protection and Labour Market Performance' in *Employment Outlook*, 1999, OECD, p 75. Female unemployment in the EU remains higher than male unemployment, except for in the United Kingdom and Sweden. See European Parliament Resolution on the particular impact of unemployment on women, OJ 1998 C 313/200.

[83] See Sarfati, above n 80, 311; and ECB, *Labour Market Mismatches in Euro Area Countries*, March 2002, p 4—efficiently functioning labour markets are regarded as necessary precisely because the Euro zone countries can no longer use monetary and exchange rate policy to address asymmetric economic shocks.

[84] For an account of the contribution made by Irish social partnerships see S. Ó Móráin, 'The European Employment Strategy—a Consideration of Social Partnership and Related Matters in the Irish Context' (2000) 16 *International Journal of Comparative Labour Law and Industrial Relations* 85–101.

productivity which, in turn, may be dependent on decent social protection and wages may also directly affect the level of investment in a Member State.[85] In addition, although the US has successfully maintained low levels of unemployment in the past three decades, the price has been the creation of what are sometimes referred to as the 'working poor'—low-paid employees who enjoy little or no employment protection.[86] Concerns about the importation wholesale of such an employment model is increasingly heard in the EU:

> Increases in the employment figures do not necessarily coincide with a higher quality of the jobs—the strongest category of workers have gained, but weaker areas of employment, such as "in-person services" and "routine production services", have lost. Inequality has grown also among categories of people who had a job; the rich have become richer and the poor have become poorer.[87]

In addition, some commentators point out that many European States did introduce greater flexibility measures in the 1980s in order to increase competition and reduce unemployment, but such policies have proved inadequate in themselves to stimulate employment.[88] For its part, even the ECB admits that it is difficult to assess the extent to which labour market reforms introduced in the 1990s have actually contributed to improvements in the labour market situation.

Unsurprisingly, the EU has not remained detached from the flexibility debate. Echoes of these conflicting views on the effect of a high level of labour market regulation and, specifically, employment protection legislation on employment rates are evident in the policy papers which have emerged from the Commission since the early 1990s. In 1993, the Commission issued its *Green Paper on Social Policy* which it was subsequently to publish as a *White Paper on Social Policy* the following year.[89] However, it also published a *White Paper on Growth,*

---

[85] See G. Majone, 'The European Community Between Social Policy and Social Regulation' (1993) 31 *Journal of Common Market Studies* 153–70, 160; and the Commission *Green Paper on Partnership for a New Organisation of Work* COM (97) 127, which associated enhanced competitiveness and productivity with improvements in the quality of employment and the transition to new forms of work organisation based on high skill, high trust and high quality.

[86] See also Blanpain in Blanpain *et al.* (eds), above n 74, pp 42–46; and G. Bertola, *Labour Markets in the European Union*, EUI WP, RSC No 99/24, p 12: '[the US model is] a paradigm of dubious appeal for many European voters, who would perhaps favor higher employment but would certainly resent many other aspects of American society, especially its less than ideal degree of 'social cohesion' as reflected in relatively high rates of single motherhood and crime.' Deakin and Wilkinson (1994), above n 80, 298 argue that: '[A]lthough a looser system of labour regulation, coupled with comparatively low levels of social security provision for the unemployed, may have produced a more "open" labour market with more extensive flows into and out of employment [in the US], the growth of lower wage, lower-productivity jobs has had an overall adverse effect on US economic performance relative to that of the EC.'

[87] See Sciarra in Snyder (1996) (ed), above n 58, p 197; and Deakin and Wilkinson (1994), above n 80, 308.

[88] See Lourtie, above n 68, p 57.

[89] COM (93) 551 and COM (94) 333 respectively. For a detailed account see B.-O. Kuper, 'The Green and White Papers of the European Union: the apparent goal of reduced social benefits' (1994) 4 *Journal of European Social Policy* 129–37.

Competitiveness and Employment.[90] The views of the Commission as reflected in these documents must of course be analysed in the context of the Member States' growing awareness of the need to combat unemployment (standing at around 10.5 per cent of the registered workforce at the time), as well as the EU's commitment to Economic and Monetary Union (EMU), and the adherence by Member States to stringent economic criteria in the 1990s in order to qualify for membership of EMU (albeit unemployment neither figured amongst the convergence criteria adopted in the Maastricht Treaty nor was it referred to in that Treaty).[91] Yet what is striking is the divergence in the philosophy which underlies the proposed means to respond to the Community's employment and labour market problems. The 1993 Green Paper recognised that labour standards and working conditions had to evolve to keep pace with rapid changes in technology and production organization, so as to facilitate the new forms of flexibility that enterprises needed. However, it added that necessary protection must still be afforded workers: 'Although it is a fact that in times of fierce competition enterprises need flexibility and that high unemployment reduces the bargaining power of workers, competitition within the Community on the basis of unacceptably low social standards, rather than productivity of entreprises, will undermine the economic objectives of the Union.'[92]

In contrast, the 1993 *White Paper on Growth, Competitiveness and Employment* outlined what it saw as the causes of Europe's structural unemployment problem—poor functioning of the labour market, lack of flexibility as regards the organisation of working time, wages and mobility, as well as compulsory social security deductions which were regarded as barriers to job creation, and high non-wage labour costs.[93] The flexibility sought by the Commission in this text for the employment market was clearly intended to benefit the employer and job-creator rather than employees and one commentator regarded the sub-text of the whole exercise as 'the dismantling of the frameworks built up in the past for the legal protection for workers'.[94] The specific action envisaged by the Commission to reduce unemployment involved, *inter alia*, the reduction or maintenance of labour costs, increased flexibility with Member

[90] COM (93) 700. EC. Bull. Suppl. 6/93.

[91] See also Deakin and Wilkinson (1994), above n 80, 297, on the need to include EMU in any assessment of the EU's (un)employment record; and E. Guild, 'How Can Social Protection Survive EMU? A United Kingdom Perspective' (1999) 24 *European Law Review* 22–37.

[92] See COM (93) 551, 60.

[93] These were regarded as some of the causes of structural unemployment. The White Paper also explained the causes of cyclical and technological unemployment. See the Editorial Comments, 'Growth, competitiveness and employment: the challenges facing the Union' (1994) 31 *Common Market Law Review* 1–6; and Lourtie, above n 68, p 82 *et seq.*

[94] See E. White, 'W(h)ither Social Policy?' in J. Shaw and G. More (eds) *New Legal Dynamics of European Union* (Oxford, OUP, 1996) pp 111–28, p 126. See also Lourtie, above n 68, p 88, who describes the policy change advocated by the 1993 White Paper: '[it] is not one from a regulated labour market to a totally flexible one, but a shift from policies oriented to the protection of the unemployed to policies raising the level of employment.'

States removing legal, fiscal and administrative obstacles to the changing trends and demands of the workplace, reduction in non-wage labour-costs which would eliminate some of the disincentives to employment of less skilled workers and enhancing the job creation potential of small and medium-sized enterprises (SMEs). The White Paper also sought to stimulate job creation by investments in large scale public works and infrastructure projects, but the Member States proved unwilling to increase the Commission's budget accordingly.[95] Following the 1993 White paper, it seemed unlikely, given the prevailing economic climate and the Commission's conversion, however partial, to the very neo-liberal equation of high levels of worker protection with assured negative economic and employment consequences, that future legislative proposals would involve a high level of employment protection.[96] The minimal nature of the protection afforded by the revised Acquired Rights Directive adopted in 1998, for example, and the provision in that Directive of a large number of optional clauses for Member States, seem to bear testimony to such fears.[97] The 1993 White Paper steered clear of the notion that reform of Europe's labour markets should entail wholesale deregulation, however, as one commentator pointed out:

> it is apparent that the underlying tension of *how* to regulate the labour market continues to restrict the EC Commission to an uneasy compromise between those who argue that excessively high labour standards result in costs which blunt the competitive edge of companies and those which believe that productivity is the key to competitiveness and that high labour standards have always formed an integral part of a competitive labour market.[98]

The preparation for and introduction of EMU provided further evidence of increased political support from some quarters for a scaling down of the protection afforded by existing national social and labour legislation. One of the European Central Bank's Executive Board members recognised that there was a tension between social union, which requires a large number of ever stricter regulations of the labour market and EMU, which requires the opposite, namely

---

[95] See further Deakin and Reed in Shaw (ed), above n 2, 87; and D. Ashiagbor, 'EMU and the Shift in the European Labour Law Agenda: From "Social Policy" to "Employment Policy"' (2001) 7 *European Law Journal* 311–30, 319–20.

[96] See White in Shaw and More (eds), above n 94, p 127; and generally S. Leibfried and P. Pierson, 'Social Policy' in H. Wallace and W. Wallace (eds), *Policy-making in the European Union* (Oxford, OUP, 1996) pp 185–207, p 193; and R. Geyer and B. Springer, 'EU Social Policy After Maastricht: The Works Council Directive and the British Opt-Out' in P.-H. Laurent and M. Maresceau (eds), *The State of the European Union. Deepening and Widening*, vol.4 (Boulder and London, Lynne Rienner Publishers, 1998) pp 207–23.

[97] For a discussion of Council Directive 98/50/EC of 29 June 1998 amending Directive 77/187/EEC on the approximation of the laws of the Member States relating to the safeguarding of employees' rights in the event of transfers of undertakings, businesses or parts of businesses, OJ 1998 L201/92, see below ch 6.

[98] See E. Szyszczak, 'Future Directions in European Union Social Policy Law' (1995) 24 *Industrial Law Journal* 19–32, 22; and Ashiagbor, above n 95, 314–15.

considerably greater flexibility in the labour market.[99] Similarly, the European Council Resolution on the Growth and Employment Pact of 1997, spoke of the need to make taxation and social protection schemes more employment friendly in order to improve the functioning of labour markets.[100] In the wake of the 1993 White Paper, an integrated employment strategy was launched at the 1994 European Council in Essen. Priority areas were identified requiring Member State action. These included classic deregulatory strategies such as the reduction of non-wage labour costs. The process which had begun in Essen continued at the IGC which culminated with the signing of the Amsterdam Treaty. Provisions on employment were inserted in the EC Treaty at the instigation of the Swedish delegation, which had originally sought a commitment to full employment. The Swedish proposals were watered down in the Treaty text to pursuit of a high level of employment. According to Deakin and Reed, Member State decisions to link this commitment to the pursuit of competitiveness and rejection of French proposals to establish a growth fund aimed at stimulating job creation directly are significant:

> The context in which the Employment Title was formulated was . . . one in which the Member States had rejected plans for a macro-economic policy aimed at achieving full employment through "demand-side" measures. . . . The prevailing consensus became one of support for a "stable" macro-economic policy based on meeting the convergence criteria for EMU, coupled with suggestions that Member States should take steps to implement 'structural' labour market reforms aimed at enhancing competitiveness.[101]

The Stability and Growth Pact agreed by the Member States at a summit in Dublin in 1996 also linked economic growth and employment and sought, *inter alia*, to make taxation and social protection systems more employment friendly and to lower non-wage labour costs. With the introduction of the Euro, pressure from the ECB for sustained reform of national labour markets has continued. In a report published in March 2002, strategically timed one would imagine to coincide with the Barcelona summit of the European Council, the ECB argued

---

[99] See I. Issing, *Cuadernos de Información Económica*, No 112, Madrid, July 1996, p 40 (cited by Rodríguez Ortiz, F., 'Las políticas de la convergencia, el espacio social europeo y el empleo' (1998) 18 *Cuadernos Europeos de Deusto* 143–71, 149, author's own translation); and E. Hamalainen, another Executive Board member, on the effect of the Euro on labour market reform: 'there is evidence of a very significant change in labour market behaviour in euro area countries, particularly in the field of wage negotiations' (*Financial Times*, 26 February 2002). See also Martin, above n 68, who compares the ECB's emphasis on supply side policies to remedy high unemployment in Euro Member States with demand side policies which seek to redress a deficit in demand for manpower due to excessively restrictive macroeconomic policies.

[100] OJ 1997 C 236/3.

[101] See Deakin and Reed in Shaw (ed), above n 2, 88. It is not clear, in any case, to what extent the French proposals would have added to, or differed from, the existing European Social Fund (ESF). See Articles 146 to 148 EC and Council Regulation (EC) No 1260/99 of 21 June 1999, laying down general provisions on the Structural Funds (OJ 1999 L161/1), which takes into consideration the European Employment Strategy. Objective 3 of the ESF covers the adaptation and modification of policies and systems of education, training and employment.

that: '[I]mproved job mediation, more flexible wages . . ., reforms of tax and benefit systems, less restrictive employment protection regulation [and] working time flexibility . . . all help towards making the matching process more efficient and labour markets more flexible.'[102] It acknowledged that Euro zone Member States had made some progress in reforming their labour markets but urged them to do more. The European Council in Barcelona in March 2002 echoed the ECB's calls for structual reforms to solve the EU's unemployment problem.

EMPLOYMENT POLICY IN THE EC TREATY

Absent in the main from the debates preceding the Maastricht Treaty, employment and, more specifically, the burgeoning number of unemployed in the EU workforce, was very much to the forefront of some Member States' minds when the Amsterdam Treaty was being negotiated. As a result of that Treaty, Article 2 TEU now provides that one of the Union's objectives is to promote economic and social progress and a 'high level of employment'. The means to achieve these objectives are identified as the creation of the internal market, the strengthening of economic and social cohesion and the establishment of EMU. By establishing a common market and EMU and by implementing a whole series of common policies, the Community is also charged, *inter alia*, with promoting a high level of employment and social protection, equality between men and women, the raising of the standard of living and quality of life, and economic and social cohesion and solidarity among Member States.[103] The activities of the EC now specifically include the promotion of coordination between employment policies of the Member States with a view to enhancing their effectiveness by developing a coordinated strategy for employment.[104] In all these activities the Community is obliged, by virtue of Article 3(2) EC, to aim to eliminate inequalities, and to promote equality between men and women.

As if to reinforce the connection drawn in the opening provisions of the EC Treaties between economic and social progress, Title VIII of the EC Treaty on employment follows immediately after the provisions devoted to economic and monetary policy.[105] Article 126(1) EC specifically requires Member States,

[102] ECB, *Labour Market Mismatches in Euro Area Countries*, March 2002, p 5.
[103] Article 2 EC.
[104] Article 3 EC.
[105] S. Sciarra, 'The Employment Title in the Amsterdam Treaty. A Multi-language Legal Discourse' in D. O'Keeffe and P. Twomey (eds), *Legal Issues of the Amsterdam Treaty* (Oxford, Hart Publishing, 1999) pp 157–70; M. Biagi, 'The Impact of European Employment Strategy on the Role of Labour Law and Industrial Relations' (2000) 16 *International Journal of Comparative Labour Law and Industrial Relations* 155–73; R. Blanpain et al. (eds), *Institutional Changes and European Social Policies after the Treaty of Amsterdam* (The Hague, Kluwer Law International, 1998); J. Kenner, 'Employment and Macroeconomics in the EC Treaty: A Legal and Political Symbiosis?' (2000) 7 *Maastricht Journal of European and Comparative Law* 375–97; J. Kenner, 'The EC Employment Title and the "Third Way": Making Soft Law Work?' (1999) 15 *International*

through their employment policies, to contribute to the objective of promoting a skilled, trained and adaptable workforce and labour markets responsive to economic change in a way consistent with the broad guidelines of the economic policies of the Member States and Community adopted pursuant to Title VII. The Treaty thus makes clear that the EU's economic objectives—non-inflationary growth and economic competitiveness—remain paramount.[106] This 'social market' economic approach to the EC's social dimension, which is reflected in the employment title and which, to some extent, has been championed by the Commission since the mid 1990s, is also evident elsewhere. The Council's 2000 recommendations on the broad guidelines of the economic policies of Member States noted that 'progress with the reform of labour markets is mixed: while policies towards activation and prevention were implemented in many Member States, employment disincentives in tax and benefit systems had been tackled in only a few. Moreover, excessively rigid employment protection legislation should be reassessed more actively in order to identify means to foster job creation.' Similar sentiments on the need for greater labour market flexibility have been evident in the Council's annual economic policy guidelines for a number of years, revealing, as Deakin and Reed point out, that flexibilisation of the labour market is seen as a key component of economic policy aimed at achieving high levels of employment.[107]

In accordance with Article 125 EC, Member States and the Community shall work towards developing a coordinated strategy for employment and particularly for promoting a skilled, trained and adaptable workforce and labour markets responsive to economic change with a view to achieving the objectives of the EU and EC defined in Article 2 of both Treaties. Member States are to regard promoting employment as a matter of common concern and shall coordinate their action in this respect within the Council.[108] The task of the Community is to encourage, support and complement cooperation on employment between Member States but the objective of high level of employment shall in any event be taken into consideration in the formulation and implementation of Community policies and actions.[109] The Council may adopt incentive measures designed to encourage cooperation between Member States and to support their action in the field of employment through initiatives aimed at developing

---

Journal of Comparative Labour Law and Industrial Relations 33–60; M. Biagi, 'The Implemention of the Amsterdam Treaty with Regard to Employment: Co-ordination or Convergence?' (1998) 14 *International Journal of Comparative Labour Law and Industrial Relations* 325–36; E. Szyszczak, 'The Evolving European Employment Strategy' in Shaw (ed), above n 2, pp 197–220; and S. Ball, 'The European Employment Strategy: The Will but not the Way?' (2001) 30 *Industrial Law Journal* 353–74.

[106] See Blanpain in Blanpain *et al.* (eds), above n 74, p 32, where he points out that this approach, which favours supply-side economies, is directed at the control of inflation rather than demand and full employment. See also M. Colucci, 'Searching for a European Employment Strategic Initiative' in Blanpain *et al.* (eds), above n 74, pp 101–56, p 128.

[107] Deakin and Reed in Shaw (ed), above n 2, p 90.

[108] Article 126(2) EC.

[109] Article 127(1) and (2) EC.

exchanges of information and best practices, providing comparative analysis and advice as well as promoting innovative approaches and evaluating experiences, in particular by recourse to pilot projects. The Treaty stipulates that these incentive measures shall not include harmonisation of the laws and regulations of the Member States.[110]

CONCLUDING REMARKS

The first employment policy guidelines issued by the Commission in 1998 centred on four main lines of action—entrepreneurship, employability, adaptability and equal opportunities. These four pillars have continued to inform the Community's employment strategy in subsequent years.[111] Entrepreneurship involves, *inter alia*, reducing and simplifying the administrative and tax burdens on SMEs, reducing the costs of hiring additional workers and making the taxation system more employment friendly. This entails reversing the long-term trend towards higher taxes and charges on labour (which had increased from 35 per cent in 1980 to 42 per cent in 1995) in order to encourage job creation and gradually reducing fiscal pressure on labour and non-wage labour costs, particularly those for relatively unskilled and low paid workers. The aim is essentially to make it easier to set up a business and employ people in it. Employability seeks to increase the access of the unemployed and the excluded from the labour market by providing them with the right skills and incentives. The new culture of adaptability is essentially a call for greater flexibility in the workplace. Social

---

[110] Article 129 EC. The Council is to adopt incentive measures following the codecision procedure after consulting the Economic and Social Committee and the Committee of the Regions. In a Declaration annexed to the Treaty of Amsterdam the IGC agreed that these incentive measures should always specify the grounds for taking them based on an objective assessment of their need and the existence of an added value at Community level, their duration, which should not exceed five years and the maximum amount for their financing, which should reflect the incentive nature of such measures.

The Treaty includes a multi-layered decision-making process for the adoption of measures in the employment field. The European Council is charged with the task each year of considering the employment situation in the Community and adopting conclusions thereon, on the basis of a joint annual report by the Council and the Commission. On the basis of the European Council's conclusions, each year the Council shall draw up guidelines which the Member States shall take into account in their employment policies (Article 128(2) EC). Member States shall then inform the Council and Commission of the principal measures taken to implement their employment policies in the light of the Council's guidelines (Article 128(3) EC). The Council shall examine the implementation of the Member States' employment policies in the light of the guidelines that it has established and may make recommendations, if it considers it appropriate, to the Member States (Article 128(4) EC). However, these recommendations are non-binding. A joint annual report on the employment situation in the Community and on the implementation of the Council's guidelines for employment shall be prepared by the Commission and Council and submitted to the European Council (Article 128(5) EC).

[111] European Commission, *Commission communication—Proposal for guidelines for Member States' employment policies 1998*, COM (97) 497. See 2002/177/EC Council Decision of 18 February 2002, OJ 2002 L60/60, and Council Recommendation of 18 February 2002 on the implementation of Member States' employment policies, OJ 2002 L60/70.

partners are encouraged to negotiate agreements on work organisation and flexible working arrangements, including reductions in working time, the development of part-time work, lifelong training and career breaks. More adaptable forms of work contracts are also encouraged. Clearly adaptability covers both the numerical and formal aspects of flexibility referred to earlier. Strengthening the policies for equal opportunities involves increasing employment rates for women and addressing the imbalance in the representation of women or men in certain economic sectors and occupations. Equal opportunities involves measures designed to reconcile work and family life such as policies on parental leave, part-time work and the provision of child care facilities.

Section two of this chapter looked at the case-law of the Court touching on social and labour law issues in diverse fields. No major conclusions were drawn from this analysis apart from the lack of a global vision on the part of the Court in the diverse fields where EC rules on free movement and competition in its widest sense had 'spilled over' with consequences for a wide variety of national social and labour regulations. It does not appear, at least from the case-law discussed, that the Court can be described as having the reregulatory mission which some commentators attribute to it. Having examined the Court's varied involvement with national social and labour law in the past, outlined the political context in which this jurisprudence has been delivered, at least during the last decade, and introduced the new EC Treaty provisions on employment policy, one question remains to be asked. What influence will the flexibility debate and the insertion of the employment title into the EC Treaty have on the Court's deliberation of social and specifically employment related issues in the future?

In its 2002 guidelines for Member States' employment policies, the Council calls on Member States to give particular attention to reducing significantly the overhead costs and administrative burdens for businesses, in particular when an entreprise is being set up and when hiring additional workers. Yet if this is the political spirit informing the EC's employment policy guidelines, what does the future hold for the Court's balancing of interests in, say, indirect sex discrimination cases where female workers claim, for example, that national qualifying thresholds for the enjoyment of protection against unfair dismissal are discriminatory to the extent that they affect a greater proportion of female than male workers. The Court will of course continue to assess whether such thresholds are objectively justified and proportionate, but does this new employment strategy not sanction a lower level of scrutiny than that which protection of the fundamental principle of equality actually merits? If so, then the decline in the level of judicial scrutiny in indirect discrimination cases discussed in chapter four seems perfectly in tune with what the EC's political institutions and its Member States have mandated. With reference to the adaptability pillar, the Council calls for an increase in flexible working arrangements, with the aim of making undertakings productive, competitive and adaptable to industrial change. Yet these are the very objectives which we will see identified by employers in the cases discussed once again in chapter four to legitimise business policies and practices which the Court has recognised affect a disproportionate percentage of workers of one sex and, therefore, as being in need of objective justification and proof of their proportionality.[112]

Member States are now urged, pursuant to the equal opportunities pillar of the EC's employment strategy, to increase employment rates for women. However, if the Court does not demonstrate the same sensitivity which it has in some past cases to national employment policies and practices which are capable of indirectly discriminating against female workers, it is difficult to see how the problem of women's lower pay or their slower progression to the upper echelons of the workforce will be redressed. Female representation in the workforce may increase, but if the prohibition against indirect sex discrimination is diluted by an equivocal judicial stance on objective justification and proportionality, at what price will this greater representation be achieved? In *Danfoss*, the Court recognised that a criterion of so-called adaptability for the granting of wage supplements may work to the disadvantage of female workers who, because of household and family duties for which they are frequently responsible, are not as able as men to organise their working time flexibly.[113] With flexibility now an essential aspect of the new culture of adaptability, it will be essential for the Court to ensure that reliance on criteria such as this does not work systematically against the interests of the employee.

To take just one example of where a change may be felt, in several cases the Court has recently observed that there is no distinction to be drawn between fixed term and indefinite term employment contracts in terms of the enjoyment of EC employment rights and protection.[114] However, the thrust of the new political agenda in the employment field is to reduce non wage labour costs and minimise the adminstrative and financial constraints on business. With this in mind, will the Court revert to what have been the more conservative examples of its employment case-law? In *Kirsammer-Hack*, for example, the applicant also complained that the exclusion of small businesses from the scope of application of Directive 76/207 was indirectly discriminatory. The national court indicated to the Court of Justice why it was concerned that the principle of equal treatment for men and women might preclude legislation such as that applicable in Germany—the legislation deprived part-time employees of protection from unfair dismissal and 90 per cent of all part-time workers in Germany were women.[115] The Court stated, however, that the impugned German legislation

---

[112] See in this respect Cases 96/80 *J.P. Jenkins v Kingsgate (Clothing Products) Ltd.* [1981] ECR 911; and 170/84 *Bilka-Kaufhaus GmbH v Karin Weber* [1986] ECR I–1607.

[113] Case 109/88 *Danfoss* [1989] ECR I–3199, para 21. For concerns about the ambiguous deregulatory/flexibility slant of the employment strategy see also Deakin and Reed in Shaw (ed), above n 2, pp 95–98; and on the relationship between the EC labour law 'acquis' and the European employment strategy N. Bruun, 'The European Employment Strategy and the "Acquis Communautaire" of Labour Law' (2001) 17 *International Journal of Comparative Labour Law and Industrial Relations* 309–24.

[114] See, for example, Cases C–109/00 *Tele Danmark*, paras 28–31 and C–173/99 *BECTU*.

[115] See further below ch 4.

led to a difference in treatment not between part-time employees and others but between all workers employed in small businesses not subject to the system of protection (ie those in undertakings which employ less workers than the stipulated threshold) and all workers employed in undertakings which, by reason of the fact that they employ a greater number of employees, are subject to it.[116] Workers such as the applicant did not benefit from protection against unfair dismissal, although they did not work part-time, while part-time employees benefited from the system of protection when they were employed in undertakings subject to that system; in other words, when they worked in undertakings large enough or with enough employees working enough hours to bring them outside the exemption. As a result, the Court held that the high proportion of women among part-time employees in Germany to which the national court referred did not justify the conclusion that the impugned provision constitutes indirect discrimination contrary to Directive 76/207. There would be such discrimination only if it were established that small businesses employ a considerably higher percentage of women than men and, even then, it could be objectively justified. The German government and the Commission had submitted that legislation such as that in question is objectively justified when it forms part of a series of measures intended to alleviate the constraints burdening small businesses which play an essential role in economic development and the creation of employment in the Community.[117] The Court concurred:

> by providing that directives adopted in the fields of health and safety of workers are to avoid imposing administrative, financial and legal constraints in a way which would hold back the creation and development of small and medium-sized undertakings, Article 118a of the EEC Treaty indicates that such undertakings may be the subject of special economic measures.[118]

While more recent decisions of the Court have cast some doubt on the general applicability of this statement,[119] one wonders whether this is what is to be expected from the Court in the future given the political and, to a certain extent, economic, context in which it now operates? Whether or not answers to the questions raised in this and the two previous chapters are provided in the substantive discussion of specific aspects of EC employment law that follows, these chapters provide the context in which readers are invited to read the critique provided.

---

[116] The Report for the Hearing in Case C–189/91 *Kirsammer-Hack*, p 6189, reveals that the referring court's argument was slightly more sophisticated than the Court gave it credit for. It had said that the great majority of workers whose hours of work fall below the threshold laid down in the impugned German law were women. Consequently, most of the undertakings which are excluded from the scope of the system of protection against unfair dismissal because of the number of part-time workers they employ are undertakings which employ women on a part-time basis.

[117] Advocate General Darmon (para 102 of his Opinion in Case C–189/91 *Kirsammer-Hack*) submitted that favouring the promotion of employment, and concentrating efforts in a sector of industry most able to adapt to economic changes figured amongst the objectives sought.

[118] Case C–189/91 *Kirsammer-Hack*, para 34.

[119] See Case C–173/99 *BECTU*.

4

Economic v Social Policy Considerations in Indirect Sex Discrimination Cases

INTRODUCTION

IT IS WIDELY recognised that, at least until amendments and additions following the Maastricht and Amsterdam Treaties, provision for social policy in the EC Treaty was a fairly lame duck. The former Articles 117 and 118 EEC may have contained some high-sounding objectives—*inter alia*, the promotion of improved working conditions and a raised standard of living—but these provisions were, in the words of the Court of Justice,[1] of a purely programmatic nature. Even the introduction of new provisions in the 1990s did not dispel misgivings about the Member States' and hence the Community legislator's willingness to take the area of social policy seriously. Not all Member States agreed originally, for example, to be subject to the Maastricht Social Protocol, or to adopt the related Social Policy Agreement (SPA),[2] and measures negotiated within the context of the SPA often fell short of expectations.[3]

The exception amongst the Treaty's social provisions was, of course, Article 119 EEC, now Article 141 EC, which provides that the Member States shall ensure that the principle of equal pay for male and female workers for equal work or work of equal value is applied.[4] However, even a cursory examination

---

[1] See Case 149/77 *Gabrielle Defrenne v Société Anonyme Belge de Navigation Aérienne Sabena (Defrenne III)* [1978] ECR 1365, paras 19 and 31; Case 126/86 *Fernando Roberto Giménez Zaera v Instituto Nacional de la Seguridad Social* [1987] ECR 3697, paras 11 and 13; and Case C–72/91 *Firma Sloman Neptun Schiffarts AG v Seebetriebsrat Bodo Ziesemer* [1993] ECR I–887.

[2] A number of important changes were made to the former Articles 117–20 EC by the Amsterdam Treaty and the renumbering of these provisions does not perfectly correspond to what they previously contained. See briefly E. Ellis, 'Recent Developments in European Community Sex Equality Law' (1998) 35 *Common Market Law Review* 379–408, 379–81. Following a change of government, the United Kingdom's acceptance of the Maastricht Social Chapter meant the inclusion of the SPA in the EC Treaty.

[3] See, for example, Council Directive 96/34/EC of 3 June 1996 on the framework agreement on parental leave concluded by UNICE, CEEP and the ETUC, OJ 1996 L145/4, discussed in greater detail below ch 5.

[4] The reference to work of equal value, which was previously only to be found in Article 1 of Council Directive 75/117/EEC of 10 February 1975 on the approximation of the laws of the Member States relating to the application of the principle of equal pay for men and women, OJ 1975 L45/19, was added to the EC Treaty by the Amsterdam Treaty. See generally Case 96/80

of the structure and operation of the European Union's employment market and a glance at academic literature reveals this provision's limited success. Article 141 EC has obviously not eliminated the wage gap which exists in many, if not the majority, of sectors, between the pay received by male and female workers, nor has it done away with the factors which disadvantage female workers in terms of their access to the labour market, their enjoyment of equal working conditions within it or their concentration in certain sectors.[5] But to expect a single Treaty provision, itself of limited scope, to achieve all that in little over twenty five years since its direct effect was first recognised is perhaps to expect too much; the law, as many commentators have pointed out, being but one imperfect means of bringing about social change.[6] In any case, granting individual remedies to litigants who are able either because of their own financial and legal resources, or by virtue of help from a third party, such as the British Equal Opportunities Commission, to mount legal challenges, is clearly an inadequate way to remedy problems which frequently and at their most resistant, are widespread and structural.[7] In the hands of the Judges of the European Court of

---

J. P. Jenkins v Kingsgate Clothing [1981] ECR 911, para 22 (relationship between the Directive and the principle of equal pay outlined in Article 141 EC); Case 157/86 *Murphy v Bord Telecom Eireann* [1988] ECR 673 (equal pay for work of equal value); Case C–309/97 *Angestelltenbetriebsrat der Wiener Gebietskrankenkasse v Wiener Gebietskrankenkasse* (hereafter 'AWG') [1999] ECR I–2685 (what constitutes the 'same work'); and Case C–320/00 *A. Lawrence and Others v Regent Office Care Ltd, Commercial Catering Group, Mitie Secure Services Ltd.*, judgment of 17 September 2002, nyr ECR (comparison of the pay of male and female workers under different employers).

[5] On the issue of pay see A. McColgan, *Just Wages for Women* (Oxford, Clarendon Press, 1997); C. Bourn and J. Whitmore, *Discrimination and Equal Pay* (London, Sweet & Maxwell, 1989). For a global comparison of wages see D. Robinson, 'Les rémunérations comparées des hommes et des femmes au niveau des professions' (1998) 137 *Revue internationale du travail* 3–36; and, in the specific context of the legal academy, McGlynn, C., 'Women, representation and the legal academy' (1999) 19 *Legal Studies* 68–92. On sex discrimination in the labour market generally see, *inter alia*, S. Fredman, 'European Community Discrimination Law: A Critique' (1992) 21 *Industrial Law Journal* 119–34, 119; F. Beveridge and S. Nott, 'Gender Auditing—Making the Community Work for Women' in T. Hervey and D. O'Keeffe (eds), *Sex Equality Law in the European Union* (Chichester, John Wiley, 1996) pp 383–98, p 385; B. Hepple, 'Equality and Discrimination' in P. Davies *et al* (eds), *European Community Labour Law: Principles and Perspectives. Liber Amicorum Lord Wedderburn of Charlton* (Oxford, Clarendon Press, 1996) pp 237–59, pp 240–41; S. Mazey, 'EC Action on Behalf of Women: The Limits of Legislation' (1988) 27 *Journal of Common Market Studies* 63–84; F. von Prondzynski and W. Richards, 'Equal Opportunities in the Labour Market: Tackling Indirect Sex Discrimination' (1995) 1 *European Public Law* 117–35; and R. Townshend-Smith, *Sex Discrimination in Employment* (London, Sweet & Maxwell, 1989).

[6] See, *inter alia*, C. Barnard, 'Gender Equality in the EU: A Balance Sheet' in P. Alston, (ed), *The EU and Human Rights* (Oxford, OUP, 1999) pp 215–79, p 216; and Fredman (1992), above n 5, 134, who argues that '[L]egal strategies must be accompanied by a much more radical focus on structural disadvantages and the causes thereof. The primary requirement is a restructuring of the work environment to take account of family needs, and this demands not only effective legal concepts but also more widespread political and social mobilisation and the appropriate resource allocation. . . . The law alone cannot bear the burden of radical institutional change.'

[7] Herein lies the crux of the problem. Sex segmentation in the labour market means that it is difficult, if not impossible, for industrial tribunals and labour courts to overcome wage gaps and limits cases where men and women can be regarded as similarly situated. As regards equal value claims and claims of indirect discrimination, the financial costs for potential litigants are very high and the fear of victimisation once the claim is complete must be a strong disincentive—a fact recognised by the Court in Case C–185/97 *Belinda Coote v Granada Hospitality Ltd* [1998] ECR I–5199.

Justice, what Article 141 EC has done, however, is to ensure that sex equality constitutes a general principle of EC law whose observance the Court of Justice must ensure, and the achievement of such equality figures prominently amongst the EC's objectives. The case-law which this provision and its progeny have generated has also inevitably brought the Court of Justice, for better or worse, into a spotlight to which the EU's citizens pay attention, if only cursorily.

The focus of this chapter is the case-law of the Court of Justice on indirect sex discrimination. Until the adoption of Directive 97/80 on the burden of proof,[8] EC legislation contained no definition of what constitutes indirect discrimination for the purposes of Article 141 EC and the Equality Directives. Article 2(2) of the Burden of Proof Directive states that 'indirect discrimination shall exist where an apparently neutral provision, criterion or practice disadvantages a substantially higher proportion of the members of one sex unless that provision, criterion or practice is appropriate and necessary and can be justified by objective factors unrelated to sex.'[9] This definition corresponds to that developed by the Court in case-law dating back to the early 1980s, when it handed down its ruling in the *Bilka* case.[10] As in other areas of EC law, the concept of indirect discrimination in the field of sex equality relies on the establishment of a *prima facie* case of discrimination by the complainant which is regarded as contrary to EC law unless the Member State or employer provides an objective justification unrelated to sex for the impugned measure or policy and demonstrates that the latter complies with the requirements of the principle of proportionality. In subsequent sections, the evolution of this case-law will be examined, with special attention being paid to the objective justifications relied on in indirect sex discrimination cases by Member States and private sector employers. Fundamental differences emerge in the standard of scrutiny exercised by the Court with respect to objective justifications when what is challenged as indirectly discriminatory is national legislation concerning social security or touching on some other area of domestic social policy.

This chapter also examines the tension which one finds in these cases between economic and social policy considerations and questions whether this tension is

---

[8] Council Directive 97/80/EC of 15 December 1997 on the burden of proof in cases of discrimination based on sex, OJ 1998 L14/6. Articles 2(1) and 4(1) of Council Directive 76/207/EEC of 9 February 1976 on the implementation of the principle of equal treatment for men and women as regards access to employment, vocational training and promotion and working conditions, OJ 1976 L39/40 and Council Directive 79/7/EEC of 19 December 1979 on the progressive implementation of the principle of equal treatment for men and women in matters of social security, OJ 1979 L6/24, respectively, simply referred to the prohibition of indirect discrimination without providing a definition of the latter.

[9] Compare with Article 2(2)(b) of Council Directive 2000/78/EC of 27 November 2000 establishing a general framework for equal treatment in employment and occupation, OJ 2000 L 303/16, which provides that indirect discrimination shall be taken to occur where an apparently neutral provision or practice would put persons having a particular religion or belief, a particular disability, a particular age, or a particular sexual orientation at a particular disadvantage compared with other persons.

[10] Case 170/84 *Bilka-Kaufhaus GmbH v Karin Weber von Harz* [1986] ECR 1607.

not the inevitable consequence of the Court operating in an individual rights-based legal order largely of its own creation, yet one which is bound by avowed free market goals and aspirations.[11] Article 4 EC states that, for the purposes set out in Article 2 EC (including the promotion of equality between men and women), the activities of the Member States and the Community shall include the adoption of an economic policy conducted in accordance with the principle of an open market economy with free competition.[12] Townshend-Smith points to the tension which results from the Treaty's commitment to both the freedom of the market, including the labour market, and the removal of gender discrimination in pay, which is by definition an interference with the market.[13] Pursuant to the Employment Title introduced by the Amsterdam Treaty, specifically Article 125 EC, Member States and the Community are now mandated to promote a skilled, trained and adaptable workforce and labour markets responsive to economic change. The aims and targets proposed to Member States pursuant to the Employment Title thus further underline this tension. Finally, the operation of Article 234 EC in the context of case-law on indirect sex discrimination is assessed. Given the limitations on the Court's role inherent in the preliminary reference procedure, the division of competences between national and Community courts which it demands and the ambivalent nature of the Court's adjudicative function thereunder, it is perhaps unsurprising when the latter fails to tackle indirect sex discrimination cases entirely to the satisfaction of litigants, national courts and Court-watchers and consumers generally.

[11] On the origins of Article 141 EC see, *inter alia*, C. Barnard, 'The Economic Objectives of Article 119 EC' in Hervey and O'Keeffe (eds), above n 5, pp 321–34; C. Barnard, 'EC "Social" Policy' in P. Craig and G. De Búrca (eds), *The Evolution of EU Law* (Oxford, OUP, 1999) pp 479–516, pp 498–99; S. Deakin, 'Labour Law as Market Regulation: the Economic Foundations of European Social Policy' in Davies *et al.* (eds), above n 5, pp 63–93; S. Fredman, 'Social Law in the European Union: The impact of the lawmaking process' in P. Craig and C. Harlow (eds), *Lawmaking in the European Union* (London, Kluwer Law International, 1998) pp 386–411.

[12] Although the Court has expressly rejected the argument that this provision has direct legal effects for individuals—Case C–9/99 *Echirolles Distribution SA v Association du Dauphiné and others* [2000] ECR I–8207, para 25. See G. More, 'The Principle of Equal Treatment: From Market Unifier to Fundamental Right?' in Craig and De Búrca (eds) (1999), above n 11, pp 517–53, p 542: 'the supra-national and market-based roots of Community law place particular limits on the operation of equal treatment as a constitutional principle in Community law'; H. Fenwick and T. Hervey, 'Sex Equality in the Single Market: New Directions for the European Court of Justice' (1995) 32 *Common Market Law Review* 443–70, 469; S. Simitis, 'Dismantling or Strengthening Labour Law: The Case of the European Court of Justice' (1996) 2 *European Law Journal* 156–76, 158: 'Where, like in the case of Article [141] EC, a rule as basic for the regulation of the employment relationship as the employer's duty not to discriminate and, hence, to ensure equal pay for women and men, is solely perceived through the filter of competition, little room, if any, is left for labour law.'; B. Hepple, 'Social Values and European Law' (1995) 48 *Current Legal Problems* 39–61, 42; and generally G. Majone, 'The European Community Between Social Policy and Social Regulation' (1993) 31 *Journal of Common Market Studies* 153–70, 156: 'The economic liberalism which pervades the founding Treaty and its subsequent revisions give priority to the allocation function of public policy over distributional objectives. Hence, the best rationale for social initiatives at Community level is one which stresses the efficiency-improving aspects of the proposed measures.'

[13] R. Townshend-Smith, 'Economic Defences to Equal Pay Claims' in Hervey and O'Keeffe (eds), above n 5, pp 35–48, p 36.

THE DUAL ECONOMIC AND SOCIAL AIMS OF EC SEX EQUALITY LAW:
FROM *DEFRENNE* TO *SCHRÖDER*

To examine the role which the Court of Justice has played in the field of sex discrimination it is useful, if not essential, to start at the beginning—and in the beginning there was Ms Defrenne. In three well-known cases before the Court the applicant challenged the policy of her now defunct employer, Sabena airlines, to terminate contracts of employment with female air hostesses on their reaching the age of forty. The aggrieved Ms. Defrenne refused to go quietly, however, and challenged her dismissal as contrary to the principle of equal pay in the EC Treaty.[14]

In *Defrenne I* the Court essentially held that statutory retirement pension schemes do not come within the concept of pay under Article 141 EC, a finding which had important implications in the field of pensions. Of particular interest for the purposes of this chapter is the decision of the Court in *Defrenne II*. Picking up on the reference by the Advocate General in *Defrenne I* to Article 141's economic and social foundations, the Court held that, in the light of the different stages of the development of social legislation in the various Member States, the aim of this EC Treaty provision is to avoid a situation in which undertakings established in States which have actually implemented the principle of equal pay suffer a competitive disadvantage in intra-Community competition as compared with undertakings established in States which have not yet eliminated discrimination against female workers as regards pay. In addition, Article 141 EC forms part of the social objectives of the Community, which is not merely an economic union, but is also intended to ensure social progress and seek the constant improvement of living and working conditions. This double economic and social aim of Article 141 EC indicates that the principle of equal pay forms part of the foundations of the Community.[15] The Court went on to recognise the direct effect of Article 141 EC but to limit its effect in time. Article

[14] See Case 80/70 *Defrenne I*, (on the scope and definition of the concept of pay within the meaning of Article 141 EC); Case 43/75 *Gabrielle Defrenne v Société Anonyme Belge de Navigation Aérienne Sabena (Defrenne II)* [1976] ECR 455 (on the direct effect of Article 141 EC); and Case 149/77 *Defrenne III* (on the scope of application of Article 141 EC and the existence of a general principle of equality requiring equal working conditions for men and women). On the role of Defrenne's lawyers see D. Wincott, 'The Court of Justice and the European Policy Process' in J.J. Richardson, (ed), *European Union. Power and Policy-making* (London and New York, Routledge, 1996) pp 170–84, p 178; and R. Dehousse, 'Integration Through Law Revisited: Some Thoughts on the Juridification of the European Political Process' in F. Snyder (ed), *The Europeanisation of Law: The Legal Effects of European Integration* (Oxford, Hart Publishing, 2000) pp 15–29, p 24.
[15] For Advocate General Trabucchi, Case 43/75 *Defrenne II*, although of modest financial importance, presented the Court with the opportunity to clarify certain aspects of the protection which fundamental rights receive within the framework of the Community structure. Clearly he viewed the reference procedure under Article 234 EC as a means not simply of dispute resolution at national level but also as a judicial mechanism for elaborating public interest considerations. See above ch 2 for a discussion of dispute resolution and public interest models of litigation in the context of Article 234 EC.

141 EC could not be invoked to support equal pay claims preceding the date of the Court's judgment, unless legal proceedings had already been initiated.[16] Finally, in *Defrenne III*, the Court declined to extend the principle of equality enshrined in Article 141 EC beyond pay to other working conditions. It held, however, that there can be no doubt that the elimination of discrimination based on sex forms part of the fundamental rights which the Court is bound to ensure.[17]

Almost a quarter of a century later, the Court reasserted the fundamental nature of the principle of equal pay and the consequences flowing from it. The *Schröder* case[18] concerned the discriminatory nature of the exclusion of part-time workers from occupational pension schemes, the temporal limitation applicable to retroactive requests by those part-time workers for equal treatment as regards membership of such schemes and the interaction between national, in this case German constitutional, law and EC law. Of particular interest, however, was the question whether one Member State can maintain a wide-ranging principle of equal treatment when that principle is not enforced to the same extent in all Member States, with the result that employers established in the first Member State may suffer a competitive disadvantage. The Court of Justice recalled the twofold economic and social purpose of Article 141 EC which it had first identified in *Defrenne II*. It then pointed out that it had repeatedly held that the right not to be discriminated against on grounds of sex is one of the fundamental human rights whose observance the Court has a duty to ensure. It continued: 'In view of that case-law, it must be concluded that the economic aim pursued by Article [141] of the Treaty, namely the elimination of distortions of competition between undertakings established in different Member States, is secondary to the social aim pursued by the same provision, which constitutes the expression of a fundamental human right.'[19] As a result,

---

[16] The Irish and British governments had intervened in the case to argue that allowing Article 141 EC retrospective direct effect would pose an intolerable financial burden on Member States and employers who would not be able to meet claims for arrears in pay. This was not the last time that a coalition of sorts was formed between these two Member States to press home similar arguments—see below for a discussion of Cases C–317/93 *Inge Nolte v Landsversicherungsanstalt Hannover* [1995] ECR I–4625 and C–444/93 *Ursula Megner and Hildegard Scheffel v Innungskrankenkasse Vorderpfalz* [1995] ECR I–4741.

[17] Case 149/77 *Defrenne III*, para 27. See subsequently Joined Cases 75/82 and 117/82 *Razzouk and Beydoun v Commission* [1984] ECR 1509 for recognition of the fundamental nature of this principle in the context of the EU's own staff cases; and Case C–13/94 *P. v S. and Cornwall County Council* [1996] ECR I–2143, paras 18–19, where the Court recognised that Directive 76/207 is simply the expression, in the relevant field, of the principle of equality, which is one of the fundamental principles of Community law. The Treaty of Amsterdam subsequently included the promotion of sex equality amongst the EC Treaty's tasks (Article 2 EC) and the list of its activities (Article 3 EC). In addition, the preamble to the TEU contains a title which confirms the Member States' attachment to fundamental social rights as defined in the European Social Charter and the Community Charter of the Fundamental Social Rights of Workers.

[18] Case C–50/96 *Deutsche Telekom AG v Lilli Schröder* [2000] ECR I–743.

[19] Case C–50/96 *Schröder*, para 57. See also Case C–67/96 *Albany International BV v Stichting Bedrijfspensioenfonds Textielindustrie* [1999] ECR I–5751, para 54.

the fact that, prior to *Defrenne II*, the principle of equal pay for men and women was directly applicable against employers in the Federal Republic of Germany, while that was not yet the case in other Member States, did not affect the application of national rules ensuring observance of that principle in the former State.

The recognition in *Schröder* of the primarily social objective of Article 141 EC is clearly to be welcomed. However, one cannot but wonder whether the Court's Sixth Chamber, the author of the decision, was engaged in some wishful thinking. *Defrenne II* was recognition by the Court of the inherent conflict between economic and social objectives in equal pay and, implicitly, equal treatment cases, with the fundamental principle of equality acting as a balance. *Schröder* seemed to dismiss the existence of this tension by recognising the paramount objective of Article 141 EC as social. Yet the Court's case-law indicates that the tension between the economic and fundamental principles based approach remains one of the unresolved issues of principle and policy in this area.[20] EC labour law specialists, anti-discrimination lawyers and those with an interest in EC social policy generally continue to lament the dominance of economic considerations in the sex equality case-law of the Court. Criticism has been particularly strong as regards the Court's indirect sex discrimination jurisprudence and, in particular, as regards its attitude to economic as opposed to social policy considerations when it is obliged to examine objective justifications of apparent discrimination or when it directs the national referring court to do so. An examination of this case-law in the following sections suggests that the attempt in *Schröder* to assert the fundamental rights underpinnings of EC sex equality law will prove insufficient on its own to realign the Court's approach to sex discrimination.

THE DEVELOPMENT OF THE EARLY JURISPRUDENCE OF THE COURT ON
INDIRECT SEX DISCRIMINATION

The merits and weaknesses of substantive as distinct from formal equality are generally at the heart of any academic discussion of sexual inequality and its redress. The European Union has proved to be no exception in this regard.[21] The Court of Justice is seen by most commentators, not without regret or criticism, as having favoured a formal understanding of the principle of equality

---

[20] See also C. Docksey, 'The Principle of Equality Between Women and Men as a Fundamental Right Under EC Law' (1991) 20 *Industrial Law Journal* 258–80, 275–76.
[21] See, for example, in the particular context of affirmative action, C. Barnard and T. Hervey, 'Softening the approach to quotas: positive action after *Marschall*' (1998) 20 *Journal of Social Welfare and Family Law* 333–52; or H. Fenwick, 'From Formal to Substantive Equality: the Place of Affirmative Action in EU Sex Equality Law' (1998) 4 *European Public Law* 507–16. Part of the discussion in this section comes from G.F. Mancini and S. O'Leary, 'The new frontiers of sex equality law in the European Union' (1999) 24 *European Law Review* 331–53.

whereby like is treated strictly as like, with the resulting assumption that women must in all relevant respects be like men in order to be equally treated.[22] One of the results of this approach is said to be that, whereas a few women may gain access to the preconditions necessary to assert equality on male terms, the majority do not. Other authors lament the Court's inability or unwillingness to dig out the roots of sexual inequality and the disadvantaging of women in the labour market and the resulting persistence of the structures which give rise to that disadvantage.

In contrast to formal equality, substantive equality rejects the male norm and seeks to situate notions of equality in the context of women's historically and socially inferior status and position of disadvantage.[23] It was to a substantive notion of equality that the Court was aspiring in *Marschall v Land Nordrhein-Westfalen* when it accepted that:

> even where male and female candidates are equally qualified, male candidates tend to be promoted in preference to female candidates particularly because of prejudices and stereotypes concerning the role and capacities of women in working life and the fear, for example, that women will interrupt their careers more frequently, that owing to household and family duties they will be less flexible in their working hours, or that they will be absent from work more frequently because of pregnancy, childbirth and breastfeeding.[24]

Thus women's different situation—the differences being a result of biological, social, economic, cultural and historic factors which do not affect men in the same way, if at all—is taken into consideration.

But as *Marschall* demonstrates, if the Court is criticised for its overly formal approach, the Court Reports are not without examples of such a substantive approach to equal treatment either. The Court's case-law on indirect discrimination bespeaks, at the very least, an awareness of the need for a substantive approach to equality,[25] as do aspects of its pregnancy jurisprudence.[26] As regards its early case-law on indirect discrimination, most commentators con-

---

[22] See, for example, T. Hervey and J. Shaw, 'Women, Work and Care: Women's Dual Role and Double Burden in EC Sex Equality Law' (1998) 8 *Journal of European Social Policy* 43–63, 48.

[23] See generally C.A. MacKinnon, 'Reflections on Sex Equality Under Law' (1991) 100 *Yale Law Journal* 1281–328; and, in the specific context of the EU, Hervey and Shaw (1998), *ibid.*, 48.

[24] Case C–409/95 [1997] ECR I–6363, para 29. See also Case C–158/97 *Georg Badeck and Others v Hessischer Ministerpräsident and Landesanwalt beim Staatgerichtshof des Landes Hessen* [2000] ECR I–1875, para 21. Although, as Fredman points out, the Court in Case C–409/95 *Hellmut Marschall v Land Nordrhein Westfalen* [1997] ECR I–6363 did not renounce the adherence to individuality which had been signalled so strongly in Case C–450/93 *v Eckhard Kalanke* v *Freie Hansestadt Breman* [1995] ECR I–3051 (S. Fredman, 'Affirmative Action and the European Court of Justice: A Critical Analysis' in J. Shaw (ed), *Social Law and Policy in an Evolving European Union* (Oxford, Hart Publishing, 2000) pp 171–95, p 179).

[25] See also L. Senden, 'Positive Action in the European Union Put to the Test. A Negative Score?' (1996) 3 *Maastricht Journal of International and Comparative Law* 146, 158–59.

[26] See, for example, Case C–136/95 *Caisse nationale d'assurance vieillesse des travailleurs salariés v Thibault* [1998] ECR I–2011, para 26, where the Court stated that the result pursued by Directive 76/207 is substantive, not formal, equality.

gratulated the Court for its rigorous scrutiny of apparently gender-neutral factors and its rejection of arguments to the effect that group disadvantage which appeared to be gender based had in fact come about by chance. The Court was originally seen as :

> committing itself to a substantive equality approach in its sex equality jurisprudence, an approach which attempts to recognize the real situation of many women, as opposed to a formal equality approach which goes no further than asking whether like is treated as like, and therefore cannot recognize or address the gendered social context within which women take part in employment.[27]

However, satisfaction with the rulings of the Court and its stance on equality has waned in recent years, as will be seen in subsequent sections.[28]

Uncertain Beginnings

The Court's first recognised encounter with indirect sex discrimination was in the *Jenkins* case, when a part-time female worker complained that her hourly rate of pay was lower than that paid to a male colleague employed full-time to perform the same work. Impressed, it seems, by the argument that the employer in question had not *intended* to discriminate against his part-time workers on the grounds of their sex,[29] the Court held that the fact that part-time work is paid at an hourly rate lower than that for full-time work does not amount *per se* to discrimination prohibited by Article 141 EC. According to the Court, there is no discrimination if the difference in pay between the two categories is attributable to factors which are objectively justified and are in no way related to any discrimination based on sex : 'Such may be the case, in particular, when by giving hourly rates of pay which are lower for part-time work than those for full-time work the employer is endeavouring on economic grounds which may be objectively justified, to encourage full-time work irrespective of the sex of the worker.'[30] It was for the national court to determine with respect to the facts of

---

[27] See H. Fenwick, 'Indirect Discrimination in Equal Pay Claims: Backward Steps in the European Court of Justice' (1995) 1 *European Public Law* 331–38, 332.

[28] See, *inter alia*, Ellis (1998) above n 2, who notes that at the end of the 1990s 'it is the Court of Justice which often appears to have lost sight of the objectives of the [sex equality] legislation and to be operating as the drag on the system.' Contrast this with her appraisal of the Court's earlier performance when scrutinising indirect discrimination: 'the Court's distinctly robust attitude to claims of justification have forced national courts, in particular those in the United Kingdom, to reject their former uncritical stance and to subject the argument to far closer and more demanding scrutiny than hitherto'. (E. Ellis, 'Gender Discrimination Law in the EC' in J. Dine and B. Watt (eds), *Discrimination Law: Concepts, Limitations and Justifications* (London, Longman, 1996) pp 14–30, p 30).

[29] According to the employer, the reason for the chosen pay policy was that the company wanted to discourage absenteeism, encourage all employees to work a full-time week and ensure optimum use of machinery.

[30] Case 96/80 *Jenkins*, paras 11–12. Further sympathy for the economic position of the employer can be found in the Opinion of Advocate General Warner, who pointed out that Kingsgate was a small firm, not in a strong financial position and typical of many in the United Kingdom clothing

the case, its history and the employer's intention, whether such a pay policy, although represented as a difference based on weekly working hours is, or is not, in reality discrimination based on the sex of the worker.[31]

The *Bilka* Test: Indirect Sex Discrimination and the Private Sector

Some of the uncertainty which *Jenkins* had provoked was resolved in *Bilka*, in particular as regards the treatment of economic justifications of differential treatment and the intent of the employer. Bilka-Kaufhaus, a large German department store, only admitted part-time workers to its supplementary pension scheme on condition that they had worked full-time for at least fifteen years, over a total period of twenty years. The pension scheme was considered an integral part of the employees' contract of service. Ms. Weber had been employed first as a full-time sales assistant and then, at her own request, in a part-time position. On retirement from her post, she did not fulfil the necessary conditions for admission to the company pension scheme. She claimed that the requirement of a minimum period of full-time employment for admission to the pension scheme disadvantaged female workers, since they were more likely to take part-time work to cope with family and childcare responsibilities.

In its defence, Bilka pointed to the scarcity of labour prior to 1977 and the difficulty of attracting job-seekers to the retail trade where working hours were unattractive. These reasons, in addition to the lower ancillary costs which employment of full-time workers entailed and their availability throughout opening hours, explained why full-time workers were given preferential treatment.[32] Bilka claimed that these constituted objectively justified economic reasons independent of the worker's sex. The Commission, however, emphasised the dual economic/social objectives of Article 141 EC and argued that, from the social perspective, that provision could only be effective if the employer's pay policy does in fact take into account the living and working conditions of women employed part-time. Advocate General Darmon obviously understood the drift of this argument, but was unwilling to accept its consequences for employers:

---

industry at the time. The Advocate General also pointed out that the applicant, with the support of her trade union and the Equal Opportunities Commission, had been able to present her case fully to the Court, while the Court had not had the chance to hear the arguments of her employer, who could not afford legal representation and had been turned down for legal aid. To the extent that the Court is assuming or having to assume a greater dispute resolution role, the fact that both parties to a case at national level do not have access to it, and the meagre funds it possesses for the grant of legal aid, are clearly problematic.

[31] Advocate General Warner argued that the Court had to reconcile the need to prevent disguised discrimination against women with the need to prevent injustice to an employer who differentiates between full-time and part-time workers 'for sound reasons unconnected with their sex'—Case 96/80 *Jenkins*, 936.

[32] Case 170/84 *Bilka*, 1614 of the Advocate General's Opinion and para 7 of the judgment.

The socio-cultural constraints faced by working women must not be exploited by employers. Nor, however, do they impose on employers additional obligations restricting their normal freedom to determine staff policy. An employer cannot be required to take over the rôle of the authorities in constructing a pension scheme which will compensate for special difficulties faced by workers who have family responsibilities. Article [141 EC] lays down positive duties only on the Member States and not on commercial undertakings which are subject only to an obligation not to discriminate.[33]

The Court, in accordance with the traditional division of functions in an Article 234 EC reference procedure, held that it was for the national court to determine whether and to what extent the grounds put forward by an employer explaining the adoption of a pay practice which applies independently of a worker's sex but in fact affects more women than men, may be regarded as objectively justified economic grounds. If the national court finds that the measures chosen by the employer correspond to a real need on the part of the undertaking, are appropriate with a view to achieving the objectives pursued and are necessary to that end, the fact that the measures affect a greater number[34] of women than men is not sufficient to show that they constitute an infringement of Article 141 EC. Once a case of apparent indirect discrimination is established, the burden of proof shifts to the employer, who must justify the discrimination with reference to objective factors unconnected with the worker's sex. Like the Advocate General, the Court found no basis, in Article 141 EC or the Treaty generally, for requiring an employer to organise its occupational pensions scheme in such a manner as to take into account the particular difficulties faced by persons with family responsibilities in meeting the conditions for entitlement to such a pension.

The *Rinner-Kühn* Test: Indirect Sex Discrimination and National Legislation

The first case to come before the Court of Justice in which an employee claimed that statutory provisions gave rise to indirect discrimination was *Rinner-Kühn,*[35] a case which also involved a part-time worker. Ms Rinner-Kühn, supported by her trade union, claimed that the refusal to grant sick pay to part-time workers on the grounds that they did not fulfil the conditions imposed by the relevant German law on sick pay was indirectly discriminatory against women contrary to Article 141 EC, since a significantly greater proportion of part-timers are female.

---

[33] Case 170/84 *Bilka*, 1618.

[34] Note the reference to numbers here, while percentages or proportions are favoured in other cases, a fact which, *inter alia*, prompted the House of Lords to refer Case C–167/97R. *v Secretary of State for Employment, ex parte Nicole Seymour-Smith and Laura Perez* [1999] ECR I–623.

[35] Case 171/88 *Ingrid Rinner-Kühn v FWW Spezial-Gebäudereinigung GmbH & Co. KG* [1989] ECR 2743.

146   *Employment Law at the European Court of Justice*

The national labour court which heard the case regarded this exclusion of part-time workers from entitlement to statutory sick pay as discriminatory. Part-time employment, in its opinion, is a form of gainful activity pursued mainly by married women who see in this form of work a chance to reconcile job and family. There is thus a close link between part-time work and jobs traditionally performed by women. In support of its legislation the German government maintained that part-time workers were not as integrated in, or as dependent on, the undertaking employing them as other workers and that, consequently, the conditions for obliging their employer to furnish them with assistance, including the continuation of their salary, were not met. The Commission, for its part, could not understand why it should be economically defensible and socially necessary to allow full-time workers to continue to receive their salary for six weeks while this right is refused to part-time workers who are socially less favoured. Such a rule, the Commission argued, removed protection precisely where it was most needed.

Distinguishing the approach of the Court in *Jenkins* and *Bilka* on the grounds that the former concerned an employer's wage policy while the latter involved a contractual pension scheme, Advocate General Darmon was strongly against raising a similar presumption of incompatibility as against a provision of national legislation. He felt that it should fall to the complainant to prove not only the fact of discrimination but also that there are structural labour market factors which demonstrate that the measure must be related to sex.[36] There is an essential difference, in his view, between an employer, for whom wages policy is one of the most important aspects of his undertaking, and a legislature, which is responsible for the general well-being and which must take into account a large number of social, economic and political circumstances amongst which the respective numbers of male and female workers is just one.[37] An employer may be assumed to be aware of inequality in the number of male and female workers employed by him or her, but, when adopting national legislation, a national legislature cannot.

In a remarkably brief judgment the Court rejected the Advocate General's approach.[38] It pointed instead to the obligation imposed on Member States by Article 141 EC and the statistics made available to it by the national court which showed that considerably less women than men worked the minimum number of weekly or monthly hours required to entitle them to sick pay. In those circumstances it held, as it had in *Bilka*, that it was for the Member State whose legislation was challenged to reverse the presumption of indirect discrimination

---

[36] E. Ellis, 'The Definition of Discrimination in EC Sex Equality Law' (1994) 19 *European Law Review* 563–80, 575, regarded the Advocate General's approach as 'extraordinarily generous'.

[37] Case 171/88 *Rinner-Kühn*, 2754 of the Advocate General's Opinion.

[38] Having agreed with him, however, that sick pay constitutes pay within the meaning of Article 141 EC. On the unclear consequences of this ruling for sick pay paid by the State see J. Shaw, annotation of Case 171/88 *Rinner-Kühn* (1989) 14 *European Law Review* 428–34, 429.

with reference to objective factors unrelated to any discrimination. Thus, as in *Bilka*, if the Member State could show that the means chosen met a necessary aim of its social policy and that they were suitable and requisite for attaining that aim, the mere fact that the provision affected a much greater number of female workers than male workers could not be regarded as constituting an infringement of Article 141 EC. As regards the justification put forward by the German government during the course of proceedings, the Court specifically stated that: 'those considerations, in so far as they are only generalizations about certain categories of workers, do not enable criteria which are both objective and unrelated to any discrimination on grounds of sex to be identified.'[39]

The Court's approach in this case to both the allocation of the burden of proof and the standard of scrutiny to be applied to proposed justifications by Member States was generally applauded. To impose on a complainant the burden of proof sought by the Advocate General would have greatly endangered the success of indirect discrimination challenges. The complainant would have had to produce complex statistical data and bear the cost which that would inevitably entail and be required to prove effectively an intention on the part of the State to discriminate.[40] If employers are to consider in advance the implications for employees of their employment and pay practices, national legislatures should, *a fortiori*, be required to do the same when drafting legislation. As regards the standard of scrutiny to be applied by national courts, the Court of Justice clearly indicated in its rejection of the German court's 'mere generalisations' that merely plausible explanations for the differential impact of legislation are insufficient. The aim of the legislation must be verifiable, suitable and requisite.

However, *Rinner-Kühn* is not just interesting from the point of view of the Court's extension of its approach in *Bilka* regarding indirectly discriminatory employment practices to Member State legislation; it was also an early indicator of the sensitive and indeed ambivalent nature of the Court's role in preliminary reference proceedings generally. By rejecting the 'mere generalisations' put forward by the German government in defence of its sick pay legislation, the Court was not simply guiding the national court on how to interpret EC law. It was in fact indicating that the evidence before it did not constitute sufficient, objective justification of the differential treatment. Although some commentators criticise the Court for impinging on the national court's jurisdiction in this respect, others point out that faced with a reference back without such specifications, a national court may be left unsatisfied or confused about what it is meant

---

[39] Case 171/88 *Rinner-Kühn*, para 14.
[40] See Shaw (1989), above n 38, 431; and E. Szyszczak, annotation of Case 171/89 *Rinner-Kühn* (1990) 19 *Industrial Law Journal* 114–20, 117. For references to the costly nature of such statistical data and the difficulties involved in the comparison of different labour pools see Case C–127/92 *Enderby v Frenchay Health Authority* [1993] ECR I–5535; and Case C–236/98 *Jämställdhetsombudsmannen v Örebro Läns Landsting* (hereafter *JämO*) [2000] ECR I–2189.

to do.[41] Wherever the merits lie, the fact remains that the closer and more specific to the facts of a case the Court's answer is, the more it assumes the role of dispute resolver. Furthermore, by assuming such a role it may increasingly find itself having to give equally specific answers to national judges who ask similar questions with respect to a slightly altered set of factual circumstances. Yet as Advocate General Jacobs indicated in his Opinion in the *Wiener* case discussed in chapter two, every national court confronted with a dispute turning on the application of EC law can refer a question to the Court. Their priority when referring a case is not the statement of clear legal principles which will contribute to the uniform application of EC law. They are concerned with the actual resolution of the case before them. This may explain why, once the relevant point of legal principle has already been established by the Court of Justice in a previous reference some national courts are still keen to go through the motions of an Article 234 EC reference in the hope that the Court will explain how to apply the principles of its case-law to the slightly different facts of the case before the national court.

Problematic Aspects of the Judicial Tests for Indirect Sex Discrimination

Despite the improvement which the *Bilka* and *Rinner-Kühn* tests represented in terms of the establishment of clearer points of reference for national courts, the decisions of the Court in these cases underlined the problems which were to plague the Court's indirect sex discrimination case-law thereafter. By demonstrating the disparate impact that an employment practice or piece of legislation has on one sex, an employee only establishes a *prima facie* case of indirect discrimination. It remains open to employers and Member States to defend their indirectly discriminatory measures with reference to objective factors unrelated to sex. In other words, it is too simplistic to regard the anti-discrimination principle as a fundamental right, as the Court has consistently claimed; rather it is 'merely a presumption which can be trumped by other considerations'.[42] How

---

[41] See K. Lenaerts, 'Form and Substance of the Preliminary Rulings Procedure' in D. Curtin and T. Heukels (eds), *Institutional Dynamics of European Integration. Essays in Honour of H.G. Schermers*, Vol. II (Dordrecht, Martinus Nijhoff, 1994), pp 355–80, 367–68; and A. Lester, 'The Uncertain Trumpet. References to the Court of Justice from the United Kingdom: Equal Pay and Equal Treatment Without Sex Discrimination' in H.G. Schermers *et al.* (eds), *Article 177 EEC: Experiences and Problems* (Amsterdam, North Holland, 1987) pp 164–94, who laments the Court's failure in the early equal pay cases to provide national courts with comprehensive and usable guidelines.

[42] See Fredman (1992), above n 5, 125. See also N. Bernard, 'What Are the Purposes of EC Discrimination Law' in Dine and Watt (eds), above n 28, pp 77–99, p 85, who explains that whether the practice or rule is regarded as lawful discrimination or non-discrimination is not simply a question of semantics: 'If justification is meant to establish that there is no alternative explanation for a practice apart from discrimination, the role of the proportionality test is merely to ensure adequation between the objective and the stated objective. If, on the other hand, one accepts that the existence of a justification does not signal the absence of discrimination, the question of justification takes the added dimension of a conflict between discrimination and other values (eg. economic efficiency).'

successful the Court's case-law was going to be as a means to combat indirect sex discrimination clearly depended on how easily Member States or employers could resort to objective justifications to demonstrate that any differentiation was unrelated to sex and, therefore, did not fall foul of the strictures of EC law.

As subsequent sections reveal, the ease with which this presumption can be rebutted depends on whether the source of discrimination is a policy or practice put in place by an employer or the result of national legislation or collective bargaining processes. In sex discrimination cases generally, the Court is confronted with arguments by parties, Member States and indeed Advocates General concerning the cost of equality to States and individual employers. As chapter five reveals, these arguments are also a recurring feature of case-law on pregnancy and parenthood. In indirect sex discrimination cases, employers and Member States have tried, when justifying differential treatment, to rely in particular on market forces arguments to explain away any apparent discrimination. Yet as one author has argued, since anti-discrimination legislation aims to change the behaviour of market actors, reference to market activity without more should be no defence.[43] As regards Member State legislation, including social security legislation, the cost which the abolition of discrimination will entail should not be sufficient reason on its own for the Court to accept the *status quo*.

The strength of the Court's objective justification test is that it ensures that a complainant can bring a challenge while leaving employers and Member States room to defend what may be legitimate or, at the very least, unavoidable choices regarding employment policies or social welfare entitlements.[44] From the point of view of ensuring effective, substantive equality, however, the test has its weaknesses. Firstly, its three elements give great scope for what Townshend-Smith calls 'impressionistic decision-making' which may depend on the Court's overall sympathy with the employer or Member State.[45] This, however, could be a criticism levelled at the Court generally—its reports are replete with examples of applicants whose cases clearly touched the Court's sense of equity, the case of *P.* being a particularly clear example. Secondly, although the Court may have discounted *intent* as a relevant criterion, it may simply have replaced it with an emphasis on the purpose of the particular employment policy or piece of legislation. Thus, as Somek points out: '[T]he responsible authority may demonstrate that the unequal treatment in question is not excessive if no disadvantages are inflicted on women beyond those necessary to achieve the purpose.'[46] A real balancing of the conflicting interests involved would entail an assessment of whether a certain policy which may appear gender neutral is nevertheless indefensible in the light of the burden that is imposed on one

---

[43] See Townshend-Smith in Hervey and O'Keeffe (eds), above n 5, p 40.

[44] *Ibid*, for a balanced and eloquent explanation as to why the employer's interests cannot simply be ignored and why a balancing process is inevitable when it comes to the employee's right not to be discriminated against.

[45] *Ibid*, p 38; and Hepple (1996), above n 5, p 250.

[46] See A. Somek, 'A Constitution for Anti-Discrimination: Exploring the Vanguard Moment of Community Law' (1999) 5 *European Law Journal* 243–71, 256.

sex.[47] Finally, the Court's objective tests clearly rely heavily on proportionality and this reliance can be problematic, particularly where Member State legislation is concerned. In most Member States the courts show a great deal of reserve in assessing the proportionality of normative measures, especially in a field such as social security. As Herbert asks:

> where exactly is the demarcation line between, on the one hand, a check of proportionality in relation to the adequacy, necessity or non-excessive nature of measures taken in a field which, in these times of crisis, is subject to enormous budgetary constraints, and, on the other hand, an opportunistic check, which implies that the courts should in some way take the place of the legislature or the executive?[48]

The Court of Justice seems sometimes to have fallen victim to this reticence as regards the standard of scrutiny to be applied in indirect sex discrimination cases to Member State legislation, specifically social security legislation. National courts—responsible for resolving the case on its facts and applying the guidelines passed down by the Court of Justice pursuant to what is seen as the classic division of competences in the preliminary reference procedure—will not be challenged to apply a higher standard of scrutiny of legislative provisions than that to which they are accustomed.

Where the Court insists on a high standard of scrutiny, as in *Bilka* or *Rinner-Kühn*, the risk of the fundamental principle of equality being trumped by factors which simply allow discrimination to be perpetuated is lessened.[49] Where, as we shall see it has been in subsequent decisions, that standard is lowered, one is left wondering about the value of judicial statements concerning the fundamental constitutional nature of the principle of equal pay/equal treatment and the predominant role of social objectives in this field.[50] As the 1990s drew to a

---

[47] See also Hepple (1996), above n 5, p 253: 'The immediate financial consequences of equality for [powerful vested interests influencing the Member State and the courts] have tended to outweigh the social and economic costs to individuals who suffer from discrimination and disadvantage'; and B. Hocking 'Indirect Discrimination: A Comparative Overview' (1992) *International Journal of Comparative Labour Law and Industrial Relations* 232–56, 254 (citing R. Hunter (1990) 15 *Legal Service Bulletin* 40, 41: 'If anti-discrimination law enshrined the subordination principle we would simply need to ask whether a particular practice operated to maintain women's subordination. If it did it should be changed.')

[48] See F. Herbert, 'Social Security and Indirect Discrimination' in C. McCrudden, (ed), *Equality of Treatment Between Men and Women in Social Security* (London, Butterworths, 1994) pp 117–36, p 120. See also Townshend-Smith in Hervey and O'Keeffe (eds), above n 5, p 44, where he observes, in the context of indirect discrimination claims, that, in the past at least, British courts have manifested an all-too easy assumption that the employer's or the government's aims will be attained by the means employed.

[49] See also Fredman (1992), above n 5, 132; and S. Anderman, 'Constitutional Law and Labour Law Dimensions of Article 119: The Case of Justification for Indirect Discrimination' in Dine and Watt (eds), above n 28, pp 100–09, p 102.

[50] On this point see E. Ellis, 'The Concept of Proportionality in European Community Sex Discrimination Law' in E. Ellis (ed), *The Principle of Proportionality in the Laws of Europe* (Oxford, Hart Publishing, 1999) pp 165–81, p 166: 'Since the right not to be discriminated against on the ground of sex is explicitly recognised by the ECJ as a fundamental human right, the application of the principle of proportionality in discrimination law might also be seen as an aspect of the

close the Court was increasingly charged with favouring conservative interpretations of EC sex equality law where a more radical ruling would throw an
industry or Member State legislation into confusion, impose what were claimed
to be (but not always proven) considerable financial burdens,[51] or threaten the
deregulated approach to employment rights which some Member States had
come to regard as an essential feature of their quest for high levels of employment and sustained economic growth. With the EC's employment strategy
based on notions of entrepreneurship, adaptability and employability, is it likely
that the future holds the prospect of a less conservative approach or greater
scrutiny of the market forces or social policy justifications advanced by Member
States and employers?

<h2 align="center">INDIRECTLY DISCRIMINATORY EMPLOYMENT POLICIES AND PRACTICES
AND THE STANDARD OF JUDICIAL SCRUTINY</h2>

Clearly one of the essential aspects of the Court's approach to indirect sex discrimination was its establishment of a reversed burden of proof. Underlying this
reversal, which required an employer or Member State to disprove a *prima facie*
case of sex discrimination, was concern that complainants should not be
required to surmount practically insurmountable evidential hurdles, with the
result that the effectiveness of the EC rules on sex equality would be all but rendered nugatory.

The *Danfoss* case[52] was one of the first and best expressions of the Court's
concern in this regard. The Danish Employees' Union brought a case on behalf
of two of Danfoss' female employees, claiming that in their wage groups a man's
average wage was higher than that of a woman's.[53] The system of individual
supplements to basic pay operated by Danfoss was implemented in such a way
that a female employee was unable to identify the reasons for a difference
between her pay and that of a man doing the same work and did not know the
criteria for the payment of supplements, nor how they applied to them.
Members of particular wage groups were thus unable to compare the various

---

more general principle by which the ECJ requires a restrictive interpretation to be placed on any ero-
sions into or curtailments of fundamental human rights.'

[51] See Beveridge and Nott in Hervey and O'Keeffe (eds), above n 5, p 385; and Hepple (1996),
above n 5, p 252.

[52] Case 109/88 *Handels- og Kontorfunktionaerernes Forbund i Danmark (Union of Commercial
and Clerical Employees, Denmark) v Dansk Arbejdsgiverforening (Danish Employers' Association),
acting on behalf of Danfoss* (hereafter *Danfoss*) [1989] ECR 3199.

[53] The contested wage was based on a national collective agreement. The Court has consistently
held that, since Article 141 EC is mandatory in nature, the prohibition of discrimination between
male and female workers not only applies to the actions of public authorities, but extends to all
collective agreements designed to regulate employment relationships and to contracts between
individuals. See in this respect Case C–333/97 *Susanne Lewen v Lothar Denda* [1999] ECR I–7243,
para 11. Collective agreements are dealt with in this section rather than in the section on discrimination arising from statutory provisions.

components of their pay with those of the pay of their colleagues who were in the same wage group. According to the Court, female employees who established differences in so far as average pay is concerned would be deprived of any effective means of enforcing the principle of equal pay before the national courts if the effect of adducing such evidence was not to impose upon the employer the burden of proving that his practice in the matter of wages is not in fact discriminatory.[54]

The Court was also asked whether an employer could justifiably rely on criteria relating to the payment of supplements—namely mobility, training or length of service—where it appears that the application of such criteria systematically works to the disadvantage of female employees. On occasion, the Court is careful to differentiate between its role and that of national courts under Article 234 EC. In *Danfoss*, however, it seemed happy to assess at least some of the Danish criteria itself for their compatibility with EC law. As regards mobility, the Court distinguished situations in which the criterion of mobility is used to reward the quality of work done by the employee from others in which it is used to reward the employee's adaptability to variable hours and varying places of work.[55] The criterion of mobility, as regards the former situation, was wholly neutral from the point of view of sex and were it to operate to the systematic disadvantage of women that could only be because the employer had misapplied it, it being inconceivable that the quality of work done by women should be generally less good. An employer could not therefore justify the criterion of mobility (understood as rewarding the quality of work) where its application proved to operate systematically to the disadvantage of women. Even if the criterion of mobility was understood as covering the employee's adaptability to variable hours and varying places of work, it 'may also work to the disadvantage of female employees, who, because of household and family duties for which they are frequently responsible, are not as able as men to organize their working time flexibly.'[56] The employer could only justify the reward of this type of adapt-

---

[54] Case 109/88 *Danfoss*, para 13. The *Danfoss* reversal of the burden of proof does not apply across the board. Where the discrimination claimed of is direct and the information concerning pay is transparent, the burden of proof will remain with the complainant—see Case C–381/99 *Susanna Brunnhofer v Bank der österreichischen Postsparkasse AG* [2001] ECR I–4961. For positive legislation on the burden of proof in sex discrimination cases see also Article 10 of Council Directive 2000/78.

[55] In this context the Court encountered what is arguably a classic, oft-repeated and inherent problem in the Article 234 EC reference system. In para 18 of its judgment it admitted that 'the documents before the Court do not clearly disclose what is meant' by the criterion of mobility. It then proceeded to cite the explanation given by the Employers' Association, probably at the oral hearing, of what this criterion meant. By the time the Court had sat down to draft its decision it was clearly no longer possible to get more information from the parties or, at the time, the national referring court. Nevertheless, the Court was still required to give a principled judgment on the interpretation of EC law, useful to the Court in *Danfoss* for the resolution of the dispute before it, yet sufficiently clear and principled to allow other national courts with similar problems to be guided by it.

[56] Case 109/88 *Danfoss*, para 21, a statement which seems at odds with the Court's refusal to countenance such considerations in Case 170/84 *Bilka*, paras 41–43.

ability by showing that it was of importance for the performance of specific tasks entrusted to the employee.

As regards the criterion of training, the Court held that it is not to be excluded that it may work to the disadvantage of women, in so far as they have had less opportunity than men for training or have taken less advantage of such opportunity. However, like the criterion of mobility, the employer could justify remuneration of special training by showing that it is of importance for the performance of specific tasks entrusted to the employee. Finally, the criterion of length of service may, the Court recognised, involve less advantageous treatment of women than of men in so far as women have entered the labour market more recently than men or more frequently suffer an interruption of their career. However, the Court stated that, 'since length of service goes hand in hand with experience and since experience generally enables the employee to perform his duties better, the employer is free to reward it without having to establish the importance it has in the performance of specific tasks entrusted to the employer.'

Danfoss is an extraordinary case in that the Court really manages to give with one hand what it takes away with another. Underlying the decision of the Court, and indeed this is what the case is most frequently remembered for, is its concern that complainants be able to effectively enforce the principle of equal pay before the national courts. However, the transparency demanded by the Court simply concerned openness in the implementation of the employer's decisions rather than in his/her prior decision to rely on particular criteria for the determination of levels of pay.[57] Furthermore, when it came to the various criteria on which the employer relied to give different pay supplements to employees, the Court gave national courts plenty of room to enable employers to justify their use of criteria which the Court clearly regarded as suspect. Although adaptability, training and length of service were all factors which might affect women differently to men—due essentially to their household/childcare responsibilities—an employer need only show that adaptability or training were of importance for the performance of specific tasks entrusted to the employee. In the case of length of service, the employer did not even have to show that.

Compare the Court's ruling in respect of length of service in *Danfoss*, with its later decision in *Nimz*.[58] In the latter case the Court was asked whether Article 141 EC precluded a collective agreement from providing that the period of service of workers employed for at least three-quarters of normal working time be taken fully into account for reclassification in a higher salary grade, but that only half of such period of service be taken into account in the case of employees whose working hours are between one-half and three-quarters of such normal working time. The latter group of employees was comprised of an appreciably larger percentage of female than male workers. The City of

---

[57] See Townshend-Smith in Hervey and O'Keeffe (eds), above n 5, p 43.
[58] See Case C–184/89 *Helga Nimz v Freie und Hansestadt Hamburg* [1991] ECR I–297.

Hamburg, the employer in *Nimz*, had argued that those who work normal, or three-quarters of normal, working time acquire more quickly than others the abilities and skills relating to their particular job. Echoing its position in *Rinner-Kühn*, the Court in *Nimz* regarded such considerations as mere generalizations about certain categories of workers and, as such, insufficient to justify the difference in treatment. It continued:

> Although experience goes hand in hand with length of service, and experience enables the worker in principle to improve performance of the tasks allotted to him, the objectivity of such a criterion depends on all the circumstances in a particular case, and in particular on the relationship between the nature of the work performed and the experience gained from the performance of that work upon completion of a certain number of working hours.[59]

A length of service justification must be objectively proved; its legitimacy cannot be presumed.

The more nuanced approach displayed in *Nimz* was lacking in *Danfoss*.[60] At issue in the latter case were two wage groups chosen at random by the Employees' Union to mount their case against Danfoss, specifically laboratory staff and depot staff. Nowhere in the Report for the Hearing, the Opinion of the Advocate General or the decision of the Court was any indication given as to what the staff involved actually did. By adapting the approach in *Nimz* and examining the relationship between the nature of the work performed and the experience gained from the performance of that work upon completion of a certain number of working hours, a national court would be in a better position to tailor its response to the nature of the individual type of work.[61] Seniority may seem a reasonable criterion for an employer to use to differentiate between employees,[62] but the Court, if it is really seeking effective implementation of the principle of equal pay, cannot simply presume or allow the national court to presume it is reasonable. As McColgan points out, even where employers do not consciously discriminate against women, stereotypical assumptions about women's attitudes and commitment are common and reliance upon factors such as labour market experience, continuity of employment etc. disadvantages

---

[59] See Case C–184/89 *Helga Nimz v Freie und Hansestadt Hamburg* [1991] ECR I–297, para 14. It was for the national court to carry out such an investigation.

[60] See Townshend-Smith in Hervey and O'Keeffe (eds), above n 5, p 44.

[61] See also the example of a case where seniority may not indicate greater experience provided by Advocate General La Pergola in Case C–100/95 *Brigitte Kording v Senator für Finanzen* [1997] ECR I–5289, fn.30 of his Opinion; and Ellis (1994), above n 36, 578, who questions what extra experience or lengthy training, for that matter, is actually required to perform a repetitive, low-skilled job. Of course even the approach in Case C–184/89 *Nimz* does nothing to alter the structure of the employment market or contribute to its desegregation, but that is a different story.

[62] See in this respect Townshend-Smith in Hervey and O'Keeffe (eds), above n 5, p 43–44, who argues that 'at a time when women are acquiring greater seniority, it would be perverse and over-interventionist to hold that rewarding seniority was normally impermissible'. He adds that this criterion, without more, should not be enough for an employer to allege greater productivity or lower costs.

female workers.[63] The purpose of an indirect discrimination inquiry is surely to expose such assumptions and allow them to be forcefully challenged. Also of interest in *Danfoss* is the complete absence of a reference to the principle of proportionality and the criteria of necessity and appropriateness which should be central to the balancing act which the national court is obliged to carry out in this context.[64] It has been suggested that the Court's ambivalence to indirect discrimination manifested itself in the early to mid 1990s—when it seems to have lost its sure footing in the field of equality. I would suggest that a lack of assurance, albeit not as marked as it is nowadays, about the objectives, scope and direction of EC sex equality law was evident in much earlier rulings and *Danfoss* is an example of this. Ellis commented in 1998, in connection with the *Helmig* case, that '[A]lthough indirect discrimination aims to tackle the hidden obstacles that stand in the way of women at work, it only discounts those obstacles where they are genuinely irrelevant to the work performed.'[65] *Danfoss*, despite its recognition of the problems that hamper the enjoyment of equality by female workers and its concern with effectiveness, is excellent early proof of her thesis.

In *Enderby*, the Court was asked to work on the assumption that the posts involved were of equal value and on the basis of that assumption determine whether the difference in pay complained of was indirectly discriminatory.[66] Senior speech therapists working for a British regional health authority claimed that they were performing work of equal value to that performed by senior clinical psychologists and pharmacists and that the higher rates of pay received by the latter gave rise to indirect discrimination since speech therapy, at junior and senior level, was almost exclusively a female profession. By contrast, the other two professions, although employing male and female workers at lower grades, consisted mainly of men in senior positions. Their employer rejected the argument that the two categories performed work of equal value but added, in any event, that the difference in pay could be justified by two factors. On the one hand, it was the result of different collective bargaining structures. On the other,

---

[63] See McColgan, above n 5, p 242.

[64] See also Case C–33/89 *Maria Kowalska v Freie und Hansestadt Hamburg* [1990] ECR I–2591, paras 13, 15 and 16, where the Court simply referred to the employer's duty to show that the greater exclusion of female workers from the enjoyment of a severance grant on termination of their employment is based on objectively justified factors unrelated to any discrimination on grounds of sex; G. More, annotation of Case C–33/89 *Kowalska* (1991) 16 *European Law Review* 58–64; and Case C–184/89 *Nimz*, para 14, although this paragraph of the decision on objective justification was arguably framed with necessity and appropriateness in mind.

[65] See Ellis (1998), above n 2, 383.

[66] In another equal value case—Case C–236/98 *JämO*—the Court was asked to rule on whether an inconvenient hours pay supplement and a reduction in working time should be taken into account in calculating the salary used as the basis for a pay comparison, despite the fact that the national court had not yet decided whether the two jobs in question (midwives and laboratory technicians in Swedish hospitals) involved work of equal value. Preliminary references of this type present the Court with particular problems since it is being asked to hand down a ruling of general application with reference to the facts of a specific case (of which it has limited knowledge) and on the basis of a legal hypothesis which has not yet been proved.

pharmacists were in great demand and thus had a higher market value than speech therapists.

In accordance with the reversed burden of proof which it had already applied in *Bilka* and other indirect discrimination cases,[67] the Court pointed out that if an employee establishes, in relation to a relatively large number of employees, that the average pay of a female worker is lower than that of a male worker, it is up to employers to demonstrate that their pay policies are not discriminatory. Workers would be unable to enforce the principle of equal pay before national courts if evidence of a *prima facie* case of discrimination did not shift to the employer the onus of showing that the pay differential is not in fact discriminatory.[68] It thus rejected arguments concerning the neutrality and autonomy of the wage-setting process, the effect of such a process being the essential point. The existence of separate collective bargaining processes was insufficient justification for the lower pay of speech therapists. In *Enderby* the Court was thus directing national courts to put aside issues of fault or intent and focus on 'the extent to which entrenched social institutions and forces operate to perpetuate inequalities regardless of individual actions.'[69] Had the Court held otherwise, the principle of equal pay could easily have been avoided by resorting to separate collective bargaining processes for the determination of pay.[70]

However, by accepting the market forces argument raised by the health authority—the alleged shortage of pharmacists and the effect this had on their market value—the Court accepted that if an employer raised pay for a particular job in response to the demand in the employment market, the latter may constitute an objectively justified economic ground for the difference in pay.[71] It is with this part of the Court's judgment that commentators have expressed most disappointment. By accepting market forces arguments as potential justifications for indirect discrimination the Court was ignoring the possibility that, in highly segregated sectors of the employment market such as those at issue in *Enderby*, market forces may themselves maintain or reinforce inequalities. As Fredman argues: 'low pay for work with part-time job opportunities [such as speech therapy] may be explained in market terms by the over-supply of women

---

[67] Case C–33/89 *Kowalska* [1990] ECR I–2591; and Case 109/88 *Danfoss* [1989] ECR 3199.

[68] Case C–127/92 *Enderby*, paras 14 and 18. See Ellis (1994), above n 36, 574, on the implications of this finding on the burden of proof beyond equal pay claims.

[69] S. Fredman, 'Equal Pay and Justification' (1994) 23 *Industrial Law Journal*, 37–41, 40; Fenwick, above n 21; Fenwick and Hervey (1995), above n 12, who observe that 'freedom of contract, in the hands of male-oriented unions, can mean freedom to perpetuate sex based assumptions and practices concerning the status and value of jobs.'; and Townshend-Smith in Hervey and O'Keeffe (eds), above n 5, p 43: 'It should be a basic aim of the law to force employers to consider *in advance*, the equality consequences of their payment strategies; concessions to a union for the sake of compromise cannot provide a defence.'

[70] Case C–127/92 *Enderby*, para 22. See, however, the Court's apparent change of tack in Case C–400/93 *Royal Copenhagen* [1995] ECR I–1275, para 46: 'the national court may take [the fact that the elements of pay were determined by collective bargaining at local level] into account in its assessment of whether differences between the average pay of two groups of workers are due to objective factors unrelated to any discrimination on grounds of sex.'

[71] Case C–127/92 *Enderby*, para 26.

requiring part-time work. Yet the underlying reason for such an over-supply is that women remain primarily responsible for child-care and there is insufficient public provision.'[72] The upshot of the Court's decision in *Enderby* is that 'employers can exploit the weaker position of women in the labour market by paying them less, provided that this practice is sufficiently generalised to be reflected in lower market rates for predominantly female jobs.'[73] *Enderby* is a classic example of how the concept of indirect discrimination, even in the hands of a court seemingly aware of its purpose, can nevertheless be applied while turning a blind eye to (or even sanctioning) the structures which give rise to the disadvantage complained of.[74] If, as Fredman explains, market forces may be used to justify indirect discrimination, there is a distinct danger that discriminatory practices which are functional to the market will simply be perpetuated.[75] For example, discriminatory practices with respect to part time workers may be in the financial interests of employers (the *Bilka* case) since part-time employment provides a large pool of cheaper, flexible labour.

In *Enderby*, the Court was clearly aware of the delicate nature of the balancing act to be performed and instructed the national court to assess whether the role of market forces in determining the rate of pay was sufficiently significant to provide objective justification for part or all of the difference in pay. It concluded, however, rather strangely given the content of the judicial tests for indirect discrimination outlined above, that: 'it is for the national court to determine, *if necessary by applying the principle of proportionality*, whether and to what extent the shortage of candidates for a job and the need to attract them by higher pay constitutes an objectively justified economic ground for the difference in pay between the jobs in question.'[76] Since proportionality was a central part of the test worked out in *Bilka* why was the national court, when examining the objective justification proposed by the health authority in *Enderby*, only to apply it if necessary?

---

[72] See Fredman (1994), above n 69, 41; Fenwick, above n 21, 334–35, who suggests that the Court's acceptance of a market forces justification sits uneasily with its recognition that apparently neutral bargaining processes might be influenced by a gendered social context; and Fenwick and Hervey (1995), above n 12, 447 and 467, who argue that judges are likely to be convinced by the assertions of employers regarding the cost of equality in pregnancy and equal pay claims, since those assertions are based on principles of law and conceptions of individuals which seem 'natural' and 'equitable' in the legal system pertaining to a free market economy. For a case where the provision of childcare was in fact the central issue and the Court's failure to tackle the indirect discrimination problem which the impugned legislation raised see Case C–249/97 *Gabriele Gruber v Silhouette International Schmied GmbH & Co. KG* [1999] ECR I–5295, discussed below ch 5.

[73] See Bernard in Dine and Watt (eds), above n 28, p 86.

[74] Advocate General Lenz was certainly aware of what an indirect sex discrimination claim is all about. At para 49 of his Opinion he stated: 'The historical and social context of a 'purely female profession' is most probably sex related. If an explanatory approach were accepted as sufficient justification, that would lead to the perpetuation of sexual roles in working life. Instead of the equality of treatment which is sought, there would be afforded a legal argument for maintaining the status quo.'

[75] S.Fredman, 'European Community Discrimination Law: a Critique' (1992) 21 *Industrial Law Journal* 119-34, 131.

[76] Case C–127/92 *Enderby*, para 29 (emphasis added).

Yet even in more recent years when the Court has seemed less assured in its treatment of sex equality cases, it can still surprise its audience. In *Hill and Stapleton*, it had to consider whether there was discrimination in a case where clerical assistants who, on converting from job-sharing to full-time employment, regressed on the incremental scale and hence on their salary scale, due to the application by their employer of the criterion of service calculated by the length of time actually worked in the post.[77] Since the case-file revealed that 99.2 per cent of clerical assistants who job-share were women (as indeed were 98 per cent of all civil servants employed on job-share contracts), it was clear that, in the absence of an objective justification, the impugned Irish civil service rules would constitute unlawful sex discrimination.[78]

Having set out the classic statement on the division of functions between the national court and the Court of Justice—it being up to the former to assess the facts and interpret the national legislation to determine whether, despite its adverse effects for a greater proportion of female than male workers, that legislation is justified by objective reasons unrelated to any discrimination on grounds of sex—the Court was eager, on the basis of the documents provided in the main proceedings, as well as the written and oral observations submitted to it, to provide the referring court with concrete guidance in order to enable it to give judgment. It rejected the justification submitted by the applicants' employers to the effect that there was an established practice of crediting actual service and that the impugned rules established an award system which maintained staff motivation, commitment and morale. In line with some of its previous more robust decisions, the Court stated that general assertions unsupported by objective criteria were not enough to justify rules which impacted adversely on women. Similarly, to accord job-sharers the same point on the incremental salary scale as full-time employees once the former converted to full-time employment did not amount to discrimination in favour of female workers since, as the Court had already explained, the hourly pay of the two categories of worker was identical at each point along the scale. Justification based on economic grounds, namely that avoidance of such discrimination would involve increased costs, was also given short shrift. Finally, the Court pointed out that almost all job-sharers in the Irish public service were women and that approximately 83 per cent of those who job-shared did so in order to be able to combine work and family responsibilities which invariably involve caring for children. According to the Court, Community policy in this area is to encourage and, if

[77] Case C–243/95 *Kathleen Hill and Ann Stapleton v Revenue Commissioners and Department of Finance* [1998] ECR I–3739. At issue was legislation governing employment in the national civil service and it is here treated as rules laid down by the employer for that reason, albeit the employer was the State.

[78] With reference to the findings of the Labour Court in Case C–243/95 *Hill and Stapleton*, the Court of Justice emphasised that the qualitative assessment of the two categories of worker in question was identical—job-sharers progressed along the pay scale in parallel to full-time workers. The only difference between a job-sharer and a colleague working full-time lay in the time actually worked during the period of job-sharing.

possible, adapt working conditions to family responsibilities, which invariably involve childcare. Reconciling family life and professional activities was, the Court stated, a principle widely recognised in Member State legal systems and in Community law, as the natural corollary of equality between men and women. Although it was for the Labour Court to determine whether the Irish public service's reliance on the criterion of service was justified by objective factors unrelated to any discrimination on grounds of sex, the Court of Justice left that court in little doubt, given the justifications advanced and rejected, that it considered the impugned rules to be indirectly discriminatory.

INDIRECTLY DISCRIMINATORY NATIONAL LEGISLATION AND THE
STANDARD OF SCRUTINY

The basic principle established in *Rinner-Kühn* was that if a Member State can show that the means chosen meet a necessary aim of its social policy and that they are suitable and requisite for attaining that aim, the mere fact that its legislation affects a much greater proportion of female workers than male workers cannot be regarded as constituting an infringement of Article 141 EC. This principle has been reiterated frequently by the Court, not, however, without undergoing sometimes subtle, and at other times fundamental, modifications.

Indirect Sex Discrimination of Part-time Workers

In *Bötel*[79] the Court of Justice reiterated that any difference in the treatment of part-time and full-time employees gave rise to a *prima facie* case of indirect discrimination requiring objective justification unrelated to sex. The German Federal Law on industrial relations provided that staff council members should be released without loss of pay from their normal work to perform their duties and that, as compensation for staff council work which takes place outside working hours, they should be entitled to a corresponding amount of paid leave. Mrs Bötel, a part-time worker, was chairman of a staff council. She was delegated to attend a series of training courses which were spread over whole days. Her employer paid her, up to the limit of her individual normal working week, for the hours she had not worked due to her course attendance. Mrs Bötel claimed that she was entitled to compensation for the total number of hours spent on the training course, including those outside her normal individual working hours. Had Mrs Bötel been working full-time, her employer would have been obliged, pursuant to the national legislation on industrial relations, to grant compensation up to the limit of the full-time working week.

---

[79] Case C–360/90 *Arbeiterwohlfahrt der Stadt Berlin e.V. v Monika Bötel* [1992] ECR I–3589.

In *Bötel*, both part-time workers and full-time workers devoted the same number of hours attending training courses, but the former received less compensation than staff council members who were employed full-time. According to the Court:

> if it were to prove that the percentage of female staff council members employed on a full-time basis is much lower than the percentage of male members, the difference of treatment suffered by staff council members employed on a part-time basis would be contrary to Article [141] of the Treaty and to Directive 75/117 where, having regard to the difficulties encountered by female workers in working on a full-time basis, that lower level of compensation cannot be accounted for by factors other than discrimination on grounds of sex.[80]

The Court accepted that amongst the members of the employer's staff council there was a far greater number of women than men working on a part-time basis and held that the application of the German legislation on compensation for participation in training courses gave rise to indirect sex discrimination against women. On the question of justification, the Court held that the fact that part-time workers receive less compensation is likely to deter employees in the part-time category from serving on staff councils or from acquiring the knowledge needed in order to serve on them, thus making it more difficult for that category of worker to be represented by qualified staff council members. It remained up to the Member State, therefore, to prove to the national court that the difference in treatment between part-time and full-time workers could be justified by objective factors unrelated to any discrimination on grounds of sex. Clearly the justifications set before the Court of Justice were once again regarded as insufficient to justify the difference in treatment complained of.

However, in subsequent preliminary references from German courts on the issue of compensation payable by employers to employees who are members of staff councils or committees—*Lewark*[81] and *Freers and Speckmann*[82]—it seemed that the Court was being asked by the German government and perhaps even by the referring courts, to re-examine its ruling in *Bötel*.[83] As in *Bötel*, the

---

[80] Case C–360/90 *Bötel*, para 18. The Court remarked on the difficulties encountered by female workers in working on a full-time basis.

[81] Case C–457/93 *Kuratorium für Dialyse und Nierentransplantation e.V. v Johanna Lewark* [1996] ECR I–243.

[82] Case C–278/93 *Edith Freers and Hannelore Speckmann v Deutsche Bundespost* [1996] ECR I–1165.

[83] Following Case C–360/90 *Bötel*, Chancellor Kohl had accused the Court of going beyond its competences (*Europe*, 14 October 1992, p 9). *Bötel* had been a decision of the Sixth Chamber, signed by five Judges. The Court sat in its full plenary formation in Case C–457/93 *Lewark*, however, and the judgment was signed by thirteen Judges (only four of whom had signed *Bötel*). Germany had probably requested that the case be heard in plenary in accordance with its right under Article 221 EC. Case C–278/93 *Freers* was, once again, a decision of the Sixth Chamber (signed by four of the original signatories of *Bötel*, who clearly felt bound to follow the revised position of the full Court in *Lewark*). See G. More, 'The Concept of 'undertaking' in the Acquired Rights Directive: the Court of Justice under pressure (again)' (1995) 15 *Yearbook of European Law* 135–55, at 153–54, on the influence of the composition of the Court on the outcome of a judgment. The statement of M. Volcansek, *Judicial Politics in Europe. An Impact Analysis* (New York, Peter Lang Publishing

Court in *Lewark* held that the application of the German provisions gave rise to indirect discrimination. The German government argued that, presuming there was a difference in treatment, it was justified by the principle that staff council members are not paid—a measure intended to ensure their independence from internal and external pressures. The German government also insisted that its wish to place the independence of staff councils above financial inducements for the performance of their functions was an aim of social policy.[84] The Court accepted that the concern to ensure the independence of members of staff committees reflected a legitimate aim of social policy. Councils have the task of promoting harmonious labour relations within undertakings and in their interest. Surprisingly, the Court concluded that: '[I]f a Member State is able to show that the measures chosen reflect a legitimate aim of its social policy, are appropriate to achieve that aim and are necessary in order to do so, the mere fact that the legislative provision affects far more women workers than men cannot be regarded as a breach of Article [141].'[85] The departure from *Bötel* and new-found deference to the justification proposed by the Member State was unmistakeable. Why in *Bötel* had the Member State's social policy not been mentioned if in *Lewark* it was more or less to carry the day? True, the Court in *Lewark* did instruct the national court to assess the social policy justification proposed to ascertain whether it was suitable and necessary to achieve the aim pursued. The Court also drew the national court's attention to the likely effect which the difference in treatment between part-time and full-time workers would have on the participation of the former in staff councils. Nevertheless, the shift in the Court's position in *Lewark* from that adopted in *Bötel* was clear and the whole saga seems to provide some substance to the theory that there is a nexus between the Court's jurisprudence and the environment in which it operates. It may, as Schepel has rather criptically argued, develop the case-law with reference to 'the expansive logic of its own interpretative devices', but it consistently probes the tolerance levels of its interlocutors.[86]

Inc., 1986) p 28, to the effect that a national court that does not find the prevailing precedent palatable, may take a chance that the Court will alter its decision when presented with a new preliminary ruling seems pertinent.

[84] Case C–457/93 *Lewark*, paras 33–34. The decision of the Court in *Lewark* was handed down on 6 February 1996. Its decisions in Cases C–317/93 *Nolte* and C–444/93 *Megner and Scheffel*, in which the Court accepted very wide Member State discretion with respect to the determination and content of domestic social policy, had been handed down on 14 December 1995. The German government, when presenting its submissions in *Lewark* had clearly argued for an extension, beyond the field of social security, for the wide margin of discretion which it had been calling for in *Nolte*.

[85] Case C–457/93 *Lewark*, para 36 (emphasis added). Note the change from a *necessary* aim of social policy in Case C–171/88 *Rinner-Kühn* to a *legitimate* aim in *Lewark*.

[86] See the book review of R. Dehousse, *The European Court of Justice. The Politics of Integration*, by H. Schepel, 'Reconstructing Constitutionalism: Law and Politics in the European Court of Justice' (2000) 20 *Oxford Journal of Legal Studies* 457–68, 460; and J. Shaw, 'Gender and the Court of Justice' in G. De Búrca and J.H.H. Weiler, *The European Court of Justice* (Oxford, OUP, 2001) pp 87–42, p 127.

What is also of interest in these cases is the Court's emphasis on its role pursuant to Article 234 EC. Although it is for the national court to establish whether objective factors exist to justify any established difference in treatment, the Court now frequently refers to its duty in preliminary reference proceedings to provide the national court with helpful answers and insists that it may provide guidance on the basis of the documents before the national court and the written and oral arguments submitted to it. Yet the answers it gives to the national court often mean that the resolution of the whole case at national level depends merely on application of the principle of proportionality. At times the Court is willing to more or less apply this principle or sanction the national court's non-appliance of it,[87] at others, as in *Lewark*, it fails to give the national court *clear* guidance as to its own appreciation of the suitability and necessity of the national rules.[88] Indeed in *Lewark*, it cited, on the one hand, case-law on the legitimacy of Member States' social policy aims; case-law in which the Court had recognised a wide, almost unlimited, discretion for Member States in this respect. On the other, it reiterated its finding in *Bötel* on the effect which the German rules were likely to have on the participation of part-time workers in staff councils and the result this would have for the representation of part-time workers on councils. In these cases the Court has found it difficult to articulate a principled way in which to balance the commercial and other interests of employers or, as the case may be, Member States, as authors of *prima facie* discriminatory rules or practices, with the right of employees not to be discrim-

---

[87] See Case C–273/97 *Angela María Sirdar v The Army Board and Secretary of State for Defence* [1999] ECR I–7403, paras 30–31.

[88] Note that Advocate General Darmon in Case C–278/93 *Freers*, regarded the German rules as disproportionate, while Advocate General Jacobs in Case C–457/93 *Lewark* accepted the underlying aim of the legislation as an objective justification for the difference in treatment. Advocate General Jacobs (para 38) drew a distinction between economic and social policy grounds of justification. Economic justifications mean that it is usually necessary to evaluate the specific circumstances of the case, taking into account *inter alia* the requirements of the market and of the employer concerned. Where a difference in treatment arises directly from national legislation and a social policy justification is alleged 'it is less likely that the specific circumstances of the employees and of the employer concerned will be of decisive influence. In such a case, it may be possible for this Court to give more detailed guidance to the national court.' In his Opinion in *Lewark* he argued that complete equality of treatment between the two categories of workers was simply unattainable and that the difference in treatment witnessed in this case was inherent in the nature of part-time work. Any disadvantage which part-time workers suffer as a result of the German measures is only an accidental consequence of the principle of compensation for loss of earnings. As a result, Advocate General Jacobs was prepared to accept Germany's arguments as going far towards providing a sufficient objective justification. In contrast, Advocate General Darmon in *Freers and Speckmann* (para 61) concentrated on the effect of the rules on part-time workers: 'a part-time worker is prompted not to take part in the training necessary for the performance of duties as a representative, and therefore to leave that post—and the shorter the working week, the greater is the incentive to leave.' He concluded that the effect of the German rules was to jeopardise the standing of part-time workers as staff representatives (since they would be less likely to accept additional training) and their representation (since they might be inclined no longer to go forward for such posts). These factors were, he argued, no less important than the independence of staff councils. Finally, he pointed out that the training courses in question could be readjusted in order to adapt them to the working hours of part-time workers.

inated against.[89] Yet, clearly articulating principled guidelines is the essence of the Court's function under Article 234 EC. Cases in which the Court wavers between detailed guidance for national referring courts and those in which no guidance at all is forthcoming on application, for example, of the principle of proportionality, are symptomatic of the Court hesitating between its role as a clarifier of public interest principles and as a dispute resolver, ultimately fulfilling neither task satisfactorily.

Unfair Dismissal Legislation

The issue of objective justification also arose in *Seymour-Smith*, a case in which the Court was asked whether a rule requiring two years service in order to entitle an employee to complain against unfair dismissal indirectly discriminated against women and, if so, whether it was justified. Of particular interest is the standard of scrutiny elaborated by the Court as regards the question of objective justification of a *prima facie* case of indirect discrimination. In two previous decisions involving indirect sex discrimination claims against national social security legislation in *Nolte* and *Megner and Scheffel* the Court had held that where measures chosen by a Member State reflect a necessary aim of its social policy and are suitable and necessary for achieving that aim, such measures will not violate Article 141 EC merely because far more female than male workers are affected by the measure.[90] These cases will be discussed in detail in a subsequent section. Of interest in *Seymour Smith* was the fact that the Court relied on these previous decisions beyond the field of social security. The Court regarded the United Kingdom's desire to encourage recruitment as a legitimate aim of its social policy.[91] The United Kingdom government had argued in *Seymour-Smith*, relying on *Nolte*, that it need only show that it was reasonably entitled to consider that the measure would advance this social policy aim. In this respect the Court held that, although Member States' enjoy a wide margin of

[89] Ellis (1998), above n 2, 384.

[90] Case C–167/97 *Seymour-Smith*, para 69. The Report for the Hearing in the case reveals that there was considerable disagreement between the parties regarding whether the position in Cases C–317/93 *Nolte* and C–444/93 *Megner and Scheffel*, which were social security cases, should be extended to a case concerning qualifying periods in national legislation for the enjoyment of protection from unfair dismissal.

[91] The switch from *necessary* to *legitimate* aims of national social policy seemed permanent at this stage. The United Kingdom had argued that exposing employers to proceedings for unfair dismissal brought by employees who had only fairly recently been engaged could act as a deterrent to recruitment. Townshend-Smith in Hervey and O'Keeffe (eds), above n 5, p 41, points out that there is little or no empirical foundation for the British belief that labour market regulation is harmful to job creation, citing S. Deakin, 'Labour Law and Industrial Relations' in Mickie, *The EC Legacy 1979–1992* (1992). For further discussion see above ch 3. Even before the decision in Case C–167/97 *Seymour-Smith* was reached, the United Kingdom government declared its intention to replace the two-year rule with a one-year qualifying period for protection. The two year qualifying period was subsequently reduced to one year in 1999 (S.I. 1999 No 1436).

discretion as regards the requirements of their social policies, the exercise of that discretion could not have the effect of frustrating the implementation of a fundamental principle of Community law such as that of equal pay for men and women: 'mere generalizations concerning the capacity of a specific measure to encourage recruitment are not enough to show that the aim of the rule is unrelated to any discrimination based on sex or to provide evidence on the basis of which it could reasonably be considered that the means chosen were suitable for achieving that aim.'[92] Although the Court did not attribute this rejection of 'mere generalisations' to *Rinner-Kühn*, the standard of scrutiny established therein was no doubt what it had in mind when it exhorted Member States to come up with better reasons to meet *prima facie* claims of indirect discrimination.

Some commentators have suggested that, given the answers of the Court in *Seymour Smith* (implicitly their lack of quality and breadth), the House of Lords would have been better to decide the case itself, thus saving the national judges and the parties involved, the inevitable delay which a preliminary reference procedure involves.[93] Barnard and Hepple chastise the Court for its decision on disparate impact where it held that:

---

[92] Case C–167/97 *Seymour-Smith*, para 76. This aspect of *Seymour-Smith* is reminiscent of the approach of the House of Lords in *R v Secretary of State for Employment, ex parte Equal Opportunities Commission (EOC)*, [1994] 2 WLR 409. In that case, the EOC successfully challenged as incompatible with Directive 76/207 and Article 141 EC a provision of the Employment Protection (Consolidation) Act 1978 which provided that employees who worked for less than 16 hours a week were subject to different conditions for claiming compensation for unfair dismissal and redundancy pay than those working for more than 16 hours a week. Statistics revealed that 87% of those working part-time in the United Kingdom were female. To justify the difference in treatment the British government argued that removing unfair dismissal protection from part-time employees would reduce the costs to employers of employing part-time workers. Although the House of Lords accepted that the creation of more part-time work might constitute a proper aim of social policy, the two year threshold in order to benefit from certain types of employment protection measures had not been shown to result in the creation of more part-time jobs and could not, therefore, be considered appropriate and necessary to achieve the objective pursued. According to Lord Keith, 421: 'The evidence for the Secretary of State consisted principally of an affidavit by an official of the Department of Employment which set out the views of the Department but did not contain anything capable of being regarded as factual evidence demonstrating the correctness of these views.'

[93] See C. Barnard and B. Hepple, 'Indirect Discrimination: Interpreting *Seymour-Smith*' (1999) *Cambridge Law Journal* 399–412, who emphasise that the Court's ruling came 'nearly two years [after the House of Lords reference] and eight years after the employees were dismissed'. Although delay is clearly a problem with the preliminary reference procedure, the assumption that blame always lies with the inefficiency of the Court is mistaken. On the one hand, much of the time a case spends at the Court is spent in the process of translation and it is difficult to envisage how the Court might alleviate the translation problems it faces other than restricting the written submissions of parties. On the other hand, several months sometimes elapse between the decision of a national court to refer and the lodging of the reference with the Court registry. This delay seems partly attributable, at least in the United Kingdom, to the involvement of the parties' counsel in the formulation of the questions. See also S. Moore, annotation of Case C–167/97 *R v Secretary of State for Employment, ex parte Nicole Seymour-Smith and Laura Perez* (2000) 37 *Common Market Law Review* 157–65, 164, who remarks on the applicants' delay in bringing their case—they waited almost 6 years after they had been dismissed.

the best approach to the comparison of statistics is to consider, on the one hand, the respective proportions of men in the workforce able to satisfy the requirement of two years' employment under the disputed rule and those unable to do so and, on the other, to compare those proportions as regards women in the workforce.

They call for a rather nebulous test based on 'substantial or practically import-ant' difference, yet concede that disparate impact is ultimately a matter of judg-ment for national courts, that it usually requires large, visible and substantial differences between the groups, and that this is best ascertained by looking at the usual pattern of behaviour of the majority group.[94] It is doubtful that the Court of Justice would disagree with their analysis. Indeed the difficulties the Court experiences when asked abstract questions the answer to which must sim-ply ensure that the national courts continue to carry out a task which only they can do while keeping within the limits of EC law are fairly clear. If the Court were to resolve the dispute in *Seymour-Smith* it should have before it a full and complete case file and the judicial freedom allowing it to do so. Since its role pursuant to Article 234 EC is supposedly more limited, the difficulties it encoun-ters when answering ever more detailed questions formulated with reference to the facts of a particular case, where the legal principles it announces must be transposable to other indirect discrimination cases, is plain to see.

Where *Seymour-Smith* clearly falls short of the clarity which it is incumbent on the Court to demonstrate in its rulings pursuant to Article 234 EC is in rela-tion to the question of objective justification. It vacillated between the *Rinner-Kühn* and *Nolte*-tests, ultimately blending the two. Barnard and Hepple conclude that:

it appears that the judges could not agree between them which way to go and so the resulting judgment reflects the competing views, with those favouring a more rigorous approach to equality getting their way in paragraphs 75 and 76; those favouring a more market-oriented concept, winning through in paragraph 77.[95]

The Court is to be criticised for not giving a clearer indication of what test to apply and the permissive approach with respect to justifications deriving from Member States' social policy arguments is, once again, disappointing. Indeed *Seymour-Smith* is an excellent example of the tension inherent in the balancing

---

[94] Barnard and Hepple, *ibid*, 407–08. Regarding the difficulties faced by the Court when pre-sented with conflicting (and often incomplete) statistical evidence see Case C–127/92 *Enderby*, paras 16–17, where the Court stated that a situation may only reveal a *prima facie* case of indirect dis-crimination if the statistics describing that situation are valid—if they cover enough individuals, do not illustrate purely fortuitous or short-term phenomena, and appear, in general, to be significant. See also Advocate General Léger in Case C–317/93 *Nolte*, paras 53–54: ' "the battle of the figures" in which the parties engaged at the hearing precludes any definitive conclusion . . . two statistical studies were produced: according to one, women account for almost 75% of persons in this type of work, whereas according to the other, they account for only 60%. The national court should there-fore establish what the factual position actually is.' See Case C–226/98 *Birgitte Jorgensen v Foreningen af Speciallaeger and Sygesikringens Forhandlingsudvalg* [2000] ECR I–2447, para 54, on what constitutes a significant sample.

[95] Barnard and Hepple, above n 93, 411.

process in which the Court is forced to participate in indirect sex discrimination cases. Member State employment policy objectives vie with the fundamental principle of equality; judicial scrutiny can be either strict or lenient; and the Court may itself intervene to reject generalisations presented by Member States to justify difference in treatment or leave it to the national court to assess the justifications presented. It is unfortunate that what could have been regarded as the anomaly which was *Nolte* and *Megner and Scheffel* has been allowed by the Court to extend beyond the field of social security into the judicial test for objective justifications of indirectly discriminatory Member State legislation, for which a perfectly good test had been in operation since *Rinner-Kühn*. Those who long for a resurrection of the latter test will have to cling to the *effet utile*-type argument on which the Court itself partially relied in *Seymour-Smith*, in relation to the fundamental principle of equal pay and its rejection, as in *Rinner-Kühn*, of mere generalisations, rather than compelling evidence as to the necessity or suitability of the means chosen to achieve the Member State's stated social policy aim.[96] However, with calls for substantial labour market reforms coming from the ECB and Member States, it will be difficult for the Court's appreciation of the proportionality and necessity of domestic social policy measures to ignore the changed political climate in the EU on the subject of employment protection.

The ambiguous nature of the test it laid down for national courts on the issue of objective justification and its reference in *Seymour-Smith* to *Nolte* and *Megner and Scheffel* was a regressive step and, unfortunately, as regards challenges to non social security legislation on grounds of indirect discrimination, not an isolated one. In *Kachelmann*, the applicant challenged as indirectly discriminatory a German law which provided that when selecting employees for dismissal according to social criteria, employers did not have to compare the work of part-time workers with that of full-time workers. It was common ground that part-time workers in Germany were far more likely to be women than men. The Court noted that Member States must be allowed a reasonable margin of discretion as regards the nature of social protection measures. It held that a comparison of part-time and full-time workers would put the former at an advantage (since, in the event of their jobs being abolished they would have to be offered a full-time job) and maintained that the question whether part-time workers should enjoy such an advantage was for the national legislature to decide. In its view, the German legislation was based on considerations unrelated to the sex of the workers. The Court's statement to the effect that '[the national legislature] must alone find a fair balance in employment law between

---

[96] Compare, in this respect, Moore (2000), above n 93, 162 with Barnard and Hepple, above n 93 One commentator regarded this part of the Court's decision as an attempt to close the door which had been opened by Case C–317/93 *Nolte*. See '*Seymour-Smith and Perez* after the European Court of Justice' (1999) *Scots Law Times* no 10, 71–74, 73. See below, where there is some discussion of a containment of the reasoning in *Nolte*.

the various interests concerned'[97] is too far-reaching and disregards the fundamental fact that, when formulating and implementing national employment policy, Member States must comply with EC law obligations as regards sex equality.[98]

Access to Training

Finally, at issue in the *Schnorbus* case were German rules on legal training which provided that completion of compulsory military service should be considered as a case of 'particular hardship', entitling an applicant for legal training to preferential treatment, namely automatic entry into a legal training course, as opposed to a twelve month deferral in the event that there were too many applicants.[99] The Court held that by giving priority to applicants who have completed compulsory military or civilian service, the German rules themselves were evidence of indirect discrimination since, under the relevant national legislation, women were not required to do military or civilian service and therefore could not benefit from the priority accorded to applications in circumstances regarded as cases of hardship.[100] On the question of justification, the Court dismissed the applicant's claim with remarkable brevity. The German rules, it held, which take account of the delay experienced in the progress of their education by legal training applicants who have been required to do military or civilian service were

---

[97] Case C–322/98 *Bärbel Kachelmann v Bankhaus Hermann Lampe KG* [2000] ECR I–7505, para 34.

[98] For another case involving different treatment of part-time workers see Case C–1/95 *Hellen Gerster v Freistaat Bayern* [1997] ECR I–5253. Bavarian civil service rules provided that since part-time employees accrued length of service more slowly, they gained promotion later. The statistics before the Court indicated that the vast majority (87%) of part-time employees in the public service were women. The Court held: 'If [the referring court] finds—despite the fact that Mrs. Gerster has already carried out on a part-time basis the duties attaching to the grade to which she aspires to be promoted, and that length of service was not calculated in accordance with criterion of strict proportionality—that part-time employees are generally slower than full-time employees in acquiring job-related abilities and skills, and that the competent authorities are in a position to establish that the measures chosen reflect a legitimate social policy aim, are an appropriate means of achieving that aim and are necessary in order to do so, the mere fact that the legislative provision affects far more women than men cannot be regarded as an infringement of Directive 76/207.' See also Case C–100/95 *Brigitte Kording v Senator für Finanzen* [1997] ECR I–5289, a case decided on the same day, by the same Chamber, as *Gerster* and involving length of service based criteria for entry to the profession of tax administrator. Those working less than half time received no service credit, while those working longer had their service credited on a *pro rata* basis. In that case, appropriateness and necessity failed to make an appearance.

[99] Case C–79/99 *Julia Schnorbus v Land Hessen* [2000] ECR I–10997.

[100] Curiously, the Court had just rejected the idea that priority rules could be regarded as directly discriminatory. Surely if women are excluded from military or civilian service then priority on that basis could of course be regarded as direct discrimination. Advocate General Jacobs did allude to this possibility but excluded a comparison with Case C–177/88 *Elisabeth Johanna Pacifica Dekker v Stichting Vormingscentrum voor Jong Volwassen (VJV-Centrum Plus)* [1990] ECR I–3941 on the grounds that, at issue was a criterion based on obligation imposed by law rather than a criterion based on a physical characteristic of one sex alone.

regarded as objective in nature and prompted solely by the desire to counterbalance to some extent the effects of that delay. This of course did not answer the question whether they were, in effect, rather than in purpose or object, discriminatory. The Court added, however, that the advantage conferred on male applicants, whose entrance may defer that of others by only twelve months, was not disproportionate, since the delay they have suffered on account of the activities referred to is at least equal to that period. Is one to infer from this that the type of compensatory measure sanctioned by the Court in *Abdoulaye*[101] could go as far as compensating women for the negative effects which childbearing and rearing have on their careers? A wider problem with *Schnorbus* is the Court's reliance on one form of discrimination (the fact that only German males could be or were required to do military service) to justify another (the favouring of military service veterans as regards access to training).

MEMBER STATE SOCIAL POLICIES AND SUPRANATIONAL JUDICIAL SCRUTINY

Directive 79/7 was intended as the first step in a process of progressive implementation of equal treatment in the field of social security. Essentially it provides that there shall be no discrimination on grounds of sex against those in the working population claiming benefits under statutory schemes providing protection against sickness, invalidity, old age, accidents at work and occupational diseases, and unemployment, or social assistance in so far as this is intended to supplement or replace statutory schemes.[102] If the Court's case-law on indirect discrimination reflects an ambivalence about the nature and quality of the equality it is seeking to ensure, namely formal or substantive, its decisions in the field of social security, give rise to particular cause for concern.

   In the *Teuling* case, the applicant claimed that national legislation which took into account a claimant's marital status or the existence of dependent children was indirectly discriminatory and contrary to Article 4(1) of Directive 79/7.[103] According to statistics provided by the Commission and the Dutch government,

---

[101] Case C–218/98 *Oumar Dabo Abdoulaye v Régie nationales des usines Renault SA* [1999] ECR I–5723, discussed below ch 5.

[102] See Articles 2, 3(1) and 4(1) of Directive 79/7. For a discussion of the limits of the notion of 'working population' pursuant to Article 2 see Case C–317/93 *Nolte*. For a discussion of the benefits which fall within the material scope of the Directive see Case C–382/98 *R v Secretary of State for Social Security, ex parte John Henry Taylor* [1999] ECR I–8955, para 14: 'in order to fall within the scope of the Directive, a benefit must constitute the whole or part of a statutory scheme providing protection against one of the risks listed in Article 3(1) of the Directive, or a form of social assistance having the same objective, and be directly and effectively linked to protection against one of those risks.' See generally M. Cousins, 'Equal Treatment and Social Security' (1994) 19 *European Law Review* 123–45; J.A. Sohrab, 'Women and Social Security: the Limits of EEC Equality Law' (1994) *Journal of Social Welfare and Family Law* 5–17; J. Steiner, 'The Principle of Equal Treatment for Men and Women in Social Security' in Hervey and O'Keeffe (eds), above n 5, pp 111–36; and L. Luckhaus, 'Egalité de traitement, protection sociale et garantie de ressources pour les femmes' (2000) 139 *Revue internationale du Travail* 163–99.

[103] Case 30/85 *Teuling* [1987] ECR 2497.

a significantly greater number of married men than married women received a supplement linked to family responsibilities. On the issue of justification of what was therefore, on its face, an indirectly discriminatory piece of legislation, the Court noted that the aim of the Dutch law was not to link benefits to the salary previously earned by beneficiaries but to provide a minimum subsistence income to persons with no income from work. It considered that such a guarantee to persons who would otherwise be destitute constituted an integral part of national social policy. It then held that increases designed to meet the additional costs of family dependants and thus to ensure that awards to beneficiaries with such dependants did not fall below a certain minimum could be justified under the Directive and left it up to the national court to verify the proportionality of such measures. The Dutch government had also argued that the impugned legislation sought to provide, having regard to the resources available, a minimum subsistence income for all workers suffering from an incapacity to work. The Court recognised the legitimacy of this aim and stated that Community law does not prevent a Member State, in controlling its social expenditure, from taking into account the greater needs of those with a dependent spouse and children.

Teuling seemed to confirm the irrelevance of intention when it comes to denying indirect discrimination. It also, like the case-law discussed above, set out fairly detailed criteria for establishing whether an apparently discriminatory practice can in fact be justified. However, as commentators pointed out in the aftermath of the Court's ruling, no matter how welcome its decision was from the point of view of extending the basics of the indirect sex discrimination doctrine to the field of social security, from the perspective of the promotion of substantive equality, the decision in *Teuling* disappointed. Essentially the Court 'implies that any sex neutral social security provision operating to women's disadvantage will be permitted if the purpose of the provision is to ensure a minimum subsistence level of income in order to protect people from poverty'.[104] In other words, the fundamental EC principle of equality may simply be trumped by a Member State pointing to the laudable social policy objectives behind its social security legislation and relying on presumably, straitened, budgetary circumstances. However, as Sohrab points out, some of this *prima facie* indirectly discriminatory legislation is really national legislatures' attempts to turn around previously directly discriminatory national social security rules. Rather than embarking on costly levelling up of rights, benefits are redesigned so that they are gender neutral; albeit they continue to channel benefits to, for example, the family 'breadwinner', thereby disadvantaging women, who traditionally have not fulfilled this role.

---

[104] See Luckhaus, above n 102, 57. In other words, the Court seemed to indicate that the disadvantages suffered by women were not disproportionate to the purpose sought to be achieved. It did not examine whether that purpose was indefensible given the burden it imposed on the female sex. See also the criticism by Somek, above n 46, of the Court's purpose-based test of indirect discrimination.

As we will see in subsequent cases, Member States tend to plead, generally with success, the primacy of their social policy objectives in order to defend their social security legislation from challenges of indirect discrimination and national budgetary constraints rarely fail to make an appearance. Full equality, as More points out, may not be achieved where the cost is prohibitive.[105] That is clearly the message which the Court (*Defrenne II*, *Barber*) and indeed the Member States (*Barber* protocol) have transmitted in their use of temporal limitations. But it is also visible in many, if not most, of the Court's rulings on indirect sex discrimination, particularly in the field of social security. More notes, in the context of temporal limitations on the Court's sex equality rulings, that cost considerations can operate as a limit in any constitutional system but that such a limit 'is more pronounced in the case of a supranational court, which is conscious of the reaction of not just one, but numerous governments, to its judgments.'[106] Her comments can equally be extended beyond temporal limitations to the Court's sex discrimination case-law generally and the standard of scrutiny it is prepared to apply to Member State legislation and, in particular, national social security legislation.

Some applicants in social security cases before the Court have been more successful. *M.L. Ruzius-Wilbrink v Bestuur van de Bedrijfsvereniging voor Overheidsdiensten*[107] concerned Dutch legislation on invalidity benefits guaranteeing a minimum subsistence income. While full-time workers and other groups, such as students and the self-employed, were entitled to claim this minimum income regardless of their previous earnings, the entitlement of part-time workers was linked to their previous income. The claimant, who had worked part-time and found that her earnings were insufficient to enable her to claim the full minimum income, claimed that the Dutch provisions were indirectly discriminatory. In defence of its legislation the Dutch government argued that it would be unfair to full-time workers to allow part-time workers to benefit under the scheme from an income higher than that they would have received had they been employed. The Court rejected this social justification of the differential treatment. The purported aim of the Dutch system was to provide assistance to those in need but its effect was to deprive those who most needed it of assistance. According to the Court, the different treatment afforded part-time workers could not be justified on the proposed ground, since the benefit received by students and self-employed workers might also be substantially above their previous income.[108] It has been suggested—as an explanation for the different

---

[105] See More in Craig and De Búrca, above n 12, p 543.

[106] *Ibid*, p 543. See also Steiner in Hervey and O'Keeffe, above n 5, p 112, where she argues that Directive 79/7 was crafted in such a way as to avoid disrupting the financial equilibrium of national social security schemes and that this factor has no doubt tempered the Court's approach to its interpretation.

[107] Case C–102/88 [1989] ECR 4311.

[108] Case C–102/88 *Ruzius-Wilbrink*, para 16. The relevant test proposed by the Court to the national court was based on its decision in Case 171/88 *Rinner-Kühn*.

fortunes of Member States' social justifications in *Teuling* and *Ruzius-Wilbrink*—that the Court is unprepared to accept such justifications where they operate to the disadvantage of an already disadvantaged group such as part-time workers (*Ruzius-Wilbrink*). Where, in contrast, the criteria for a benefit are linked to objective factors such as responsibility for dependants (*Teuling*), or partner's income, the Court is prepared to apply a more lenient standard of scrutiny and accepts social justifications more readily.[109]

Further proof of this distinction can be found in other cases concerning Directive 79/7 such as *Commission v Belgium*[110] and *Molenbroek*[111]. The former, the Commission's first Article 226 EC action with respect to the Directive, concerned Belgian legislation on unemployment benefits and invalidity assurance. For the purposes of calculating such benefits Belgian legislation gave preferential treatment to unemployed persons who, in their capacity as head of household, had a spouse, cohabitee, parent or child as a dependant. These benefits were calculated on a less favourable basis for unemployed workers who lived alone or, less favourably still for those unemployed workers who lived with another person receiving a salary or replacement income. The Commission argued that the Belgian system was indirectly discriminatory since men predominated in the category treated most favourably, namely that of workers with dependants, while women made up the bulk of the group which was treated least favourably.[112]

The Belgian government argued that the difference in incidence as between men and women in the three categories of beneficiaries reflects a social phenomenon, namely the fact that there are fewer women than men in the working population. This argument held no sway with the Court, which stated that it was not possible to derive from such considerations objective criteria unrelated to any discrimination on grounds of sex capable of justifying discrimination. In contrast, the Court did accept the Belgian government's argument to the effect that the aim of its legislation was to provide beneficiaries, within the limits necessarily imposed by budgetary resources, with a minimum replacement income, having regard to the family situation of the beneficiary. According to the Court, the impugned legislation took into consideration the existence of different needs—the greater burdens resulting from unemployment for households with only one income and the financial aid which a spouse's income may represent

---

[109] See Steiner in Hervey and O'Keeffe (eds), above n 5, p 124; and J.A. Sohrab, *Sexing the Benefit: Women, Social Security and Financial Independence in EC Equality Law* (Aldershot, Dartmouth, 1996), p 125.

[110] Case C–229/89 [1991] ECR I–2205.

[111] Case C–226/91 *Jan Molenbroek v Bestuur van de Sociale Verzekeringsbank* [1992] ECR I–5943.

[112] The statistics provided by the Belgium government at the request of the Commission (based on a survey of 6% of wholly unemployed persons in receipt of benefit in June 1982) revealed that 81.4% of unemployed persons in group 1 were men whereas 65.25% of those in group 3 were women. See Banks, K., 'Social Security—Objective Justification in the Context of Indirect Discrimination' (1991) *Industrial Law Journal* 220–23, 220, for a detailed description of the system.

for the unemployed: 'Those principles and objectives form part of a social policy which in the current state of Community law is a matter for the Member States which enjoy a *reasonable* margin of discretion as regards both the nature of the protective measures and the detailed arrangements for their implementation.'[113] The Court found that Belgium was permitted to control its social expenditure and take into account the greater needs of certain beneficiaries.

It is interesting in *Commission v Belgium* to compare the technique and approach of the Court to the case file and the issues in this, an Article 226 EC infringement case, compared to a preliminary reference procedure under Article 234 EC. It was for the Court and the Court alone to accept or reject the factual and legal analysis presented to it by the Commission. In addition, it was for the Court to grapple with the various elements of the *Rinner-Kühn* test, including the suitability and appropriateness of the Belgian rules for the attainment of the social policy aim proposed. Although the Court recognised the Member State's discretion with respect to the determination and organization of its own social policy it remarked that they simply enjoyed a *reasonable* margin of discretion, rather than the *wide* margin conceded in later cases. In addition, the Court maintained proportionality as an essential element of the standard of scrutiny with which Member States' social policy measures had to comply. Nevertheless, the Court's recognition of even this degree of Member State discretion as regards the scope and implementation of domestic social policy objectives was rightly regarded as ominous.[114] It has been suggested in fact that it was the extent of the margin of discretion conceded Member States by the Court which dissuaded the Commission from bringing more Article 226 EC actions in the social security field.[115] Finally, what has been identified as the Court's 'ready acceptance of the characterisation by Member State governments of the purposes of national schemes'[116] may be explicable in the context of Article 234 EC references, where the resolution of the case is ultimately for the national court, but it is inexplicable in the context of infringement proceedings under Article 226 EC, where the Court sits as court of first and final instance and where its duty is to root out and condemn failures by Member States to fulfil their Treaty

---

[113] Case C–229/89 *Commission v Belgium*, para 22 (emphasis added). On Member States' continued competence in the field of social policy see Case C–343/92 *M.A. De Weerd, née Roks, and Others v Bestuur van de Bedrijfsvereniging voor de Gezondheid, Geestelijke en Maatschappelijke Belangen and Others* [1994] ECR I–571, para 26: 'Directive 79/7 leaves intact the powers reserved by Articles [136 and 137] of the Treaty to the Member States to define their social policy within the framework of close cooperation organised by the Commission, and consequently the nature and extent of measures of social protection, including those relating to social security, and the way in which they are implemented'; and Advocate General Darmon in Case 192/85 *Newstead v Department of Transport* [1987] ECR 4753, 4773: '[Member States] must retain the power to control their own social policy and, of course, its financial implications.'

[114] See Banks, above n 112, 223.

[115] See T. Hervey, 'Sex Equality in Social Protection: New Institutionalist Perspectives on Allocation of Competence' (1998) 4 *European Law Journal* 196–219.

[116] See Sohrab (1996), above n 109, p 132.

obligations. In *Commission v Belgium*, the Court approved of the aim, principle and objective behind the Belgian system. But it did not examine whether the effect of that system was acceptable from the point of view of the principle of equality or whether the disadvantages, if any, suffered by female benefit recipients as a result of that legislative choice, or the budgetary constraints which dictated it, were necessary for the attainment of the objective in question. The legitimacy of the Belgian objective seemed to suffice and no explicit balancing of the interests at stake was undertaken.

Reference was made previously to the *Nolte* and *Megner and Scheffel* cases and, indeed, in terms of the evolving standard of scrutiny which the Court is willing to apply to allegedly discriminatory national legislation they are cases of the utmost importance, representing, as they do, one of the lowest points of the Court's work in this field. German legislation excluded persons in minor or short-term employment from the benefit of compulsory invalidity and old-age insurance and sickness insurance, as well as from the obligation to contribute to the national unemployment insurance scheme. The applicant in *Nolte*, who had previously been employed in a normal job subject to compulsory insurance contributions, subsequently worked in minor employment,[117] a job which she was then forced to give up due to illness. She appealed against a decision by the competent authorities refusing her an invalidity pension on account of the fact that she had not made the necessary insurance contributions. The Court of Justice was in turn asked whether the exclusion of minor employment from compulsory insurance constitutes indirect discrimination contrary to Article 4(1) of Directive 79/7.

As regards the personal scope of Directive 79/7, the Court held that minor employment of the type referred to in the reference fell within the scope *ratione personae* of the Directive and that it was up to the national court to resolve any doubts surrounding Ms. Nolte's employment status when she applied for invalidity benefit.[118] On the question of the indirectly discriminatory effects of the statutory exclusion of minor employment from the statutory old-age insurance scheme, the Irish and British governments intervened to emphasise the need to protect the financial equilibrium of the Member States' contributory schemes; an argument reminiscent of that which had previously carried the day in cases

---

[117] Thereafter she ceased to carry out activities covered by the statutory social security scheme and paid no further compulsory contributions—the Court stated that this was on account of having to bring up her children and consequently being in minor employment.

[118] The Court's inclusion of minor employment within the personal scope of the Directive is to be welcomed. As S. Deakins points out, 'Equality Under a Market Order: The Employment Act 1989' (1990) *ILJ* 1–18, 18: 'a meaningful strategy for employment opportunities for women would aim to extend social protection to non-standard working arrangements and would seek to raise the attractiveness of "atypical" work.' This aspect of the decision in Case C–317/93 *Nolte* underlines, however, why the Court's finding on objective justification was so disappointing. On the factual circumstances surrounding the applicant's claim see the Opinion of Advocate General Léger in Case C–317/93 *Nolte*, paras 24–25.

like *Defrenne II* and *Barber*.[119] The German government argued that it had to respond to a social and presumably economic demand for minor employment by fostering the existence and supply of such employment. The only way to do this within the structural framework of the German social security scheme was to exclude minor employment from compulsory insurance, thereby making minor employees attractive to employers. The German government also warned that full-time or part-time jobs would not replace minor employment were the legislation altered following a decision of the Court. Instead, there would be an increase in black market employment and other circumventing devices.[120]

Perhaps it is useful to remember before explaining the Court's response to these arguments, that the decision, handed down in December 1995, must have been deliberated that Autumn. At the time, few Member States were in a position to comply with the Maastricht convergence criteria for EMU, unemployment in the EC generally was rising to alarming levels, not least in Germany and the latter had begun to realise the full cost of reintegrating Eastern Germany. One can only speculate whether or not these considerations had some bearing on the Court's response. That response was as follows:

> in the current state of Community law, social policy is a matter for the Member States. Consequently, it is for the Member States to choose the measures capable of achieving the aim of their social and employment policy. In exercising that competence, the Member States have a broad margin of discretion [. . . .] the social and employment policy aim relied on by the German Government is objectively unrelated to any discrimination on grounds of sex and that, in exercising its competence, the national legislature was reasonably entitled to consider that the legislation in question was necessary in order to achieve that aim. In those circumstances, the legislation in question cannot be described as indirect discrimination within the meaning of Article 4(1) of the directive.[121]

---

[119] Essentially their argument consisted of the following: contributory schemes required equivalence to be maintained between the contributions paid by employees and employers and the benefits paid in the event of the materialization of one of the risks covered by the scheme. The structure of these schemes could not be maintained in their present form if the impugned provisions had to be abolished. It should be added, however, that even the requirements of free movement in the internal market have sometimes given way to similar claims—see Case C–204/90 *Hans Martin Bachmann v Belgian State* [1992] ECR I–249, paras 21–28.

[120] Case C–317/93 *Nolte*, paras 31–32. For a similar doomsday scenario see the submissions of the United Kingdom government in Case C–9/91 *R v Secretary of State for Social Security, ex parte Equal Opportunities Commission* [1992] ECR I–4297.

[121] Case C–317/93 *Nolte*, paras 33–35 and Case C–444/93 *Megner and Scheffel*, paras 29–31. Advocate General Léger had identified the objective justifications proposed by the German government as the need to safeguard a structural principle of the German social security system, the need to avoid financial disequilibrium and serious problems generally for the statutory old-age insurance scheme and the need to avoid the adverse repercussions on employment policy (ie the reduction in minor employment and the resulting rise in unemployment and increase in black market employment). He regarded only the latter justification as one to which the national court should give serious attention but seemed to doubt whether any of the drawbacks suggested by the German government constituted a sufficiently serious objective justification of the disadvantage caused by the legislation.

The Court accepted that, in the context of social security, where a Member State is reasonably entitled to regard legislative measures as necessary to achieve a social and employment policy aim, that legislation passes muster. Member States enjoy a wide margin of discretion in relation to their social and employment policy and it is not for the Court, even with reference to its time-honoured principle of proportionality, to second guess that discretion.[122] Despite the fact that proportionality had previously been part and parcel of the judicial test of the objective justification of *prima facie* discriminatory national legislation, even that relating to social security, in *Nolte* and *Megner and Scheffel* the need to examine appropriateness and necessity were jettisoned.[123]

In the light of these decisions, Ellis argues that, in order to justify apparent indirect sex discrimination, a Member State may need only show that it reasonably believed the measure to be necessary to achieve a social policy aim, not that it actually and demonstrably is necessary in order to achieve that aim.[124] She also points out that if anti-sex discrimination law is to have the remedial effect intended, it must impose a rigid requirement on employers and, as the case may be, the legislator, to examine exactly how and why their *prima facie* discriminatory practices or rules are essential. If they are not essential, then they should be forbidden because of their discriminatory effect.[125] This was not the case in *Nolte* and *Megner and Scheffel*. In *Rinner-Kühn* the Court had chosen not to follow Advocate General Darmon's advice to the effect that national legislation should only be regarded as incompatible with EC law if it was intended to

---

[122] W. Niemayer, (Director General at the time in the German Federal Ministry of Labour and Social Affairs), commenting in McCrudden (ed), above n 48, pp 143–46, p 146, on Case C–317/93 *Nolte* claims that if the Court of Justice had accepted the discrimination claim, forcing the German government to abolish the exemption of minor employment from compulsory insurance and rearrange its social insurance scheme, it would have been engaging in law-making in the field of social security, despite the limited Community competence in this respect. See further, on the role of proportionality in the context of Directive 79/7 (specifically Article 7(1)(a)), Case C–9/91 *R v Secretary of State for Social Security, ex parte Equal Opportunities Commission* [1992] ECR I–4297, para 13 of Advocate General Van Gerven's Opinion: 'in a context such as the present the principle of proportionality plays a smaller role than is usual. The principle of proportionality requires the Court to weigh the interest pursued by the rule in question against the interest which that rule infringes. Where the relevant rules lay down a procedure involving the balancing of interests, it is not as a rule for the Court to undertake such a balancing of interests itself . . . it may do so only exceptionally because it appears that the discrimination may be eliminated without excessive legislative or financial difficulties.'

[123] According to Hervey (1998), above n 115, the Court has more or less forfeited control over the issue of justification. See also B. Fitzpatrick, 'Converse Pyramids and the EU Social Constitution' in Shaw (ed), above n 24, pp 303–24, pp 319–20; and Case C–8/94 *C.B. Laperre v Bestuurscommissie Beroepszaken in de Provincie Zuid-Holland* [1996] ECR I–273, which involved two Dutch unemployment benefit schemes: one which provided benefits to unemployed workers without sufficient resources to ensure their subsistence, subject to their resources being modest, the other providing benefits for older or partially incapacitated long-term unemployed persons. The applicant argued that the conditions and age in the second scheme favoured more men than women. The Court applied its hands-off approach to social policy legislation and held that the Dutch legislature was reasonably entitled to consider that the rules in question were necessary to achieve the social policy aims.

[124] See Ellis in Ellis (ed) (1999), above n 50, p 179.

[125] See Ellis above n 36, 574.

discriminate. However, it is arguable that, over time and overall, specifically in the context of Member State social security legislation, Darmon's suggested level of scrutiny has won through.

What is to be hoped, following *Nolte* and *Megner and Scheffel*, is that the Court does not forget its other judicial pronouncements on the limits to Member States' discretion in the field of social policy. In *De Weerd*, for example, the Court recognised that budgetary considerations may influence a Member State's choice of social policy and affect the nature or scope of the social protection measures which it wishes to adopt, but that they cannot in themselves constitute the aim pursued by that social policy and cannot, therefore, justify discrimination against one of the sexes. To concede that budgetary considerations may justify a difference in treatment as between men and women which would otherwise constitute indirect discrimination on grounds of sex would be, said the Court, to accept that the application and scope of as fundamental a rule of EC law as that of equal treatment between men and women might vary in time and place according to the state of the public finances of the Member States.[126]

Equally, in *Buchner*, which involved national legislation establishing a different minimum age for male and female workers for entitlement to old-age pensions due to incapacity for work, the Court was not content to accept the loosely framed social policy arguments of the Member State in question and pointed out that, apart from general considerations of a budgetary nature, no argument had been put forward to demonstrate any interdependence between social security systems which might be affected by removal of the discrimination at issue. The Court concluded that the removal of such discrimination could not have any serious effect on the financial equilibrium of the social security systems as a whole. Equally, the Court refused to accept Member State requests for the imposition of a temporal limitation to avoid major financial repercussions pointing out that the financial consequences which might ensue for a Member State from a preliminary ruling do not in themselves justify limiting the temporal effect of a Court ruling.[127]

---

[126] See Case C–343/92 *De Weerd*, para 36. Compare Case C–226/98 *Jorgensen* paras 40–41: reasons relating to the need to ensure sound management of public expenditure on specialised medical care and to guarantee people's access to such care are legitimate and may justify measures of social policy. They must be suitable and requisite for attaining that end; and Case C–280/94 *Posthuma-van Damme v Bestuur van de Bedrijfsvereniging voor Detailhandel, Ambachten en Huisvrouwen* [1996] ECR I–179. See further Herbert in McCrudden (ed), above n 48, p 133, who maintains that it would be shocking if measures having a budgetary objective with regard to the cost of the health insurance system should not be able to justify discriminatory measures in the field of the free movement of goods (Case 238/82 *Duphar v Netherlands* [1984] ECR 523) but that the same kind of measures would in themselves justify an infringement of equality between men and women. See also, in the context of the free provision of services, Case C–158/96 *Raymond Kohll v Union des caisses de maladie* [1998] ECR I–1931.

[127] See also Case C–328/91 *Secretary of State for Social Security v Evelyn Thomas and Others* [1993] ECR I–1247.

Decisions following *Nolte* and *Megner and Scheffel* provide evidence of resistance within the Court, whether intentional or fortuitous, to application of the lower level of judicial scrutiny to Member State justifications of indirect sex discrimination beyond the field of social security. In *Seymour-Smith*, the Court seemed partly to resist the wholesale extension of this laxer approach to review of Member State social policy legislation in the broader sense. It specified, in a case concerning national legislation on unfair dismissal protection, that the Member States' broad margin of discretion in the area of social policy cannot have the effect of frustrating the implementation of the fundamental principle of equal pay for men and women. Member States still have to provide evidence on the basis of which it could reasonably be considered that the means chosen to achieve a particular social policy aim are suitable for achieving it.[128]

Similar resistance was evident in the *Krüger*[129] case, which involved a nurse who had worked full-time in a post covered by the provisions of German collective agreements on public sector employees (otherwise known as the BAT) until the birth of her child. Thereafter she took some leave and received a child-care allowance before returning to work in a minor employment post, which was not covered by the BAT. She claimed that the hospital's refusal to pay her a special Christmas bonus on the grounds that the allowance is payable only to those covered by the BAT was discriminatory.

Did the exclusion of persons in minor employment from the scope of the BAT constitute indirect sex discrimination? The Court reiterated its finding in *Nolte* and *Megner and Scheffel* to the effect that the exclusion of persons in minor employment from social insurance is intended to meet a social demand for minor employment which the German government considered it should respond to in the context of its social and employment policy. However, exclusion of persons in minor employment from the BAT cannot alter the principle that male and female workers should receive equal pay for equal work as laid down in Article 141 EC. In this respect the Court emphasised its position in *Seymour-Smith* to the effect that a national rule cannot have the effect of rendering a fundamental principle of Community law meaningless. The Court accepted that, as Community law stands, social policy is a matter for the Member States, that it is for them to choose measures capable of achieving their social and employment policy aims and that, in this respect, they enjoy a broad margin of discretion. However, the Court then distinguished *Nolte* and *Megner and Scheffel* from the instant case:

> In this case, it is not a question of either a measure adopted by the national legislature in the context of its discretionary power or a basic principle of the German social security system, but of the exclusion of persons in minor employment from the benefit of a

---

[128] See Case C–167/97 *Seymour-Smith*, paras 75–76. L. Flynn, 'Equality between Men and Women in the Court of Justice' (1998) 18 *Yearbook of European Law* 259–87, 278, suggests that these statements are likely to receive considerable scrutiny to determine how they affect Member States' freedom of manoeuvre.

[129] Case C–281/97 *Andrea Krüger v Kreiskrankenhaus Ebersberg* [1999] ECR I–5127.

collective agreement which provides for the grant of a special annual bonus, the result of this being that, in respect of pay, those persons are treated differently from those governed by that collective agreement.[130]

The Court found that such an exclusion constitutes indirect discrimination based on sex, where that exclusion applies independently of the sex of the worker but actually affects a considerably higher percentage of women than men. The broad margin of discretion which the German government had wanted to wield beyond the field of social security was thus not permitted. *Krüger* confirms that the highest standard of scrutiny in indirect discrimination cases is reserved by the Court for the justification of employers' practices, albeit in the instant case a public service employer.

Clearly the Court must respect the Treaty's division of competences between Member States and the EC in the field of social policy and the delicate nature of the balancing process inherent in its consideration of objective justifications is undeniable. Nevertheless, if the Court is to ensure that the fundamental principles of equal treatment and/or equal pay between male and female workers are to be upheld, it must surely demand a high level of justification from Member States whose employment policies or practices appear to thwart those principles, even if they do so in the context of social security provision. The indirect discrimination case-law of the Court was acclaimed precisely because it would allow the law and its users to pry behind apparently gender neutral constructs and challenge what may be a gendered division of society. In the context of social security legislation, indirect discrimination is a tool of crucial importance precisely because traditional divisions of labour in the home and employment market have meant that women have to date enjoyed a very different relationship with the social security system than men.[131] Women, for example, may move in and out of employment more frequently because of childcare/elderly care/homecare responsibilities.[132] As a result, they sometimes do not belong to the 'working population'[133] or, if they do, they often do not comply with employers' and the law's penchant for long-term, stable employment relationships and other models which the law has adopted for the distribution of benefits, such as 'head of household' allowances.[134] It is for legislators primarily to

---

[130] Case C–281/97 *Krüger*, para 29.

[131] See Sohrab (1994), above n 102, 5; and Luckhaus (2000), above n 102.

[132] A fact explicitly recognised by the Court itself in Case 109/88 *Danfoss*, para 24: 'the criterion of length of service may involve less advantageous treatment of women than of men in so far as women have entered the labour market more recently than men or more frequently suffer an interruption of their career.' See generally E.J. McCaffrey, 'Slouching Towards Equality: Gender Discrimination, Market Efficiency and Social Change' (1993) 103 *Yale Law Journal* 595–675.

[133] See, for example, Case C–77/95 *Bruna-Alessandra Züchner v Handelskrankenkasse (Ersatzkasse) Bremen* [1996] ECR I–5689, on the exclusion from the personal scope of Directive 79/7 of a woman who undertook, as an unremunerated activity, the care of her handicapped spouse.

[134] See also Beveridge and Nott in Hervey and O'Keeffe (eds), above n 5, p 387: 'Women's work patterns, their role in childcare and elder care and the segregated nature of the labour market are implicated. Women are more likely than men to take career breaks or work part-time with adverse consequences for earnings, for occupational benefits and for State benefits.' See also D. Meulders

take on these gendered structures and adapt them. However, by adopting Directive 79/7, albeit a measure which is only intended as a progressive first step involving several exclusions and derogations, this is what the Member States had committed themselves to do. Surely the Court must realise that anything short of a high level of scrutiny of Member State justifications of discrimination in this field will mean that the fundamental nature of the equality principle and its social objectives ring untrue.[135] In addition, as Sohrab points out, in implementing the Directive it can be easy for a Member State to substitute directly discriminatory rules for rules which are *prima facie* gender neutral but which favour certain groups financially and which, in fact, continue to be a source of indirect discrimination.[136] They do so in the knowledge that the wide margin of discretion which the Court affords them in the social policy sphere means it is likely the objective justifications they put forward in their defence will successfully excuse any difference in treatment.

ARTICLE 234 EC AND INDIRECT SEX DISCRIMINATION CASES

The jurisprudence of the Court in the field of indirect sex discrimination highlights the difficulties which beset the development of EC law on the basis of a procedure which dictates a particular relationship between the Court of Justice and national courts and a peculiar division of functions between them. According to this jurisdictional dividing line, it is for the former to interpret EC law and for the latter to apply that law to the specific facts in the legal disputes with which they are seised. Yet what exactly are national courts asking the Court of Justice to do when they refer questions concerning alleged cases of indirect sex discrimination? The Court is often being asked whether the specific employment practice, rule or legislative provision gives rise to a *prima facie* case of indirect discrimination when a group of workers of one sex, usually female, are disadvantaged, in law or in fact, by the rule in question to a greater extent than their male colleagues. To determine whether this is the case, national courts have requested guidance from the Court on whether disadvantages complained of could point to indirect discrimination by an employer or the legislator and have sought to establish what level of disparate impact is necessary for

and R. Plasman, 'European Economic Policies and Social Quality' in W. Beck, L. van der Maesen and A. Walker (eds), *The Social Quality of Europe* (1997), pp 15–33, p 27.

[135] See also Cousins (1994), above n 102, 143–44, who argues that by delimiting the personal and material scope of the Directive in a manner which allows discrimination against women to be perpetuated and by accepting economic factors and a wide margin of discretion for Member States to justify differences in treatment, the Court has failed to promote a strong interpretation of the existing legislation and has weakened the potentialities of the Directive.

[136] Sohrab (1994), above n 102, 15. These formally equal benefit rules help those women gain access to benefits who most closely conform to underlying structures of benefit entitlement, and underlying structures which disadvantage women who do not conform remain untouched.

such a case of *prima facie* indirect discrimination to be established. National referring courts also seek to establish whether the justifications put forward by employers and, as the case may be, the legislator, may excuse what appear at first sight to be discriminatory rules or practices, thereby bringing them beyond the sanction of EC sex equality law.

If the Court is simply to provide referring courts with principled statements as to the law and its interpretation, which is what the orthodox approach to the preliminary reference procedure would seem to suggest, there is little in fact it can do beyond restating the principles it established in its early indirect discrimination cases. As the case-law discussed in previous sections reveals, however, this is not, in reality, how the dialogue between national courts and the Court of Justice has been evolving. As the law develops and the Court's interlocutors become more aware of the difficulties they face applying it what seems to happen is that the questions referred become increasingly more complex and indeed more specifically linked to the factual circumstances which inspire them. On occasion, the Court does essentially repeat the essence of its already established case-law.[137] The difficulty which such an approach presents, however, is that a national referring court which has stayed the proceedings before it may be extremely disappointed, even exasperated, to find that the answers from the Court of Justice are of little help and could actually have been gleaned from the Court reports themselves without a stay on proceedings at national level of approximately twenty two months and without the additional financial cost for litigants that a reference entails. To date, however, the Court of Justice's insistence on the cooperative nature of its relationship with national courts (and the interpretation/application distinction which follows from it) has been due to its conviction, well-founded to a certain extent, that the success of the preliminary reference procedure and indeed its own standing and legitimacy, depended on the extent to which national courts were prepared to enter into a judicial dialogue between equals and apply EC law more or less uniformly and in accordance with the Court's rulings.

Rather than simply referring back to the essence of its previous case-law, the Court has also tried to adapt the essential principles of that case-law to the facts underpinning the particular case before it. This of course has its own perils. On the one hand, if the Court is to be in a position to provide a useful, even correct, ruling, it is essential in indirect sex discrimination cases that the picture of facts and problems is clear and complete and, in particular, that the reasons presented

---

[137] In Case C–33/89 *Kowalska v Freie und Hansestadt Hamburg* [1990] ECR I–2591, the City of Hamburg argued that a collective agreement which excluded part-time workers from severance pay was justified by the fact that part-time workers do not provide for their needs and those of their families exclusively out of their earned income, so that employers need not provide temporary assistance to them in the form of severance pay on the termination of their employment. Rather than rebutting this stereotypical argument the Court merely stated that it was for the national court to assess the justifications put forward.

as justification have been discussed before the national court.[138] This is very often not the case, the point at which national proceedings are stayed varying according to the eagerness of the referring judge to send the case to Luxembourg or to the determination of one or both of the parties at national level to get the case out of the national forum to Luxembourg. Furthermore, as *Enderby* and *JamO* demonstrated, national courts may, in some circumstances, prefer issues of EC law to be clarified before proceeding with lengthy and costly inquiries into, for example, the question whether the jobs involved are of equal value. On the other hand, the closer the Court gets to the facts of the case and, inevitably, to applying and adapting EC law to those facts, the more open it is to challenge for having breached the jurisdictional line which is meant to separate it from the national referring court. Thus, in *Seymour-Smith*, where the Court was asked a number of highly specific questions, including one as to whether disparate impact could be established, it was said to have sailed 'perilously close to the jurisdictional dividing line between itself and the national court' when it had observed that the statistics before it did not appear to show that a considerably smaller percentage of women than men was able to fulfil the requirement imposed by the disputed rule.[139] That jurisdictional dividing line may appear particularly fragile and the dialogue between the courts somewhat meaningless when, as sometimes happens, the national court comes to a different conclusion to that intimated by the Court on the basis of the facts before it.

As the law on indirect sex discrimination stands, the Court has elucidated a hierarchy of tests intended to enable national courts to determine whether an indirectly discriminatory rule or practice is objectively justified. The robustness of the judicial test of indirect sex discrimination has depended, as we have seen, on whether the rule or practice is attributable to an individual employer or the result of legislation and, in turn, whether that legislation concerns the field of social security. In addition, as several commentators have pointed out, given the

---

[138] S. Prechal, 'Combatting Indirect Discrimination in Community Law Context' (1993) *Legal Issues of European Integration* 81–97, 93. See also Case C–66/96 *Handels- og Kontorfunktionaerernes Forbund i Danmark, acting on behalf of Hoj Pedersen v Faellesforeningen for Danmarks Brugsforeninger* [1998] ECR I–7327, para 45: 'the need to afford an interpretation of Community law which is helpful for the national court makes it essential to define the legal context in which the interpretation requested should be placed. From that point of view it may, depending on the circumstances, be an advantage for the facts in the case to be established and for questions of purely national law to be settled at the time the reference is made to the Court of Justice so that it can be in a position to take cognisance of all the factual and legal elements which may be relevant to the interpretation of Community law which it is called upon to give.' This was, however, a case of direct discrimination; and Case C–333/97 *Susanne Lewen v Lothar Denda* [1999] ECR I–7243, where the Court had to base its ruling on indirect discrimination on two different hypotheses since it was unclear from the information available to it what the purpose and objective of the impugned national rule were.

[139] See E. Ellis 'The Recent Jurisprudence of the Court of Justice in the Field of Sex Equality' (2000) 37 *Common Market Law Review* 1403-26, 1409–10. See also E. Ellis, 'Recent Case Law of the Court of Justice on the Equal Treatment of Men and Women' (1994) 31 *European Law Review* 43–75, 75, where she regarded the Court's approach in indirect sex discrimination cases to what constitutes justification as (at that time) strict and even 'verging on the interfering'.

division of judicial functions on which Article 234 EC was originally based, it has been for the national court to determine the question of whether an indirectly discriminatory provision of national law is justified. This has limited the development of a uniform concept of justification at EU level.[140] As regards the field of social security and other sensitive areas of national law touching, for example, on employment creation and promotion, the Court has been far from rigorous in the application of the objective justification test which it created, appearing to accept the word of national governments that the rules complained of were intended to achieve a legitimate objective, without more. Yet, as Hepple points out, the impact which the potentially powerful tool of indirect discrimination has on the labour market will depend upon how sympathetic a court is to the employer's, and from a broader perspective, the legislator's business or policy needs.[141]

The preliminary reference procedure has obviously been of fundamental importance in the development and acceptance of EC law, not least EC sex equality law. However, since sex discrimination is something suffered by a group collectively, there are limits to the extent to which a procedure involving the elevation to a European court of individual disputes between litigants can effectively combat the disadvantage suffered by a group as a whole. Article 226 EC does of course provide the Commission with a tool for combatting statutory discriminatory measures and practices and, as Fredman points out, may lighten the financial and psychological burden on the individual litigant. However, as the discussion of the *Commission v Belgium* case revealed, the Commission seems to have been loath, at least in the field of social security, to bring more cases to the Court given the wide margin of discretion afforded the Member States by its past jurisprudence.

Finally, if the Court's stance on indirect discrimination and the issue of objective justification in particular is seen to have gone from robust to downright confused and indeed to be far too permissive of practices and rules which disadvantage one sex over another, then there must be some reason for this. One reason for the lack of coherence and predictability in the Court's case-law could be that the collegiate principles which have brought the Court so far, are making it difficult, at this later stage in the process of European integration, for its jurisprudence to advance and mature further. If indeed the questions being referred by national courts are more complex and demanding now that the basic principles of EC sex discrimination law have been established both at a legislative and judicial level, it is questionable whether the sometimes elliptical manner in which the Court's decisions are constructed and the lack of dissenting opinions are conducive to the achievement of the objective behind the preliminary reference procedure, namely coherent, principled interpretations of EC

---

[140] Hervey (1998), above n 115; Townshend-Smith in Hervey and O'Keeffe (eds), above n 5, p 44; and Fredman (1992), above n 5, 133.
[141] See Hepple in Davies *et al.* (eds), above n 5, 250.

law intended to facilitate the uniform application of that law by national courts. There seems to be a distinct possibility, even probability that, with successive renewals and changes in the composition of the Court, the majorities within the Court whether in Chambers or in the plenary have been shifting and that those who hold sway within the institution may have a different approach from their predecessors to the principle of equality, including sex equality, or to the role of the EC's judicial body in ensuring respect for the fundamental principle of equality in the different Member States.

5

Reconciling Pregnancy, Maternity and Family Responsibilities with the Fundamental Principle of Equality and the Demands of the Workplace

INTRODUCTION

WOMEN'S CHILD-BEARING CAPACITY, the traditional assumption, and indeed the fact, that they take prime, often sole, responsibility for rearing children, is widely regarded as one of the greatest obstacles to full and equal female participation in the employment market.[1] In the Court's own words:

> ... even where male and female candidates are equally qualified, male candidates tend to be promoted in preference to female candidates particularly because of prejudices and stereotypes concerning the role and capacities of women in working life and the fear, for example, that women will interrupt their careers more frequently, that owing to household and family duties they will be less flexible in their working hours or that they will be absent from work more frequently because of pregnancy, childbirth and breastfeeding.[2]

It is somewhat ironic then that the first preliminary reference concerning pregnancy and maternity rights to reach the Court of Justice involved a male complainant.[3] It was only in 1988, with the arrival at the Court of the *Dekker* case,[4] involving a female job applicant who was refused employment on grounds of her pregnancy, despite having been selected as the best candidate for the job, that the Court was obliged, in the words of one of its Advocates

---

[1] See variously L. Finlay, 'Transcending Equality Theory: A Way Out of the Maternity and Workplace Debate' (1986) 86 *Columbia Law Review* 1118–82; E. Szyszczak, 'Community Law on Pregnancy and Maternity' in T. Hervey and D. O'Keeffe (eds), *Sex Equality Law in the European Union* (Chichester, John Wiley & Sons Ltd, 1996) pp 51–62; T. Hervey and J. Shaw, 'Women, Work and Care: Women's Dual Role and Double Burden in EC Sex Equality Law' (1998) 8 *Journal of European Social Policy* 43–63; S. Bailey, 'Equal Treatment/Special Treatment: The Dilemma of the Dismissed Pregnant Employee' (1989) *Journal of Social Welfare Law* 85–100.

[2] See Case C–409/95 *Hellmut Marschall v Land Nordrhein-Westfalen* [1997] ECR I–6363, para 29.

[3] Case 184/83 *Ulrich Hofmann v Barmer Ersatzkasse* [1984] ECR 3047.

[4] Case C–177/88 *Johanna Dekker v Stichting Vormingscentrum voor Jong Volwassenen (VJV-Centrum) Plus* [1990] ECR I–3941.

General, to 'consider generally the question of maternity and the status to be accorded to it, in the light of the Community law principle of equal treatment of male and female workers, within the economic and social life of the European peoples.'[5]

EC sex equality law has developed on the basis of a patchwork of Treaty provisions, essentially the principle of equal pay in Article 141 EC and the provisions of directives adopted on the basis of Articles 94 and 308 EC. These directives were conceived, as previous chapters have observed, not simply as a means to achieve equality between male and female workers in terms of pay, working conditions, social security provision and equal access to employment and vocational training,[6] but also, if not principally, in terms of their effect on the establishment and functioning of the common market.[7] The purpose of this chapter is first to assess, within the context of these early equality directives, the Court's performance in preliminary references which have required it to reconcile pregnancy, maternity and the family responsibilities of workers with the demands of employers and the workplace. Thereafter, legislative developments in this field, specifically the adoption of directives concerning the protection of pregnant workers and those on maternity leave and parental leave, are outlined with a view to determining whether the subsequent adoption of more focused legislation at Community level provides a juridical framework within which these issues can be better addressed. As elsewhere in the book, the chapter reflects on the interaction between the fundamental principles developed by the Court in its jurisprudence in this field and the EC's employment policy objectives and, on the other, on the ambivalent nature of the Court's role in preliminary reference proceedings.

PREGNANCY AND MATERNITY PROTECTION THROUGH THE CASE-LAW
OF THE COURT OF JUSTICE

The contrast between formal as distinct from substantive approaches to sex equality was already discussed in chapter four. Much of the criticism levelled at the formal approach concerns, as we saw, the preponderant role given the male norm; a comparator which fails to take account of the considerations which often disadvantage female workers vis-à-vis their male colleagues—first and foremost their role as child-bearers, thereafter traditional divisions of responsibility in child-rearing and the partition of household duties and even precon-

---

[5] Case C–177/88 *Dekker*, Opinion of Advocate General Darmon, para 1.

[6] For criticism of the division entrenched in these Directives and in EC sex equality law generally between work in the public and private spheres see J.A. Sohrab, *Women, Social Security and Financial Independence in EC Equality Law* (Aldershot, Dartmouth, 1996); Hervey and Shaw (1998), above n 1; and H. Cullen, 'The Subsidiary Woman' (1994) *Journal of Social Welfare and Family Law* 407–21.

[7] See above Introduction and ch 4 for details of the principal Equality Directives.

ceptions about the capabilities, or lack thereof, of female workers.[8] As one commentator has remarked:

> [I]n an employment market arranged around the assumption of constant availability for work of employees, with no career breaks, or parental duties, women employees who have children . . . are perceived as more costly employees since, first, the woman will be unavailable for work during maternity leave, and, second, there is no guarantee for the employer that the woman will return to work after the child is born.[9]

Reference to the male norm—perceived (whether rightly or wrongly[10]) as a full-time worker employed continuously without career breaks until retirement and who is unencumbered by external commitments—therefore overlooks women's difference, whether physiological or socially constructed. In no context, however, can reference to a male norm be more controversial than with respect to cases where the rights of female workers who are pregnant or on maternity leave are at issue.

Until the adoption of Directive 92/85,[11] provision for pregnancy and maternity in the equality directives was scant and formulated essentially in negative terms. Specifically, Article 2(3) of Directive 76/207 provided that 'This Directive shall be without prejudice to provisions concerning the protection of women, particularly as regards pregnancy and maternity.' As an exception to the fundamental principle of equal treatment for men and women, this provision must be interpreted strictly. The Court has tended to limit application of Article 2(3) to situations where it considers a woman's biological condition is in need of protection and to what has been termed the 'special relationship' which exists

---

[8] Of particular interest in this respect have been cases before the Court involving women excluded from traditionally male posts in the police and armed forces who have claimed discrimination contrary to EC sex equality law. Compare, for example, Case C–273/97 *Angela María Sirdar v The Army Board, Secretary of State for Defence* [1999] ECR I–7403 (justified and proportionate exclusion of women from the Royal Marines Corps); Case C–285/98 *Tanja Kreil v Bundesrepublik Deutschland* [2000] ECR I–69 (impermissible exclusion of women from the German army); and Case C–186/01 *Alexander Dory v Bundesrepublik Deutschland* OJ 2001 C 200/49, pending (where a German court has referred a question to determine if the exclusion of women from the obligation to do military service is discriminatory).

[9] See in this respect H. Fenwick and T. Hervey, 'Sex Equality in the Single Market: new directions for the European Court of Justice' (1995) 32 *Common Market Law Review* 443–470, 443–447; Hervey and Shaw (1998), above n 1, 48 on formal as distinct from substantive approaches to sex equality; A. Morris and S. Nott, 'The legal response to pregnancy' (1992) 12 *Legal Studies* 54–73, for discussion of the confused legislative and judicial responses to pregnancy, particularly in the United Kingdom, and the different philosophies (legal paternalism, special protection, equal treatment) behind those responses; and Fredman, S., 'A Difference with Distinction: Pregnancy and Parenthood Reassessed' (1994) 110 *Law Quarterly Review* 106–23, for a historical insight into women's position in the home and the workplace.

[10] See the discussion in G.F. Mancini and S. O'Leary, 'The new frontiers of EC sex equality law' (1999) 24 *European Law Review* 331–53, 335–36.

[11] Council Directive 92/85/EEC of 19 October 1992 on the introduction of measures to encourage improvements in the safety and health at work of pregnant workers and workers who have recently given birth or are breast-feeding (tenth individual Directive within the meaning of Article 16(1) of Directive 89/391/EEC), OJ 1992 L 348/1.

between a woman and her child.[12] Thus, in the *Johnston* case[13] it held that Article 2(3) does not allow women to be excluded from certain types of employment on the ground that public opinion demands that women be given greater protection than men against risks which affect men and women in the same way and which are distinct from what the Court and, it seems, the Community legislature, regard as a woman's specific need for protection. A total exclusion of women from the Northern Ireland police force, which was imposed for reasons of public safety was thus not one of the differences in treatment that Article 2(3) of the Equal Treatment Directive allowed out of a concern to protect women.[14] For some, Article 2(3) should not be seen in the light of a derogation from the principle of equality. Since it is a woman's special condition in the period before and immediately after childbirth that is the subject of special protection, Advocate General Tesauro argued in *Habermann-Beltermann* that this provision seeks rather to ensure that the principle of equal treatment operates in substance, by permitting such 'inequalities' as are necessary in order to achieve equality : 'different treatment is allowed or imposed, in favour of and to protect female workers, in order to arrive at material and not formal equality, since that would constitute a denial of equality.'[15] The fact remains, however, that provision for pregnancy and maternity in early Community secondary legislation was limited and when cases began arriving at the Court in the late 1980s, the latter was forced to address, within this existing, partial legal framework, whether the protection of the employment rights and working conditions of women during specific periods of their working lives which are unique to their sex can be reconciled with the fundamentals of the principle of equality.

Refusal to Employ, or Dismissal of, Pregnant Workers

Unlike the courts or tribunals in some Member States and, indeed, unlike the U.S. Supreme Court, the Court of Justice chose, at the first opportunity, not to apply a comparator or seek a male norm when determining whether the dismissal or refusal to employ pregnant workers was discriminatory. Whereas other jurisdictions had originally held that distinctions concerning pregnancy are not based on sex because the group of non-pregnant persons consists of

---

[12] See, for example, Case 184/83 *Hofmann*; Cf. Case 312/86 *Commission v France* [1988] ECR 6315.

[13] Case 222/84 *Marguerite Johnston v Chief Constable of the Royal Ulster Constabulary* [1986] ECR 1651, para 44.

[14] By accepting, however, with reference to Article 2(2) of Directive 76/207, that the sex of a police officer could constitute a determining factor for carrying out certain policing activities, the Court arguably resorted to the traditional view of women's different biological make-up. See also Case C–273/97 *Sirdar*, para 31 and G. More, 'Reflections on pregnancy discrimination under European Community law' (1992) *Journal of Social Welfare and Family Law* 48–56, 49.

[15] See para 11 of his Opinion in Case C–421/92 *Habermann-Beltermann* [1994] ECR I–1657.

members of both sexes,[16] the Court of Justice in *Dekker* decided that since only women can be refused employment on grounds of pregnancy, such a refusal constitutes direct discrimination on grounds of sex contrary to the provisions of the Equal Treatment Directive.[17] Furthermore, there was no need for the claimant to show fault on the part of the employer or the absence of any grounds of justification recognised in national law. The Court held that such discrimination cannot be justified in terms of the financial loss which an employer might suffer during the maternity leave due to his insurer not covering the cost of a replacement.[18] The upshot of *Dekker* is that refusal to employ a female worker on grounds of pregnancy constitutes direct discrimination. At least pursuant to the traditional tenets of EC discrimination law, it is thus not open to an employer to argue that such discrimination is objectively justified.[19] This identification of the cause of discrimination as sex rather than pregnancy, was clearly down to a policy choice or realisation on the part of the Court, namely that, in the absence of specific secondary legislation addressing pregnancy and maternity issues affecting women at work, it had to protect pregnant employees within the limits available under Directive 76/207.[20]

As the 1990s progressed, further pregnancy cases arrived at the Court. In *Webb v EMO Air Cargo (UK) Ltd*,[21] a female employee who was meant to

---

[16] See *Geduldig v Aiello*, 417 US 484 (1974) and *General Electric Co. v Gilbert*, 429 US 125 (1976). See also *Bliss* [1978] 6 WWR 711, a decision of the Supreme Court of Canada prior to the adoption of the Canadian Charter of Rights and Freedoms. These precedents have since been overridden: see s 701(k) of the Civil Rights Act, added by way of amendment in 1978 and *Brooks v Canada Safeway Ltd* [1989] 1 SCR 1219.

In the United Kingdom the Industrial Tribunal in *Turley v Allders Stores* [1980] IRLR 4 held that dismissal by reason of pregnancy was incapable, as a matter of law, of amounting to sex discrimination because a man can never be dismissed on the same ground. In *Hayes v Malleable* [1985] IRLR 367, however, the Employment Appeal Tribunal reasoned that it was not the pregnancy as such which gave rise to dismissal but the consequences of pregnancy and it therefore compared a pregnant employee with a male employee suffering a long-term illness.

[17] Case C–177/88 *Dekker*, para 12. The fact that there were no male candidates for the job did not affect the Court's ruling. Mrs Dekker had applied for a post as instructor in a training centre for young adults run by VJV. She informed the committee dealing with applications that she was three months pregnant but her name was sent forward, nonetheless, as the most suitable candidate for the job. VJV subsequently informed her, however, that she would not be appointed. Its insurer, applying Dutch law on sickness benefits which equated pregnancy with sickness and refused payment of daily benefits in cases of 'forseeable sickness ', had previously refused to bear the cost in similar circumstances. As a result, VJV believed that it would be financially impossible to employ a replacement during Mrs Dekker's absence on maternity leave.

[18] Case C–177/88 *Dekker*, paras 12–13.

[19] See also A. Arnull, 'When is pregnancy like an arthritic hip ?' (1992) 17 *European Law Review* 265–73, 269. On the subject of justification of sex discrimination see generally ch 4 and, in the specific context of pregnant employees on fixed term contracts, the discussion below.

[20] See also E. Ellis, annotation of Case C–394/96 *Brown v Rentokil Ltd.* (1999) 36 *Common Market Law Review* 624–33, 631.

[21] Case C–32/93 [1994] ECR I–3567. Mrs Webb was to replace an employee who was absent on maternity leave. Her contract was for an indefinite period as it was intended that she would stay on when her pregnant colleague returned. See further Arnull, above n 19 and E. Szyszczak, 'Pregnancy and Sex Discrimination' (1996) 21 *European Law Review* 79–82.

replace another during her maternity leave found herself to be pregnant, shortly after being engaged, and was dismissed by her employer.[22] The latter argued that the dismissal did not constitute direct discrimination as it was due to her anticipated inability to carry out the task for which she had been recruited, specifically covering the job of an absent pregnant colleague. As a preliminary, the Court seemed to emphasise that the question submitted to it related to a contract concluded for an indefinite period, leading to speculation thereafter that fixed term contracts were not covered. It held that the dismissal of a pregnant worker in these circumstances on account of pregnancy constituted direct discrimination on grounds of sex. Accordingly, the Court held that 'there can be no question of comparing the situation of a woman who finds herself incapable, by reason of pregnancy discovered shortly after the conclusion of the employment contract, of performing the task for which she was recruited with that of a man similarly incapable for medical or other reasons.'[23] Pregnancy, according to the Court, is not in any way comparable with a pathological condition and the dismissal of a pregnant woman recruited for an indefinite period cannot be justified on grounds relating to her inability to fulfil the fundamental condition of her employment contract. Although the availability of an employee is necessarily a precondition for the proper performance of the employment contract, the protection afforded by EC law to a woman during her pregnancy and after childbirth cannot be dependent on whether her presence at work during maternity is essential to the proper functioning of the undertaking in which she is employed. The pregnant employee was going to be absent from work on a purely temporary basis and termination of her contract could not be justified by the fact that she would be prevented from performing the work for which she had been engaged during that period.

The Court has subsequently confirmed (a) that refusal of or dismissal from employment on grounds of pregnancy constitutes direct discrimination on grounds of sex;[24] (b) that the protection afforded by Community law during pregnancy and after childbirth cannot be dependent on whether the presence at work of the employee during maternity is essential to the proper functioning of the undertaking by which she is employed;[25] (c) that a refusal to employ a preg-

---

[22] The United Kingdom Employment Protection (Consolidation) Act 1978 provided that dismissal on grounds of pregnancy constituted unfair dismissal but specified, at the time, that employees who had been employed for less than two years were not entitled to claim that protection. As a result, the applicant mounted her claim on the basis of the 1975 Sex Discrimination Act. See further S. Fredman, 'A Difference with Distinction: Pregnancy and Parenthood Reassessed' (1994) 110 *Law Quarterly Review* 106–23, 109.

[23] Case C–32/93 *Webb*, para 24.

[24] See, for example, Case C–207/98 *Silke-Karin Mahlburg v Land Mecklenburg-Vorpommern* [2000] ECR I–549; or Case T–45/90 *Alicia Speybrouck v European Parliament* [1992] ECR II–33, para 49, where, in the context of an EU staff case, the Court of First Instance confirmed the decision in Case C–177/88 *Dekker*, but specified that such protection, deriving for EU staff members from the fundamental principle of equality, only applied to employees dismissed on account of pregnancy.

[25] See, for example, Case C–109/00 *Tele Danmark*, [2001] ECR I–6993, paras 29–30.

nant worker and, presumably, her dismissal, cannot be justified on grounds relating to the financial loss which an employer would suffer for the duration of her maternity leave;[26] and (d) that in the case of a contract for an indefinite period a statutory prohibition on, for example, night-time work by pregnant women, takes effect only for a limited time in relation to the total length of the contract and cannot serve as a basis for dismissal.[27]

In the *Mahlburg* case, a nurse who had been working on a fixed-term contract applied for a permanent post as an operating-theatre nurse but was refused on account of her pregnancy. Her employer claimed that provisions of the applicable German law on the protection of working mothers expressly prohibited employers from employing pregnant women in areas in which they would be exposed to the harmful effects of dangerous substances, a hospital operating-theatre being one such example. As in *Habermann-Beltermann*, the Court in *Mahlburg* held that the application of provisions concerning the protection of pregnant women cannot result in unfavourable treatment regarding their access to employment. It is thus not permissible for an employer to refuse to take on a pregnant woman on the ground that a prohibition on employment arising on account of the pregnancy would prevent her from being employed from the outset and for the duration of the pregnancy in a post of unlimited duration.[28] Curiously, the Court in *Mahlburg* stated, contrary to *Dekker*, that the unequal treatment complained of was not based directly on the woman's pregnancy but on a statutory prohibition on employment attaching to that condition.[29] However, the employer in *Dekker* had also claimed that any discrimination experienced by Ms Dekker was not the result of her pregnancy but was due to provisions of Dutch law which permitted an insurer to refuse to reimburse an employer who, having taken on a pregnant woman who would in the forseeable future be absent from work, needed to pay a replacement during her absence.[30] In *Mahlburg*, when it came to arguments about the possible financial consequences of an obligation to take on pregnant women, in particular for small and medium-sized entreprises, the Court relied on *Dekker*, however, and its statement to the effect that a refusal to employ a woman on account of her pregnancy cannot be justified on grounds relating to the financial loss which an employer who appointed her would suffer for the duration of her maternity leave. The same conclusion had to be drawn in *Mahlburg* as regards the financial loss

---

[26] Cases C–207/98 *Mahlburg* and C–109/00 *Tele Danmark*, para 28.

[27] See Case C–421/92 *Gabriele Habermann-Beltermann v Arbeiterwohlfahrt, Bezirksverband Ndb./Opf.ev* [1994] ECR I–1657.

[28] Case C–207/98 *Mahlburg*, para 27. Since Ms Mahlburg was applying for a position covered by a contract of indefinite duration, the speculation which Case C–32/93 *Webb* and C–421/92 *Habermann-Beltermann* had caused about the possibility of justifying dismissal or exclusion from a fixed-term post was not relevant.

[29] Case C–207/98 *Mahlburg*, para 21.

[30] See also J. Jacqmain, 'Pregnancy as grounds for dismissal' (1994) 23 *Industrial Law Journal* 355–59, 356.

caused by the fact that the woman appointed cannot be employed, for safety reasons, in the post concerned for the duration of her pregnancy.[31]

Over ten years after the *Dekker* case had been decided, the Court had yet to bite that most difficult of bullets: was a female worker employed on a fixed term basis also entitled to protection against dismissal or refusal of employment on the grounds of her pregnancy or was protection deriving from EC law limited to workers on indefinite contracts as some commentators had suggested?[32] The fact that the Court seemed to link its ruling in *Webb* to the circumstance that the pregnant complainant had in fact been employed on a pemanent basis led some to believe that fixed term contracts were not covered.

In *Tele Danmark A/S v Handels- og Kontorfunktionaererernes Forbund i Danmark (HK)*,[33] the Court of Justice was asked whether Articles 5(1) of Directive 76/207 and 10 of Directive 92/85 must be interpreted as precluding a worker from being dismissed on the grounds of pregnancy where the employee in question had been recruited for a fixed term, had failed to inform the employer that she was pregnant even though she was aware of this when the contract of employment was concluded and because of her pregnancy she was unable to work for a substantial part of the term of that contract. Having reiterated the essence of *Dekker* and observed that the purpose of the special protection from dismissal afforded pregnant workers by Article 10 of Directive 92/85 was to protect pregnant workers from the risk that a possible dismissal may pose for the physical and mental state of pregnant workers, workers who have recently given birth or those who are breastfeeding, including the particularly serious risk that they may be encouraged to have abortions.[34] Since the dismissal of a worker on account of pregnancy constitutes direct sex discrimination, whatever the nature and extent of the economic loss incurred by the employer as a result of her absence, the duration of the contract of employment has no bearing on the discriminatory character of the dismissal. Whether the

---

[31] Case C–207/98 *Mahlburg*, para 29; and the Opinion of Advocate General Saggio at paras 33–36. He suggested that action be taken in the context of Member States' social policies to protect the more fragile businesses from the financial burden resulting from this protection. Such action would not, in his view, be contrary to the principle of protecting women through pregnancy and maternity but would, on the contrary, contribute to the elimination of the *raison d'être* of much discriminatory treatment.

[32] See, for example, Szyszczak (1996), above n 21, 81–82 and 'Pregnancy Discrimination' (1996) 59 *Modern Law Review* 589–92; S. Fredman, 'Parenthood and the Right to Work' (1995) 111 *Law Quarterly Review* 220–23, 221–22; and Lord Keith in the House of Lords judgment giving effect to the preliminary ruling in *Webb*, [1995] All ER 577, 582: 'It does not necessarily follow that pregnancy would be a relevant circumstance in the situation where the woman is denied employment for a fixed period in the future during the whole of which her pregnancy would make her unavailable for work, nor in the situation where after engagement for such a period the discovery of her pregnancy leads to cancellation of the engagement.' See also E. Caracciolo di Torella, 'The "Family-Friendly Workplace": the EC Position' (2001) 17 *International Journal of Comparative Labour Law and Industrial Relations* 325–44, 333.

[33] Case C–109/00 *Tele Danmark*. See also Case C–438/99 *María Luisa Jiménez Melgar v Ayuntamiento de los Barrios* [2001] ECR I–6915, paras 43 and 44.

[34] Case C–109/00 *Tele Danmark*, para 26.

employee's contract is fixed term or indefinite, her inability to perform the contract is due to the pregnancy. The Directives make no distinction, as regards the scope of equal treatment, according to the duration of the employment relationship and, in the opinion of the Court, if the Community legislature had wished to make such a distinction it would have done so expressly. Consequently, Articles 5(1) of Directive 76/207 and 10 of Directive 92/85 were interpreted as precluding the dismissal of a pregnant worker employed on a fixed term contract in the circumstances described in the questions referred.

Thus, the duration of the employment relationship may have consequences for the maternity benefits payable to the worker in question but it has no bearing on the extent of protection otherwise afforded by EC law. In addition, Directives 76/207 and 92/85 do not distinguish, as regards the scope of the prohibitions they lay down and the rights they guarantee, according to the size of the undertaking concerned. The Court's decision is interesting for a number of reasons. In the first place, regardless of whether good faith in this case was on the side of the employer or the newly recruited employee, the Court stood by the principles which it had championed in relation to the protection from dismissal of pregnant employees. It decided the case as a matter of principle—the protection of pregnant workers regardless of the duration of their employment contract—as it would seem Article 234 EC demands. Its answer to the national referring court in *Tele Danmark*—which had framed its question with reference to the specific facts of the case before it (the employee's failure to inform her employer of her pregnancy when it was clear that she would not be in a position to perform her duties for the greater part of its duration)—was not determined by those circumstances. The Court was also clearly conscious of the widespread use of fixed term contracts in today's labour market. In its view, even if a worker is recruited under a fixed term contract, their employment relationship may be for a longer or shorter period, and is moreover liable to be renewed or extended. As Advocate General Ruiz Jarabo pointed out in his Opinion, if fixed term contracts were excluded from the scope of application of Directive 76/207, the latter would be deprived on much of its *effet utile* and employers might be encouraged to resort to the use of such contracts given the lower level of protection they afforded.[35] From an employer's perspective, the decision was an unequivocal indication that they assume the 'risk' when recruiting staff, for whatever duration, that those employees may legitimately absent themselves from work for certain periods in the event of pregnancy regardless of the cost which that might entail.

Pregnancy Related Illnesses

A difficult and, as it has transpired, contradictory aspect of the Court's jurisprudence in this field is that some of the consequences of pregnancy, in particular

---

[35] C–109/00 *Tele Danmark*, para 28 of his Opinion.

pregnancy related illnesses leading to absences from work, or medical advice requiring the same, have been separated from the pregnancy itself and a male comparator has been reintroduced in order to assess how a man in a similar situation would have been treated. The comparator becomes relevant again—it seems—because it is the effects of pregnancy rather than the pregnancy itself which are at issue. A bizarre turn of events if one considers that this was precisely the argument rejected by the Court in *Webb* as justification for the dismissal of a pregnant worker employed to cover the post of another worker absent on maternity leave and as justification in *Dekker* for the refusal to employ a pregnant candidate for a job.

In *Hertz*,[36] a case decided on the same day as *Dekker*, the Court held that beyond the period of protected maternity leave, any illness, even if it is a consequence of the pregnancy, is to be treated as sex-neutral, since both men and women could become ill in the ordinary course of events. According to the Court, when it came to illnesses manifesting themselves after the maternity leave, the only question is whether a woman is dismissed on account of absence due to illness in the same circumstances as a man. If that is the case, there is no direct discrimination on grounds of sex.[37] The decision of the Court in *Hertz*, however, was problematic. Although the Court had referred in its judgment to illness manifesting itself after the maternity leave and had held in that context that there is no reason to distinguish such illness from any other, the operative part of the judgment simply stated that the Equal Treatment Directive does not preclude dismissals which are the result of absences due to an illness attributable to pregnancy or confinement, without specifying whether this covered pregnancy related illness manifesting itself before the end of the protected period of maternity leave or simply illness manifesting itself thereafter.

The answer to any doubts raised by the elliptic nature of the operative part of the *Hertz* ruling seemed to come in *Larsson v Føtex Supermarkked*.[38] In this case, which involved a worker absent from work due to pregnancy-related illness prior to the protected period of maternity leave, the Sixth Chamber of the

---

[36] Case C–179/88 *Handels-og Kontorfunktionoererernes Forbund i Danmark v Dansk Arbejdsgiverforening* (hereafter '*Hertz*') [1990] ECtR I–3979. Having worked for her employer for several years, Mrs Hertz gave birth in June 1983 and resumed her duties at the end of her maternity leave. However, after an absence due to illness for a period of 100 working days between June 1984 and June 1985, she received notice of her dismissal. It was common ground that these periods of sick leave were related to her pregnancy.

[37] Case C–179/88 *Hertz*, para 17.

[38] Case C–400/95 [1997] ECR I–2757. The plaintiff informed her employer that she was pregnant in August 1991. She took sick leave twice during her pregnancy, once for eighteen days and the second time, on account of a pelvic prolapse, for four and a half months. At the end of the maternity leave, she took her annual leave until 16 October 1992. She remained on sick leave, being treated for the pelvic prolapse until 4 January 1993. Her employer informed her soon after her return that she was to be dismissed due to these long periods of absence from work and the unlikelihood, for health reasons, that she would be able to carry out her tasks satisfactorily. Apart from the periods of absence during her pregnancy, maternity leave and annual leave, it emerged that Mrs Larsson had in fact only been absent from work for a period of less than four weeks.

Court, applying what it must have thought was the rationale of the plenary in *Hertz*, made no distinction between pregnancy related illnesses which had manifested themselves pre and post the period of confinement. According to the Sixth Chamber, the Court in *Hertz* did not draw a distinction in its decision on the basis of the moment of onset or first appearance of the illness :

> It merely held that, *in the factual situation submitted to it on that occasion*, there was no reason to distinguish, from the point of view of the principle of equal treatment enshrined in the Directive, between an illness attributable to pregnancy or confinement and any other illness. That interpretation is confirmed, moreover, by the absence of any reference in the operative part of the *Hertz* judgment to the moment of onset or first appearance of the illness.[39]

The Court thus concluded in *Larsson* that, outside of the periods of maternity leave laid down by the Member States, a woman is not protected under the Directive against dismissal on grounds of periods of absence due to an illness originating in pregnancy.[40]

Just over a year after the decision in *Larsson* was handed down it was unequivocally and unceremoniously overturned by a plenary formation. Clearly, the deliberation of a case by one formation over another may have fundamental consequences for the outcome, but when it comes to the establishment of legal principles, so too may the specific factual context with reference to which the questions are submitted. The *Brown*[41] case also involved a pregnant female worker who had been absent from work due to difficulties associated with her pregnancy for considerable periods of time prior to the commencement of her maternity leave. Her employment contract stipulated that if an employee was absent because of sickness for more than twenty six weeks continuously he or she would be dismissed. The Court recalled its decisions in *Dekker* and *Hertz* and the reasons for the protection of women during pregnancy and confinement and pointed to the adoption of Directive 92/85. The reply to the question referred by the national court must be given, it stipulated, taking into account this general context, despite the fact that the 1992 Directive was not in force at the material

---

[39] Case C–400/95 *Larsson*, para 17 (emphasis added). An omission recognised by Advocate General Ruiz-Jarabo in his Opinion in Case C–394/96 *Mary Brown v Rentokil Initial UK Ltd (formerly Rentokil Ltd)* [1998] ECR I–4185, para 36. At para 31 of his Opinion in Case C–400/95 *Larsson* he had been of the view, however, that the law governing periods of absence on medical grounds during pregnancy had not yet been decided by the Court of Justice. Some commentators felt it was clear that the decision in Case C–179/88 *Hertz* only applied to illness arising after the period of maternity leave. See, for example, N. Burrows, 'Maternity Rights in Europe—An Embryonic Legal Regime' (1991) 11 *Yearbook of European Law* 273–93, 282.

[40] Case C–400/95 *Larsson*, para 23.

[41] Case C–394/96 *Brown v Rentokil Ltd* [1998] ECR I–4185. For a criticism of what she regarded as the Court's well-intentioned but ultimately mistaken approach in this case see E. Ellis, annotation of Case C–394/96 *Brown v Rentokil Ltd* (1999) 36 *Common Market Law Review* 624–33. See also C. Boch, 'Official : During Pregnancy, Females Are Pregnant' (1998) 23 *European Law Review* 488–94; and M. Wynn, 'Pregnancy Discrimination : Equality, Protection or Reconciliation ?' (1999) 62 *Modern Law Review* 435–47.

time. In agreement with its Advocate General, the Court pointed out that pregnancy is a period during which disorders and complications may arise compelling a woman to undergo strict medical supervision and, in some cases, to rest absolutely for all or part of her pregnancy. Those disorders and complications form part of the risks inherent in the condition of pregnancy and are thus a specific feature of that condition. Dismissal of a female worker during pregnancy for absences due to incapacity to work resulting from her pregnancy must therefore be regarded as essentially based on the fact of pregnancy. Since such a dismissal can affect only women, it constitutes direct discrimination on grounds of sex.[42] Contrary to its ruling in *Larsson*, the Court in *Brown* specified that absence from work not only during maternity leave but also during the period extending from the start of pregnancy to the start of maternity leave cannot be taken into account for the computation of the period justifying dismissal under national law.[43] In contrast, where pathological conditions caused by pregnancy or childbirth arise after the end of maternity leave, they are covered by the general rules applicable in the event of illness.

Thus, the Court has devised the following, somewhat convoluted position in its case-law: dismissal for absences due to pregnancy-related illnesses which manifest themselves or continue after the maternity leave comes to an end is not discriminatory since sick male workers can be discharged in similar circumstances (*Hertz*),[44] while dismissal for absences due to pregnancy-related illnesses which manifest themselves during the pregnancy itself is 'linked to the occurrence of risks inherent in pregnancy and must therefore be regarded as essentially based on the fact of pregnancy'[45] (*Brown*). The upshot of this jurisprudence—admittedly a questionable one—is that only the latter type of dismissal is regarded as constituting direct discrimination on grounds of sex, despite the fact that the absence from work in both cases is due to the pregnancy.

---

[42] Case C–394/96 *Brown*, paras 22 and 24. Rather illogically, Advocate General Ruiz-Jarabo (para 62 of his Opinion), while supporting a finding of direct discrimination and therefore a substantive approach to pregnant workers absent from work due to obstetric complaints argued that: 'it is inappropriate to draw parallels or distinctions between two pregnant women experiencing more or less easy or problematical pregnancies—the point of reference continues to be the male worker.' He then goes on to say that 'for the purposes of dismissal the situation of a pregnant woman whose pregnancy prevents her from working and that of a man who is unwell are not comparable.'

[43] Furthermore, in those circumstances, application of a contractual term which brings a contract to an end as a result of absence over and above a specified period also constitutes direct discrimination: see Case C–394/96 *Brown*, para 32. When it came to the solution of the case before it, the national court in *Larsson* disregarded the Court's ruling and applied its decision in *Brown* instead.

[44] Although Advocate General Ruiz-Jarabo stated in Case C–400/95 *Larsson*, para 40, without distinguishing between periods prior to or post maternity leave: 'It seems to me to be obvious that, as pregnancy is a situation which can only affect women, problems of health attributable to it cannot be covered by the general rules applicable to both men and women in the event of illness.'

[45] Case C–394/95 *Brown*, para 24.

Pay, Employment Benefits and Working Conditions During and After Maternity Leave

Further incoherence in the Court's case-law on pregnancy and maternity is evident in its decisions on entitlement to equality with respect to pay and working conditions. The plaintiffs in *Joan Gillespie and Others v Northern Health and Social Services Board and Others*[46] were nurses who, pursuant to a collective agreement, were entitled to receive full weekly pay for the first four weeks of their maternity leave, nine-tenths of their full weekly pay for two weeks thereafter and one-half of their full weekly pay for the remaining twelve weeks. Negotiations with the Northern Ireland health services resulted in pay increases backdated to the beginning of April 1988. However, the plaintiffs were unable to receive the increase because the reference pay used for the calculation of the benefit payable to them during maternity leave did not take the increase into account. The Court was asked, on the one hand, whether women on maternity leave must continue to receive full pay and, if not, how was the amount of their maternity benefit to be determined and, on the other, whether they must receive a pay rise awarded before or during maternity leave.

The Court observed that a woman on maternity leave is in a special position which requires her to be afforded special protection, but which is not comparable either with that of a man or with that of a woman actually at work. Once again, as it was to do in subsequent cases such as *Brown* and *Larsson*, the Court referred to the, as yet, inapplicable Directive 92/85, and noted that it simply required payment of an adequate allowance to female workers on maternity leave. With the 1992 Directive not yet in force, the Court still held that nothing in Article 141 EC or the Equal Pay Directive requires that employees should receive full pay when on maternity leave. It was up to the Member States to set the amount of benefit to which they are entitled. In doing so they must simply ensure, with reference to the length of the maternity leave and the availability of other forms of national social protection in the case of justified absence from work, that a woman receives an adequate amount which should not be so low as to undermine the purpose of maternity leave, namely the protection of women before and after giving birth.[47] Ultimately the application of the non-comparator approach originating in *Dekker* to the question of the salary entitlement of workers on maternity leave worked to their disadvantage in

---

[46] Case C–342/93 [1996] ECR I–475.

[47] Case C–342/93 *Gillespie*, paras 19–20. Advocate General Léger had come to the same conclusion as the Court but resolved matters on the basis of Directive 76/207 rather than 75/117: 'The Court has refused to extend the scope *ratione materiae* of the protection for pregnant workers provided for by Directive 76/207, in the absence of national rules adopted pursuant to Article 2(3) of Directive 76/207. For that reason, the Court cannot accept that a provision of national law, whether statutory or contractual, which does not require employers to maintain full pay for women on maternity leave is contrary to Community law.'

Gillespie. The uniqueness of their position legitimated the exclusion of a comparison with workers who continued to be in employment. Essentially employees on maternity leave are no longer treated as workers, not even as workers with special needs, as they are when pregnant. Instead they are mothers not actually in active employment, albeit temporarily.[48]

In contrast, the Court held that the principle of non-discrimination requires that a woman who is still linked to her employer by a contract of employment or by an employment relationship during maternity leave must, like any other worker, benefit from a pay rise, even if backdated, which is awarded between the beginning of the period covered by reference pay and the end of maternity leave: 'To deny such an increase to a woman on maternity leave would discriminate against her purely in her capacity as a worker since, had she not been pregnant, she would have received the pay rise.'[49] But is the same not true of the maternity benefit which a worker receives? Had the applicants not become pregnant and given birth they would have been working just like male workers and other non-pregnant female workers. Since they were absent from work because of pregnancy and confinement, why were they not entitled to their full pay during that period? The reversion to comparators when dealing with the equal pay claim of women on maternity leave led the Court to hold that, when on maternity leave, women are in a unique situation which is not comparable to that of a man or woman at work. Hence part of the nurses' pay discrimination claim failed. This despite the fact that the uniqueness of pregnancy and, by implication, the maternity period, did not stand in the way of a finding of discrimination in *Dekker* and *Webb* (albeit not with respect to pay).[50] Furthermore, as we will see in a subsequent case on the receipt of full pay by pregnant workers absent from work due to pregnancy-related illness, depriving pregnant women of full pay can be regarded as being based on their pregnancy, with the result, following the logic in *Dekker*, that such a reduction is discriminatory.[51] The *Dekker* approach seems not to apply to equal pay claims, an argument which could be said to find further support in the next case discussed—*Thibault*—a preliminary ruling which focused on the Equal Treatment Directive rather than Article 141 EC.[52]

---

[48] For an excellent classification of the Court's case-law with reference to whether issues of family life or employment are affected see E. Caracciolo di Torella and A. Masselot, 'Pregnancy, maternity and the organisation of family life: an attempt to classify the case law of the Court of Justice' (2001) 26 *European Law Review* 239–60.

[49] Case C–342/93 *Gillespie*, para 22.

[50] See C. McGlynn, 'Equality, Maternity and Questions of Pay' (1996) 21 *European Law Review* 327–32, for similar criticism of the case.

[51] See Case C–66/96 *Handels- og Kontorfunktionaerernes Forbund I Danmark, acting on behalf of Berit Hoj Pedersen e.a. v Faellesforeningen for Danmarks Brugsforeninger e.a* (hereafter *Pedersen*) [1998] ECR I–7327.

[52] See also P. Lewis, 'Pregnant Workers and Sex Discrimination: the Limits of Purposive Non-comparative Methodology' (2000) *International Journal of Comparative Labour Law and Industrial Relations* 55–69, 68: 'Purposive, non-comparative methodology has been used to create significant protection against dismissal and other detriment. The . . . same methodology has also restricted the rights of the pregnant worker in respect of maternity pay because the purpose of the legislation itself is limited.'

The decision in *Gillespie* was clearly dictated by policy. By opting for the guarantee of merely an adequate allowance for female workers on maternity leave, the Court endorsed the solution already negotiated at the political level between the Member States in the form of Directive 92/85. The success of the plaintiffs' demands for full pay would inevitably have led to the maternity allowance provisions of the Directive being challenged as incompatible with EC sex equality law.[53] McGlynn suggests that, in favouring the solution it did in *Gillespie*, the Court may have tested the political climate existing in the Member States and concluded that the backlash against a judgment guaranteeing women on maternity leave a right to full pay 'may ultimately have been more to the detriment of women'.[54] The upshot of the case is that neither individual employers nor Member States are saddled with too great a financial burden when it comes to the benefits payable to employees absent from work on maternity leave.[55]

At the heart of *Gillespie* is a glaring contradiction which sits uneasily with the Court's judicial and moral determination to protect pregnant workers and those who have recently given birth. In this case the Court sanctioned the provision of an 'adequate' amount of pay for women on maternity leave. This is similar to the provision made in Directive 92/85, which requires Member States to ensure provision of an income at least equivalent to that which the worker concerned would receive in the event of a break in her activities on grounds connected with her state of health, subject to any ceiling laid down under national legislation. Yet in other cases on the protection of pregnant workers or those on maternity leave, *Tele Danmark* being a case in point, the Court seems filled with social and even moral concern that an employee's fears about the consequences of her pregnancy for her employment status and rights should not be allowed to interfere with her well-being or that of her unborn child. Neither the Court nor the Community legislature seems untowardly concerned about the very real economic concerns which a pregnant worker or one on maternity leave may face when forced to meet their normal living expenses and those of a newborn child

---

[53] Pursuant to Articles 2, 8 and 11 of Directive 92/85, workers on maternity leave covered by the Directive are entitled to the payment of an adequate allowance. The latter is deemed adequate if it guarantees income at least equivalent to that which the worker concerned would receive in the event of a break in her activities on grounds connected with her state of health, subject to any national ceiling. At para 49 of his Opinion in Case C–342/93 *Gillespie*, Advocate General Léger emphasised that the initial Commission proposal included provision for the maintenance of full pay but that this had been rejected in favour of the adequate allowance solution.

[54] See McGlynn (1996), above n 50, 330 and 332; and Lewis, above n 52, 65–66. Such a hypothesis has some resonance with what American scholars call Bickel's theory of 'passive virtues'—techniques for not deciding controversial political questions before the public and their political representatives have reached at least minimum consensus (see A.-M. Slaughter Burley, 'New Directions in Legal Research on the European Community' (1993) 31 *Journal of Common Market Studies* 391–400, 393). In the instant case, the Member States' political representatives had discounted the possibility of full pay for women on maternity leave when negotiating the 1992 pregnancy directive.

[55] See Hervey and Shaw (1998), above n 1, 52; R. Wintemute, 'When is Pregnancy Discrimination Indirect Sex Discrimination?' (1998) 27 *Industrial Law Journal* 23–36, 34.

from a salary suddenly reduced to an amount equivalent to statutory sick pay simply by virtue of the employee being absent from work on maternity leave. In the United Kingdom, for example, all women are entitled to eighteen weeks maternity *leave*, with those with one year or more continuous service (at the beginning of the eleventh week before the expected week of confinement) entitled to leave up to twenty nine weeks from the week of birth.[56] However, entitlement to eighteen weeks statutory maternity *pay* is dependent on, *inter alia*, twenty six weeks continuous service at the fifteenth week before the expected week of confinement.[57] The rate of statutory maternity pay does not correspond to the employee's usual rate of pay but consists of a higher rate of ninety per cent of normal weekly earnings for the first six weeks of leave, followed by a reduced rate set in line with statutory sick pay of around £62 for the remaining twelve weeks. Those who do not qualify for this statutory maternity pay can get a maternity allowance paid by the Benefits Agency if their earnings reached the national insurance threshold. Otherwise they receive a one-off maternity grant.[58] It is difficult not to speculate that traditional assumptions about two parent families, with the male partner presumed to perform the primary breadwinning function, were somewhere at work when the issue of maternity pay was discussed in both the Council and the Court.[59]

Employed since 1973 with the CNAVTS, the plaintiff in the *Thibault* case[60] was not perhaps, from her employer's perspective, a model employee. In 1983, due to illness, maternity leave and child-care leave, she had been at work for around one hundred and fifty five days.[61] As a result of this low attendance, her employer refused to draw up a performance assessment for the year in question, as he would normally do pursuant to the provisions of the relevant French

[56] Maternity and Parental Leave etc. Regulations 1999 (S.I. 1999 No 3312).

[57] Social Security Contributions and Benefits Act 1992.

[58] See A. McColgan, 'Family Friendly Frolics? The Maternity and Parental Leave etc. Regulations 1999' (2000) 29 *Industrial Law Journal* 125–43; C. Palmer and J. Wade, *Maternity and Parental Rights*, 2nd ed. (London, Legal Action Group, 2001); and generally N. Busby, 'Divisions of Labour: Maternity Protection in Europe' (2000) 22 *Journal of Social Welfare and Family Law* 277–94.

[59] See A. McColgan, *Just Wages for Women* (Oxford, Clarendon Press, 1997) p 140, on the effect which this 'breadwinner' ideology has had on women's wages generally; and the Report of the House of Lords Select Committee on the European Communities, p 18 for the EOC submissions in written evidence. In Case C–33/89 *Maria Kowalska v Freie und Hansestadt Hamburg* [1990] ECR I–2591, the City of Hamburg argued, in an attempt to justify its discriminatory treatment of part-time workers when it came to entitlement to severance pay, that part-time workers do not provide for their needs and those of their families exclusively out of their own income and that employers were under no duty, therefore, to provide them with temporary assistance in the event of redundancy. The Court of Justice simply left it to the national court to assess the legitimacy and proportionality of this proposed justification.

[60] Case C–136/95 *Caisse Nationale d'Assurance Vieillesse des Travailleurs Salariés (CNAVTS) v Évelyne Thibault* [1998] ECR I–2011.

[61] Note that the applicable collective agreement provided that maternity leave (which could range from sixteen to twenty-eight weeks) could not be counted in the computation of sick leave and could not lead to a reduction in annual leave. At the end of maternity leave a woman could also take three months' leave on half-pay or one-and-a-half months' leave on full pay.

collective agreement for the staff of social security institutions.[62] As a result, the plaintiff could not be included on the list of staff which was used annually for the purpose of awarding advancements on merit equivalent to 2 per cent of salary. She claimed that the lack of an assessment, due essentially to her absence from work on maternity leave, and her resulting exclusion from the advancement system, constituted discrimination. The question referred by the national court was drafted with reference to the Equal Treatment Directive. The Court pointed out that the exercise of the rights conferred on women under Article 2(3) of this Directive cannot be the subject of unfavourable treatment regarding their access to employment or their working conditions.[63] The result pursued by Directive 76/207 is—according to the Court—substantive, not formal, equality.[64] The right to have one's performance assessed and, consequently, to qualify for promotion, constitutes a working condition within the meaning of Article 5(1) of the Equal Treatment Directive. According to the Court, the principle of non-discrimination requires that a woman who continues to be bound to her employer by her contract of employment during maternity leave should not be deprived of the benefit of working conditions which apply to both men and women and are the result of that employment relationship. It concluded that denying a female employee the right to have her performance assessed annually would discriminate against her merely in her capacity as a worker because, if she had not been pregnant and had not taken the maternity leave to which she was entitled, she would have been assessed for the year in question and could therefore have qualified for promotion.[65] The denial of such a right constitutes discrimination based directly on grounds of sex contrary to Articles 2(3) and 5(1) of Directive 76/207.

[62] The standard service regulations for the application of the collective agreements applicable to the CNAVTS provided that employees who are present for at least six months in any year must be the subject of an assessment by their superiors. However, the French labour code provided that periods of maternity leave should be treated as periods of actual work for the purpose of determining a worker's rights by virtue of length of service.

[63] The choice of words here—rights conferred under Article 2(3)—is open to question, given that the latter merely states that Directive 76/207 shall be without prejudice to provisions concerning the protection of women, particularly as regards pregnancy and maternity. However, it is perhaps this notion of Article 2(3) conferring rights on women during these periods which explains the result in Case C–342/93 *Gillespie*, where no corresponding right to full pay was identified under Article 141 EC or Directive 75/117. See E. Ellis, 'The Recent Jurisprudence of the Court of Justice in the Field of Sex Equality' (2000) 37 *Common Market Law Review* 1403–26, 1417, who comments on the Court's crafty disposal of Case C–136/95 *Thibault* with reference to Directive 76/207, which helped avoid the constraints of the reasoning in the *Gillespie* decision. See also Advocate General La Pergola in Case C–1/95 *Hellen Gerster v Freistaat Bayern* [1997] ECR I–5253, who suggested that the law on equal treatment seeks to ensure that men and women gain access to employment in conditions of substantive equality while the law on equal pay demands merely formal equality.

[64] Case C–136/95 *Thibault*, para 26.

[65] This conclusion reinforces criticism of the reasoning on pay entitlements on maternity leave in C–342/93 *Gillespie*: had the nurses absent from work on maternity leave not been pregnant, or had they not given birth, they would have been at work and would thus have been entitled to receive full pay. At para 36 of his Opinion in Case C–136/95 *Thibault*, Advocate General Ruiz-Jarabo, who was such a staunch supporter of protecting pregnant workers in Case C–394/96 *Brown*, regarded the solution in Case C–342/95 *Gillespie* as regards the reduced pay entitlement on maternity leave as 'logical'.

The reasoning of the Court in *Thibault* contrasts sharply with that in the *Abdoulaye* case[66] where male employees of Renault, the car manufacturer, claimed that they were being discriminated against. Female workers who were due to be absent from work on maternity leave were paid an allowance which was not awarded to male workers who were expecting a child. The latter argued that certain measures directed uniquely at female workers, such as the protected period of maternity leave, may be justified from a physiological point of view, but that the same was not true for the payment of a one off benefit to expectant mothers departing on maternity leave. The birth of a child, they argued, may principally involve the mother but it is a social act which concerns the whole family, including the father, and the latter should not be deprived of such a benefit.

The Court in *Abdoulaye* held first of all that, despite the periodic character of the allowance and the fact that it was not salary indexed, it constituted remuneration within the meaning of Article 141 EC. Secondly, as regards the question whether female workers absent on maternity leave were in a situation comparable to that of male workers, the Court recited the various occupational disadvantages which Renault had submitted female employees may suffer as a result of being away from work during maternity leave: they cannot be promoted during that period and their period of service is reduced as a result of their absence; they cannot claim performance-related salary increases; they cannot participate in training; and they may lose out when it comes to understanding and adapting to the new technology constantly being introduced into the workplace. The Court held that the payment of a lump sum to employees on maternity leave was designed to offset the occupational disadvantages inherent in that leave. Although it was for the national court to verify that male and female workers were not in a comparable situation in this respect—which would preclude any breach of the principle of equal pay—the Court clearly indicated to the national court that it was of the view that their situations were different.

Abdoulaye, like many other cases in this field, although ostensibly seeking to protect the position of female workers when on maternity leave, actually undermines their position by reinforcing the notion that women are and should remain primarily responsible for childcare.[67] The Court was unwilling to contemplate that the arrival of a new baby is something which concerns both parents and that the exclusion of one set of parents from the grant of an allowance on such an occasion is discriminatory. What is truly remarkable about the judgment, however, is that the justifications advanced by Renault, and accepted by the Court, for limiting the allowance to female employees— such as not being proposed for promotion or loss of performance-related salary

---

[66] Case C–218/98 *Abdoulaye*.
[67] See generally for this criticism C. McGlynn, 'Ideologies of Motherhood in European Community Sex Equality Law' (2000) 6 *European Law Journal* 29–44 and 'Pregnancy, Parenthood and the Court of Justice in *Abdoulaye*' (2000) 25 *European Law Review* 654–62.

increases—are, as *Thibault* demonstrated, actually unlawful![68] In other words, the Court referred to unlawful, discriminatory criteria in *Abdoulaye* to find that the male and female workers in question were in a different position, thereby excluding any breach of the principle of equal pay. As one commentator has justifiably remarked, it seems strange that the Court accepts in one case what it has admonished national courts not to accept in other indirect sex discrimination cases, namely general assertions unsupported by objective criteria, all the more so when some of those general assertions relate to grounds of unlawful discrimination.[69] It is impossible to deny that the position of women in the labour market is affected by having children. The question, however, is how best to redress this problem while respecting the fundamental tenets of equality. Although the provision of special protection for women about to give birth is understandable from a political and even legal point of view, *Abdoulaye* and the child care cases which follow show that the Court's attempts to tackle the inequalities in the labour market which motherhood may provoke are inconsistent with each other and ultimately do not seek to alter the stereotypical assumption that women are and should remain the primary carers.

The Danish law on non-manual workers at issue in the *Pedersen* case[70] provided, *inter alia*, that pregnant employees who, for a reason connected with pregnancy, were unfit for work before the beginning of the three month period preceding their confinement were not entitled to full pay, while an employee who was unfit for work on grounds of illness was, in principle, entitled to full pay. Some of the applicants in the *Pedersen* case were declared totally unfit for work and ceased to be paid by their employers, while others were either declared only partially unfit or, according to the Court, doubt remained as to the nature of their incapacity. They were advised to claim the benefits paid, in accordance with this Danish legislation, by local authorities to pregnant workers in the event of incapacity for work.

The Court reiterated the essence of its rulings in *Webb* and *Brown* and held that the fact that a woman is deprived, before the beginning of her maternity leave, of her full pay when her incapacity for work is the result of a pathological condition connected with the pregnancy must be regarded as treatment based essentially on the pregnancy and thus as discriminatory.[71] Even if the benefits received by employees in lieu of salary were equal to their full salary, the national court would still have to determine whether the circumstance that the benefits are paid by a local authority is such as to bring about discrimination in breach of Article 141 EC. As regards the ceiling authorised by Article 11 of Directive 92/85 on the allowance which employees may claim in the event of

---

[68] See also Case C–333/97 *Susanne Lewen v Lothar Denda* [1999] ECR I–7243, discussed below; Article 11(2)(a) of Directive 92/85, which provides that the rights connected with the worker's employment contract must be ensured during maternity leave; and McGlynn (2000), *ibid*, 657.

[69] See McGlynn (2000), *ibid*, 658.

[70] Case C–66/96 *Pedersen*.

[71] *Ibid*, para 35.

pregnancy and possible justification of the lower pay received by absent pregnant employees the Court held, on the one hand, that Directive 92/85 authorised a reduced allowance only during the period of maternity leave and not during the pregnancy itself. On the other hand, it stated that pay discrimination against pregnant workers could not be justified by the aim of equitably sharing the risks and economic costs connected with pregnancy between the pregnant worker, the employer and society as a whole.[72]

The national court had also asked whether it is contrary to the principle of equal pay that a pregnant woman is not entitled to receive her pay from her employer where she is absent from work by reason either of routine pregnancy-related inconveniences, when there is in fact no incapacity for work, or of medical recommendation intended to protect the unborn child but not based on an actual pathological condition or any special risks for the unborn child, while any worker who is unfit for work on grounds of illness is in principle entitled to pay. In these circumstances the Court held that the fact that the employee forfeits some, or even all, of her salary by reason of such absences which are not based on an incapacity for work cannot be regarded as treatment based essentially on the pregnancy but rather as based on the choice made by the employee not to work and as such there was no discrimination.

Finally, the Danish court had asked whether the Equal Treatment or Pregnant Workers' Directives preclude national legislation providing that an employer may send home an employee who is pregnant, although not unfit for work, without paying her salary in full when he considers that he cannot provide work for her. The Court held that, although Article 2(3) of Directive 76/207 authorised national legislation intended to protect women in connection with pregnancy and maternity, the impugned Danish legislation was aimed not so much at protecting the pregnant woman's biological condition as at preserving the interests of her employer. In addition, the legislation did not satisfy the substantive and formal conditions laid down by Directive 92/85 in respect of activities liable to involve a risk to the health and safety of a pregnant worker.[73] The decision to suspend the activities of a pregnant worker cannot only reflect the interest of the employer. The latter must first examine the possibility of adjusting the pregnant employee's working conditions, working hours or even the possibility of moving her to another job and only if this is not possible is the worker granted leave.

---

[72] Case C–66/96 *Pedersen*, paras 38 and 40. The case involved direct discrimination. Although the Court did not discuss the issue whether direct discrimination could in fact be justified, which would be at odds with its classic discrimination case-law, the drafting of para 40 and its reference to Case C–457/93 *Kuratorium für Dialyse und Nierentransplantation e.V. v Johanna Lewark* [1996] ECR I–243 (discussed above ch 4) could have suggested that that was the case. See L. Flynn, 'Equality Between Men and Women in the Court of Justice' (1998) 18 *Yearbook of European Law* 259–87, 270.

[73] See Articles 4 (Assessment of information) and 5 (Action upon the results of the assessment) of Directive 92/85.

Finally, the *Lewen* case involved the question of the entitlement to a Christmas bonus of an employee on parenting leave.[74] Prior to her pregnancy and associated leave, the applicant, like other employees, had received a Christmas bonus. She had also been required to sign a declaration recognising that the bonus constituted a single, voluntary social benefit which could be revoked at any time and created no future entitlement. The bonus was to be repaid if the contract was terminated before July of the coming year. When refused her bonus in 1996 while absent on parenting leave, the applicant brought an action against her employer seeking its payment.

A Christmas bonus of the kind at issue constituted pay, according to the Court, within the meaning of Article 141 EC. Did, however, Article 11(2) of Directive 92/85 and Clause 2(6) of the Annex to Directive 96/34 on parental leave preclude an employer from excluding a female employee from the benefit of a bonus paid voluntarily at Christmas if, at the time of payment of the bonus, they are on parenting leave, without taking into account the work done during the year in which the bonus is paid or of the statutory periods of protected leave enjoyed by the mother, during which time she was prohibited from working? There being some confusion as to whether the Christmas bonus was intended to encourage those in 'active' employment to work hard in the coming months, the Court proceeded on the assumption that it was an exceptional allowance at Christmas, did not constitute retroactive pay for work performed and was subject only to the condition that the worker be in active employment when it is awarded. The Court ruled that the voluntary payment of a bonus at Christmas by an employer or, more to the point, the withholding of such a voluntary payment, did not constitute direct discrimination, since it applies without distinction to male and female workers. As to a claim of indirect discrimination, the Court reasoned *à la Gillespie*, that a worker who exercises a statutory right to take parenting leave is in a special situation which cannot be assimilated to that of a man or woman at work. Such leave involves suspension of the contract of employment and, therefore, of the respective obligations of the employer and the worker. Although it had been established by the national court as a matter of fact that far more women avail of parenting leave than men, the Court concluded that the refusal to pay a female employee on parenting leave the special Christmas bonus does not constitute discrimination within the meaning of Article 141 EC, where the award of that allowance is subject only to the

---

[74] Case C–333/97 *Lewen*. The applicant had worked full time in her employer's firm for several years before becoming pregnant. She was absent from work on leave for some weeks before her maternity leave began in May 1996. Her child was born in July and, pursuant to the relevant provisions of German law, her period of protected maternity leave ended in September, from which time she took parenting leave. Under German law, this is a facility available to both parents until a child reaches the age of three. During the period of parenting leave, the contract of employment is suspended. The employee on parenting leave does not have to receive monthly remuneration but receives an income based parenting allowance instead from the State.

condition that the worker is in active employment when it is awarded.[75] The Court stated that the position would be different if the national court classified the bonus as retroactive pay for work performed in the course of the year in which the bonus is awarded. Only then would the refusal to grant the bonus constitute indirect discrimination. The Court also stated that, were the national court to classify the bonus at issue under national law as retroactive pay for work performed in the course of the previous year, the periods for the protection of mothers—in other words those periods when they are prohibited by law from working—must be assimilated to periods worked for the purpose of the calculation of the bonus since, had they not been pregnant, those periods would have had to be counted as periods of work. In the same vein, the Court held that although an employer cannot take periods of protection for mothers into account in order to reduce the bonus *pro rata*, he cannot be prevented from taking periods of parenting leave into account for that purpose.

Analysing the Judicial Approach to Pregnancy and Maternity

While the Court's jettisoning of the need for a pregnant complainant to point to a comparator has been praised by some for having 'eschewed the minefield of the comparative approach to pregnancy' and adopted a substantive test of equality,[76] it has been the object of considerable criticism in other quarters. Ellis, for example, argues that an element of comparability is important to the component of adverse impact which is at the heart of anti-discrimination law. If direct discrimination were defined simply as 'nasty treatment' on the ground of sex, enormous discretion would be left in the hands of persistently male courts and tribunals to decide what is to the detriment or advantage of complainants, the majority of whom are female.[77] While the same author recognises that pregnancy is the one truly exceptional situation affecting women and not men, she urges the Court to measure the treatment received by pregnant complainants by means of a comparison with the treatment received or receivable by a member of the opposite sex, placed in broadly the same circumstances as the complainant. Another proposed solution, also centred on the need for a comparator in cases of alleged discrimination, is to treat discrimination against pregnant

---

[75] See also the Opinion of Advocate General Ruiz-Jarabo Colomer, para 46: 'the fact that [exclusion from receipt of the Christmas bonus] applies more frequently to women will result from the exercise of the right to parenting leave, which is not a working condition but a special advantage available to workers only on grounds of recent paternity or maternity'; and Case C–411/96 *Margaret Boyle and Others v Equal Opportunities Commission* [1998] ECR I–6401, paras 77–79, discussed below.

[76] See, for example, Hervey and Shaw, above n 1, 51.

[77] See E. Ellis, 'The Definition of Discrimination in European Community Sex Equality Law' (1994) 19 *European Law Review* 563–80, 571. See also S. Honeyball, 'Pregnancy and Sex Discrimination' (2000) 29 *Industrial Law Journal* 43–52; and Lewis, above n 52.

women as *prima facie* indirect discrimination.[78] The treatment of a pregnant woman, this argument goes, is always compared, implicitly if not explicitly, with that of a non-pregnant person to show that the less favourable treatment would not have occurred had the woman not been pregnant.

Yet, since the female sex's unique biological capacity to bear children and society's traditional assumption that women are more apt to rear them are at the heart of much of the less advantageous treatment which women receive in the labour market, surely no Court should ignore this fact by searching for comparable situations affecting men which do not in reality exist. Furthermore, the dangers inherent in the treatment of pregnancy and maternity discrimination as indirect sex discrimination are evident. Quite apart from the prejudice which the comparison of pregnancy with illness is capable of propagating, the prospect of employers being able to justify discrimination against pregnant women or those on maternity leave and courts being too willing to accept those justifications when faced with tales of woe regarding the financial implications for employers of recruiting and maintaining pregnant workers, is not an attractive one.[79] Although the Court has laid down standards by which cases of apparent discrimination should be judged, chapter four clearly indicates how difficult the application of those criteria may sometimes be.

However, fears about the damage which abuse of the concept of discrimination, no matter how well-intentioned, could entail, are understandable.[80] Indeed, the fact that the Court has been unable to adopt a consistent approach in its case-law to pregnancy and maternity and its consequences for employment, dismissal, pay and working conditions, suggests that it is also a well-founded fear and those confused by what could be regarded as its 'multi-speed' approach to pregnant workers and those on maternity leave are to be forgiven.[81] The Court has chosen to apply a substantive approach to equality in some cases where the refusal to appoint or dismissal of pregnant workers is concerned, regarding both as direct discrimination even in the absence of a male comparator (*Dekker*, *Webb*), and in others where plaintiffs have claimed entitlement to the same working conditions as male/non-pregnant workers during the course

---

[78] See Wintemute (1998), above n 55.

[79] As Wintemute himself admits (1998), above n 55, 35. See the rejection of his thesis by Honeyball, above n 77.

[80] See Ellis (1999), above n 20; and the concerns raised by Honeyball, above n 77.

[81] See also Hervey and Shaw (1998), above n 1, 45: 'the Court of Justice appears, depending on the circumstances, to have been impressed by different "standards" of equality in different sets of circumstances.' Compare Lewis, above n 52, who argues that the Court's case-law provides a fair and coherent scheme for the protection of pregnant workers. The central principle, in his opinion, is that the pregnant worker is in a unique or special position, not to be compared with a man in comparable circumstances (illness) nor with a non-pregnant woman. Decisions of the Court such as C–179/88 *Hertz* or C–342/93 *Gillespie* seem to belie this analysis. See also Caracciolo di Torella and Masselot, above n 48, who provide a more convincing classification of the Court's case-law based on a distinction between cases dealing with pregnancy and maternity within family life and those within the employment market.

of their pregnancy or when on maternity leave (*Pedersen, Thibault*).[82] In other cases it has opted for a straightforward formal comparison of like with like, equating pregnancy and illness, so that women absent from work following maternity leave due to pregnancy related illnesses have been compared with men absent from work due to illness (*Hertz*). In yet other cases the Court has preferred to premise its response on the notion of the special protection permitted under Article 2(3) of the Equal Treatment Directive, so that, for example, an employer may not dismiss a pregnant worker engaged on an indefinite contract due to a statutory prohibition on nightwork for pregnant employees, since to allow the employer to avoid the contract would be contrary to the objective of protecting women during pregnancy and maternity (*Habermann-Beltermann*). However, it emerges from the case-law that special protection and/or resorting to the principle of non-discrimination can prove a double edged sword. According to the Court, women on maternity leave are in a special position which requires them to be afforded special protection, with the result that their position is not comparable either with that of a man or woman actually at work and, as a result, the principle of equal pay does not, therefore, preclude them receiving an allowance which is lower than their usual pay during this period (*Gillespie*) or a Christmas bonus, depending on how it is classified (*Lewen*). Finally, although the Court has reiterated on several occasions that pregnancy is not in any way comparable to a pathological condition, it has come very close in others to comparing pregnancy and illness (*Pedersen*), and has stated that:

> the fact remains . . . that pregnancy is a period during which disorders and complications may arise compelling a woman to undergo strict medical supervision and, in some cases, to rest absolutely for all or part of her pregnancy. Those disorders and complications, which may cause incapacity for work, form part of the risks inherent in the condition of pregnancy and are thus a specific feature of that condition.[83]

The Opinion of Advocate General Darmon in *Hertz* highlights the difficulties facing the Court when trying to reconcile pregnancy and maternity protection with the principle of equal treatment, particularly when all that was available to it was the Equal Treatment Directive and its negative provision of a derogation from that principle for the protection by Member States of pregnancy and maternity. Advocate General Darmon confessed in *Hertz* to having been:

> tempted to propose a solution whereby medical conditions which were directly, definitely and preponderantly due to pregnancy or confinement would enjoy a sort of "immunity", in the sense that the principle of equality of treatment would restrain the employer from dismissing his employee for a reasonable period after the event in question.[84]

---

[82] See the Court in Case C–136/95 *Thibault*, para 26; and Advocate General Tesauro in Case C–32/93 *Webb*, para 8, where he stated that it follows from the reasoning underlying the pregnancy cases 'that the [Equal Treatment] directive must be construed so as to achieve substantive equality, and not mere formal equality which would constitute the very denial of the concept of equality.'

[83] Case C–394/96 *Brown*, para 22.

[84] See his joint Opinion in Cases C–177/88 *Dekker* and C–179/88 *Hertz*, para 43.

However, he resisted this temptation on the grounds that Community law as it stood did not envisage such a requirement[85] and that this ostensibly attractive expedient would be sure to produce a number of negative effects which it would be hard to remedy: namely an obligation on employers to maintain a female employee unable to work for several years after pregnancy while contributing towards the social benefits payable to her,[86] the difficulties which national courts and employers would face in defining the circumstances meriting protection and the risk that a device protecting a few women affected by severe post-natal problems might jeopardise the chances of all women wishing to enter the labour market.[87] Thus, once a female worker has exhausted her entitlement to the various types of maternity leave, her periods of absence for reasons of sickness, even if those reasons can be traced back to pregnancy or confinement, cannot be attributed to the normal risks of maternity and must accordingly be viewed in the same light as the absences of any other worker, unless the national legislature provides special protection.[88]

What one finds in these cases is noble sentiment : 'What is involved here, ultimately, is the duty incumbent upon us all of progressively removing all traces of the discrimination which women have suffered over the centuries, a duty to which the institutions of the European Union are so deeply committed'[89] versus the dictates of political and economic reality: '[Directive 76/207] only contemplates the adoption of measures for the protection of women in [cases of pregnancy and maternity] as an exception to that principle; it does not oblige the Member States to legislate to that effect'[90]. The Court has been forced in these cases to make policy choices but the way in which it has chosen to answer national courts in preliminary reference proceedings added to the absence of dissenting opinions means that there is no discussion of the reasons for its

[85] Article 2(3) of the Equal Treatment Directive merely left to the Member States the task of adopting appropriate provisions concerning the protection of women, particularly, as regards pregnancy and maternity.

[86] In his Opinion in Case C–394/96 *Brown*, para 39, Advocate General Ruiz-Jarabo expressed similar concerns in the context of the possibility of dismissing pregnant workers or those who have given birth: 'If, as a result of having given birth at any time in their lives, women could claim what amounted to a sort of insurance against dismissal for the rest of their working lives, as a result of which no account would be taken for such purposes of periods of incapacity for work following maternity leave, whose origin might be attributable to their pregnancy or confinement, that would amount to a privilege contrary to the principle of equal treatment.'

[87] Opinion of Advocate General Darmon in Case C–179/88 *Hertz*, paras 45–47. In Case 184/83 *Hofmann*, where a man had argued that limiting the possibility of taking additional maternity leave to women risked having adverse effects on their recruitment chances, Advocate General Darmon, p 3086, had rejected the possibility of such adverse effects as a mere possibility which had not been demonstrated. Fears that high regulatory standards may ultimately damage women's employment opportunities pervade the field of pregnancy and maternity protection and were a factor in discussions prior to the adoption of the 1992 pregnancy directive, see K.A. Armstrong and S.J. Bulmer, *The Governance of the Single European Market* (Manchester, Manchester University Press, 1998) 'The protection of pregnant women at the workplace' pp 226–54, pp 241 and 251.

[88] Case C–179/88 *Hertz*, para 48 of the Opinion and para 16 of the decision.

[89] See the Opinion of Advocate General Ruiz Jarabo in Case C–394/96 *Brown*, para 51.

[90] *Ibid.*, para 74.

choices and preferences and indeed little discussion in the Opinions of Advocate Generals' either.[91] Even the reversal by the plenary in *Brown* of the decision of the Sixth Chamber in *Larsson* was supported by no clear explanation as to the reason. As many commentators have suggested, a clearer recognition of the economic concerns which have dictated some of the questionable distinctions in the Court's case-law would have been more helpful, not least for national courts seeking to extract a clear ratio from the Court's often difficult rulings.

As chapter four indicated in the context of market forces justifications in indirect sex discrimination cases, the sympathy of a court may often lie with an employer or Member State obliged to bear the costs of equality or special protection.[92] When the *Webb* case came before the Court of Appeal in the United Kingdom, for example, Balcombe LJ. was quick to reveal where his sympathy lay:

> . . . many people would consider it highly unjust if the dismissal of Ms. Webb in the circumstances of this case amounted to sex discrimination for which her employers, EMO, were financially liable. I would myself share that view, and the real question on this appeal is whether the law, whether domestic or European, compels us to arrive at a conclusion contrary to the justice of the case.[93]

Yet, once again, the Court's decisions contain no discussion of what those financial repercussions might actually be. Cases like *Jiménez Melgar* or *Jenkins* point to the vulnerability of small and medium-sized entreprises when faced with the demands which pregnancy/maternity legislation places on them. However, a survey of the experience of employees and employers of maternity rights in the United Kingdom—not a Member State renowned for its love of employment protection legislation—reveals some surprising results. The survey concentrated on small employers and reported that: 'such firms were much less likely than larger employers to have reported any difficulties associated with matern-

---

[91] See also N. Bamforth, 'The Treatment of Pregnancy Under European Community Sex Discrimination Law' (1995) 1 *European Public Law* 59–68, 61; and S. Simon, 'Discrimination on the Ground of Pregnancy: Chaos or Consistency from the ECJ?' (1999) 3 *The Edinburgh Law Review* 217–28, 228.

[92] See Boch, above n 41, 493; Burrows (1991), above n 39, 283; and Bailey (1989), above n 1, 93, who, writing in the British context, prior to the decisions of the Court of Justice in *Dekker* and *Webb*, stated that: 'past decisions have indicated that the smaller the firm the more likely a tribunal will decide that a pregnant employee has been dismissed because she has become incapable of doing her job, either because she is continually or frequently absent or is unable to do her job when she is at work. Further, it is also more likely that a small firm will be held not to have been in a position to have offered the pregnant employee a suitable alternative vacancy, or to have acted unreasonably in dismissing the employee.'

[93] [1992] 1 *CMLR* 793–819. See also Lord Griffiths in *Stockton on Tees Borough Co. v Brown* [1988] 2 All ER 129, 133: 'I have no doubt that it is often a considerable inconvenience to an employer to have to make the necessary arrangements to keep a woman's job open for her whilst she is absent from work in order to have a baby, but this is a price that has to be paid as part of the social and legislative recognition of the equal status of women in the workplace.'

ity rights. Indeed, the larger the workplace, the more likely employers were to have experienced problems with maternity rights . . .'[94]

The Court of Justice, in balancing the interests of working mothers, those of employers and, one would hope, the interests of society as a whole, has sought to delimit its protection of mothers before and after birth with reference to temporal barriers and the degree of risk associated with the mother's condition.[95] Since it is difficult to imagine male workers suffering from the various complications to which pregnancy may give rise and which the Court's Reports most genteelly decline to discuss,[96] and since it is impossible for them to be absent from work on maternity leave, these limits can be attributed to the utilitarian concerns which Advocate General Darmon vocalised in *Hertz*. Yet the Court is far from consistent when it comes to economic justifications for the treatment of pregnant workers. In *Dekker* the Court rejected arguments about the cost to the employer of recruiting a woman who would be absent in the not too distant future from work due to maternity leave. In *Pedersen*, the pregnant applicants were deprived, before the beginning of their maternity leave, of their full pay when their incapacity for work was the result of a pathological condition connected with pregnancy. The Court explicitly stated that such treatment, which it qualified as discriminatory, could not be justified by the aim of sharing the risks and economic costs connected with pregnancy between the pregnant worker, the employer and society as a whole. That goal, in the view of the Court, could not be regarded as an objective factor unrelated to any discrimination based on sex within the meaning of the Court's case-law.[97]

This complex, differentiated judicial approach to the protection of female workers during pregnancy and maternity was clearly to be expected: determining how the workplace is to deal with pregnancy and homecare is highly problematic and relying on the principle of equal treatment as a means to distribute the burden was always likely to prove insufficient. On the one hand, formal equal treatment simply requires consistency of treatment between men and women, with the result that women's rights are entirely dependent on the extent to which comparable rights are afforded to comparable men. However, despite the long list of suggestions provided in the case-law and doctrine—ranging from absence from work due to participation in the Olympics, the playing of rugby,

---

[94] See S. McRae, *Maternity Rights in Britain. The Experience of Women and Employers* (London, Policy Studies Institute) p 17. Compare the Report of the House of Lords Select Committee on the European Communities, *Protection at work of pregnant women and women who have recently given birth and child care*, HOL Session 1991–92, 2nd report, particularly the submissions of employers' representatives and the Department of Employment, pp 8–9 and pp 35 *et seq.* of the written evidence.

[95] See M. Wynn, 'Pregnancy Discrimination: Equality, Protection or Reconciliation' (1999) 62 *Modern Law Review* 435–47, 439.

[96] With the brave exception of Advocate General Ruiz-Jarabo in Case C–394/96 *Brown*, para 59.

[97] See Case C–66/96 *Pedersen*, paras 35 and 40.

or because of operations for, variously, arthritic hips, hernias or tonsils[98]—the problem with pregnancy and maternity leave is, of course, the difficulty in finding a comparable male situation.[99] As Wynn points out 'the delineation of women on maternity leave as dependant mothers as opposed to productive workers has allowed the Court to by-pass notions of equality and locate the problem in the realm of social protection where economic justifications are more likely to gain recognition.'[100] *Gillespie* bears clear testimony to this.

On the other hand, the Court's case-law tends to place the social cost of pregnancy and child-bearing on individual employers or, in the alternative, if and when it is deemed justified, on those female workers who bear children. Nowhere is the State factored into the equation as a third, yet implicated party, to which costs can be spread.[101] A good example of how this works is provided by the *Dekker* case, where Dutch legislation allowed an insurer to refuse wholly or in part to refund daily benefits to an employer where the employee's incapacity arose within six months following recruitment and was forseeable at the time of recruitment. The employer was thus obliged to meet the cost of temporarily replacing the incapacitated pregnant worker as well as the cost of her maternity entitlements while on leave. Although from the point of view of the protection of pregnant female employees and the effectiveness of that protection the Court's finding that the absence of fault or the existence of national legislation on the subject did not alter the obligations of an employer pursuant to Community law, it is not hard to imagine how put upon an employer might feel. In *Tele Danmark* the Court explicitly stated that the size of an undertaking is of no relevance to the interpretation of Articles 5(1) of Directive 76/207 and 10 of Directive 92/85, despite the fact that the preamble of the latter Directive evokes Article 137(2) EC and its commitment to a limitation of the administrative, financial and legislative constraints imposed on small and medium sized undertakings. It is short-sighted simply to ignore the costs to employers of the absence of female workers from the workforce due to pregnancy and maternity, if only because, left to shoulder the financial burden alone employers may prove reluctant to hire or promote women of child-bearing age. As Ellis has remarked:

[98] See Simon, above n 91.

[99] E. Szyszczak, 'Community Law on Pregnancy and Maternity' in Hervey and O'Keeffe (eds), above n 1, pp 51–62, p 61: 'David Pannick QC asks why then are men not protected against sex specific discrimination—hernia operations, discrimination as a result of dress codes, for example, growing a beard. The short answer is that, at least for the present, growing beards is not seen as important as producing babies.'

[100] See M. Wynn, 'Pregnancy Discrimination: Equality Protection or Reconciliation?' (1999) 62 *Modern Law Review* 435–47, 442.

[101] On the subject of who should bear the cost of pregnancy and maternity see variously M. Wynn, *ibid*, 441; Bamforth (1995), above n 91, 65; Fredman (1994), above n 9, 111; F. Winch, 'Maternity Rights Provisions—A New Approach' (1981) *Journal of Social Welfare* 321–28; Advocate General Saggio in Case C–207/98 *Mahlburg*, paras 33–36, on the vulnerable position of small businesses; and the Report of the House of Lords Select Committee, above n 94, p 13, for discussion of the creation of a maternity fund.

When an employer dismisses a pregnant employee who has been absent from work for a long time, it is of no interest to that employer, nor any necessary part of his/her reasoning, to know the nature of the employee's illness; it is, in other words, not the illness which the law should fasten on as the practical cause of the dismissal, but the fact of absence from the workplace. This is not to say that the economic or administrative arguments of employers should be allowed to trump the fundamental right to equal treatment, but simply to acknowledge that there are a number of conflicting interests to be balanced in this complex situation.[102]

One way of addressing the cost issue is to pool the risk, either through a mainly state-funded programme or by devising some sort of insurance model to which employers and employees could contribute.[103] The advantage of adopting special protection pregnancy legislation is that the issue of cost can be specifically addressed, although, as discussion of implementation of the Pregnant Workers' Directive reveals, the implementation of that legislation in the Member States is not always to the advantage of employers.[104] With only an equality tool at its disposal the Court could have factored employer liability more in to the equation, with the 'risk' to the employer being passed on, albeit imperfectly, to the consumer in the form of business costs.

There is no doubt that the scant provision in Community secondary legislation for pregnancy and maternity up until the mid 1990s has contributed to the lack of consistency in the Court's case-law on pregnancy and maternity. As Boch writes:

since the principles of equal pay and treatment are not really accompanied by measures designed to finance the cost of pregnancy and maternity, these costs must be supported by employers and, in the absence of a political decision, it is up to the Judge to set limits and reconcile the interests and rights of employers with these employees.[105]

Equipped with merely the Equal Treatment Directive the Court did succeed in providing a fair degree of protection which, admittedly, a strict legal interpretation of EC law might not have managed. However, it is also submitted that the Court has demonstrated a distinct lack of vision when it comes to reconciling the position of female workers pregnant or on maternity leave with the

---

[102] Ellis (1999), above n 41, 632. Contrast the legislative and judicial approach in the EU with the decision of the Supreme Court of Canada in *Brookes v Canada Safeway*, 1243: 'Combining paid work with motherhood and accomodating the childbearing needs of working women are ever-increasing imperatives. That those who bear children and benefit society as a whole thereby should not be economically or socially disadvantaged thereby seems to bespeak the obvious.'

[103] See further S. Issacharoff and E. Rosenblum, 'Women and the Workplace: Accommodating the Demands of Pregnancy' (1994) 94 *Columbia Law Review* 2154–221.

[104] See Armstrong and Bulmer, above n 87, p 251, where they describe the discontent in the United Kingdom, following the implementation of Directive 92/85 (Pregnant Workers Directive), that the government chose to pass the burden of additional maternity costs to employers rather than increasing the statutory maternity pay scheme which is funded by the State.

[105] See C. Boch, 'Où s'arrête le principe de l'égalité ou de l'importance d'être bien-portante (à propos de l'arrêt *Larsson* de la Cour de justice' *(1998) Cahiers de droit européen* 177–90, 180.

demands of the workplace and the understandable constraints on employers. In *Gillespie*, for example, the Court refused to accept the argument that a provision of national law which does not require employers to maintain full pay for female employees on maternity leave was contrary to EC law. The legal reason for its decision seemed to be, if the Advocate General's Opinion is anything to go by, a reluctance to extend the material scope of Directive 76/207. A similar reluctance seems absent, however, from other decisions such as that in *Brown*. While the institutional and structural constraints on the Court discussed elsewhere in the book have clearly contributed to this state of affairs, its policy choices in this field demonstrate, once again, that when it comes to choosing between enforcing the fundamental principle of equality and economic justifications in favour of limiting that principle, the latter may often win the day.[106]

JUDICIAL ENDEAVOURS TO CATER FOR WORKING WOMEN'S FAMILY RESPONSIBILITIES

A quick perusal of a variety of EC sex discrimination cases underlines how closely women's so-called family responsibilities—a term covering anything from childcare, to homecare, to care of the elderly—are bound up with the type of posts they occupy, their conditions of employment and the social and employment benefits to which they are entitled or from which they are excluded by law. *Enderby* provides a good example of the segregated nature of the labour market, with women dominating particular professions—in that instance speech therapy—despite the relatively lower pay on offer, since the nature of the work allowed employees to work part-time.[107] In the field of equal pay, the plaintiff in *Bilka* was employed full-time for 11 years in a department store before she asked to be downgraded to a part-time job in order, it seems, to take care of her family and children.[108] The same reason for their choice of employ-

---

[106] See C. Boch, 'Où s'arrête le principe de l'égalité ou de l'importance d'être bien-portante (à propos de l'arrêt *Larsson* de la Cour de justice' *(1998) Cahiers de droit européen* 187–89.

[107] Case C–127/92 *Dr. Pamela Mary Enderby v Frenchay Health Authority and Secretary of State for Health* [1993] ECR I–5535, p 5542 of the Report for the Hearing. Note also the disproportionately high number of pregnancy and maternity cases which the Court has heard where the plaintiffs involved work as nurses or in the health care sector generally. The concentration of these sex discrimination cases in certain sectors emphasise the fact that female workers tend to congregate in certain types of employment but also indicate society's priorities when it comes to remunerating those who perform essential functions in the health and eduction spheres of the public sector.

[108] Case 170/84 *Bilka-Kaufhaus GmbH v Karin Weber von Harz* [1986] ECR 1607. See also Case C–297/93 *Rita Grau-Hupka v Stadtgemeinde Bremen* [1994] ECR I–5535, para 5 of the Report for the Hearing and paras 23–28 of the decision; and Case C–226/98 *Birgitte Jorgensen v Foreningen af Speciallaeger, Sygesikringens Forhandlingsudvalg* [2000] ECR I–2447, involving a doctor who, for many years, limited herself to her own medical practice, with the result that her turnover was low, in order to be able to devote herself in part to family commitments. Danish rules on the classification of medical practices provided that a practise with such a low turnover could be regarded as full-time. However, were she to sell her practice, it would be converted to a part-time practice, with the result that the annual fees paid by the health insurance body which the purchaser could receive

ment is proferred by other female workers engaged in what national law sometimes qualifies as 'minor' employment—essentially jobs where the number of hours worked per week is low with correspondingly low social insurance obligations and rights—or those who job share.[109] Finally, other female plaintiffs who have appeared before the Court have worked for years but not, it must be added, in a capacity recognised by the Community's social security or equality legislation, as these home-carers who look after sick, elderly and disabled children have been deemed to fall outside the personal scope of the relevant EC equality directives.[110] The list goes on.

Yet, the EC has long since claimed that it recognises the importance of an equal opportunities approach to employment from the point of view of the employee, the employer and society at large. In its 1989 action programme in relation to social rights the Commission pointed out that:

> . . . recruitment opportunities, protection against dismissal and maintaining of employment and accrued rights in the case of pregnancy and maternity have implications for the propensity of girls to undergo training and further training and as regards the birthrate. If women consider that pregnancy weakens their chances at work, they will be less inclined to have children, and if they want to have children, they risk foregoing opportunities for appropriate training. As a result, women will continue to be employed in low level jobs.[111]

The EC's equal opportunities strategies rarely miss an opportunity to recall the need for men and women, without discrimination on grounds of sex, to reconcile

---

would be limited. The Danish rules did provide, however, that if special circumstances such as illness caused the turnover to be low and therefore caused the practise to fall within this band, previous years turnover would be taken into consideration. The applicant claimed that this treatment of her practice as part-time was indirectly discriminatory.

[109] See Case C–243/95 *Hill and Stapleton v The Revenue Commissioners and the Department of Finance* [1998] ECR I–3739.

[110] See Case C–77/95 *Bruna-Alessandra Züchner v Handelskrankenkasse (Ersatzkasse) Bremen* [1996] ECR I–5689 (a wife working as a home carer who did not give up her employment but who, as a result of the home care she provided, was not in a position to look for other work); and Case C–66/05 *R v Secretary of State for Social Security, ex parte Eunice Sutton* [1997] ECR I–2163 (homecare for a sick child affecting the pension rights of the applicant who had been in part-time employment when the child fell ill). See also Case C–31/90 *Elsie Rita Johnson v Chief Adjudication Officer* [1991] ECR I–3723, para 19: 'a person who has given up his or her occupational activity in order to attend to the upbringing of his or her children does not fall within the scope of Directive 79/7/EEC as a worker whose activity has been interrupted by one of the risks specified in the directive'. In response to submissions to the effect that it is mainly women who interrupt their occupational activities in order to attend to the upbringing of their children and therefore suffer the consequences of the limited personal and material scope of Directive 79/7, the Court in *Johnson* emphasised that the Directive seeks only progressive implementation of the principle of equal treatment for men and women in matters of social security. The social protection of mothers remaining at home is still a matter for the Member States to regulate. An individual must have been in employment or seeking employment when one of the risks covered by Directive 79/7 materialises—see Case 150/85 *Drake v Chief Adjudication Officer* [1986] ECR 1995. Directive 79/7 is said to have embraced a deeply entrenched public/private dichotomy in relation to the principle of equality. See Hervey and Shaw (1998), above n 1, 56; and H. Cullen, 'The Subsidiary Woman' (1994) *Journal of Social Welfare and Family Law* 407–421.

[111] COM (89) 568 final, 37.

their family and working lives[112] and calls for such measures now regularly feature in the EC's employment guidelines.[113]

However, when it comes to the reconciliation of these family responsibilites with the obligations imposed by and operation of the workplace, the response of the Court of Justice can, more often than not, be characterised as unsympathetic. In the *Bilka* case,[114] for example, the plaintiff successfully challenged her exclusion as a part-time worker from her employer's occupational pension scheme. Her employer, as we saw in chapter four, had to demonstrate that this exclusion was based on objectively justified factors unrelated to any discrimination on grounds of sex. However, the national referring court had also asked the Court of Justice whether an employer is obliged under Article 141 EC to organise its occupational pension scheme in such a manner as to take into account the fact that family responsibilities prevent female workers from fulfilling the requirements for such a pension. The Court responded to this, admittedly daring, argument, by pointing to the division of functions of Articles 141 EC on the one hand and Articles 136 and 137 EC on the other. The imposition of an obligation such as that envisaged by the national court in its question went beyond the scope of Article 141 EC, held the Court, and had no other basis in Community law as it then stood.[115] Although aware, it seemed, of the 'socio-cultural constraints faced by working women', the Advocate General maintained that employers cannot be required to take over the role of the authorities in constructing a pension scheme which will compensate for the special difficulties faced by workers who have family responsibilities.[116] The Court, when seised of such cases, is clearly in the unenviable position of having to reconcile the demands of equality with the economic reality in which business, not least small and medium-sized entreprises, operates. Yet if it is recognised that women's ability to bear children and their involvement in and responsibility for their upbringing is the 'major impediment to women becoming fully integrated into the public world of the workplace'[117], one should surely question why, twenty five years after the equal pay principle was deemed directly effective and

---

[112] Resolution of the Council and of the Ministers for Employment and Social Policy meeting within the Council of 29 June 2000 on the balanced participation of women and men in family and working life, OJ 2000 C218/5.

[113] See, for example, Council Decision 2000/228/EC of 13 March 2000 on guidelines for Member States' employment policies for the year 2000, OJ 2000 L72/15, Annex IV: 'Policies on career breaks, parental leave and part-time work, as well as flexible working arrangements which serve the interests of both employers and employees, are of particular importance to women and men. . . . An equal sharing of family responsibilities is crucial in this respect.'

[114] Case 170/84 *Bilka.*

[115] *Ibid*, para 42.

[116] *Ibid*, Opinion of Advocate General Darmon, para 14. See also the Opinion of Advocate General Darmon in Joined Cases C–399/92, C–409/92, C–425/92, C–34/93, C–50/93 and C–78/93 *Stadt Lengerich and Others v Angelika Helmig and Others* [1994] ECR I–5727, paras 41–42.

[117] See Findlay (1986), above n 1, 1119.

more or less the same time since the equality directives were adopted, women are still, literally, left holding the baby.[118]

The *Hofmann* case, which first brought the issue of pregnancy and childcare before the Court in the context of a sex discrimination claim, involved the father of a child who obtained unpaid leave from his employer in order to care for his child from the end of his partner's statutory period of maternity leave to the day on which the child reached six months.[119] His partner had recently qualified as a teacher and in order not to interfere with the development of her new career, the couple had decided that, at the end of the compulsory period of maternity leave, the father would stay at home to take care of the baby. He requested that the allowance normally paid to mothers who choose to remain off work for the additional period of maternity leave be paid to him and when he was refused he claimed that he was being discriminated against contrary to Directive 76/207.[120]

In its preliminary ruling in the case the Court pointed out that the Directive, specifically Article 2(3), recognised the legitimacy of protecting a woman's needs in two respects. On the one hand, it is legitimate to ensure the protection of a woman's biological condition during pregnancy and thereafter until such time as her physiological and mental functions have returned to normal after childbirth. On the other, it is legitimate to protect the special relationship between a woman and her child over the period which follows pregnancy and childbirth, by preventing that relationship from being disturbed by the multiple burdens which would result from the simultaneous pursuit of employment.[121] The Court concluded that the German law came within the scope of Article 2(3) of the Equal Treatment Directive and that the type of additional maternity leave which it afforded could legitimately be reserved to the mother to the exclusion of any other person, in view of the fact that it is only the mother who may find herself subject to undesirable pressures to return to work prematurely. Finally,

---

[118] See further A.M. Parkman, 'Why Are Married Women Working So Hard?' (1998) 18 *International Review of Law and Economics* 41–49, who notes that between 1960 and 1986, married women increased the total number of hours that they worked per week by 4 hours, while their husbands were decreasing theirs by 2.5 hours; and A.C. Neal, 'United Kingdom' in *The Harmonization of Working Life and Family Life* (1995) 30 *Bulletin of Comparative Labour Relations* 105–22, 115, particularly the literature cited in fn.30.

[119] The *Mutterschutzgesetz* provided that mothers were to enjoy a compulsory convalescence period of eight weeks' leave after childbirth. During that period they were relieved of all their duties at work and continued to receive their net remuneration, which was paid to them by the sickness fund and/or their employer. A mother could, on expiry of the compulsory period, and until the day on which the child reached six months, take a so-called maternity leave, during which period she would receive from the state, via the sickness fund, a daily allowance and at the end of which she enjoyed a guaranteed right to resume her employment on the same conditions as before.

[120] In Case 163/82 *Commission v Italy* [1982] ECR 3273, the Commission had challenged Italian legislation which provided adoptive mothers with compulsory leave and a financial allowance during the first three months after the child enters the adoptive family, without according the adoptive father similar rights. The Court held that the difference in treatment was justified by the legitimate concern to assimilate as far as possible the conditions of entry of the child into the adoptive family to those of the arrival of a newborn child in the family during the very delicate initial period. After that period, the adoptive father has the same rights as the mother.

[121] Case 184/83 *Hofmann*, para 25.

Member States enjoy a reasonable margin of discretion as regards both the nature of the measures which they adopt to protect women in connection with pregnancy and maternity and to offset the disadvantages which women, by comparison with men, suffer with regard to the retention of employment, as well as the arrangements for their implementation. Directive 76/207, it concluded, 'is not designed to settle questions concerned with the organization of the family, or to alter the division of responsibility between parents.'[122]

A number of aspects of the *Hofmann* case are perplexing. In the first place, the allowance being claimed by Mr Hofmann was in lieu of the period following the expiry of the compulsory period of maternity leave. As such, the first grounds for the protection of women cited by the Court, namely protection of her biological condition after childbirth, should not have been in question, since Member States' provision for a compulsory period of maternity leave is intended to respond to this legitimate need.[123] The reasoning of Advocate General Rozès in *Commission v Italy*, the infringement proceedings concerning the exclusion of adoptive fathers from the right to take leave and receive a financial allowance on the arrival of a child into the adoptive family, is instructive in this regard. She distinguished, on the one hand, between leave after giving birth to a child which is intended to allow the mother to rest and can be regarded as protection of women in relation to maternity and, on the other, leave after adoption. The latter, in her view, benefits the child and is intended to foster the emotional ties necessary to settle the child in the adoptive family. As such, she concluded, unlike the Court in that case, that adoptive fathers should be equally entitled to avail of the right to leave and to an allowance provided for that purpose by Italian law.

The crux of the problem in *Hofmann* was thus the Court's determination to protect what it deemed the special relationship between a woman and her child and its unwillingness to allow the Equal Treatment Directive to be used to upset that relationship.[124] By condoning Germany's refusal of the additional maternity allowance to a father who wished to remain at home with his child it was reinforcing the traditional approach to childcare which has played such a part in limiting, impeding or preventing women's full and equal participation in the

---

[122] Case 184/83 *Hofmann*, para 24. Advocate General Darmon, p 3081, argued that offering a choice designed to promote a better distribution of responsibilities between the partners is, for the time being, a matter for Member States alone. See also the submissions of the French government in Case C–312/86 *Commission v France* [1988] ECR 6315, para 11; and the judgment of the Court of First Instance in Case T–51/98 *Ann Ruth Burrill and Alberto Noriega Guerra v Commission* [1999] ECR II–1059, IA–203, limiting provision of maternity leave in the EU staff regulations to female employees who have had a child to the exclusion of the child's father.

[123] See later Advocate General Ruiz-Jarabo in Case C–394/96 *Brown*, para 39, where, when trying to reconcile the decisions in Cases C–177/88 *Dekker* and C–179/88 *Hertz*, he states that 'once a woman has given birth and returned from maternity leave, her physiological state is no different from that of male workers.'

[124] Advocate General Darmon, Case 184/83 *Hofmann*, 3083, maintained that the Equal Treatment Directive is not intended to create rights where none exist but that it seeks to equalize rights at work wherever the development of social attitudes so permits.

labour market and it was penalising a couple who wished to share family responsibilities from doing so, since they thereby forfeited the right to a supplementary maternity allowance.[125] The Court was thus entrenching social attitudes about a mother's special relationship with her child beyond, it must be remembered, the compulsory period of maternity leave. Furthermore, it seems that one of the objectives behind the German legislation was to allow/encourage women to remain at home for a further period with their child, while facilitating their eventual return to work at a later stage.[126] Yet, that is precisely what Mr Hofmann's partner wanted to do—to return to work—and he was willing and able to facilitate her return. As the approach of Advocate General Rozès in the context of care of an adoptive child in *Commission v Italy* demonstrates, it is possible for the law to protect a mother and child while conceding that, after a certain period of time, maternal care in the post-birth period can and should evolve into a simple case of parenting by one or other parent.[127]

It could of course be argued that the case, decided in 1984, would be decided differently nowadays. In infringement proceedings brought by the Commission against France and decided just a few years after *Hofmann*, what was at issue was whether reservation of a whole range of rights for women was compatible with Article 2(3) and (4) of the Equal Treatment Directive.[128] Advocate General Slynn was unwilling to accept that some of these special rights were related solely to the biological condition of women or that men would not, in certain circumstances, also have need of such privileges:

> A father, in modern social conditions, may just as much be responsible for looking after sick children or need to pay childminders . . . .France's insistence on the traditional role of mother, as I see it, ignores developments in society whereby some men in "single-parent families" have the sole responsibility for children or whereby parents living together decide that the father will look after the children, in what would traditionally have been the mother's role, because of the nature of the mother's employment.

The Court was also concerned about the generality of the French measures and was unwilling to regard the grant of these special rights as coming within the scope of the derogations from the principle of equal treatment provided in

---

[125] It would be interesting to get statistics on the number of women in Germany and in Italy who return to work and to compare childbirth/childcare legislation in the two Member States.

[126] Statistics revealed that, at the time, one German woman in two gave up her employment following the birth of children.

[127] See also E. Ellis, *EC Sex Equality Law* (Oxford, Oxford University Press, 1991) p 172; Hervey and Shaw (1998), above n 1, 51; and J.K. Mills, 'Childcare Leave: Unequal Treatment in the European Economic Community' (1992) *The University of Chicago Legal Forum* 497–515, 505.

[128] See Case C–312/86 *Commission v France* [1988] ECR 6315. The special rights at issue included the extension of maternity leave, the shortening of working hours for women over fifty-nine, the obtaining of leave when a child is ill, the granting of leave at the beginning of the school year and on Mother's Day, the granting of an allowance to mothers who have to meet the cost of nurseries or childcare, daily breaks for women working on keyboard equipment or as typists or switchboard operators, and the grant of extra pension rights to those with two children or more.

Article 2(3) and (4) of Directive 76/207, unless they related to pregnancy and maternity.

Similarly, as chapter four revealed in the context of indirect sex discrimination cases —particularly *Gerster* and *Hill*—the Court has stated that: 'The protection of women—and men—both in family life and in the workplace is a principle broadly accepted in the legal systems of the Member States as a natural corollary of the fact that men and women are equal, and is upheld by Community law.'[129] This dictum is remarkable, not just because the Court's judgment provided at least the makings of a legal basis for claims to parental leave and a general principle of Community law that family and work responsibilities should be reconciled, but also because, in the *Gerster* case where it originated, there seemed little need for its addition. The case concerned rules for the calculation of length of service for the purpose of promotion and possible indirect discrimination against part-time workers, the vast majority of whom (87 per cent) are women.[130] Nowhere in the judgment was a link made between these statistics and a child-bearing or child-minding role of either the plaintiff in particular or part-time female workers generally. Advocate General La Pergola drew an explicit connection between part-time work and the dual burden of home and work responsibilities and stated, in characteristically lyrical style, that the protection of women in family life and in the workplace is accepted as a natural corollary of the fact that men and women are equal, is a feature of our shared constitutional heritage and is recognised in the Treaty as one of the guarantees afforded as part of the European venture.[131] The Court simply stated that the amendment of the national law in question equating part-time and full-time work was to assist in making working life more compatible with family life.

Yet, when it comes to facilitating the access to work and benefits of persons with children, the Court's case-law is riddled with confusion and contradiction. A particular relationship between a woman and her child may be the basis for special protection but this is the case only for a short period and parents, particularly mothers, who find themselves trying to juggle jobs and childcare will not necessarily find a sympathetic ear in Luxembourg when they attempt to challenge national legislation which renders this task even more difficult.

---

[129] Case C–1/95 *Gerster*, para 38. This statement is reminiscent of para 16 of the Community Charter of the Fundamental Social Rights of Workers which provides, *inter alia*, that measures should be developed to enable men and women to reconcile their occupational and family obligations. For criticism of Case C–243/95 *Hill and Stapleton* as an extension of the Court's ideology of motherhood as stated in Case 184/85 *Hofmann* see McGlynn (2000), above n 67, 41.

[130] Note in this respect that the Court simply reproduced Mrs Gerster's submission to the effect that '87% of part-time employees are women' and the finding of the national court that this percentage reflects the situation right across the board in the Bavarian civil service. Advocate General La Pergola, Case C–1/95 *Gerster*, para 36 of his Opinion, specified that the plaintiff's figures related to the department in which she worked.

[131] Case C–1/95 *Gerster*, para 48 of the Advocate General's Opinion.

In the *Gruber* case,[132] a decision handed down long after *Hofmann* had passed its acceptable sell-by date, the Court demonstrated itself to be either still unwilling or unable to challenge the type of employment conditions which clearly do not favour full and equal female participation in the labour market. The Austrian Law on Employees provided that if an employment relationship which has lasted, without interruption, for three years is ended, the employee is entitled to a termination payment. This is not payable, however, if the employee terminates the contract without 'important reasons'. The important reasons for which an employee may terminate his contract range from his being unfit for work or being unable to continue to work without damage to his health or moral welfare, to the employer improperly withholding pay due to the worker or failing to abide by other important terms of the contract. In contrast to the full termination payment received by employees who terminate their contracts for these important reasons, the legislation provides that female employees who have been employed without interruption for five years are to be entitled to one half of the termination payment if they give notice of resignation, after a live birth, within a specified period. A termination payment is also payable to male employees who have exercised their statutory right to parental leave. The plaintiff in the case was an employee of Silhouette who, following the birth of her two children, had been absent from work first on maternity leave and then on parental leave. She experienced difficulties arranging for the care of her children owing to a lack of child-care facilities and, despite a real desire to continue in employment, she terminated her contract of employment in November 1995 in order to take care of her children.[133] She claimed that she had resigned for important reasons, namely the lack of child-care facilities for children under three years of age, and challenged the reduced amount of her termination payment before the Courts. Since it is likely to be predominantly female employees who are forced to resign due to a lack of childcare facilities, the failure by the legislature to consider this reason for the termination of an employment contract as important was, she claimed, indirectly discriminatory on grounds of sex.

The Court of Justice stated that it was being asked:

whether Article [141] of the Treaty precludes national legislation under which a termination payment is granted to workers who end their employment relationship prematurely in order to take care of their children owing to a lack of child-care facilities

---

[132] Case C–249/97 *Gabriele Gruber v Silhouette International Schmied GmbH & Co. KG* [1999] ECR I–5295.

[133] Mrs Gruber's second child had been born on 19 May 1995 so that, when she resigned, she could in fact have taken further parental leave. This led Silhouette to argue that the questions referred by the Court were inadmissible. Mrs Gruber admitted that she could have taken additional parental leave but added that the problem raised by the reference would have arisen anyway at the end of that leave, since children can be placed in nurseries only after the age of three. The Court did not accept that the questions referred were inadmissible but left it to the national court to determine whether the impugned Austrian provisions applied on the facts of the case.

for them, where that payment is reduced in relation to that received, for the same actual period of employment, by workers who give notice to resignation for an important reason, if the workers who receive the reduced termination payment are predominantly women.

The case hinged on which comparator the Court was willing to choose—either a worker who had resigned for one of the enumerated important reasons or those who resign voluntarily for no important reason or for reasons of personal convenience. Despite the fact that the question referred by the national court was premised on a comparison of resignation for reasons relating to childcare with the important reasons enumerated in the Austrian employment legislation, the Court questioned whether the situation in which workers who resign in order to take care of their children find themselves is, in substance and origin, similar to the situation of those workers. According to the Court, this was not the case. The important reasons established in the Austrian law on employees and the trade and industry code 'have the common characteristic of being related to the working conditions in the undertaking or to the conduct of the employer, rendering continued work impossible, so that no worker could be expected to maintain his employment relationship, even during the period of notice normally provided for in the event of resignation.'[134] These situations were said to be, in substance and origin, different from that of a worker like Mrs Gruber, with the result that the exclusion of such a worker from the provision of a full termination payment did not constitute indirect discrimination.

It is arguable that the Court in *Gruber* essentially failed to carry out the legal analysis which indirect discrimination cases require. Being forced to give up one's employment because of a lack of childcare facilities is not a question of personal preference and it is difficult to understand why the frustration of a contract on this basis is not comparable to one of the important reasons established in the national law as leading to entitlement to a termination payment. A lack of childcare facilities means that, for one of the parents, work is impossible. Reduced to its bare essentials, the Court's reasoning seems to be as follows: termination of a contract of employment in order to look after children cannot be compared to termination for one of the important reasons provided in the Austrian legislation because the latter does not regard these situations as comparable! It was incumbent on the Court to establish whether, by not equating the former with the latter, the Austrian legislation had a disparate impact on female workers and whether that impact could be objectively justified on grounds other than sex. The Court completely missed the point.

At issue in the *Lommers* case was a circular of the Dutch Ministry of Agriculture which, save in cases of emergency, reserved available nursery places to female employees. Mr Lommers, an official of the Ministry, claimed that the refusal to allow him to reserve a nursery place for his child was discriminatory. For its part, the Ministry claimed that the reservation of places for the children

---

[134] Case C–249/97 *Gruber*, para 32.

of female staff was its way of tackling the under-representation of women in its higher echelons. The Dutch Higher Social Security Court, seised of Mr Lommers' appeal, asked the Court whether Article 2(1) and (4) of Directive 76/207 preclude measures of this type. The Dutch reference seemed partly informed by, on the one hand, understandable confusion as to what degree of 'positive discrimination' the judgments of the Court in *Kalanke* and *Marschall* permitted. On the other, the referring court noted that, according to a body of academic legal opinion, measures such as those provided for in the impugned circular are likely to perpetuate and legitimise the traditional division of roles between men and women. Were, it wanted to know, such measures permissible?

The Court stated that a scheme under which nursery places made available by an employer to his staff (a measure qualified as a working condition) are reserved only for female employees does in fact create a difference in treatment on grounds of sex, within the meaning of Articles 2(1) and 5 of Directive 76/207: 'The situation of a male worker and a female worker, respectively father and mother of children of low age, are comparable as regards the necessity in which both may find themselves, with both having to use nursery facilities on account of the fact that they are in employment.'[135] The Court proceeded to examine the legitimacy of such a measure by virtue of Article 2(4) of the Directive, which authorises national rules relating to access to employment, including promotion, which give a specific advantage to women with a view to improving their ability to compete on the labour market and to pursue a career on an equal footing with men. It noted that, at the time the circular was adopted, the employment situation in the Ministry concerned was characterised by a significant under-representation of women, both in terms of the number of women working there and their occupation of higher grades. It also stated, citing the Council's recommendation on childcare[136], that a proven insufficiency of suitable and affordable child-care facilities is particularly likely to induce more female employees to give up their jobs. In these circumstances it concluded that a measure such as that at issue falls, in principle, amongst those measures permitted by Article 2(4).[137]

The Court saw no problem either with a measure such as that at issue from the perspective of the principle of proportionality. Firstly, as regards the body of academic legal opinion cited by the referring court, the Court simply noted that there was an insufficiency of supply of nursery places, with the result that all female employees did not enjoy a guaranteed place. Secondly, it observed that the measure does not deprive male employees of all access to nursery places for their children since 'such places still remain accessible on the relevant

---

[135] See Case C–476/99 *Lommers* [2002] ECR I–2891, para 30.

[136] Council Recommendation 92/241/EEC of 31 March 1992, OJ 1992 L123/16.

[137] The Court noted that the Dutch rule forms part of the restricted concept of equality of opportunity in so far as it is not places of employment which are reserved for women but enjoyment of certain working conditions designed to facilitate their pursuit of, and progresssion in, their career. See, in particular, Case C–476/99, para 38.

services market'. Thirdly, male employees could still be granted places for their children in cases of emergency, with the result that male employees who bring their children up by themselves should have access to the nursery scheme.[138] Finally, as regards the difficulties in pursuing a career which might be encountered by the spouse of a male employee because of the need to take care of the couples' young children due to their exclusion by a measure such as that at issue from the nursery scheme, the Court regarded such difficulties as being of no relevance for the assessment of the validity of the rule in relation to Article 2(1) and (4). The latter provision cannot be construed as requiring an employer who adopts a measure to tackle under-representation of women amongst his or her own staff to take account of considerations related to the maintenance in employment of women not belonging to that staff.

Lommers is confirmation, if confirmation is indeed needed, that the Court's contribution to the development of EU sex equality law cannot always be considered a blessing. *Commission v France*, which involved special rights for female employees, including the payment of an allowance to mothers to help meet the costs of nurseries or childminders, is summarily dismissed in *Lommers* as an irrelevant precedent. The French government had defended the special rights in that case as being designed to take account of the situation existing in the majority of French households. The Court held, however, that the contested provisions of the French collective agreements could not find justification in Article 2(3) of Directive 76/207, since 'some of the special rights preserved related to the protection of women in their capacity as [. . .] parents—categories to which both men and women may equally belong.'[139] True, the Court in *Commission v France* had also held, as regards Article 2(4), that nothing in the papers before it made it possible to conclude that a generalised preservation of special rights for women 'may correspond to the situation envisaged in that provision.' Arguably, however, what the Court was referring to was the fact that no evidence had been produced by the defendant government (it being an infringement action) to show that inequalities did in fact exist which affected women's opportunities.

In *Lommers* the applicant had argued both at national and European Court level that regardless of whether or not women were underrepresented in the Ministry, it had not been demonstrated that the number of women staying in their jobs after taking maternity leave had increased as a result of the subsidised nursery scheme. This surely was a relevant consideration when it came to an assessment of the impugned measure's proportionality.[140] Furthermore, it

---

[138] The Court specified in this context that a measure which excluded access to nursery places to male employees who brought up their children on their own would go beyond the derogation in Article 2(4) Directive 76/207.

[139] Cited with approval in Case C–366/99 *Griesmar v French Republic* [2001] ECR I–9383, para 44, discussed below.

[140] As regards the principle of proportionality, Case C–476/99 *Lommers*, para 39, states that the latter 'requires that derogations must remain within the limits of what is appropriate and necessary in order to achieve the aim in view and that the principle of equal treatment be reconciled as far as

would appear from the decision of the Court that the rule applies across the board to all grades of female staff in the Ministry. The judgment of the Court is silent as regards the proportion of female staff in the Ministry or their distribution across different grades. The Advocate General's Opinion reveals that only 25 per cent of the Ministry's staff is female, while only 14 per cent of higher grade posts are occupied by female staff. However, it would not be surprising to find their equal or even overrepresentation at the lower levels of the administration and in the secretariat. Since the purpose for and justification of the positive action in question is to tackle the underrepresentation of female staff in the Ministry, logic dictates that the reservation of nursery places is not justified in those grades where they are not underrepresented. In reality, however, this would mean that female employees in lower grades who are least able economically to compete for private childcare places would not be reserved places whereas those in the upper echelons would, despite the fact that they would most probably have less financial difficulty seeking alternative arrangements.[141] This argument simply seeks to demonstrate that blanket provisions of one type or another are dangerous. The generality of the Dutch rule undermines its ability to deliver full professional equality for men and women and to redress the imbalance in the Ministry's workforce to date.

Behind *Lommers* lies the Court's apparent sympathy with measures which seek to tackle the underrepresentation of women in the workforce; a sympathy which was distinctly lacking in *Gruber* when it discussed the potentially discriminatory nature of Austrian rules on compensation in the event of the termination of employment contracts for reasons related to childcare. The reservation of nursery places for female employees is seen as legitimate because the *purpose* of such a rule is to increase female representation in the workforce by diminishing one of the primary factors which works against women entering or re-entering the workforce, namely the lack of sufficient and affordable childcare facilities. However, nowhere does the Court discuss the *effect* of such a rule; neither the effect in terms of whether the measure has been successful in terms of the numbers of women remaining in or returning to their jobs in the Ministry nor, perhaps more importantly, the *effect* which a rule such as this has on the 'employability' of female staff in general. Female workers who have children are, it follows from *Lommers*, seen as bearing primary responsibility for the care of those children. The present writer must admit that part of her criticism of the decision in *Lommers* is attributable to a stance on affirmative action which is diametrically opposed to that which the Court has favoured since

possible with the requirements of the aim thus pursued.' This statement, which is derived from Cases 222/84 *Johnson*, C–273/97 *Sirdar* and C–285/98 *Kreil* (all very particular precedents relating to the role of women in the security and armed forces), arguably turns the principle on its head. It is surely the aim pursued which must be reconciled as far as possible with the requirements of the fundamental principle of equal treatment!

[141] See also McRae, above n 94, pp 10–12, for discussion of the fact that the lowest paid workers are the least likely to return to work after having a baby and that those who are better paid and in more senior jobs are the most likely.

Marschall. The Court (and indeed the EC Treaty) now recognise gender as a legitimate basis for positive action, the aim of the latter being to rectify the underrepresentation of female workers in certain posts or certains echelons. However, the prejudice or exclusion which a worker may experience in the labour market is not merely down to gender but concerns also, if not more so, race, class and the effects of mature capitalism.[142] It is one thing to argue in favour of legislation providing for childcare facilities and another to legitimise a measure which gives automatic, priority access to female employees to child-care facilities without reference to income, personal circumstance etc. If the law identifies working mothers as being primarily/solely responsible, in practice and principle, for their young children, is it surprising that employers have 'prejudices and stereotypes about the role and capacities of women in working life'[143], the very thing which affirmative action seeks to counteract.

Lommers is also disappointing because it highlights a complete lack of coherence in the case-law of the Court. Just under four months previously, in its decision in *Griesmar*, the Court had held that the exclusion of male employees from entitlement to service credits granted to retired civil servants who are mothers was contrary to the principle of equal pay if those fathers can prove that they brought up their children. The Court held that retirement pensions for civil servants constituted pay, within the meaning of Article 141 EC, since they are directly linked to the post previously occupied. It therefore examined whether the service credit granted female employees in respect of each of their children was linked to the career-related disadvantages incurred during maternity leave or whether it was intended to offset disadvantages that result from bringing up a child, in which case male civil servants would be entitled to claim it.[144]

As it had already done in *Commission v France*, the French government argued in *Griesmar* that the service credit had been reserved to female civil servants who have had children in order to address a social reality, namely the disadvantages which they incur in the course of their professional career by virtue of the predominant role assigned to them in bringing up children. The Court referred to this explanation and concluded that there was no link between the credit and the maternity period but rather that the credit is linked to a separate period devoted to bringing up the children. The national legislation used a single criterion for granting the credit and took for granted the fact that children are brought up at home by their mother despite the fact that 'the situations of a male civil servant and a female civil servant may be comparable as regards the bringing-up of children'.[145] The impugned national legislation did not permit a

---

[142] See also Mancini and O'Leary, above n 10, 335–36.

[143] Case C–409/95 *Marschall*, para 29.

[144] See also Case C–206/00 *Mouflin v Recteur de l'Academie de Reims* [2001] ECR I–10201, where the Court regarded as incompatible with the principle of equal treatment another provision of the French civil and military code which reserved the right to immediate enjoyment of their pension rights to female civil servants who wished to take care of an ill spouse.

[145] Case C–366/99 *Griesmar*, paras 55 and 56.

male civil servant who has assumed the task of bringing up his children (the language of the Court still leaves something to be desired in *Griesmar*) to receive the credit even if he is in a position to prove that he did in fact assume that task.

Read side by side, *Lommers* and *Griesmar* appear not only contradictory, but bizarrely so given their proximity in time and subject matter. The Court's discussion in *Griesmar* of the relevance of Article 6(3) of the Agreement on Social Policy is a particularly good illustration. According to the Court, Article 6(3) of the Agreement authorises national measures intended to eliminate or reduce actual instances of inequality which result from the reality of social life and affect women in their professional life. As the French government had pointed out, the bringing-up of children is an important factor, perhaps the most important factor, in explaining the shorter duration of the careers of female civil servants at the date of their retirement. Nevertheless, the Court in *Griesmar* held that in the light of the arguments raised and the information before it:

> the measure at issue in the main proceedings does not appear to be of a nature such as to offset the disadvantages to which the careers of female civil servants are exposed by helping those women in their professional life. On the contrary, that measure is limited to granting female civil servants who are mothers a service credit at the date of their retirement, without providing a remedy for the problems which they may encounter in the course of their professional career.[146]

So what do *Griesmar* and *Lommers* leave us with? On the one hand, male and female employees are regarded in one case as comparable as regards the bringing-up of children (*Griesmar*), while in the other (*Lommers*), they are not. On the other hand, a measure which reserves nursery places to female employees can be considered as belonging to a group of measures designed to improve the ability of women to compete on the labour market and pursue a career on an equal footing with men (*Lommers*), while a measure reserving to female employees with children the right to a service credit for the calculation of their retirement pension is not of a nature such as to offset the disadvantages to which the careers of female civil servants are exposed by helping them in their professional careers (*Griesmar*).

Of course a subtle, legalistic reading of the two cases might argue that the reservation of nursery places is considered legitimate because it seeks to provide equal opportunities, while a service credit on retirement is not, because it pursues an equality of results rather than tackling the causes of inequality. Yet compensation for occupational disadvantage was considered perfectly legitimate in *Abdoulaye*. It could also be argued that, although the Court may have seemed to recognise 'parenting' responsibilities in one case and only 'maternal' responsibilities in another, the fact that it required proof in *Griesmar* that the father had cared for the children could mean that that decision is limited to widowed

---

[146] *Ibid*, para 65. The impugned provision of the French code on civil and military retirement pensions dated from 1924, since which time it had not succeeded in resolving the problems which a female civil servant might encounter in her career!

or divorced fathers who have brought up their children alone or those who have actually taken career breaks to do so.[147] At first sight, *Lommers* may seem impressive. However, what the Court has done is arguably to legitimise a practice which benefits a small minority of employees in one section of the Dutch public service while regarding as incompatible with EC law a provision of the French civil service code reserving a service credit for the calculation of pensions which benefited many thousands.[148] In doing so, it has not indicated to national courts coherent legal principles with which to resolve this type of case in the future, since it remains unclear, in particular, whether national legislation reserving aspects of pay or working conditions to workers of one sex due to their childcare responsibilities is legitimate.

References turning on Directive 79/7 have fared no better. The plaintiffs in *Jackson and Cresswell*,[149] who were in receipt of income support or supplementary allowances, but who subsequently undertook part-time work for less than 24 hours a week or a vocational training course, wanted to have their childminding expenses deducted from their incomes for the purposes of determining the amount of benefit to which they were still entitled under United Kingdom law.[150] The Court held that benefits such as supplementary allowances or income support, which may be granted in a variety of personal situations to persons whose means are insufficient to meet their needs, do not come within the material scope of Directive 79/7. As regards the application of the Equal Treatment Directive, it held that the fact that the method of calculating claimants' actual earnings (ie the failure to deduct childminding expenses), which are used as the basis for determining the amount of the benefits, might affect single mothers' ability to take up access to vocational training or part-time employment, was not sufficient to bring income support and supplementary allowance schemes within the scope of the Directive. Only those social-security schemes whose subject-matter is access to employment, including vocational training, promotion or working conditions fall within the scope of Directive 76/207.[151]

---

[147] *Liaisons Sociales*, 13 December 2001.

[148] In the immediate aftermath of the Court's judgment, in which the possibility of a temporal limitation on its effect had been rejected, the upshot seemed likely to be that the French government would seek not to extend the credit to male civil servants but rather to eliminate it, see *Le Monde*, 5 December 2001. If the Court had thought it was championing substantive equality in Case C–366/99 *Griesmar*, it will no doubt be disappointed.

[149] Joined Cases C–63/91 and C–64/91 *Sonia Jackson and Patricia Cresswell* [1992] ECR I–4737.

[150] Childminding expenses were not deductible, according to the applicable United Kingdom legislation, from allowances paid during vocational training organised by the national body responsible for vocational training, Manpower, or for persons engaged in less than twenty four hours work a week.

[151] See also Case C–245/94 and C–312/94 *Hoever and Zachow v Land Nordrhein Westfalen* [1996] ECR I–4895, where the Court was asked whether a child-raising allowance intended to secure the maintenance of the family while children were being raised fell within the scope of Directive 79/7. Concentrating on the measure's aim, the Court held that it did not. For possible reasons for the Court's failure, in cases like this, to engage in important substantive questions as regards the effect of such social and financial structures see L. Luckhaus, 'Egalité de traitement, protection

Unlike the Court, Advocate General Van Gerven was of the view in *Jackson and Cresswell* that Directive 79/7 did apply. He thus proceeded to apply the principles underlying the Court's well-developed case-law on indirect discrimination. If the national court found that the British schemes affected a higher percentage of women than of men, it was up to the United Kingdom to demonstrate that there were objective factors unrelated to any discrimination on grounds of sex for not taking childminding costs into account when calculating the plaintiffs' benefit entitlements. Admittedly, when assessing the United Kingdom's proposed justifications, he conceded that allowance must be made for the reasonable discretion which each Member State enjoys with regard to social protection measures.[152] The upshot of the impugned national legislation in this case was that the opportunities for divorced or single parents like Ms. Jackson and Cresswell to undertake successfully vocational training or part-time work were likely to be severely affected if their overall financial position worsened as a result. Advocate General Van Gerven seemed fully aware of this problem when he urged the Court, as regards examination of the question whether the national legislation led to indirect discrimination contrary to Directive 76/207, to concentrate on the impact of the national rules on the possibility to engage in vocational training or to take up a job.[153]

In contrast, it appears from the *Meyers* case that another type of benefit granted in the United Kingdom—family benefit—which aims to keep poorly paid workers in employment and to meet family expenses, has, by virtue of its first function, an objective which brings it within the scope of the Equal Treatment Directive. The *Meyers* case also concerned the deduction of childcare costs from gross income, this time in order to allow the claimant to qualify for family credit. The plaintiff argued that the failure to deduct those expenses meant that her income exceeded the ceiling for qualification for family credit and that this discriminated against single parents, who usually have no choice when it comes to resorting to paid childcare and who are, in the majority, women. In determining whether family credit fell within the personal scope of Directive 76/207, the Court emphasised that a social security scheme may come within the scope of Directive 76/207 if its subject-matter is access to

---

sociale et garantie de ressources pour les femmes' (2000) 139 *Revue internationale du Travail* 163–99, 170: 'Chercher à promouvoir l'intégrité de la personne et à faire respecter le droit sont des objectifs louables, mais qui ne concernent pas spécifiquement la protection sociale, et qui ne visent pas à modifier la structure existante des relations financières et sociales.'

[152] For further discussion of indirect discrimination see above ch 4. Note the Advocate General's reliance in Joined Cases C–63/91 and C–64/91 *Jackson and Cresswell* on the word reasonable to describe the extent of the Member States' discretion, which is arguably more limited than the qualifications used by the Court in some of the social security cases discussed in ch 4.

[153] *Ibid*, 4769–4770. He rejected the idea that his position in the case could be regarded as an example of 'positive discrimination' in the sense that legal corrective action was being taken with respect to a group of the population which is disadvantaged by sociological circumstances. On the contrary: 'The development of objective criteria in the legislation which take account of the family costs of a lone parent [regardless of sex] does not disadvantage the male population.'

employment.[154] In the Court's view, one of the functions of family credit was to ensure that families do not find themselves worse off in work than they would be if they were not working and it was therefore clearly concerned with access to employment.[155] In addition, the Court stated that compliance with the fundamental principle of equal treatment presupposes that a benefit such as family credit, which is necessarily linked to an employment relationship, constitutes a working condition within the meaning of Article 5 of Directive 76/207.

At issue in *Jackson and Cresswell* was the topping up of a part-time salary or the income received during a vocational training course with income support or supplementary allowances. The Court in *Meyers* distinguished *Jackson and Cresswell* by stating that the Directive is not rendered applicable simply because the conditions of entitlement for receipt of benefits may be such as to affect the ability of a single parent to take up employment. Yet it is difficult to square the two cases. The purpose of the family credit benefit was to ensure a minimum level of income for poor families. Admittedly, by virtue of United Kingdom law on income support, single parents, unlike other recipients, are not obliged to make themselves available for work. But does the fact that they are not *obliged* to work mean that single parents, the majority of whom are women, should be actually *discouraged* from taking up employment by benefit rules which mean they are actually or relatively worse off as a result, since their salaries are low and their childcare expenses are not deducted for the purpose of calculating supplementary benefits. It is arguable that in *Jackson and Cresswell* the Court fell into the trap which it should, in cases of indirect discrimination cases, take the utmost care to avoid: it is not, as Advocate General Van Gerven emphasised in his Opinion in that case, the *intention* of the legislature which is relevant, it is the actual *impact* or *effect* which its rules and actions have on the disadvantaged group, in this context single parents.[156] Furthermore, as other Advocates General have emphasised, the vital question raised under Directive 76/207 is how to ensure that men and women can gain access to employment in conditions of substantive equality.[157] Given that the majority of single parents are

---

[154] Case C–116/94 *Jennifer Meyers v Adjudication Officer* [1995] ECR I–2131, para 13.

[155] *Ibid*, paras 20–21. According to Advocate General Lenz (para 47 of his Opinion) the prospect of receiving family credit if he accepts low-paid work encourages an unemployed worker to accept such work, with the result that the benefit is related to considerations governing access to employment.

[156] *Ibid* (para 43 of Advocate General Lenz's Opinion), where he stated that the Court had decided against the application of Directive 76/207 in Joined Cases C–63/91 and C–64/91 *Jackson and Cresswell* 'because there was no intention in that case to affect access to employment'. This 'intention' trap is one into which the Court has regularly and sometimes apparently willingly fallen.

[157] See Advocate General La Pergola's Opinion in Case C–1/95 *Gerster*, para 41; and the substantive thrust of Advocate General Tesauro's Opinion in Case C–450/93 *Kalanke* [1995] ECR I–3051. For an excellent discussion of whether the kinds of assumptions about households, family units and female participation in the labour market upon which the British legislator operates in relation to labour law matters are correct see Neal, above n 118.

women, failure to deduct childcare costs from their income for the calculation of supplementary benefits disadvantages them when compared to male workers who do not need to pay such childcare costs. It should be irrelevant from the point of view of equality that income support was nevertheless available for those who chose not to work.[158]

LEGISLATING FOR SPECIAL PROTECTION

Pregnancy and Maternity

Unlike Directive 76/207, which was adopted on the basis of Article 308 EC and which seeks to achieve equal treatment for men and women in a variety of fields, Directive 92/85, which was adopted on the basis of the health and safety provisions of the former Article 118a EC, is concerned with the protection of pregnant women, those who have recently given birth and those who are breastfeeding, and thus seeks to provide different treatment for women in any of these situations.[159] According to Advocate General Ruiz Jarabo in the *Brown* case, both the aims and provisions of the two Directives differ.[160] The preamble of Directive 92/85 reflects the (political) need to place this piece of legislation within the context of the Treaty's health and safety legal basis and the concern that the protection of pregnant women, those on maternity leave and those breastfeeding should not result in unfavourable treatment or work to the detriment of directives concerning equal treatment for men and women.[161] Although the Pregnant Workers' Directive is the Community's first move into the field of

---

[158] Perhaps one relevant factor to be taken into consideration when comparing the two cases is that Joined Cases C–63/91 and C–64/91 *Jackson and Cresswell* was decided in 1992 by the full Court, while C–116/94 *Meyers*, decided in 1995, was a decision of a Chamber of three Judges. On the social exclusion of single parent/female families from the labour market see S. Vousden, 'Gender, exclusion and governance by guideline' (1998) 20 *Journal of Social Welfare and Family Law* 468–479.

[159] For discussion of the legislative background to Directive 92/85 as well as its content and effect see variously the report of the House of Lords Select Committee on the European Communities, above n 94; Armstrong and Bulmer, above n 87; N. Burrows, 'Maternity Rights in Europe—An Embryonic Legal Regime' (1991) 11 *Yearbook of European Law* 273–93; E. Ellis, 'Protection of Pregnancy and Maternity' (1993) 22 *Industrial Law Journal* 63–67; V. Cromack, 'The E.C. Pregnancy Directive—Principle or Pragmatism' (1993) *Journal of Social Welfare and Family Law* 261–72.

[160] See the Opinion of Advocate General Ruiz-Jarabo in Case C–394/96 *Brown*, para 20.

[161] Opposition to the use of the former Article 118a EC as the legal basis for legislation with social and employment protection objectives was voiced by the House of Lords Select Committee, above n 94, p 12; see also the memorandum by the Confederation of British Industry annexed to the House of Lord's Report, p 12. It is well-know that, at least during the reign of the Conservative government in the 1980s and early 1990s, the British government opposed expansive use of the health and safety legal basis; see above ch 3 for an account of its attempts to annul Directive 93/104 on working time.

special protection, the Directive does not, as some of its provisions reveal, move entirely away from the equal treatment underpinnings of much of the Court's early case-law.

The Directive applies to pregnant workers who inform their employers of their condition, workers who have recently given birth and workers who are breastfeeding. Articles 3–6 of the same Directive deal with the hazards (chemical, physical, biological) which may be encountered by pregnant workers or those who have recently given birth, while Article 7 covers night work. Article 8 of the Directive provides that Member States shall take the necessary measures to ensure that pregnant workers are entitled to a continuous period of maternity leave of at least fourteen weeks allocated before and/or after confinement in accordance with national legislation and/or practice. This leave must include compulsory maternity leave of at least two weeks allocated before and/or after confinement. Pregnant workers are also entitled to time off, without loss of pay, in order to attend ante-natal examinations. Article 10, which codifies the jurisprudence of the Court in *Dekker*, deals with protection from dismissal. It is prohibited to dismiss pregnant workers from the beginning of their pregnancy to the end of the fourteen weeks (minimum) maternity leave, save in exceptional cases unconnected with their condition which are permitted under national legislation and/or practice. It is up to the employer to explain, with reference to duly substantiated grounds, the reasons why a pregnant employee has been dismissed during this protected period. Member States are to take the necessary measures to protect pregnant workers from dismissal which is unlawful by virtue of Article 10. The prohibition against dismissal in Article 10 applies to absence from work during pregnancy and maternity but has no effect with respect to absence from work due to pregnancy related illness following the end of the protected maternity leave period, which means that the principles established in *Hertz* still apply. During the course of maternity leave Article 11(2) provides that the rights connected with the employment contract must be ensured, as must the maintenance of the worker's pay or payment of an adequate allowance. The latter shall be deemed adequate if, according to Article 11(3), it guarantees income at least equivalent to that which the worker concerned would receive in the event of a break in her activities on grounds connected with her state of health, subject to any ceiling laid down under national legislation. Pursuant to Article 11(4), Member States may make entitlement to pay or to the allowance described above conditional upon the worker concerned fulfilling the conditions of eligibility for such benefits laid down under national legislation, but a period of employment in excess of twelve months immediately prior to the presumed date of confinement cannot be required. Member States are obliged to introduce into their national legal systems such measures as are necessary to enable all workers who should themselves be wronged by failure to comply with the obligations arising from this Directive to pursue their claims by judicial process and/or by recourse to other competent authorities.

Whether or not Directive 92/85 brings about improvements in the safety and health at work of pregnant workers and workers who have recently given birth or are breastfeeding,[162] it certainly represents a departure from the equality-difference rationale which has pervaded much of the Court's case-law. The Directive may at least mean that the Court need no longer wrestle to find solutions in the equal treatment/non-discrimination tools which were at its disposal in an area where comparisons of male and female are often if not always untenable. It remains to be seen, of course, whether Directive 92/85 is any more successful than the principle of equal treatment in protecting pregnant workers before and after the birth of their children. The legislative history of the Directive reveals to what extent more stringent protection had to be sacrificed on the altar of compromise in order for its adoption to be secured.[163] Furthermore, even this special protection instrument is not free from the difficulties which dogged the Court's pregnancy and maternity jurisprudence in the past. Thus, only mothers benefit from maternity leave pursuant to the Directive and they will not necessarily receive their full pay, or a high percentage thereof, during this period but may simply receive an income equivalent to the standard rate of sick pay. The Directive, though it guarantees a minimum period of maternity leave, may leave the most vulnerable employees with little if any protection as, if they do not qualify under national law for statutory sick pay, they may be entitled to, at most, a one off compensation payment during their maternity leave. As a result, they will inevitably be forced back to work before their fourteen weeks entitlement has expired out of sheer economic necessity.[164]

Clearly the Directive has not signalled the end of assumptions about the division of employment and childcare responsibilities and use of the sick male employee comparator, despite the fact that the preamble states that this fixing of the minimum level of protection should in no circumstances be interpreted as suggesting an analogy between pregnancy and illness. Although the minimalist regime introduced by the Directive—in terms of the protected period of maternity leave and the maternity pay or allowance payable to female workers on leave—may have been an improvement on the existing statutory position in some Member States such as the United Kingdom, it could be regarded with distinct disappointment in other Member States where far more generous statutory provisions were already in operation.[165] The disappointing nature of the Directive's provisions on maternity pay are emphasised by the ILO Maternity Convention 2000, which provides that, where a ratifying state is 'insufficiently

---

[162] The Report from the Commission on the implementation of Council Directive 92/85/EEC of 19 October 1992, COM (99) 100 final reveals that the Directive brought about a substantive improvement in the level of protection in very few Member States.

[163] See Ellis, above n 159.

[164] *Ibid*, 67. See also Fredman (1995), above n 32, 223, on the high percentage of women who are excluded from the scope of application of the provisions of the Directive on pay because of their low incomes.

[165] See, for example, the details provided in the Houses of Lords Select Committee Report, above n 94, p 7.

developed', it may pay cash benefits during maternity leave at a level no less than sickness or temporary disability benefits. Otherwise, ratifying States should provide not less than two thirds of the woman's previous income. Not surprisingly, the Member States of the European Union were not those the ILO had in mind when referring to insufficiently developed States.

The applicants in the *Boyle* case, employees of the United Kingdom's Equal Opportunities Commission, were the first to bring a case to the Court of Justice under Directive 92/85 when they challenged the compatibility with Directive 92/85 of certain clauses of the EOC's maternity scheme.[166] In answer to the complicated and detailed questions referred to it, the Court emphasised the special protection underpinnings of the 1992 Directive. Maternity leave is intended to protect a woman's biological condition during and after pregnancy and to protect the special relationship between a woman and her child over the period which follows pregnancy and childbirth. This special protection rationale, according to the Court, meant, first of all, that a clause in an employment contract entitling female employees to receive more than the statutory maternity pay from their employer on condition that they, unlike workers on sick leave, return to work after childbirth or, failing that, repay the contractual maternity pay in so far as it exceeds the level of the statutory payments in respect of that leave, does not constitute discrimination contrary to Article 141 EC and the Equal Pay Directive.[167] The level of payments made during maternity leave must simply satisfy the requirements in Article 11(2)(b) and (3) of Directive 92/85— i.e. they must not be lower than the income which the worker concerned would receive under the relevant national social security legislation.[168]

Secondly, the Court recalled that Directive 92/85 merely requires Member States to provide a minimum period of fourteen weeks maternity leave with two compulsory weeks before or after confinement. The Directive leaves the decision concerning the starting date of the maternity leave to the Member States. In these circumstances, a provision requiring a pregnant worker who is on sick leave due to a pregnancy-related illness before the proposed commencement of her maternity leave and who gives birth when on sick leave, to bring forward the commencement of her paid maternity leave, is not contrary to the Directive. The clause in the EOC maternity scheme simply reflected a legitimate choice made at Member State level.

Thirdly, given the purpose and scope of Article 8, the Court held that it is contrary to the Directive to require a woman on the statutory period of fourteen weeks maternity leave to return to work and terminate her maternity leave in order to take sick leave. However a similar clause prohibiting a woman from taking sick leave during a period of supplementary maternity leave granted to

---

[166] Case C–411/96 *Boyle*. See the annotation by E. Carraciolo de Torella, 'Recent Developments in Pregnancy and Maternity Rights' (1999) 28 *Industrial Law Journal* 276–82.
[167] Case C–411/96 *Boyle*, para 42.
[168] *Ibid*, para 36.

her by her employer unless she elects to return to work and thus terminate her maternity leave was considered compatible with Directive 92/85, since the objective of the latter is simply the provision of a minimum level of protection. The minimum level of protection afforded by Directive 92/85 also underpinned the Court's finding that a clause which prevents annual leave accruing during periods of supplementary maternity leave is not contrary to Directive 92/85. The applicants had argued that, since a substantially greater proportion of women than men take periods of unpaid leave because they take supplementary maternity leave, such a rule constitutes indirect discrimination against women contrary to Article 5(1) Directive 76/207. The Court accepted that, in practice, more women than men take periods of unpaid leave during their career because they take supplementary maternity leave. However, the fact that such a clause applies more frequently to women results from the exercise of the right to unpaid maternity leave granted to them by their employers in addition to the period of protection guaranteed by Article 8 Directive 92/85. Supplementary unpaid maternity leave was seen as a special advantage, over and above the protection provided for by Directive 92/85 and was available only to women, so that the fact that annual leave ceased to accrue during that period of leave could not amount to less favourable treatment of women.[169]

Finally, the Court held that the accrual of pension rights under an occupational scheme during the period of maternity leave cannot be made conditional upon the woman's receiving the pay provided for by her employment contract or statutory maternity pay during that period.[170] Member States may make entitlement to maternity pay or a maternity allowance conditional upon the worker concerned fulfilling the conditions of eligibility for such benefits laid down under national law. No such possibility exists, however, with respect to rights connected with the employment contract within the meaning of Article 11(2)(a) of the Directive.

Essentially, the upshot of the *Boyle* case is that the minimum obligations imposed on Member States by Directive 92/85, in particular by Article 8, do not cover supplemental periods of maternity leave afforded by an employer to a pregnant employee. The rights conferred by the Directive on pregnant workers and those who have recently given birth constitute a special protection regime, which may undermine any attempt by female workers to claim that legislative

---

[169] *Ibid*, paras 78–79. At para 61 of his Opinion, Advocate General Ruiz Jarabo also rejected the applicants' argument since the leave taken by the women reflected special arrangements which have no connection with unpaid leave taken voluntarily for personal reasons, which is available to both men and women. However, he insisted, at para 60, that he considered 'that reserving solely to women the availability of unpaid leave to look after a newborn child does not help promote equality of opportunity between the sexes, since what it does in reality is to perpetuate in society the idea that it is women who as a matter of priority should take care of the children—with all the concomitant adverse effects on their future careers'. For another childcare case in which the Court showed a similarly short-sighted view of the principle of indirect sex discrimination see Case C–249/97 *Gruber*, discussed above.

[170] Case C–411/96 *Boyle*, para 85.

provisions, because of the disproportionate effect they have on female workers, give rise to discrimination. Although pregnant workers may rely on the equality directives, it is clear that their legal rights once on maternity leave are governed by the special protection regime in Directive 92/85. The minimalist nature of the provisions of this compromise text will not always work in their favour, with the result that a pregnant woman or one on maternity leave can indeed be treated worse than sick male workers in terms of pay entitlement.[171]

Something which Directive 92/85 leaves unresolved is the question of Member States' contributions to the costs of maternity pay or, at the very least, discussion of how the financial consequences of maternity should be met. Indeed, the Commission was strongly criticised for its failure to make an adequate assessment of the economic implications of the Directive when it was in draft form.[172] The issue of cost was put to one side in the Directive—the solution preferred by the Member States being the provision of only a minimum floor of rights for those female workers concerned. This minimalist approach, which was already evident in the decision of the Court of Justice in *Gillespie*, has come to the fore again in *Boyle*, with the Court of Justice being called upon to interpret a safe and unchallenging legislative text. As one commentator has remarked:

> Ultimately, where the balance lies in this area between the welfare of employees and the commercial needs of employers will be a matter of public policy. For the present, the purposive methodology of the courts does not appear a likely public policy vehicle for change in that balance in favour of improved statutory maternity pay in the UK, and the principal constraint appears to be article 11 of the [Pregnant Workers' Directive] which sets the level of the floor for the payment.[173]

In submissions to the House of Lords Select Committee, the EOC—ironically, as we saw, the first defendant before the Court in a case involving the Directive—had argued in favour of an improved maternity fund to ensure that the costs of maternity pay should not be borne exclusively by employers.[174] The creation of such funds at national level could contribute to the cost to employers of providing cover during the worker's maternity leave or during absence from work due to pregnancy-related illness.

---

[171] See also A. Masselot and K. Berthou, 'La CJCE, le droit de la maternité et le principe de non discrimination—vers une clarification?' (2000) *Cahiers de droit européen* 637–56.

[172] House of Lords Select Committee Report, above n 94, p 12. An estimate of the costs of implementing EC pregnancy protection legislation was compiled by the British Department of Employment (annexed to the House of Lords Select Committee Report, above n 94, p 35). Note, however, that the estimates were based on the Commission's original proposal for a pregnancy directive which included the provision of maternity pay of at least 80% of the worker's salary.

[173] See Lewis, above n 52, 69. Bamforth, above n 91, 61, regards the choice as a political one about the role of maternity in modern society.

[174] See the memorandum on the Commission's draft pregnancy directive submitted by the EOC to the House of Lords Select Committee, above n 94, p 20.

Parental Leave

Although binding legislation on parental leave was only adopted in 1996, the Commission had, for many years, regarded the work-family interface as an essential part of its equal opportunities policy:

A *sine qua non* for the promotion of true equality at work is the sharing of family and occupational responsibilities, particularly the development of adequate child-minding facilities and a review of social infrastructure in general. In the same area, the development of parental leave and leave for family reasons and the reorganization of working time call for an open and positive approach in connection with the promotion of equality at work, a better quality of life and the campaign against unemployment.'[175]

The Parental Leave Directive was the first instrument adopted on the basis of Article 4(2) of the Agreement on Social Policy annexed to the TEU Social Policy Protocol.[176] Following several unsuccessful attempts by the Commission to introduce legislation on parental leave, Directive 96/34 transposed a framework agreement concluded by the main organisations representing confederations of European employers' and employees' representatives. Its objective is to reconcile work and family life and to promote equal opportunities and equal treatment between men and women. Clause 2 of the agreement grants male and female workers—full-time and part-time—an individual statutory right to parental leave on the grounds of the birth or adoption of a child. The leave is to enable them to take care of their child, for at least three months, until a given age up to eight years, to be specified by the Member States or the social partners. To promote equal opportunities this right is granted, in principle, on a non-transferable basis so that one parent cannot accumulate the other's entitlement to leave (Clause 2(2)). Workers who apply for or take parental leave are to be protected against dismissal and afterwards they have a right to return to their

---

[175] See EC Commission, *Equal Opportunities for Women, Medium-term Community programme 1986–1990*, Bull. EC. Supp. 3/86, p 8; the Resolution of the Council and of the Ministers for Employment and Social Policy, meeting within the Council of 29 June 2000, on the balanced participation of women and men in family and working life, OJ 2000 C218/5; Article 33(2) of the Charter of Fundamental Rights of the European Union, OJ 2000 C364/01: 'To reconcile family and professional life, everyone shall have a right to protection from dismissal for a reason unconnected with maternity and the right to paid maternity leave and to parental leave following the birth or adoption of a child.' For academic discussion and criticism see C.L. Claussen, 'Incorporating Women's Reality into Legal Neutrality in the European Community: The Sex Segregation of Labor and the Work-Family Nexus' (1991) 22 *Law & Policy in International Business* 787–811; and E. Caracciolo di Torella, 'The Family-Friendly Workplace: the EC position' (2001) 17 *International Journal of Comparative Labour Law and Industrial Relations* 325–44.

[176] Council Directive 96/34/EC of 3 June 1996 on the framework agreement on parental leave concluded by UNICE, CEEP and the ETUC, OJ 1996 L 145/4, extended to the United Kingdom by Council Directive 97/75/EC of 15 December 1997, OJ 1997 L 10/24. For an account of the adoption of Directive 96/34 see M. Schmidt, 'The EC Directive on Parental Leave' (1998) 32 *Labour Law and Industrial Relations in the European Union. Bulletin of Comparative Labour Relations* 181–92; and P. Roberts, 'Current Developments' (1997) 19 *Journal of Social Welfare and Family Law* 87–104, for a brief discussion of the Directive's scope and effects.

jobs after parental leave or to an equivalent or similar job consistent with their employment contract or relationship (Clauses 2(4) and (5)). Member States are left to determine the status of the employment contract or relationship during parental leave and all matters relating to social security (Clauses 2(7) and (8)). The framework agreement makes no provision for remuneration or social security during the period of leave, this issue being left for determination at national level.[177] However, Clauses 2(6) and (8) provide, on the one hand, that rights acquired or in the process of being acquired by the worker on the date on which parental leave starts shall be maintained as they stand until the end of parental leave and, on the other, for the continuity of social benefits, particularly in relation to health care. The agreement does not preclude Member States from introducing more favourable provisions than those provided and the implementation of the agreement shall not constitute valid grounds for a levelling down of standards of protection in the Member States. The agreement is applicable to undertakings of all sizes although, by virtue of Clause 2(3)(f), Member States and/or management and labour are authorised to adopt special arrangements to meet the operational and organisational requirements of small undertakings. Finally, the conditions of access and detailed rules for applying parental leave shall be determined by law and/or collective agreement in the Member States. These rules can, for example, make entitlement to leave subject to a period of work qualification and/or length of service qualification not exceeding one year (Clause 2(3)(b)). In addition, they can provide that an employer is, in certain circumstances, following consultation, allowed to postpone the granting of parental leave for justifiable reasons relating to the operation of the undertaking where, for example, the work is seasonal, where a specific function is of strategic importance or where a number of employees apply for parental leave at the same time (Clause 2(3)(e)).

The Parental Leave Directive has been the subject of little case-law to date. In *Lewen* the Court held that the payment by an employer of a Christmas bonus does not fall within the scope of Clause 2(6) of the annex to the Directive, since it is paid voluntarily after the start of the parenting leave. The Directive did not preclude, therefore, a refusal to pay such a bonus to a woman on parenting leave, where the award of that allowance is subject to the sole condition that the worker must have been in active employment when it was awarded. The exclusion of the bonus in question from the scope of Clause 2(6) also led the Court to conclude that this provision does not preclude an employer, when granting such a bonus to a female worker on parenting leave, from taking periods of that leave into account so as to reduce the benefit *pro rata*. It was only periods for the protection of mothers, in other words periods in which they are prohibited by law from working, which could not, by virtue of Article 141 EC, be taken into account so as to reduce any benefit *pro rata*. In the absence of a provision in the

---

[177] For criticism of the absence of provision for pay and discussion of the likely negative impact of this omission see McColgan (2000) above n 58, 139–40.

Directive requiring financial compensation for parents who avail of their rights thereunder, Clause 2(6), on the maintenance of employment rights during this period, was potentially of considerable importance for the success of the Directive. Employees are less likely to avail of their right to leave if they risk losing not only their pay but also their enjoyment of employment rights which they would otherwise be entitled to. The exclusion of the Christmas bonus in *Lewen* from the scope of Clause 2(6) highlights the weakness of the Directive's provisions and contrasts significantly with the Court's position in *Thibault*, where the Equal Treatment Directive was interpreted as requiring the protection of a female worker's employment rights, albeit during maternity leave.[178]

---

[178] For other cases concerning the Parental Leave Directive see Case T–135/96 *UEAPME v Council of the European Union* [1998] ECR II–2335, where the UAEPME sought unsuccessfully to have the Directive annulled; Case T–51/98 *Burrill*; and Case C–243/00 *R v Secretary of State for Trade and Industry, ex parte TUC*, pending (OJ 2000 C233/23), where the Court has been asked whether Member States are obliged to accord a right to parental leave with respect to children born or adopted before the entry into force of the Directive, or whether the Directive applies only to those born or adopted thereafter.

6

Employment Protection: Struggling with Acquired Rights

INTRODUCTION

WHILE CHAPTERS FOUR and five have examined issues which can, roughly speaking, be located squarely within the parameters of EC sex equality law, the subject matter of this chapter relates to employment protection generally, regardless of the sex of the workers involved.[1] Adopted in 1977 as part of the Community's Social Action Programme, Directive 77/187 was intended both as an employment protection mechanism in the face of the major corporate restructuring which was forecast in the 1970s and also as a means to facilitate the transfer of undertakings which that restructuring was bound to entail.[2] Although the provisions of the 1977 Directive have since been amended and consolidated by Directives 98/50 and 2001/23, the jurisprudence discussed herein dates from the time when Directive 77/187 was still in force.[3]

The purpose of this chapter is to examine the difficulties that the Court of Justice has experienced when fleshing out the scope and substantive content of the Directive on Acquired Rights and how, as regards in particular the Directive's application to contracting out, insolvency and the public sector, the

---

[1] Although, when it comes to the question of whether or not EC legislation on transfers of undertakings should apply to contracting out, the sex of employees is undoubtedly an issue, since women are usually predominant in services industries, such as catering or cleaning, where contracting out is prevalent. See further A. McColgan, *Just Wages for Women* (Oxford, Clarendon Press, 1997) pp 77–81; the Report of the House of Lords Select Committee on the European Communities, *Transfer of Undertakings: Acquired Rights*, Session 1995–1996, 5th Report, p 13; and C–320/00 A.G. *Lawrence and Others v Regent Office Care Ltd. and Commercial Catering Corp*, judgment of 17 September 2002, nyr ECR.

[2] Council Directive 77/187/EEC of 14 February 1977 on the approximation of the laws of the Member States relating to the safeguarding of employees' rights in the event of transfers of undertakings, businesses or parts of businesses, OJ 1977 L61/26, often referred to as the Acquired Rights Directive. On the Community's 1974–76 Social Action Programme (Bull. EC. Suppl. 2/74) see further M. Shanks, 'Introductory Article: The Social Policy of the European Communities' (1977) 14 *Common Market Law Review* 375–83, who explains that the programme was devised with a view to avoiding political backlash. The Community had to be seen to be more than a device to enable capitalists to exploit the common market if the peoples of the Community were to be persuaded to accept the disciplines of the creation of a common market. The basic guidelines of the programme were full and better employment, better living and working conditions and greater participation.

[3] Council Directive 98/50/EC of 29 June 1998, OJ 1998 L201/88; and Council Directive 2001/23/EC of 12 March 2001, OJ 2001 L82/16.

Court has been forced to make difficult policy choices. At the heart of these choices is a tension in the Directive between, on the one hand, employment protection objectives and, in later years, the demands of labour market flexibility and, on the other, the demands of business in a changing competitive environment. This chapter also details the amendments introduced by Directive 98/50 and consolidated in Directive 2001/23 and questions whether the Community legislator has eased the Court's difficult task of providing national courts with useful and sufficiently precise interpretative guidance on how to apply the provisions of the Directive. As before, the chapter concludes with an analysis of the Court's performance under Article 234 EC with specific reference to its case-law on transfers of undertakings and of its attempts to balance employment protection objectives with business interests.

THE ORIGINAL LEGISLATIVE FRAMEWORK GOVERNING
TRANSFERS OF UNDERTAKINGS: DIRECTIVE 77/187

The Preamble of Directive 77/187 made clear the reasons for the adoption by the Community legislature, as early as 1977, of such a relatively advanced employment protection measure with the potential to fundamentally affect Member State labour laws.[4] Although the Directive did not concern the level and scope of national employment terms and conditions—its objective simply being to ensure that terms and conditions which existed prior to a transfer continued to apply thereafter—it was of fundamental importance in ensuring that employees did not lose the enjoyment of the terms and conditions applicable to their contracts as a result of the reorganisation and transfer of their employer's business. According to the first recital, economic trends were resulting, at both national and EC level, in changes to the structure of undertakings as a result of legal transfers and mergers. The purpose of the Directive was to ensure that the rights of employees, in the event of a change of employer, were safeguarded. However, the Preamble also made clear that one of the principal reasons for the introduction of a minimum level of employment protection at EC level was the fear that disparities in employment protection legislation between Member States might have a deleterious effect on the transfers and mergers which it was the common market's aim to bring about as a result of greater economic integration. Thus, the Directive reflected the dual economic and social aims that characterised

---

[4] On Directive 77/187 generally see M.C. Rodríguez-Piñero Royo, 'Transmisión de empresas y derecho europeo' in Cacucci (ed) *La transmisión de empresas en Europa*, Collana di diritto comparato e comunitario del lavoro e della sicurezza sociale (Cacucci Editor, 1999); F. Vandamme, 'Concentrations d'entreprises et protection des travailleurs' (1977) 13 *Cahiers de droit européen* pp 25–48; M.F.G.M. Legnier, 'Transferts d'entreprises et protection des travailleurs dans le cadre communautaire' (1977) *Revue du Marche Commune* 473–82; Report of the House of Lords Select Committee on the European Communities, above n 1.

much of the Community's Social Action Programme.[5] Like Article 141 EC which, as we have seen, was inserted in the Treaty to serve both economic and social aims,[6] Directive 77/187 reflected both the Community's attempts to ameliorate 'the unacceptable by-products of growth'[7] and its intention to eliminate distortions of competition. Traces of the tension between the Directive's social and economic facets can be found throughout the case-law of the Court of Justice which has been called upon, essentially, to balance the employment protection objectives of the Directive with the need to ensure that there are no untoward disincentives to transferring business in an increasingly integrated and globalised European market.

Article 1(1) indicated to which transfers Directive 77/187 would apply. It provided that the Directive should apply to the transfer of an undertaking, business or part of a business to another employer as a result of a legal transfer or merger. The Directive provided employees essentially with three forms of protection. In the first place, the transferor's rights and obligations arising from a contract of employment or from an employment relationship existing on the date of a transfer were, by reason of the transfer, to be transferred to the transferee.[8] Following the transfer, the transferee was bound to observe the terms and conditions agreed in any collective agreement on the same terms applicable to the transferor under that agreement, albeit Member States could limit the period for observing such terms and conditions (Article 3(2)). The Directive did not, however, cover employees' rights to old-age, invalidity or survivors' benefits under supplementary company or inter-company pension schemes outside the statutory social security schemes in Member States (Article 3(3)), a fact which, given that the Directive's purpose was to protect workers in a period of rapid

---

[5] Advocate General Cosmas (para 15) in Case C–472/93 *Luigi Spano and Others v Fiat Geotech SpA and Fiat Hitachi Excavators SpA (formerly Fiat Hitachi Construction Equipment SpA)* [1995] ECR I–4321 regarded the Directive as pursuing a manifestly social objective. See, however, G. More, 'The concept of 'undertaking' in the Acquired Rights Directive: the Court of Justice under pressure (again)' (1995) 15 *Yearbook of European Law* 135–55, 136–37, who contends that the social focus of the Commission's original proposal, namely ensuring that employees did not forfeit essential rights and advantages acquired prior to a change of employer (COM (74) 351 Final/2, para 7), was diluted during the process of adoption, with the need to safeguard the functioning of the common market gaining strength. She questions whether this change in emphasis was deliberate or merely a means of shaping the Directive to fit its Article 94 EC legal basis. Closely related to the adoption of the Acquired Rights Directive were Council Directive 75/129/EEC of 17 February 1975 on the approximation of the laws of the Member States relating to collective redundancies, OJ 1975 L48/29 and Council Directive 80/987/EEC of 20 October 1989 on the protection of employees in the event of the insolvency of their employer, OJ 1980 L283/23. All three Directives were intended to ensure appropriate protection for the employee in situations associated with company restructuring and long-term economic difficulties.

[6] See the discussion in ch 4.

[7] See the 1974 Social Action Programme, Bull. EC. Supp. 2/74, 13 and the discussion in M. Shanks, *European Social Policy, Today and Tomorrow* (Oxford, Pergamon, 1977).

[8] By virtue of Article 3(1) of Directive 77/187, Member States could provide that, after the date of transfer and in addition to the transferee, the transferor should continue to be liable in respect of obligations which arose from a contract of employment or an employment relationship.

economic and technological change, has been described as 'imponderable'.[9] As Davies points out, when adopting the 1977 Directive, the Member States opted for a narrow form of acquired rights: transferred employees were entitled to the same level of employment protection *vis-à-vis* the transferee as they had been *vis-à-vis* the transferor. The purpose of the Directive was not to demand any particular substantive level of employment protection but simply to ensure that the level of protection that pertained prior to the transfer continued to be guaranteed thereafter.[10] The second form of protection afforded by Directive 77/187 referred to the fact that the transfer of an undertaking did not in itself constitute grounds for dismissal of employees by the transferor or the transferee.[11] Dismissal of employees was, however, in accordance with Article 4(1), permissible for economic, technical or organisational reasons entailing changes in the workforce; a provision which underlined the compromise inherent in the Directive between the need to protect employees and the need to recognise the hard realities of business life. Thirdly, employees' representatives had to be informed by the transferor and the transferee of the reasons for the transfer, the legal, economic and social implications of the transfer for the employees and of the measures envisaged in relation to the employees (Article 6). This information was to be provided in good time before the transfer was carried out.[12]

JUDICIAL DEVELOPMENT OF DIRECTIVE 77/187

It took some years following the entry into force of Directive 77/187 for the first references involving the Directive to be lodged at the Court of Justice. Those first references were followed in the same and subsequent years by somewhat of a deluge of cases relating to the interpretation of the Acquired Rights Directive. In particular, national courts seemed to experience considerable difficulties when determining whether or not Directive 77/187 applied to the type of business arrangements before them. They repeatedly questioned the Court of Justice about the interpretation to be given the concepts 'legal transfer' and 'transfer of

---

[9] See the decision of the High Court of England and Wales in *Adams v Lincolnshire CC and BET Catering Services* [1996] IRLR 154 (ChD).

[10] See P. Davies, 'Acquired Rights, Creditors' Rights, Freedom of Contract, and Industrial Democracy' (1989) 9 *Yearbook of European Law* 21–53, 21; and R. Upex, 'The Acquired Rights Directive and its effect upon consensual variation of employees' contracts' (1999) 24 *European Law Review* 293–99.

[11] It was open to Member States not to apply Article 4(1) to specific categories of employees who were not covered by the laws or practice of the Member States in respect of protection against dismissal. Article 4(2) provided that, if the contract of employment or the employment relationship were terminated because the transfer involved a substantial change in working conditions to the detriment of the employee, the employer was to be regarded as having been responsible for termination of the contract of employment or of the employment relationship.

[12] See further Davies (1989), above n 10, 27–29, for discussion of how and why the original proposals for the 1977 Directive relating to consultation were watered down during the course of the adoption process. See also Case T–12/93 *Comité central d'entreprise de la Société anonyme Vittel and others v Commission of the European Communities* [1995] ECR II–1247, paras 62–63.

an undertaking, business or part of a business' in Article 1(1) and, subsequently, about the application of the Directive to the contracting out of services and to undertakings involved in insolvency or similar proceedings.[13] What was also striking about references concerning the transfer of undertakings was the concentration, at least in the early years, of references from Danish and Dutch courts.

WHAT CONSTITUTES A LEGAL TRANSFER?

In the *Abels* case,[14] the Court made clear that the scope of Article 1 generally, and the expression legal transfer in particular, could not be appraised solely on the basis of a textual interpretation. This was due to the differences between the language versions of this provision and the divergences between the laws of the Member States with regard to the concept of legal transfer. Reference to the purpose of the Directive—safeguarding employees in the event of a transfer of their undertaking—as well as to its scheme, ensured that a sufficiently flexible interpretation was given the concept of legal transfer, presumably to ensure that the scope of the Directive was not untowardly narrowed, thereby depriving employees of the protection which had been intended for them in the event of a transfer.[15]

The *Ny Molle Kro* case involved the owner of a leased restaurant who took over its operation following a breach of the lease by the lessee.[16] The owner had leased the restaurant in 1980 to a Mrs Larsen who undertook to comply with the terms of the collective agreements concluded by the Danish association representing hotel and restaurant employees and the corresponding Danish employers' association. Following breach of the lease by Larsen, the owner of the Ny Molle Kro rescinded the lease and took over the operation of the restaurant at the beginning of 1981.[17] In May 1983 a waitress was engaged to work in the restaurant until the end of the Summer season. She left the employ of the defendant in mid-August without giving notice. Subsequently, the Danish Trade Unions Congress ascertained that the wage paid to the said waitress did not correspond to the amount due under the relevant Danish collective agreement and it thus brought an action against the owner of the Ny Molle Kro for the arrears.

---

[13] For a fairly comprehensive synopsis of the Court's rulings on the scope and application of the Directive see the Opinion of Advocate General Ruiz Jarabo in Case C–234/98 *G.C. Allen and Others v Amalgamated Construction Co. Ltd* [1999] ECR I–8643, para 30.

[14] Case 135/83 *H.B.M. Abels v Administration Board of the Bedrijfsvereniging voor de Metaalindustrie en de Electrotechnische Industrie* [1985] ECR 469.

[15] Case 135/83 *Abels*, paras 11–13, discussed in greater detail below. See also Joined Cases C–171/94 and C–172/94 *Albert Merckx and Patrick Neuhuys v Ford Motors Company Belgium SA* [1996] ECR I–1253, para 28.

[16] Case 287/86 *Landsorganisationen i Danmark for Tjenerforbundet i Danmark v Ny Molle Kro* [1987] ECR 5465.

[17] It emerges from the Report of the Hearing that the restaurant was leased briefly to a third party during the course of the 1981 summer season.

The owner, however, denied that the collective agreement with which the former lessee had agreed to comply could be pleaded against her.

In its reference to the Court of Justice, the referring court sought to ascertain whether the notion of legal transfer in Article 1(1) of Directive 77/187 covers the situation in which the owner of a leased undertaking rescinds the lease on the ground of breach by the lessee and carries on the business himself. In its response, the Court emphasised the employment protection purpose of the Directive, which was: 'to ensure, so far as possible, that the rights of employees are safeguarded in the event of a change of employer by enabling them to remain in employment with the new employer in the terms and conditions agreed with the transferor.'[18] The Directive thus applied where, following a legal transfer or merger, there is a change in the legal or natural person who is responsible for carrying on the business and who by virtue of that fact incurs the obligations of an employer *vis-à-vis* employees of the undertaking, regardless of whether or not ownership of the undertaking is transferred.[19] According to the Court, employees of an undertaking whose employer changes (due, for example, to the original owner taking over the operation following the breach of the lease) without any change in ownership are in a situation comparable to that of employees of an undertaking that is sold, and they require equivalent protection.

In the memorably named *Daddy's Dance Hall*,[20] the owner of the Palace Theatre had leased the restaurants and bars in a theatre complex to a catering company. The lessee, pursuant to this contract, was not entitled to transfer its rights under the lease to third parties. The lease was conditional, however, on the catering company obtaining a licence to sell alcohol. When it failed to obtain that licence it gave up the lease and dismissed its staff. However, the original lessee continued to run the theatre's restaurants and bars until they were taken over by the new lessee. Without any involvement of the original lessee—in what the Advocate General described as a triangular operation—the owners of the theatre concluded a new lease with the defendant Daddy's Dance Hall. The defendants concluded a contract with the manager who had previously been employed by the original lessee, with effect from the date of the transfer of the lease. A trial period of three months was included in the manager's contract, during which each party could give 14 days notice. The Court also stated that the defendant re-employed the employees of the original lessee to do the same jobs as before.[21] The manager was dismissed just over two months after his new

---

[18] Case 287/86 *Ny Molle Kro*, para 12.

[19] *Ibid*; see also the Opinion of Advocate General Mancini, 5476, where he argued that the wide interpretation afforded by the Court to the notion of legal transfer in Article 1(1) was consistent with the spirit and purpose of the Directive, which was to render irrelevant any changes of ownership of an undertaking as regards employment relationships existing within it.

[20] Case 324/86 *Foreningen af Arbejdsledere i Danmark v Daddy's Dance Hall A/S* [1988] ECR 739.

[21] The Copenhagen Maritime and Commercial Court which had heard the case at first instance had found, as a fact, that Daddy's Dance Hall only took over the stock from the original lessee and left it to the restaurant manager which it had employed to recruit new staff. With the exception of one person, however, all of the original lessee's former employees were taken on by the new lessee.

contract with Daddy's Dance Hall had taken effect and he was given fourteen days notice.

The Court in *Daddy's Dance Hall* found that: 'where, upon the expiry of the lease, the lessee ceases to be the employer and a third party becomes the employer under a new lease concluded with the owner the resulting operation *can* fall within the scope of the directive as defined in Article 1(1).'[22] The fact that in such a case the transfer is effected in two stages, in that the undertaking is first re-transferred from the original lessee to the owner and the latter then transfers it to the new lessee, does not prevent the directive from applying, provided that the economic unit in question retains its identity. The Court emphasised that the latter is so when, as in the case of Daddy's Dance Hall, the business is carried on without interruption by the new lessee with the same staff as were employed in the business before the transfer.

The dispute in *Redmond Stichting v Hendrikus Bartol*[23] arose between the applicant foundation, which was engaged in the provision of assistance to drug addicts and alcoholics from certain minority groups in Dutch society, and the foundation's employees, who were bound to it by employment contracts to which the provisions of the Dutch Civil Code applied. The Redmond Foundation was dependent for its income on subsidies from the Municipality of Groningen. With effect from January 1991, the latter switched the available funding to a foundation called Sigma, which also provided assistance to drug addicts. The funding was conditional on the minority groups previously served by the applicant foundation being catered for. The premises, which had previously been leased to the applicants, were also made available to Sigma. The two foundations co-operated on the transfer of Redmond's patients and the Municipality made it clear that Sigma should make use of the knowledge and resources of the plaintiff foundation. Sigma did in fact offer new employment contracts to a number of Redmond Foundation employees. The plaintiff sought to have the employment contracts between it and those members of staff not taken on by Sigma set aside. In determining whether this request could be granted, the national court sought to ascertain whether Directive 77/187 applied to the dispute between the Redmond Foundation and the staff it sought to let go. The detailed questions referred by the Dutch court once again concerned the Directive's scope and, specifically, the interpretation of the expression 'legal transfer' and the expression 'transfer of an undertaking, business or part of a business'.

With regard to the notion of 'legal transfer', the Court recalled its previous case-law in *Abels, Bork, Ny Molle Kro* and *Daddy's Dance Hall*. It likened the operation effected by the Dutch Municipality to that it had dealt with in the

---

[22] Case 324/86 *Daddy's Dance Hall*, para 10 (emphasis added), reiterating and adapting its decision in Case 101/87 *P. Bork International A/S, in liquidation, and others v Foreningen Arbejdsledere i Danmark, acting on behalf of Birger E. Petersen, and Junckers Industrier A/S* [1988] ECR 3057.

[23] Case C–29/91 *Dr Sophie Redmond Stichting v Hendrikus Bartol and Others* [1992] ECR I–3189.

Bork case.[24] The transfer in *Bork*, to which the Court had held the Directive should apply, had essentially been brought about in two stages, in the sense that the undertaking was first restored by the lessee to the owner, who then transferred it to the new owner. The important point was that the undertaking retained its identity.[25] In *Redmond Stichting*, the Court stated that it was irrelevant, as regards the application of Directive 77/187, that the transfer decision was one taken unilaterally by a public authority and not the result of an agreement concluded by it with the subsidised bodies. The Court pointed out that there is a unilateral decision both where an owner decides to change his lessee and where a public body changes its policy on subsidies. The change in the recipient of the subsidy is carried out in the context of contractual relations within the meaning of the Directive.[26] It was also irrelevant from the point of view of the application of the Directive that the origin of the transfer operation at issue before the national court lay in the grant of subsidies to foundations whose services were allegedly provided without remuneration.[27] The expression legal transfer in Article 1 of Directive 77/187 thus covers a situation in which a public authority decides to terminate the subsidy paid to one legal person, as a result of which the activities of that legal person are fully and definitively terminated, and to transfer it to another legal person with a similar aim.

Thus, a combination of the Directive's aim of protecting workers, differences in the language versions of the Directive and divergences between the laws of the Member States with regard to the concept of legal transfer conspired to ensure that the Court developed a flexible interpretation of what constitutes a legal transfer within the meaning of the Directive. The latter has been held to apply: to the termination of a lease of a restaurant followed by the conclusion of a new management contract with another operator (*Daddy's Dance Hall*); to termination of a lease followed by a sale by the owner (*Bork*); to the transfer of public authority subsidies from one legal person to another with a similar aim (*Redmond Stichting*); to the discontinuance of a motor vehicle dealership with one undertaking and its award to another undertaking pursuing the same activities (*Merckx and Neuhuys*); and, in the absence of a direct contractual link between two undertakings, to the award of a public service contract pursuant to

---

[24] In Case 101/87 *Bork*, the owner of the undertaking which had been leased with its entire staff to a third party gave notice terminating the lease. The factory in question ceased to operate and the staff were dismissed. The factory was then sold on by the owner to another party, the contract for sale stipulating that the transfer of the factory was to include all land, factory buildings, machines and spare parts belonging to the factory. The new owner restarted operations and re-employed just over half the staff previously employed by the original lessee.

[25] See Case 101/87 *Bork*, para 14.

[26] Case C–29/91 *Redmond Stichting*, para 17.

[27] *Ibid*, para 18. The Court also dismissed (at para 20) an argument put forward by the plaintiff to the effect that it was in a situation comparable to insolvency. Even if the plaintiff had been experiencing difficulties in honouring its commitments at the date of the transfer, that fact alone would not be sufficient to exclude the disputed transfer from the scope of Directive 77/187.

EC public procurement legislation (*Oy Likenne*).[28] According to the Court, the fact that the transferor undertaking is not the one which concluded the first contract with the original contractor but only the subcontractor of the original cocontractor has no effect on the concept of legal transfer. For the Directive to apply, it is sufficient for that transfer to be part of a web of contractual relations, even if they are indirect.[29] The mode of transfer has thus proved unimportant and the Directive has been held to apply regardless of whether there is a change in the ownership of the undertaking or the legal relationship between the transferor and the transferee and to a variety of different contractual relations.[30] As one commentator has remarked, it is hardly possible, in the light of the Court's extensive interpretation, to regard the concept of legal transfer as a serious impediment to the application of the Directive.[31]

What Does the Expression 'Transfer of an Undertaking, Business or Part of a Business' Mean?

While it is up to the Court of Justice to assist national courts in understanding how to interpret the expression legal transfer and what criteria they must employ to determine whether there has been a transfer of an undertaking, it is up to the national court to make the necessary factual appraisal in order to establish whether there has actually been a transfer within the meaning of Directive 77/187.[32] The Court is thus obliged to steer a difficult line between guiding national courts as to the correct interpretation of the provisions of the Directive—its responsibility pursuant to Article 234 EC—and application of the Directive to the facts of the case—in principle the duty of the national court. The Court has tried to perform this task by reiterating in each case a series of guidelines and criteria that national courts must keep in mind when ascertaining whether there has been a transfer of an undertaking pursuant to Directive 77/187. What emerges from the case-law, however, is a slow but distinct movement towards application of the Court's own guiding criteria to the facts

---

[28] See Case C–172/99 *Oy Likenne Ab v Pekka Liskojärvi and Pertti Juntunen* [2001] ECR I–745, paras 29–30.

[29] Case C–51/00 *Temco Service Industries SA v Samir Imzilyen and others* [2002] ECR I–969.

[30] See generally More (1995), above n 5; and Joined Cases C–173/96 and C–247/96 *Francisca Sánchez Hidalgo and Others v Asociación de Servicios Aser and Sociedad Cooperativa Minerva* and *Horst Ziemann v Ziemann Sicherheit GmbH and Horst Bohn Sicherheitsdienst* [1998] ECR I–8237, para 22.

[31] See C. De Groot, 'The Council Directive on the Safeguarding of Employees' Rights in the Event of Transfers of Undertakings: an Overview of Recent Case Law' (1998) 35 *Common Market Law Review* 707-29, 709.

[32] See also G. More, 'The Acquired Rights Directive: Frustrating or Facilitating Labour Market Flexibility' in J. Shaw and G. More (eds), *New Legal Dynamics of European Union* (Oxford, OUP, 1995) pp 129–45, p 133.

presented to it in the order for reference.[33] One of the reasons for this tendency to apply the Directive to the facts of the case is undoubtedly the increasing detail apparent in the questions referred by national courts, unable or unwilling to apply the Court's guidelines to the concrete cases before them. It is possible that national courts feel frustrated with the answers furnished by the Court in previous references; answers which they have found incomprehensible or downright incompatible with the legislative and judicial approaches to transfers of undertakings pertaining in their own jurisdictions.

Insistent about the social objective of Directive 77/187, the Court in *Spijkers* held that the latter was to ensure the continuity of employment relationships existing within a business, irrespective of any change of ownership. The decisive criterion for national courts to consider when establishing whether or not there was a transfer for the purposes of the Directive was whether the business in question retains its identity, in the sense that it was disposed of as a going concern. This was indicated *inter alia* by the fact that its operation was actually continued or resumed by the new employer, with the same or similar activities.[34] The Court in *Spijkers* then listed some of the elements characterising a transaction which the national court had to keep in mind when determining whether the undertaking had retained its identity:

> including the type of undertaking or business, whether or not the business's [*sic*] tangible assets, such as buildings and movable property, are transferred, the value of its intangible assets at the time of the transfer, whether or not the majority of its employees are taken over by the new employer, whether or not its customers are transferred and the degree of similarity between the activities carried on before and after the transfer and the period, if any, for which those activities were suspended.[35]

The Court emphasised, however, that the assessment to be undertaken by the national court was a global one, that the circumstances listed were merely single factors in this overall assessment and that they could not therefore be considered in isolation. True to its word that it was for the national court to carry out the necessary factual appraisal of whether or not there had been a transfer, the Court refused to answer the specifics of the nationals court's questions in *Spijkers* and indicated instead, in the operative part of its judgment, what national courts must look for and how they should proceed when making their appraisal regarding the existence of a transfer within the meaning of the Directive. It interpreted Article 1(1) of Directive 77/187 for the guidance of the national court but did not determine its application to the facts of the case.

Redmond Stichting provides another clear example of the Court using this technique of enumerating the criteria that the national court must consider to ascertain whether the disputed transaction comes within the scope of the

---

[33] See further above ch 2 for discussion of the interpretation *v* application conundrum posed by Article 234 EC.

[34] Case 24/85 *Jozef Maria Antonius Spijkers v Gebroeders Benedik Abattoir CV and Alfred Benedik en Zonen BV* [1986] ECR 1119, paras 11–12.

[35] Case 24/85 *Spijkers*, para 13.

Directive. Once again, the Court emphasised that the decisive criterion for establishing whether there is a transfer for the purposes of the directive is whether the entity in question retains its identity, as indicated *inter alia* by the fact that its operation is actually continued or resumed.[36] In order to determine whether that condition is met, the national court was instructed to consider all the facts characterising the transaction in question, including the list of factors already outlined in *Spijkers*.[37] The Court stressed in *Redmond Stichting* that all these elements were 'merely single factors in the overall assessment which must be made and cannot therefore be considered in isolation' and indicated that the details contained in the order for reference in the case concerning the transfer of subsidies from one foundation to the other were all essential to the assessment the national court had to perform in interpreting and applying Article 1 of the Directive.[38]

Yet the national court had included in its reference to the Court detailed questions concerning the particular circumstances in which certain property was used and certain activities carried on. Clearly, the risk was that the Court would be drawn inexorably away from simply interpreting the Directive to actual application of its provisions to the facts of the case in hand.[39] The Court indicated, with respect to movable property, that the fact that these assets were not transferred did not *seem* in itself to prevent the Directive from applying, but stressed that it was for the national court to appraise their importance by incorporating them into the overall assessment which has to be made to determine whether or not there was a transfer.[40] The Redmond Foundation had also carried out social and recreational functions and the national court asked whether it made any difference, in terms of determining whether a transfer had occurred, whether those activities were regarded as constituting a separate object or solely as an aid for the purposes of the optimum provision of assistance. Once again, the Court stressed the importance of the global nature of the appraisal which the national court had to undertake, but it added that the mere fact that social and recreational activities constituted an independent function of the plaintiff was not sufficient to rule out the application of the relevant provisions of Directive 77/187. Activities of a special nature, which constitute independent functions, could be equated with the transfer of businesses or parts of businesses to which Article 1 also applied.[41]

---

[36] Case C–29/91 *Redmond Stichting*, para 23; and previously Case 101/87 *Bork*, para 14.
[37] Case C–29/91 *Redmond Stichting*, para 24; and previously Case 101/87 *Bork*, para 15.
[38] Case C–29/91 *Redmond Stichting*, paras 24 and 26.
[39] Advocate General Van Gerven was clearly aware of this risk in Case C–29/91 *Redmond Stichting*, as he repeated continually that it was for the national court to determine the importance to be attached to the circumstances adverted to in its second, third and fourth questions.
[40] Case C–29/91 *Redmond Stichting*, para 29.
[41] *Ibid*, para 30.

Contracting Out

Particularly problematic from the point of view of the scope of Directive 77/187 and the protection afforded employees has been the question whether the contracting out or outsourcing of services comes within the notion of 'transfer of an undertaking, business or part of a business' in Article 1(1). It goes without saying that the principal reason for an undertaking to contract out services is to ensure that those services are provided at the most competitive rate possible. One of the most obvious ways for a firm to gain a competitive edge (while, of course, ensuring as much profit as possible[42]) when taking over the provision of certain services from another firm is to alter the rates of pay and employment conditions previously offered to employees when the services were provided in-house or by another contractor.[43] Contracting out is a particularly acute example of the numerical form of flexibility referred to in chapter three. More identifies two aspects of contracting out which favour employment flexibility: (i) the undertaking contracting out the services shifts any responsibility towards employees onto the contractor and can forget about employee-related costs; and (ii) the contractor may use short-term, 'flexible' contracts of employment which entail fewer employment protection rights.[44] Clearly, whether or not Directive 77/187 and the guarantees which it entails for the rights and conditions of employment of employees applied to contracting out was of paramount importance for business and, increasingly, for the public sector. As the Court had made clear in *Wendelboe*, Directive 77/187 was intended to ensure, as far as possible, that the employment relationship continues unchanged with the transferee, in particularly by obliging the transferee to continue observing the terms and conditions of any collective agreement and by protecting workers against dismissals motivated solely by the fact of the transfer.[45] In fact, the introduction of Directive 77/187 meant that when negotiating and concluding transfer deals, commercial lawyers finally had to pay some attention at least to the requirements of employment law, EC employment law at that. As Davies observes,

---

[42] In the words of one newspaper correspondent following the judgment in Case C–13/95 *Ayse Süzen v Zehnacker Gebäudereinigung GmbH Krankenhausservice* [1997] ECR I–1259: 'There is only one reason to outsource, . . ., and that is to save money. There are really only two ways of doing this too. You work people harder or you pay them less—ideally both, if you can get away with it' (*The Times*, 12 March 1997). It is not just in the context of reduced employment protection that labour is losing out. Between 1980 and 1994, the implicit tax rate on employed labour increased from 34.7% to 40.5% in the Member States. Over the same period the tax rate decreased from 44.1% to 35.2% for other factors of production, including capital. See B. Schulte, 'The Welfare State and European Integration' (1999) 1 *European Journal of Social Security* 7–61, 31.

[43] See J. Hunt, 'The Court of Justice as a policy actor: the case of the Acquired Rights Directive' (1998) 18 *Legal Studies* 336–59, 337. On contracting out and flexibility see J. Bennett and S.L. Belgrave, 'Taking Stock after *Rygaard*' (1996) 5 *Public Procurement Law Review* CS16-CS25, CS16: 'There are contractual business relationships which, in current economic thinking, need to be as uncluttered as possible to ensure maximum flexibility for businessmen.'

[44] More (1995), above n 5, p 141.

[45] Case 19/83 *Knud Wendelboe*, para 15.

they became 'aware of labour law as a major impediment to their traditional way of doing things, and they did not like what they saw.'[46] Within the United Kingdom their response was threefold—they argued for a narrow interpretation of the national regulations transposing the 1977 Directive, embarked on long drawn-out litigation concentrating on the applicability of the Directive to the contracting out of services and relied on the 'economic, technical or organisational' defence to dismissals in Article 4(1) of the Directive.[47]

The Court's initial response to the question of the Directive's applicability to contracting out bore close resemblance to its previous case-law on 'standard' transfers, where it had offered referring courts guidance on how to determine whether a disputed transaction constituted a transfer of an undertaking within the meaning of the 1977 Directive. It also closely resembled previous case-law in terms of the paramount importance attributed the protection of employees. The *Rask* case concerned a dispute between the applicants and their employer, ISS Kantineservice, over the date of payment of their wages and the payment of certain allowances.[48] The applicants worked in the Philips' company canteen when the management of the canteen was handed over to ISS. Under the terms of the transfer agreement, Philips agreed to pay ISS a fixed monthly fee to cover wages, insurance, work clothes and management costs. It also made available to ISS the necessary premises, equipment, heating, electricity, telephone, cloakroom and refuse removal service. ISS assumed the responsibility for managing the canteen together with recruitment and staff training. It undertook to offer jobs to Philips permanent canteen staff on the same terms and conditions as regards pay, seniority and notice as they had previously enjoyed. Their wages were to consist of the basic ISS wage plus a transfer supplement to ensure that they would incur no loss of income. However, the applicants disputed ISS' decision to pay them on a day other than Philips' pay day and the fact that they no longer received allowances for laundry, footwear and so on, which had formed part of their pay package with Philips, albeit the total amount of their wages remained unchanged. The transfer, if indeed there had been one, between Philips and ISS, had been of the operation of Philips' works canteen, a service that it had previously provided in-house. There had been no transfer of assets, Philips had

---

[46] P. Davies, *The Relationship between the European Court of Justice and the British Courts over the Interpretation of Directive 77/187/EC*, EUI WP Law No 97/2, p 5. In the Report of the House of Lords Select Committee, above n 1, p 12, the British Department of Trade and Industry submitted that the application of the Directive to contracting for services restricts entrepreneurial freedom, may inhibit quality improvements as well as denying the client the benefit of substantial cost reductions, is damaging to competition and thus inhibits the prospects for enterprises within the EU to compete and prosper in increasingly global markets. According to the Confederation of British Industry (CBI), which also submitted evidence, application of the Directive to contracting out meant delays, higher legal and administrative costs, weakened and distorted competition and even damage to the interests of employees.

[47] See Davies (1997) EUI WP, *ibid*, p 6.

[48] Case C–209/91 *Anne Watson Rask and Kirsten Christensen v ISS Kantineservice A/S* [1992] ECR I–5755.

simply let ISS make use of its facilities, and the service or activity contracted out was ancillary, in the sense that it did not constitute Philips' main business activity.

As before, the Court emphasised that the Directive is applicable whenever, in the context of contractual relations, there is a change in the legal or natural person who is responsible for carrying on the business and who, by virtue of that fact, incurs the obligations of an employer *vis-à-vis* the employees of the undertaking, regardless of whether or not ownership is transferred. This principle had become clear in previous decisions of the Court in cases such as *Daddy's Dance Hall*, where a lease rather than the ownership of the transferred undertaking had been at issue. The Court in *Rask* held that 'where one businessman entrusts, by means of an agreement, responsibility for running a facility of his undertaking, such as a canteen, to another businessman who thereby assumes the obligations of employer *vis-à-vis* the employees assigned to that facility, the resulting transaction may fall within the scope of the Directive, as defined in Article 1(1).'[49] The fact that in such a case the activity transferred is merely an ancillary activity for the transferor without a necessary connection with its company objectives cannot have the effect of excluding the transaction from the scope of the Directive. Nor does the fact that the agreement between the transferor and the transferee relates to a provision of services exclusively for the benefit of the transferor in return for a fee preclude the applicability of the Directive. To determine whether the facts of the case pointed to a 'transfer of an undertaking', the national court in *Rask* was directed, as the referring courts had been in *Spijkers* and *Redmond Stichting*, to determine whether the entity in question retained its identity.[50] The Court of Justice thus indicated to the referring court that Directive 77/187 may apply to a contracting out of a facility for staff, but left it to the national court to determine whether the actual facts of the case before it characterised a transfer of an undertaking, business or part of a business within the meaning of Article 1(1) of the Directive.

References concerning contracting out did not end, however, following the fairly clear and well-established instructions given the national court in *Rask*. In the controversial *Schmidt* case,[51] the applicant was employed as the only cleaner at one of the defendant's savings banks. In February 1992 the defendant terminated its employment relationship with Mrs Schmidt on the ground that the branch where she worked had been renovated and extended and that the cleaning of the new premises would take far more time than had previously been agreed with her. Cleaning of the new premises was taken over by a cleaning firm which was responsible for cleaning most of the bank's other premises. The cleaning firm approached the applicant to work for it for an increased net

---

[49] Case C–209/91 *Rask*, para 17.
[50] *Ibid*, paras 18–19.
[51] Case C–392/92 *Christel Schmidt v Spar- und Leihkasse der früheren Ämter Bordesholm, Kiel und Cronshagen* [1994] ECR I–1311.

monthly wage. However, Mrs Schmidt was not prepared to accept this offer of employment; the considerable increase in the surface area which required cleaning meant that her hourly wage would in fact be lower. The applicant brought an action challenging her dismissal by the savings bank and, on appeal, the referring court sought guidance from the Court as to whether there had been in the instant case 'transfer of an undertaking, business or part of a business' within the meaning of Article 1(1) of Directive 77/187. In particular, it asked the Court whether the cleaning operations of a branch of an undertaking could be treated as part of a business within the meaning of Directive 77/187 and whether it was possible to do so where the work was performed by a single employee before being transferred by contract to an outside firm. Of particular importance in *Schmidt* was the fact that at issue was the transfer of a bare contract for services employing one employee and involving the transfer of neither tangible nor intangible assets of any significance.

In the light of the Court's decision in *Rask*, the answer to the first part of the referred question in *Schmidt* should arguably have been clear. However, the defendant, in line with the governments of Germany and the United Kingdom, argued that, since the performance of cleaning operations was neither the main nor an ancillary function of the undertaking, the Directive did not apply. In *Rask*, however, the Court had made clear that the fact that the activity transferred was for the transferor merely an ancillary activity not necessarily connected with its objects could not have the effect of excluding the operation from the scope of the Directive.[52] The Court in *Schmidt* also regarded the other factor cited by the national court—the fact that the activity was performed by a single employee—as irrelevant from the point of view of application of Directive 77/187. The application of the latter, it insisted, did not depend on the number of employees assigned to the part of the undertaking that is the subject of the transfer. The protection which the Directive is intended to extend to the employees of a transferred undertaking must be guaranteed even where only one employee is affected by that transfer.[53] Both the United Kingdom and Germany had argued that the absence of any transfer of tangible assets—one of the factors characterising a transfer which the Court had listed in *Redmond Stichting* and *Rask*—indicated the non-applicability of the Directive. The Court gave this argument short shrift. It pointed out that the fact that the transfer of tangible assets figured amongst the list of factors to be taken into account by national courts when they make their complex, global assessment of whether an undertaking has been transferred did not mean that the absence of such a factor

---

[52] *Ibid*, para 14.

[53] *Ibid*, para 15. Advocate General Van Gerven, para 15 of his Opinion in that case, was somewhat more circumspect. He stated that although it is not desirable to introduce strict quantitative criterion by which to delimit the scope of the Directive, the fact that the economic activity in question is performed by a single employee should be taken into consideration in determining whether there is an organisational unit. He regarded the latter as a prerequisite for the transfer of an undertaking within the meaning of Directive 77/187.

necessarily precluded the existence of a transfer. The employment protection afforded by the Directive could not be made exclusively dependent on consideration of a factor that the Court had, in any event, held not to be decisive on its own.[54] The decisive criteria for national courts remained whether the business in question had retained its identity, as indicated *inter alia* by the transferee/new employer continuing or resuming the same or similar activities. With rather more of an inclination to actually provide the national court with the answer it sought than it had displayed in previous cases, the Court held that:

> where all the relevant information is contained in the order for reference, the similarity in the cleaning work performed before and after the transfer, which is reflected, moreover, in the offer to re-engage the employee in question, is typical of an operation which comes within the scope of the directive and which gives the employee whose activity has been transferred the protection afforded to him by that directive.[55]

However, having been particularly clear in its instructions to the national court in *Schmidt* as regards the application of Directive 77/187 to the disputed transfer, the Court then proceeded to muddy the waters. It pointed out, on the one hand, that although Article 4(1) of the Directive provided protection against dismissal by the transferor or the transferee, that provision did not stand in the way of dismissals for economic, technical or organisational reasons entailing changes in the workplace.[56] At national level, the first instance court which rejected Mrs Schmidt's challenge of her dismissal had already held that the bank was able to rely on business-related grounds (the renovation and extension of the bank's premises) in order to justify the dismissal of the plaintiff. So although the Directive would undoubtedly be found by the referring court to apply, Mrs Schmidt might not benefit from its guarantee of protection against dismissal. The Court also pointed out that the Acquired Rights Directive did not preclude an amendment to the employment relationship with the new employer, in so far as national law allowed such an amendment otherwise than through a transfer of the undertaking.

---

[54] Case C–392/92 *Schmidt*, para 16. In Case 24/85 *Spijkers*, para 12, the Court had held that a transfer of an undertaking, business or part of a business does not occur merely because its assets are disposed of. More (1995), above n 32, 143, points out that although *Schmidt* follows on from *Spijkers*, the Court nevertheless altered the *Spijkers* test in *Schmidt* by emphasising that the essential factors characterising the transfer of an undertaking, business or part of a business as the being the continuation of a similar activity and the re-employment of the workers.

[55] Case C–392/92 *Schmidt*, para 17. Cf Advocate General Van Gerven who, in his Opinion in Case C–392/92, had left this determination to the national court. In his Opinion in Joined Cases C–171/94 and C–172/94 *Merckx and Neuhuys*, para 18, Advocate General Lenz remarked on this unprecedented intervention by the Court in *Schmidt*.

[56] Case C–392/92 *Schmidt*, para 18. Cf Advocate General Van Gerven in Case C–362/89 *Giuseppe d'Urso, Adriana Ventadori and Others v Ercole Marelli Elettromeccanica Generale SpA and Others* [1991] ECR I–4105, para 35 of his Opinion: 'I do not share the view that the directive allows any kind of dismissal on economic, technical or organizational grounds. . . . It is only where the dismissals have already taken place, for example if they had already been decided on before the question of any transfer of the undertaking arose, that they come under that derogation.'

The decision of the Court in *Schmidt* was received extremely negatively in Germany and in some quarters in the United Kingdom. German commentators were particularly unhappy with the Court's approach to what constitutes an undertaking and its acceptance that there can be a transfer within the meaning of the Directive without the transfer of tangible assets, business goodwill or know-how.[57] The Court was seen in *Schmidt* as having given too much weight to the protection of employees and too little to the need for business to respond to an increasingly competitive climate. In the United Kingdom, the inclusion by the Court of contracting out within the regulatory, protective framework of the 1977 Directive was regarded as being in direct opposition to prevailing government policy on compulsory competitive tendering.[58] While in other Member States, not least France and Italy, the decision of the Court conflicted with long-standing national jurisprudence on the issue.[59]

The Court's decisions in *Rask* and *Schmidt* were also followed by what can only be interpreted as criticism from another unlikely source—the Commission. The opening recitals of the Commission's 1994 proposal for a new Directive on transfers of undertakings stated that:

> considerations of legal security and transparency . . . demand, in the light of the case law of the Court of Justice, that a clear distinction be made between transfers of undertakings, businesses or parts of businesses and the transfer of only an activity of an undertaking.

The amended Article 1(1) of the proposed Directive provided that:

> The transfer of an activity which is accompanied by the transfer of an economic entity which retains its identity shall be deemed to be a transfer within the meaning of this Directive. The transfer of only an activity of an undertaking, business or part of a business, whether or not it was previously carried out directly, does not of itself constitute a transfer within the meaning of the Directive.[60]

---

[57] See further More (1995), above n 32, pp 144–48; C. Bourn, 'When Does the Transfer of a Service Contract Constitute the Transfer of an Undertaking?' (1998) 23 *European Law Review* 59–64, 60; and generally M. Körner, 'The Impact of Community Law on German Labour Law—the example of transfer of undertakings' EUI WP Law No 96/8. See also the Opinion of Advocate General Cosmas in Joined Cases C–127/96, C–229/96 and C–74/97 *Francisco Hernández Vidal SA v Prudencia Gómez Pérez and Others, Friedrich Santner v Hoechst AG and Mercedes Gómez Montaña v Claro Sol SA and Red Nacional de Ferrocarriles Españoles (Renfe)* [1998] ECR I–8179, fn 36, where he remarked on the poor reception of the *Schmidt* decision and the Commission's incorporation in its proposals for the amendment of Directive 77/187 of a clear limitation of that decision.

[58] See the definition of compulsory competitive tendering provided by the Report of the House of Lords Select Committee on transfers of undertakings (1995–96), above n 1, p 11: 'the process by which public authorities, especially the National Health Service and local authorities, subject the supply of services to bids from in-house and outside service providers.' See also S. Arrowsmith, 'Developments in Compulsory Competitive Tendering' (1994) 3 *Public Procurement Law Review* CS153-CS172; and N. O'Loan, 'Acquired Rights and the Contracting Out of Services in the United Kingdom' (1993) 2 *Public Procurement Law Review* CS74-CS78.

[59] See P. Davies, 'Transfers of Undertakings' in S. Sciarra (ed), *Labour Law in the Courts. National Judges and the European Court of Justice* (Oxford, Hart Publishing, 2001) pp 131–44.

[60] Com (94) 300 final; OJ 1994 C274/10.

The Commission's proposal, which met with opposition from the European Parliament, the Economic and Social Committee and certain Member States was subsequently amended. Nevertheless, its proposed amendment clearly served as a shot across the bows of the Court and tallied with the keen criticism which had met the equation in the *Schmidt* decision of the transfer of an activity with the transfer of an undertaking.[61]

The Court had heretofore been regarded as a champion of employment protection in its case-law relating to the Acquired Rights Directive. It was soon to draw criticism both from its previous supporters for what they perceived as its more limited commitment to employment protection and from Member State governments and contractors generally due to the confusion its jurisprudence was creating as regards the application of Directive 77/187 to contracting out. The first signs of the Court's change of heart came in the *Rygaard* case.[62] The referring court sought to determine whether the Acquired Rights Directive applied to a situation where one contractor continues work begun by another contractor when there was a period where both contractors were working on site at the same time. Specifically, did the taking over of works started by another undertaking, with a view to completing them and with the consent of the awarder of the main building contract, which involved taking on two apprentices and an employee, together with the materials assigned to those works, constitute a transfer of an undertaking, business or part of a business, within the meaning of Article 1(1) of the Directive? The Court of Justice in *Rygaard* once again explained the procedure which national courts should follow in order to determine whether there had been a transfer within the meaning of the Directive—the national court must apply the *Spijkers* identity test and the check-list of evidential factors already outlined in that case. However, in *Rygaard*, the Court included, for the first time, the requirement that a transfer within the meaning of the Directive must relate to a *stable* economic entity, a requirement that it claimed had underpinned its previous decisions in *Spijkers* or *Schmidt*.[63] According to the Court in *Rygaard*, the transfer must relate to a stable economic entity whose activity is not limited to performing one specific works contract. That is not the case where an undertaking transfers to another undertaking one of its building works with a view to the completion of that

---

[61] For discussion in this particular context of the role of the Court as a political institution and policy actor see Hunt, above n 43. See also Bennett and Belgrave, above n 43, CS24, who submitted, following the decision of the Court in Case C–48/94 *Rygaard*, that both the Court and the Commission seemed to share the view that it is only certain types of contracting out which should provide employment protection.

[62] Case C–48/94 *Ledernes Hovedorganisation, acting on behalf of Ole Rygaard v Dansk Arbejdsgiverforening, acting on behalf of Stro Molle Akustik A/S* [1995] ECR I–2745. Significantly, as More points out (1995), above n 32, 151, while Case C–209/91 *Rask* and Case C–392/92 *Schmidt* had been decided by Chambers of three and five Judges, respectively, *Rygaard* was referred to a small plenary.

[63] Case C–48/94 *Rygaard*, para 20. See also the Opinions of Advocate General Van Gerven (para 13) in Case C–392/92 *Schmidt* and Advocate General Cosmas (para 12) in Case C–48/94 *Rygaard*.

work. Such a transfer could come within the scope of the Directive only if it included 'the transfer of a body of assets enabling the activities or certain activities of the transferor undertaking to be carried on in a stable way.'[64] The Court thus answered the national court's question in the negative—the situation described did not constitute a transfer within the meaning of Article 1(1) of Directive 77/187.

In *Rygaard*, once again, the national court called on to apply the Directive to the facts of the case was left little, if any, room for manoeuvre. There could be no doubt, given the way in which the Court drafted its decision and, particularly, the clarity of its answer in the operative part of its judgment, that the Directive should not apply. What the referring court and other courts may not have found clear following *Rygaard* was why, all of a sudden, the Court was attributing such importance to the stability of the economic entity purportedly transferred. Admittedly, as long ago as the *Spijkers* case the Court had referred to the need for the business to be transferred as a 'going concern'. The inclusion of this new or revamped criterion in *Rygaard* probably owed more to concern that the Court had gone too far in *Schmidt*.[65] In particular, although the Court had not heeded his advice at the time, Advocate General Van Gerven had insisted in *Schmidt* that the concepts 'transfer of an undertaking', 'business' and 'part of a business' be underpinned by the need for an economic unit with a minimum level of organisational independence.

The next employee to test the Court's grasp of acquired rights was a school cleaner employed by a contract cleaning company.[66] Ms Süzen was informed that her company's cleaning contract with the school was expected to end and that the defendant would, as a result, be forced to terminate her employment, which it subsequently did. The defendant's contractual relationship with the school was brought to an end and the cleaning was contracted out to another company. The applicant meanwhile instituted proceedings against the defendant

---

[64] Case C–48/94 *Rygaard*, para 21. Advocate General Cosmas (para 16) had argued that the specific activity being transferred must be characterised by a certain autonomy of organisation in the sense that in carrying on that activity one or more workers together possibly with materials have been assigned thereto.

[65] Cf Bennett and Belgrave, above n 43, CS20, who contend that decision in Case C–392/92 *Schmidt* did not support the view that assets are generally to be regarded as irrelevant or that a transfer of a single individual will always trigger acquired rights protection. In their view, *Schmidt*, like Case C–48/94 *Rygaard*, simply supports the proposition that the decisive criterion sought by the Court is a degree of permanence in the identity of the business undertaking; something which was present in the former case, but absent in the latter.

[66] Second generation contracting out refers to trilateral situations where a recipient of services replaces the contractor who was providing those services with another contractor providing the same or similar services. The award of the contract is usually the result of competitive tendering. In contrast, first generation contracting out involves a bilateral relationship between a company which decides to make use of the services of an outside contractor for an activity which it previously performed in-house using its own workers. A good example is the contract between Philips and ISS to run the company canteen in Case C–209/91 *Rask*. Finally, contracting in is sometimes used to describe the situation where a firm which previously contracted out certain services reverts to performance of those services in-house by its own employees.

seeking a declaration that her dismissal was invalid. To determine the lawfulness of that dismissal, the national court sought to ascertain whether the Directive applied to this so-called second generation contracting out.

No doubt due to the furore which the *Schmidt* decision had provoked in Germany, the referring German court was asking the Court of Justice to determine whether, following that controversial ruling, the Directive was also to be held to apply to second generation contracting out.[67] Advocate General La Pergola argued that the *Süzen* reference gave the Court an opportunity to reflect on the criteria laid down in previous rulings for determining the scope of application of the Directive. In his view, the concept of transfer of undertakings set out in Directive 77/187 called for a better definition: the Community legislature had simply taken for granted the standard content of what transactions constituted a transfer of an undertaking or business, despite the fact that the concept varied from one Member State legal system to the next. The criteria laid down by the Court since *Spijkers* may have pointed to the type of situation where the features of a transfer are present, but he submitted that it had not provided a definite distinction between a situation in which an undertaking is transferred and a situation where the features of a transfer are not present.[68] A transfer must always involve, according to the Advocate General, the actual transfer of tangible or intangible assets.[69] In the specific context of contracting out, the Advocate General was unconvinced that the *Schmidt* precedent should be applied: 'To transfer the facilities (of whatever kind) required by an undertaking to another body is a decision made in competitive circumstances, which ensures a choice between several competing rivals.'[70] He did not feel that there was any justification for requiring the new contractor to keep on the staff of the undertaking which provided the services in the past and whose tender has proved unsuccessful.

The tightening in the *Rygaard* decision of what type of economic entities are susceptible to transfer may indeed have seemed curious. However, the decision of the Court in *Süzen* led many commentators (and even contractors opposed, in principle, to application of the Directive to contracting out) to conclude that the Court had lost the plot previously of its own making. The Court first

---

[67] Specifically, the referring court asked the Court of Justice whether, in the light of the Court's decisions in Case C–392/92 *Schmidt* and Case C–29/91 *Redmond Stichting*, the Directive applied if an undertaking terminates a contract with an outside undertaking in order to transfer it to another outside undertaking and whether there was a legal transfer within the meaning of the Directive even if no tangible or intangible business assets are transferred.

[68] Case C–13/95 *Süzen*, paras 8–9 of Advocate General La Pergola's Opinion.

[69] *Ibid*, para 9 of Advocate General La Pergola's Opinion. He was clearly building on the Court's more narrow approach in Case C–48/94 *Rygaard*.

[70] *Ibid*, para 7 of Advocate General La Pergola's Opinion. See also the primary purpose attributed to contracting out by the report written by P. Davies, commissioned by Commission DG V, *Interim Report on the Application of the Acquired Rights Directive in the context of contracting out in UK, Ireland and Denmark*, October 1993, p 42: 'to enable the client to bring the forces of competition to bear on the provision of the services that it requires.'

repeated, *à la Spijkers*, that the decisive criteria for establishing the existence of a transfer within the meaning of the Directive is whether the entity in question retains its identity, as indicated *inter alia* by the fact that its operation is actually continued or resumed. The absence of any contractual link between the two undertakings successively entrusted with the cleaning of a school may point to the absence of a transfer but it is certainly not conclusive, since the Directive is applicable wherever, in the context of contractual relations, there is a change in the natural or legal person who is responsible for carrying on the business and who incurs the obligations of an employer towards employees of the undertaking. As in previous cases, the Court repeated its extensive list of factors to which a national court must refer in order to determine whether the conditions for the transfer of an entity within the meaning of the Directive have been met.

But therein ended the similarity with the Court's previous rulings on what constitutes a 'transfer of an undertaking' within the meaning of Directive 77/187. Something more was needed for the Directive to apply. Following *Rygaard*, the Court in *Süzen* held that the transfer must relate to a stable economic entity, in the sense of 'an organized grouping of persons and assets facilitating the exercise of an economic activity which pursues a specific objective',[71] whose activity is not limited to performing one specific works contract. Though the intention behind the refinements in *Süzen* may have been to clarify the law, the Court's ruling contained a series of confusing and sometimes circular indications to the national court regarding what it must and need not take into consideration when determining whether there has been a transfer within the meaning of the Directive. Thus, at paragraph 15, the Court stated that the mere fact that the service provided by the old and the new awardees of a contract is similar does not support the conclusion that an economic entity has been transferred, since an entity cannot simply be reduced to the activity entrusted to it. However, the Court then held that:

> the factual circumstances to be taken into account in determining whether the conditions for a transfer are met include *in particular*, the degree of similarity of the activity carried on before and after the transfer and the type of undertaking or business concerned and the question whether or not the majority of the employees were taken over by the new employer.[72]

In *Süzen*, distancing itself from the stark terms of its judgment in *Schmidt*, the Court seemed to be introducing more detailed and previously unused criteria which national courts would henceforth have to refer to when resolving disputes regarding the application of the Directive to contracting out. Its definition of what constitutes a stable economic entity—an organised grouping of persons and assets facilitating the exercise of an economic activity which pursues a

---

[71] Case C–13/95 *Süzen*, para 13.
[72] *Ibid*, para 20 (emphasis added).

specific objective—was new,[73] as were some of the factors which national courts must assess in order to determine whether the identity of such an entity has been retained—its workforce, management staff, the way in which work is organised, its operating methods or, where appropriate, the operational resources available to it. The national court was also directed to take into account, in assessing the facts characterising the transaction in question, the type of undertaking or business concerned. The degree of importance to be attached to all the different criteria mentioned would vary according to the activity carried on, or indeed the production or operating methods employed in the relevant undertaking. By way of example the Court pointed out that where an economic entity is able to function without any significant tangible or intangible assets, the maintenance of its identity following the transaction affecting it could not, logically, be dependent on the transfer of such assets. Similarly, in certain labour-intensive sectors, where a group of workers engaged in a joint activity on a permanent basis may constitute an economic entity, the Court held that such an entity is capable of maintaining its identity after it has been transferred where the new employer does not merely pursue a similar activity but also takes over a major part, in terms of their numbers and skills, of the employees specially assigned by the previous employer to that task.

Although the Court stipulated that it was for the national court to establish, in the light of the interpretative guidance provided by it, whether a transfer had occurred in the *Süzen* case, the operative part of its decision once again left the national court in little doubt as to the answer:

> Article 1(1) of . . . Directive 77/187 . . . does not apply to a situation in which a person who had entrusted the cleaning of his premises to a first undertaking terminates his contract with the latter and, for the performance of similar work, enters into a new contract with a second undertaking, if there is no concomitant transfer from one undertaking to the other of significant tangible or intangible assets or taking over by the new employer of a major part of the workforce, in terms of their numbers and skills, assigned by his predecessor to the performance of the contract.[74]

---

[73] In Case C–392/92 *Schmidt*, the German government had argued unsuccessfully that the Court's case-law since *Spijkers* implied that a clearly defined economic objective is being pursued within the context of an autonomous organisation. In his Opinion in Case C–392/92 *Schmidt* (para 14), Advocate General Van Gerven also submitted that the phrase 'transfer of an undertaking' in Article 1(1) of the Directive is underpinned by the concept of an economic unit which refers to an organised whole consisting of persons and (tangible and/or intangible) assets by means of which an economic activity is carried on having an objective of its own, albeit ancillary to the objects of the undertaking. His argument seems to have been taken up by Advocates General Cosmas in Case C–48/94 *Rygaard* and La Pergola in Case C–13/95 *Süzen*.

[74] Case C–13/95 *Süzen*, para 22 and the operative part of the judgment. Compare the Opinion of Advocate General Slynn in Case 24/85 *Spijkers*, 1121–22, where he argued that the fact that good will or existing contracts are not transferred is not conclusive against there being a transfer. In addition, he submitted that there may be a transfer in some cases where goodwill or existing contracts or lists of customers are sold without there being a transfer of physical assets. In Case E–3/96 *Tor Angeir Ask and Others v ABB Offshore Technology AS and Aker Offshore Partner AS*, judgment of 14 March 1997, the EFTA Court followed the decision of the Court of Justice in Case C–13/95 *Süzen* in its advisory opinion. It also held that the fact that a transaction is subject to the public procurement Directives does not by itself prevent Directive 77/187 from being applicable.

The upshot of the case was that, when the disputed transfer concerns the contracting out of a service or specific activity, national courts will first have to establish the existence of a stable economic entity capable of transfer and then to ensure that the transfer of the activity was accompanied by the transfer of significant assets or, in labour-intensive sectors, the transfer of a major part of the workforce, in terms of skill and numbers. The transfer of a service contract will not necessarily amount to a transfer of part of a business within the meaning of the Directive. In the case of labour intensive services such as cleaning, the transferee will have to take on a major part of the workforce for the protection afforded by the Directive to apply.

If the Court was under the impression that its decision in *Süzen* would relieve it of any further need to answer questions concerning contracting out, it was quickly disabused of this notion. In *Hernández Vidal*[75] and *Sánchez Hidalgo*,[76] references which had been lodged while the *Süzen* case was pending, the referring courts, although asked following the decision in *Süzen* whether they wanted to maintain their questions, decided, not surprisingly perhaps, that they did.[77] The first case, *Hernández Vidal*, concerned cleaners employed in Spain and Germany by contract cleaning companies who were dismissed when the undertakings which had originally contracted those cleaning companies decided to assume the responsibility of cleaning their own premises themselves (or partly with the assistance of outside cleaning firms). Thus, while *Süzen* concerned the contracting out of a service previously performed in-house, in these cases, the referring courts questioned whether Directive 77/187 applies when an undertaking which used to rely on outside contractors decided to perform the services in question in-house.

Following *Rygaard* and *Süzen*, a national court does not simply have to determine whether there has been a legal transfer and what constitutes a transfer of an undertaking, it must also first determine, with respect to the latter appraisal, whether there exists a stable economic entity capable of being transferred. According to the Court in *Hernández Vidal*, just as the contracting out of cleaning operations previously performed by a company directly (*Schmidt*), or the conclusion of a new contracted out cleaning contract with a new undertaking (*Süzen*), with the result that a cleaning contract with a previous undertaking is terminated, may come within the scope of Directive 77/187, so too the Directive

[75] Joined Cases C–127/96, C–229/96 and C–74/97 *Hernández Vidal and others*.
[76] Joined Cases C–173/96 and C–247/96 *Sánchez Hidalgo and others*.
[77] Advocate General Cosmas was clearly unimpressed by the referring courts' persistence. At para 55 of his Opinion he pointed out that, with the exception of Case C–247/96 concerning the concept of a transferable economic entity, the remaining cases could be answered on the basis of the Court's existing case-law and, in particular, Case C–13/95 *Süzen*, which he said gave detailed indications to national courts as to the criteria to be employed and the relative weight to be attached to them. As a result: 'the national courts should be given general answers providing them with interpretative criteria that will enable them to classify the facts, a task which it is not for the Court itself to perform. Any other course would divert the Court from its true function, as defined in Article [234], and would diminish the role of the national court in the administration of ordinary law within the Community legal order.'

could be held to apply when an undertaking which used to contract out its cleaning contract to another undertaking decides to terminate that contract and undertake the cleaning work itself.[78] However, as in *Süzen*, the national court was directed to establish whether the transfer relates to a stable economic entity (in the sense of an organised grouping of persons and of assets enabling an economic activity which pursues a specific objective to be exercised[79]) and whether the activity of that entity is not simply limited to performing one specific works contract.

For the most part, the Court in *Hernández Vidal* simply reproduced entire paragraphs of the *Süzen* decision.[80] However, it also emphasised that, in particular sectors, such as cleaning, assets are often unimportant or reduced to their most basic and the activity of the undertaking is essentially based on manpower. In such circumstances 'an organized group of wage earners who are specifically and permanently assigned to a common task may, in the absence of other factors of production, amount to an economic entity.'[81] In this respect the Court seems to have been persuaded by the concerns expressed in the Opinion of Advocate General Cosmas, who had urged the Court to clearly state that its definition of economic entity did not mean that sectors in which the workforce is the main factor and the undertaking's tangible or intangible assets were negligible, fell automatically outside the scope of the Directive.[82] The Advocate General had been concerned that the importance attached in *Süzen* to the transferee taking over a major part of the transferor's employees was capable of giving rise to extreme confusion. He argued that this criterion could not be decisive as it would mean that the protection afforded by the Directive depends essentially on the parties, something which the Court had previously been unwilling

---

[78] Joined Cases C–127/96, C–229/96 and C–74/97 *Hernández Vidal*, para 25.

[79] Note that in Joined Cases C–173/96 and C–247/96 *Sánchez Hidalgo*, para 27, the Court stipulated that: 'The presence of a sufficiently structured and autonomous entity within the undertaking awarded the contract is, in principle, not affected by the circumstances which occurs quite frequently, that the undertaking is subject to observance of precise obligations imposed on it by the contract-awarding body. Although the influence which the contract-awarding body has on the service provided by the undertaking concerned may be extensive, the service-providing undertaking nevertheless normally retains a certain degree of freedom, albeit reduced, in organising and performing the service in question, without its task being capable of being interpreted as simply one of making personnel available to the contract-awarding body.' This stipulation was due to the fact that in Case C–247/96 *Horst Ziemann*, the German Federal Armed Forces, the body awarding the surveillance contract, defined in detail the rules of organisation and exercise of the services contracted out and the national court questioned whether, in these circumstances, an economic entity could be said to exist.

[80] Paras 22, 23, 26, 29–32 of the decision in Joined Cases C–127/96, C–229/96 and C–74/97 *Hernández Vidal* were taken directly from Case C–13/95 *Süzen*. See also Joined Cases C–173/96 and C–247/96 *Sánchez Hidalgo* for a similar response to Spanish and German courts in references involving home-helps who had worked for a local authority on a contracted out basis but were then taken on by the local authority itself and a security guard employed by successive firms on contract to the German Federal Armed Forces for surveillance.

[81] Joined Cases C–127/96, C–229/96 and C–74/97 *Hernández Vidal*, para 27.

[82] Opinion of Advocate General Cosmas in Joined Cases C–127/96, C–229/96 and C–74/97 *Hernández Vidal*, paras 66–69.

to countenance.[83] Indeed, imposing such a criterion begs the question—'the result achieved by applying the Directive becomes a condition determining whether it is to apply. . . . The negative repercussions for employees of admitting readiness to take over staff as a decisive criterion for the application of the Directive cannot be neglected.'[84] Similar concerns had been expressed by academic commentators following the *Süzen* decision. Shrubsall pointed out, for example, that the transferee needs to consent to take at least enough of the workforce to amount to 'a major part' before the Directive can be held to apply, despite the fact that the Court had previously regarded the intentions of the parties as irrelevant when it came to determining whether they were bound by the Directive's obligations.[85] The Court in *Hernández Vidal* seemed willing to take these concerns about *Süzen* on board, at least in so far as undertakings or businesses in which manpower is the main consideration is concerned.[86]

Subsequent decisions reveal that the Court is not slow to differentiate between economic activities—such as cleaning—based essentially on manpower and others—such as transport or driveage work in mines—which require substantial plant and equipment.[87] In *Oy Likenne*, for example, a public service contract to operate bus services was awarded to one contractor whose tender beat the previous operator. The new operator took on some of the previous operator's employees on less advantageous terms and conditions and the employees complained, claiming that they were, in accordance with the Acquired Rights Directive, entitled to the same terms and conditions as before. The new operator was clearly carrying on the same activity as before—running bus services—but had significant tangible assets or a major part of the workforce been taken over, as was required by *Süzen*? Where tangible assets play a significant part in the performance of the activity in question, the Court held that the absence of a transfer to a significant extent of such assets from the old to the new contractor indicates that the entity has not retained its identity and the Directive does not, therefore, apply. However, as Davies points out, the upshot of the Court's case-law on contracting out from *Süzen* onwards means that application of the Directive is highly contingent on the structuring of the

---

[83] See, in this respect, Case C–305/94 *Rotsart de Hertaing* [1996] ECR I–5927, para 20.

[84] Opinion of Advocate General Cosmas in Joined Cases C–127/96, C–229/96 and C–74/97 *Hernández Vidal*, para 80.

[85] See V. Shrubsall, 'Competitive Tendering, Out-sourcing and the Acquired Rights Directive' (1998) 61 *Modern Law Review* 85–92, 87; Bourn (1998), above n 57, 63; and at national judicial level the comments of Justice Morrison in *ECM (Vehicle Delivery Service) v Cox and others* [1998] IRLR 419, para 24, where he stated that: 'The issue as to whether employees should have been taken on cannot be determined by asking whether they were taken on.'

[86] See also Case C–234/98 *G.C. Allen*, where the Court held that the Directive can apply to a transfer between two companies in the same corporate group which have the same ownership, management and premises and which are engaged in the same works. In determining whether there was an economic entity capable of being transferred and whether a transfer had occurred, it reiterated in detail the criteria set out in Cases C–13/95 *Süzen*, C–127/96, C–229/96 and C–74/97 *Hernández Vidal* and C–173/96 and C–247/96 *Sánchez Hidalgo*.

[87] See Cases C–172/99 *Oy Likenne*, para 39 and C–234/98 *G.C. Allen*, para 30.

deal by which the contracting out is effected. Where assets are an essential part of the business, the application of the Directive can be avoided by not transferring the assets; where the business is based essentially on manpower, it can be avoided *ex ante* by the new employer not offering jobs to the former employer's workforce.[88] Where once the Directive as applied by the Court made commercial lawyers pay attention and factor employment law into their deal-making equation, it now simply encourages them to apply their legal skills with as much ingenuity as possible in order to avoid its application.

In the *Süzen* case, and in its subsequent decisions on contracting out, the Court did not overrule previous case-law on what constitutes a transfer within the meaning of the Directive or how to determine whether the Directive covers contracting out. It did, however, qualify that case-law considerably.[89] *Süzen*, in particular, is seen as 'a substantial re-evaluation by the Court of the balance to be struck between the economic imperative to pursue the most cost-efficient forms of organisation and the need for the protection of workers' interests in a changing labour market.'[90] Indeed, the intention in that case seems to have been to ensure that the Directive did not interfere untowardly with competitive contracting out and tendering; in other words with the business world's need for greater labour market flexibility. The consequence, of course, 'is to allow a competitor to an existing supplier of services to tender on the basis that he does not have to take on existing staff on existing employment terms.'[91] The service provider may take the activity but decline to take the workforce and, as a result, the Directive, which was intended to protect that workforce, is inapplicable. There was a time when the Court thought otherwise. When confronted in *d'Urso* with complaints that Directive 77/187 would curtail the freedom to carry on business the Court replied that 'such a restrictive effect is inherent in the very purpose of the Directive which is to ensure that in the interests of employees the obligations arising under contracts or relationships of employment are transferred to the transferee.'[92] The Court also discussed in that case the dissuasive

---

[88] See P. Davies, 'Transfers—the United Kingdom Will Have to Make Up its own Mind' (2001) 30 *Industrial Law Journal* 231–35, 234.

[89] See the Opinion of Advocate General Ruiz Jarabo in Case C–234/98 *G.C. Allen*, para 33. See also Kennedy LJ in *Betts v Brintel Helicopters Ltd and KLM ERA Helicopters (UK) Ltd* [1997] IRLR 361, 366, who regarded the decision in *Süzen* as representing 'a shift of emphasis, or at least a clarification of the law.' See also *The Times* 12 March 1997, which reported the decision as 'a complete about-face in only three years'.

[90] See Bourn (1998), above n 57, 63.

[91] See Shrubsall (1998), above n 85, 87; and P. Bramhall, 'Application of the Acquired Rights Directive to Contracting Out of Services: The Decision of the European Court of Justice in the Case of *Süzen*' (1997) 6 *Public Procurement Law Review*. 179–81, 181. See also J. Hunt, 'Success at last? The amendment of the Acquired Rights Directive' (1999) 24 *European Law Review* 215–30, 226, who submits that Case C–13/95 *Süzen* operates an *ex post* test in the sense that interested parties and courts may rely on it to assess whether a transfer has actually taken place, but it does not provide them with the clarity they need, when entering into a contract, as regards whether or Directive 77/187's protection of transfer rights applies.

[92] Case C–362/89 *d'Urso*, para 15. See also Bourn, above n 57, 60: 'the Acquired Rights Directive limits price competition amongst service providers.'

effect on a potential transferee of the obligation to assume the surplus personnel of the transferred undertaking. Its solution was not to exclude application of the Directive,[93] but to refer the national court to the provision in Article 4(1) for dismissals for economic, technical or organisational reasons and to the existing possibility for national law to allow the burdens connected with the employment of surplus employees to be alleviated or removed.[94] The Directive does not provide harmonised, comprehensive protection to workers of transferred undertakings, but it is surely preferable that the limited protection which it does provide is extended to those workers engaged on contract precarious forms of employment in the service sector who most need it.

Whether national courts find the Court's instructions clear or not remains to be seen—and certainly in the immediate aftermath of *Süzen* references continued. Those instructions are essentially as follows. In order to determine whether there has been a transfer within the meaning of Article 1(1) of Directive 77/187, national courts must establish that: there is an economic entity, defined as an organised grouping of persons and assets for the exercise of an economic activity which pursues a specific objective; that entity is organised in a stable manner; that entity is not limited to performing one specific works contract; there is a change, in terms of contractual relations, in the legal or natural person who is responsible for carrying on the business and who incurs the obligations of an employer towards employees of the entity; the economic entity must retain its identity, which is marked both by the continuation by the new employer of the same activities and by the continuity of its workforce, its management staff, the way in which its work is organised, its operating methods or the operational resources available to it.[95] The fact that the engagement of part of the staff of the previous contractor is imposed on the new contractor by a collective agreement does not preclude the conclusion that the transfer concerns an economic entity within the meaning of the Directive.[96] All these circumstances are but single factors in the overall assessment which must be made, at least in theory, by the national court. They must not, for this purpose, be considered in isolation.

The Special Case of Insolvency

Another issue that has caused the Court of Justice a number of headaches is the applicability of the Directive to transfers in the context of insolvency or similar proceedings. In the *Abels* case, the applicant's former employer ran into financial

---

[93] For discussion of the applicability of the Directive to insolvency and similar proceedings see below.

[94] Presumably what would then be incurred are obligations to give notice of termination and make redundancy payments, which may sometimes prove costly. See further Davies, (1997) EUI WP, above n 46, pp 21–22.

[95] See the Opinion of Advocate General Ruiz Jarabo in Case C–234/98 G.C. *Allen*, para 34.

[96] Case C–51/00 *Temco Industries*, para 27.

difficulties, as a result of which the company was granted judicial leave to suspend payment of debts and was subsequently put into liquidation. The liquidator made an agreement with another company, TTP, that the latter would take over the business. The applicant and most of the insolvent company's employees were taken on by TTP, but their wages, arrears of holiday pay and allowances for the period between the declaration of insolvency and the transfer of the business were paid neither by their previous nor by their new employer. The plaintiff sought therefore to recover these sums from his trade association, which in turn claimed that TTP was liable. The national court seised of the case asked the Court of Justice whether Directive 77/187 applies to a situation in which the transferor of an undertaking is adjudged insolvent or granted judicial leave to suspend payment of debts. At the heart of the problem in *Abels*, and subsequent cases, was the fact that certain Member States regarded a sale of a business in the context of liquidation proceedings as a normal contractual sale, regardless of the need for judicial intervention for the conclusion of such a contract. For others such a sale could not be considered genuinely consensual, since it took place by virtue of a measure adopted by a public authority.[97] Insolvency proceedings entail a clear conflict between the acquired rights of employees and those of other creditors. Compounding this problem was the existence of terminological divergences in the different language versions of Directive 77/187 as regards the notion of transfer of undertakings.

In determining whether or not Directive 77/187 applied in the instant case, the Court first concentrated on the specifics of insolvency law as reflected both in Community and national law:

> [I]nsolvency law is characterized by special procedures intended to weigh up the various interests involved, in particular those of the various classes of creditors; consequently, in all the Member States there are specific rules which may derogate, at least partially, from other provisions, of a general nature, including provisions of social law.[98]

The Court concluded that if Directive 77/187 had been intended to apply also to transfers of undertakings in the context of such proceedings, an express provision would have been included for that purpose. It argued that support for this conclusion could be found in the very purpose of the Directive, which was to ensure that the restructuring of undertakings within the common market did not adversely affect the employees of the undertakings concerned. The Court explained that the parties were divided as to the possible effects of the Directive being held applicable to liquidation or similar proceedings. On the one hand, the Danish Trade Association and Danish government considered that the

---

[97] See the Opinion of Advocate General Slynn in Case 135/83 *Abels*, 474, for a discussion of the differences between Member State legislation; and similar arguments in Joined Cases 144 and 145/87 *Harry Berg and Johannes Theodorus Maria Busschers v Ivo Marten Besselsen* [1988] ECR 2559, para 16 (retransfer of a lease-purchase agreement by judicial decision).

[98] Case 135/83 *Abels*, para 15.

Directive must apply, particularly since employees whose employer has been adjudged insolvent are those most in need of the protection afforded by the Directive. In contrast, the Dutch government and Commission had argued that applying the Directive to insolvency or similar proceedings would actually detract from the protection of workers that the Directive sought. Potential purchasers/transferees might be dissuaded from acquiring an undertaking on condition that they take on all former employees. More jobs might be lost if purchasers were deterred by rules which obliged them to take on all employees and satisfy all pre-existing obligations to them. If purchasers were deterred, the assets of the undertaking might have to be sold separately, with the result that all the jobs in the undertaking would be lost.[99]

Faced with these conflicting arguments, the Court stated that 'at the present stage of economic development, considerable uncertainty exists regarding the impact on the labour market of transfers of undertakings in the event of an employer's insolvency and the appropriate measures to be taken in order to ensure the best protection of the workers' interests.'[100] In the Court's view, a serious risk of general deterioration in working and living conditions of workers, contrary to the social objectives of the Treaty, could not be ruled out if the Directive were applied. It concluded, therefore, that Directive 77/187 did not require Member States to extend its provisions to transfers in the context of insolvency proceedings instituted with a view to the liquidation of the assets of the transferor under the supervision of the competent judicial authority.[101]

Curiously, the Court then distinguished between a sale in the context of liquidation proceedings and a transfer which took place in the context of proceedings such as judicial leave to suspend payment of debts. The latter, according to the Court of Justice, albeit that it involves proceedings of a judicial nature, differs from liquidation proceedings in a number of respects—the exercise of judicial supervision is more limited, the object of such proceedings is to safeguard the assets of the insolvent undertaking and to allow it to continue to operate. As a result, the reasons for not applying Directive 77/187 to transfers of undertakings taking place in liquidation proceedings were found not to be applicable to proceedings such as judicial leave to suspend payment of debts, which take place at an earlier stage.

The decision of the Court in *Abels* was confirmed in *Industriebond FNV, Botzen, Wendelboe* and *Danmols Inventar.*[102] As a result of these rulings, the

[99] See the Opinion of Advocate General Slynn in Case 135/83 *Abels*, 474, for a detailed discussion of the Dutch and Commission arguments; and subsequently the Opinion of Advocate General Lenz in Case C–319/94 *Jules Dethier Équipement SA v Jules Dassy and Sovam SPRL, in liquidation* [1998] ECR I–1061, para 22.

[100] Case 135/83 *Abels*, para 22.

[101] *Ibid*, para 23, following the approach of Advocate General Slynn, 475.

[102] Cases 179/83 *Industriebond FNV and Federatie Nederlandse Vakbeweging (FNV) v The Netherlands State* [1985] ECR 511; 186/83 *Arie Botzen and Others v Rotterdamsche Droogdok Maatschappij BV* [1985] ECR 519; and 105/84 *Foreningen af Arbejdsledere i Danmark v A/S Danmols Inventar, in liquidation* [1985] ECR 2639.

limited employment protection afforded by Directive 77/187 to employees in the event of a transfer is available to those employed in undertakings which are subject to a variety of what can be termed pre-liquidation proceedings. By contrast, the unfortunate employees of undertakings subject to liquidation proceedings receive no such protection. Davies has suggested that one of the reasons the Court came up with this rather illogical distinction was to take some of the sting out of its acceptance in *Abels* that, given the specificity of insolvency, the purpose of the Directive and the uncertain consequences for that purpose of application of the Directive to the transfer of insolvent undertakings, the employment protection offered by the Directive would have to be denied the employees of insolvent transferred undertakings.[103] In a classic trade off between the need to protect employees and the dictates of what it perceived as commercial reality, the Court was, in essence, asking the employees of insolvent undertakings to accept a diminution of their rights in the hope that (some of) their jobs would actually be preserved. As Davies has stated:

> [T]he argument of the Court was that insolvency necessarily involves the potential overriding of rights that can be claimed against a solvent debtor and that the employees' protection of their acquired rights should be subject to the same risk in order to maximise the chances of the viable parts of the business being sold off as going concerns with, therefore, the maximum preservation of jobs. In principle the argument is attractive, but the defect with it is that it requires employees to take a lot on trust.[104]

Furthermore, although the Court had been faced with competing arguments concerning the effect of the applicability of the Directive to the transfer of insolvent undertakings and had accepted that it was not clear how the transfer of insolvent undertakings impacted the labour market or how best to protect workers' interests in such circumstances, it favoured the solution which would least impinge on the priorities of business rather than that which favoured the protection of vulnerable employees. As Davies points out, the Court was unable (indeed did not attempt) to demonstrate an empirical link between the scaling down of employees' rights and the preservation of business. In *Abels* it referred to the uncertain effects for the labour market, 'at the present stage of economic development', which applying the Directive to insolvency proceedings might have, but it has subsequently relied on *Abels* on several occasions without once questioning whether that stage of economic development has altered.[105]

The limited scope of application of the Directive to pre-liquidation and insolvency proceedings has also provided a good example of the Court being drawn

---

[103] See Davies (1989), above n 10, 46–47.

[104] *Ibid*, 51.

[105] See also the evidence submitted by P. Davies to the House of Lords Select Committee for its report on transfers of undertakings (1995–96), above n 1, pp 2–3 of the evidence, where he argued that the Commission's 1994 proposals to amend Directive 77/187 as regards its application to insolvency were premised on the notion that there is a conflict between legal rights for employees and the maintenance of jobs: 'it has not yet been demonstrated by reliable research that the problem actually exists in practice or, if it does, what the extent of the problem is.'

into the minutiae of the legal and factual appraisals to be made by national courts and, increasingly, to case-by-case determinations of whether or not the Directive applies. At issue in the *d'Urso* case was the special administration procedure established under Italian law for large undertakings in critical difficulties.[106] The Court was asked whether Directive 77/187 applies to the transfer of business by an undertaking subject to special administration. The plaintiffs in the case were originally employed by a company (EMG) which was made the subject of the special administration procedure by a decree of the Italian Minister for Industry but which was authorised to continue trading under the supervision of an auditor in accordance with Italian law. In his Opinion, Advocate General Van Gerven explains that the special administration procedure for large undertakings in critical difficulty provided for by Italian law is one of the procedures provided in the event that an undertaking is not in a position to meet its obligations, in particular when its debts to credit institutions and social security institutions exceed both a set minimum and five times the paid-up capital. The decision to apply the procedure is taken by ministerial decree but it is first necessary for the court to have found that the undertaking is insolvent or that at least three months' salaries have not been paid.[107] In trying to decide whether or not the Directive applied to a transfer within the context of the special administration procedure, the Court was obviously obliged to examine the purpose of that procedure. Yet, in doing so, it was clearly being drawn nearer factual details and specific interpretations of the domestic law of one Member State which is not its, but the national court's, province. Advocate General Van Gerven seemed more conscious than the Court of the need to avoid defining the scope of Directive 77/187 by reference only to a specific procedure existing in the legal system of an individual Member State.[108] Yet, he was also aware that, if his reply to the referring court was to be at all useful, he had to relate it to the specific purpose of the Italian procedure and highlight the criteria which, in view

---

[106] Case C–362/89 *d'Urso*.

[107] Opinion of Advocate General Van Gerven in Case C–362/89 *d'Urso*, para 5. The dispute before the national court followed on the transfer of EMG to Ercole Marelli Nuova Elettromeccanica Generale (Nuova EMG), pursuant to which almost two thirds of EMG's employees were transferred to the new company, while the remaining third remained in the service of EMG. The employment relationships of these employees, the applicants amongst them, were, however, suspended and their wages were covered by a wage supplement fund. They applied for a declaration to the referring court to the effect that their employment relationship had continued with the transferor in accordance with the relevant provisions of the Italian Civil Code. EMG argued, however, that in the case of undertakings placed under the special administration procedure, the said provision of the Civil Code did not apply to staff who were not transferred at the same time as the undertaking.

[108] See para 4 of his Opinion in Case C–362/89 *d'Urso*. See also paras 55–56 of the Opinion of Advocate General Cosmas in Joined Cases C–127/96, C–229/96 and C–74/97 *Hernández Vidal*, where he indicates that the referring courts could themselves have answered a number of questions concerning the application of the Directive to contracting out. He also referred to the Opinion of Advocate General Jacobs in Case C–338/95 *Wiener S.I. GmbH v Hauptzollamt Emmerich* [1997] ECR I–6495, in which he raised the issue of the correct division of tasks between the Court and national courts. See above ch 2.

of the case-law of the Court, the national court should consider decisive in ascertaining whether the Directive applies. According to the referring court, the Italian procedure was mainly intended to restructure the undertaking, having regard, above all, to the safeguarding of jobs. The referring court also emphasised, unlike the defendants, that the protection of creditors' interests under the special administration procedure was less extensive than in other liquidation procedures. The Commission, in contrast, argued that the main emphasis of the procedure was placed on winding-up the business. The Italian government stated that the aim of the procedure is to save as far as possible the viable parts of the undertakings by transferring them to a new employer so as to limit the economic and social damage which may be caused when large undertakings cease to operate.[109]

In *d'Urso*, the Court of Justice first rejected the idea that the scope of the Directive is to be determined according to the kind of supervision exercised by the administrative or judicial authority over transfers of undertakings in the course of a specific creditors' arrangement procedure. The decisive test for determining the scope of the Directive is the purpose of the contested procedure. Regardless of the fact that the case-file contained clearly conflicting interpretations of what the purpose of the Italian procedure actually was, the Court stated that a ministerial decree providing for the special administration procedure may have two effects: (i) it may apply the law on insolvency in all its effects, in which case the special administration procedure must be assimilated to the law ordering compulsory administrative liquidation; or (ii) it may authorise the undertaking to continue trading under the supervision of an auditor who may draw up, as far as possible taking account of creditors' interests, a restructuring plan compatible with the trends of industrial policy, specifying the plants to be brought back into operation and those to be expanded, as well as the plants or business to be transferred. The Court held that where the undertaking had not been authorised to continue trading or where that authorisation had expired, the aim, consequences and risks of the contested procedure were comparable to those which led it to conclude in *Abels* that Article 1(1) of the Directive did not apply. Such a procedure is designed to liquidate the debtor's assets in order to satisfy the body of creditors and transfers effected under such a legal framework are excluded from the scope of the Directive.

In contrast, where the undertaking is authorised to continue trading, the primary purpose of the special administration procedure is to give the undertaking some stability, allowing its future activity to be safeguarded. The Court added that: 'The social and economic objectives thus pursued cannot explain nor justify the circumstance that, when all or part of the undertaking concerned

---

[109] According to Advocate General Van Gerven, para 26 of his Opinion in Case C–362/89 *d'Urso*, the difference of opinion between the parties regarding the purpose of the special administration procedure was based on a misunderstanding or confusion between (compulsory) liquidation of the assets and the continuity of the undertaking transferred.

is transferred, its employees lose the rights which the Directive confers on them under the conditions which it lays down.'[110] In support of this conclusion the Court pointed to several factors adduced by the referring court explaining the purpose and operation of the special administration procedure, at least when accompanied by authorisation to continue trading—an undertaking may obtain loans, for the purpose of resuming operations and supplementing plant, land and industrial equipment, whose repayment is guaranteed by the State; the protection of creditors' interests is less extensive under the special administration procedure than in other liquidation procedures; and creditors are not involved in decisions concerning the continued operation of the undertaking. Thus Directive 77/187 applies to the special administration procedure under Italian law, but only where it has been decided that the undertaking is to continue trading for as long as that decision remains in effect.

The Court has also been questioned, again by an Italian court, about the Directive's applicability to procedures by which an undertaking is declared to be in critical difficulties. In the *Spano* case the order for reference specified that such a procedure is intended to stabilise the undertaking with a view to protecting jobs and providing workers with financial support for as long as those difficulties persist.[111] The Court pointed out that a declaration that an undertaking is in critical difficulties, which is based on assessments of both an economic and financial nature and of a social nature, is conditional on the submission of a recovery plan, which must include measures to resolve employment problems. In addition, the economic situation of the undertakings concerned is such that they can continue, without any significant hiatus, their production activities and have real prospects of recovery. The Court held that the economic and social objective pursued by the contested procedure cannot explain or justify the circumstance that, when all or part of the undertaking concerned is transferred, its employees lose the rights which the Directive confers on them.[112]

In *Abels*, *d'Urso* and *Spano*, the Court had emphasised that the decisive factor to be taken into consideration when determining whether the Directive applies to the transfer of an undertaking subject to an administrative or judicial

---

[110] Case C–362/89 *d'Urso*, para 32. In contrast, Advocate General Van Gerven concluded that a procedure of the special administration kind provided for by Italian law must be treated, for the purposes of Directive 77/187, as a bankruptcy procedure, with the result that the Directive does not apply once the debtor is adjudged insolvent. The Advocate General accepted (para 26) that particular emphasis is placed in the special administration procedure on the protection of jobs but stated that 'the risk of a counterproductive effect which prompted the Court to exclude bankruptcy proceedings from the scope of the directive . . . must be regarded as providing an additional reason for treating the special administration procedure in a way analogous to bankruptcy proceedings for the purposes of the directive.'

[111] Case C–472/93 *Spano*, paras 26 of the Opinion of Advocate General Cosmas and the judgment.

[112] *Ibid*, para 30 of the judgment. The fact that, pursuant to the impugned national legislation, the workforce has been consulted through their representatives on the preservation of at least some jobs, could not, given the mandatory nature of the provisions of Directive 77/187, detract from its application to the transfer of an undertaking declared to be in critical difficulties (paras 31–32).

procedure is the purpose of the procedure in question. In *Dethier Équipement*,[113] however, the purpose of the procedure no longer appeared to be regarded as conclusive. The Court held that account should also be taken of the form of the procedure in question (whether it means the undertaking continues or ceases trading) and of the Directive's objectives. Confronted with a question concerning the applicability of the Directive to the transfer of an undertaking which was being wound up by a court but which was continuing to trade, the Court seized upon the differences between the objectives pursued in the winding up of a company (as here) and those in an insolvency procedure and examined the form of the winding up procedure in detail.[114] According to the Court, the situation of an undertaking being wound up by the court presents considerable differences from that of an undertaking subject to insolvency proceedings:

> in the case of a liquidation the liquidator, although appointed by the court, is an organ of the company who sells the assets under the supervision of the general meeting; there is no special procedure for establishing liabilities under the supervision of the court; and a creditor may as a rule enforce his debt against the company and obtain judgment against it. By contrast, in the case of an insolvency, the administrator, inasmuch as he represents the creditors, is a third party *vis-à-vis* the company and realises the assets under the supervision of the court; the liabilities of the company are established in accordance with a special procedure and individual enforcement actions are prohibited.[115]

The Court concluded that the reasons which had led it to rule out application of the Directive in insolvency situations *may*, despite the similarities between the two procedures, be absent in the case of an undertaking being wound up by the court.[116] The Directive was held to apply where the undertaking continues to trade while it is being wound up by the court since, in such circumstances, continuity of the business is assured when the undertaking is transferred and there is thus no justification for depriving the employees of the rights which the Directive guarantees them.[117] The primacy which this decision gave the fact that the undertaking continued to trade after the liquidation process was

---

[113] Case C–319/94 *Dethier Équipement*. At issue in the case was a company which got into financial difficulty and which, in the absence of agreement between the shareholders on the course to be followed, applied to be wound up by the local commercial court in Belgium. The latter made an order putting the company into liquidation under supervision of the Court and appointed a liquidator. The employment contract of the applicant in the case, Mr. Dassy, was terminated by the liquidator, who subsequently transferred the assets of the company in liquidation to Dethier Équipement. The applicant then brought an action against the latter claiming that it was jointly and severally liable for payment of the sums due from his previous employer.

[114] See Case C–319/94 *Dethier Équipement*, para 9 for details.

[115] *Ibid*, para 29.

[116] *Ibid*, para 30 (emphasis added). The Court had stressed, para 27, that liquidation proceedings may be used whenever it is wished to bring a company's activities to an end and whatever the reasons for taking that course.

[117] Case C–319/94 *Dethier Équipement*, para 31.

commenced, as distinct simply from the purpose of that process, is to be welcomed.[118]

Application of Directive 77/187 to the Public Sector

Prior to the *Henke* case, the Court had not had to consider directly the applicability of Directive 77/187 to the public sector. At issue in *Redmond Stichting* had been subsidies granted by a Dutch public authority to foundations involved in the provision of assistance to drug addicts. However, the contested transfer in that case concerned merely the decision of that public authority to terminate the subsidy paid to one legal person, as a result of which its activities came fully and definitively to an end, and to transfer it to another legal person with a similar aim. It was irrelevant, said the Court, as regards the application of Directive 77/187, that the transfer decision was one taken unilaterally by a public authority. The Court had also implicitly held in *Redmond Stichting* that an intention to make profit was not necessary for an establishment to be regarded as an undertaking within the meaning of Directive 77/187.[119]

In *Henke,* by contrast, the Court was being asked whether Article 1(1) of the Directive had to be interpreted as meaning that the concept of a 'transfer of an undertaking, business or part of a business' applies to the transfer of administrative functions from a municipality to an administrative collective.[120] The

---

[118] See S. Hardy and R.W. Painter, 'The New Acquired Rights Directive and its Implications for European Employee Relations in the Twenty-First Century' (1999) 6 *Maastricht Journal of European and Comparative Law* 366–79, 373. The Court followed its judgment in Case C–319/94 *Dethier Équipement* in Case C–399/96 *Europièces SA, in liquidation v Wilfried Sanders and Automotive Industries Holding Company SA, declared insolvent* [1998] ECR I–6965, which concerned the transfer of an undertaking in voluntary liquidation. It compared winding up by a court with voluntary liquidation and pointed out that, at least in procedural terms, voluntary liquidation had even less in common with insolvency than winding up by a court. The Court's reasons in *Dethier Équipement* for confirming the application of the Directive were all the more pertinent, it held, where the undertaking transferred is being wound up voluntarily.

[119] See also Case C–382/92 *Commission of the European Communities v United Kingdom of Great Britain and Northern Ireland* [1994] ECR I–2435, para 45, where it followed from the decisions of the Court in Case C–29/91 *Redmond Stichting* (social law) and Case C–41/90 *Höfner and Elser v Macrotron* [1991] ECR I–1979 (competition law) that the fact that an undertaking was engaged in non-profit-making activities was not in itself sufficient to deprive such activities of their economic character or to remove the undertaking from the scope of Directive 77/187.

[120] Case C–298/94 *Annette Henke v Gemeinde Schierke and Verwaltungsgemeinschaft 'Brocken'* [1996] ECR I–4989. The plaintiff in the case was employed as a secretary in the mayor's office of the municipality of Schierke in 1992. In 1994, Schierke and a number of neighbouring municipalities formed, in accordance with German law on municipal co-operation, an administrative collective, to which it transferred administrative functions. The plaintiff was informed by the municipality of the termination of her contract of employment. She claimed, however, that her contract had been transferred to the new administrative collective and could not, therefore, be terminated. It emerges from the Opinion of Advocate General Lenz in Case C–298/94 *Henke*, para 5, that the plaintiff was actually offered a post with the new administrative collective, which she turned down on the ground that she could only take a post in Schierke itself because she had to look after her child. She was also unsuccessful in her application for a post at the local office of the administrative collective in Schierke.

Court held, in line with the submissions of the Commission and various Member State governments in the case, that the reorganisation of the structure of the public administration or the transfer of administrative functions between public administrative authorities does not constitute a 'transfer of an undertaking' within the meaning of the Directive.[121] It referred to a variety of language versions of the Directive in support of this conclusion. The disputed transfer in the *Henke* case involved the reorganisation of administrative structures and the transfer of administrative functions of various municipalities to a public entity specially set up for that purpose. The transfer thus only related to activities involving the exercise of public authority and even if those activities demonstrated aspects of an economic nature the Court regarded them as purely ancillary, which would be insufficient to bring the transfer within the scope of the Directive, since the latter concerned the transfer of economic entities.[122]

In his Opinion in the *Henke* case, Advocate General Lenz, unlike the Court in its judgment, dealt exhaustively with the issues at stake in the case. He was unhappy at the outset with the exclusion of the public sector *per se* from the scope of application of Directive 77/187. However, he was also unwilling to accept that the Directive's non-application should simply depend on the criterion of activity in the exercise of public powers or of activity typically of the public administration: 'What is today regarded as purely public may, in even only a few years, be carried out by a private undertaking with a view to profit.'[123] He pointed to the privatisation of *Deutsche Bundespost* as an excellent example of this. Other examples might include the policies of some Member State governments, notably the United Kingdom, to compel local authorities to put key services out to competitive tender or to alter the organisation and management of previously nationalised services such as healthcare.[124] In the Advocate General's view, if regard is had to the protective purpose of the Directive, there is no reason why employees of the public administration should be excluded from the protective ambit of the Directive merely because the authority which employs them *also* acts in the exercise of public authority. Economic developments and restructuring are liable to entail disadvantages for workers irrespective of whether they are employed in the public or private sector. The Directive should apply, according to the Advocate General, whenever employees within the meaning of the protective provisions of national employment law are employed in an undertaking or organised entity.

Advocate General Lenz's Opinion in *Henke* is of interest not because the Court followed him—it did not—but because of his appreciation of the extent to which economic development and restructuring was transforming the public

---

[121] Case C–298/94 *Henke*, para 14.
[122] *Ibid*, paras 16–17.
[123] Opinion of Advocate General Lenz in Case C–298/94 *Henke*, para 29.
[124] See further G. More, annotation of Case C–209/91 *Rask* (1993) 18 *European Law Review* 442–48.

sector in the European Union. The *Collino* case[125] bore out his arguments, as it specifically concerned the question of the applicability of the Directive to the privatisation of a public body.[126] The background to *Collino* is complicated and can be described briefly as follows. In 1992, as part of the reform of the telecommunications sector, the Italian Minister for Posts and Telecommunications was authorised to grant the exclusive concession for the telecommunications services for public use, operated until then by the State (in the form of the Azienda di Stato per i Servizi Telefonici—ASST), to a company established for that purpose by the State-owned holding company, IRI. The concession for the telecommunications services for public use passed in 1992 to Iritel SpA. Within two years, Società Italiana per le Telecommunicazioni SpA (SIP), another subsidiary of IRI, absorbed Iritel and took the name Telecom Italia SpA. The applicants had been employed by ASST, the State body. They were transferred to Iritel, then taken on by SIP, now Telecom Italia. The applicants challenged the conditions of their transfer from ASST to Iritel and in particular, national legislation applicable to them establishing a special scheme which derogated from the general rules on transfers of undertakings in the Italian Civil Code.[127]

The Court stated that the fact that the service transferred was the subject of a concession by a public body such as a municipality cannot exclude application of the Directive if the activity in question does not involve the exercise of public authority.[128] It then referred to competition law precedents which indicated, on the one hand, that the management of public telecommunications equipment and the placing of such equipment at the disposal of users on payment of a fee amounted to a business activity and, on the other, that the fact that the public telecommunications network is entrusted to a body forming part of the public administration cannot prevent that body being classified as a public

---

[125] Case C–343/98 *Renato Collino and Luisella Chiappero v Telecom Italia SpA* [2000] ECR I–6659.

[126] The referring court in Case C–343/98 *Collino* sought to ascertain whether Directive 77/187 applies to a situation in which an entity operating telecommunications services for public use managed by a public body within the State administration is, following decisions of the public authorities, the subject of a transfer for value, in the form of an administrative concession, to a private law company established by another public body which holds its entire capital.

[127] This derogating legislation provided that (i) employees of ASST could either stay in the public administration or become employees of the new company; (ii) collective bargaining at trade union level was to ensure that the new company's employees received economic treatment which overall is not less than that previously enjoyed and (iii) employees who did not opt to stay in the public administration were entitled to payment of severance pay. The applicants argued that this special regime prejudiced both calculation of their length of service and their receipt of termination payments when they subsequently retired from SIP (previously Iritel).

[128] See also Joined Cases C–173/96 and C–247/96 *Sánchez Hidalgo*, para 24, where the Court held that the fact that a service or contract has been contracted out or awarded by a public body cannot exclude the application of Directive 77/187 if neither of the activities in question (providing home-help and providing surveillance) involves the exercise of public authority; and Case C–175/99 *Didier Mayeur v Association Promotion de l'information messine (APIM)* [2000] ECR I–7755 (transfer to a municipality of publicity and information activities previously carried out by a private law, non-profit making body).

undertaking.[129] In addition, the Court pointed to its decision in *Redmond Stichting* where it had been held that the Directive can apply even where a unilateral decision of the public authority on subsidies leads to the activities of one legal person being fully terminated and the transfer of those subsidies to another legal person with a similar aim. The Court concluded that a transfer such as that at issue in *Collino* falls within the scope of the Directive. There was, however, a sting in the tail of the Court's response to the referring court concerning the applicability of the Directive. It pointed out that, in accordance with the *Danmols Inventar* case, the latter may only be relied on by persons who are protected in the Member State concerned as workers under national law. Regardless of the similarity in the tasks performed by public servants working in the telecommunications sector and the tasks performed by those in the private sector, the Court held that the case-file suggested that, at the time of the disputed transfer, ASST's employees were subject to public-law status in Italy, not to employment law. The national court was left to verify that this was the correct position, in which case those employees could not rely on the Directive.[130]

In subsequent cases involving transfers by or to public law bodies, the restrictive scope of *Henke* has arguably been even more refined. While the reorganisation of structures of the public administration or the transfer of administrative functions between public administrations are excluded from the scope of Directive 77/187, the Court held in the *Mayeur* case[131] that the transfer of an economic activity from a legal person governed by private law to a legal person governed by public law cannot be excluded from its scope simply because the transferee is a public-law body. Nevertheless, *Mayeur* also emphasises the Court's limited vision in *Henke*, despite the Advocate General's comprehensive warnings to the contrary. In *Henke* the disgruntled, dismissed employee had been working as a secretary and senior official dealing with industrial development and tourism—both activities capable of being qualified as economic in nature. In *Mayeur*, the applicant had been employed originally by a non-profit organisation involved in publicity and information activities on behalf of the City of Metz. While in *Henke* the small plenary court was content to exclude the application of the Directive, since it deemed that the transfer related only to activities involving the exercise of public authority, in *Mayeur* a larger plenary

---

[129] Case C–343/98 *Collino*, para 33. The Court has been less willing in other circumstances to rely on competition law theory or practice. See Case C–234/98 *G.C. Allen*, para 19: 'The concept of undertaking is specific to competition law. . .'

[130] See, however, the Opinion of Advocate General Alber (para 48) in Case C–343/98 *Collino*, who was adamant that, given the employment protection purpose of the 1977 Directive, public sector employees should not be excluded from the benefits which it conferred; and the decision in Case C–164/00 *Katia Beckmann v Dynamoco Whichloe Macfarlane Ltd.*, judgment of the Court of 4 June 2002, nyr. ECR., para 27, where the Court made clear that NHS employees in the United Kingdom are covered by national employment law and, therefore, are eligible to benefit from the provisions of the Directive.

[131] See Case C–175/99 *Mayeur*, paras 33.

formation held that the activities of the applicant's employer, consisting in the provision of services, were economic in nature and could not be regarded as deriving from the exercise of public authority.[132] *Mayeur* also sits uneasily with the *Collino* case, at least as regards the fate of the employees of the transferred undertaking. In *Collino* the Court left it to national definitions of who is covered by employment law to resolve whether the former employees of the State-owned telecommunications body could enjoy the protection afforded Directive 77/187 when the activities of the latter were privatised. The French government in *Mayeur* had argued that it was not possible for a public body which takes over an activity previously carried out by a legal person governed by private law to maintain contracts of employment concluded by that legal person inasmuch as public officers are officials governed by public law, recruited under special rules and procedures, whose status is determined by administrative law.[133] The Court accepted that, in certain circumstances, factors such as organisation, operation, financing, management and the applicable legal rules identify an economic entity in such a way that any alteration of those factors resulting from the transfer of that entity would lead to a change in its identity.[134] However, it added that, as regards any obligation prescribed by national law to terminate contracts of employment governed by private law in the case of transfer of an activity to a legal person governed by public law, such an obligation constitutes, in accordance with Article 4(2) of the Directive, a substantial change in working conditions to the detriment of the employee resulting directly from the transfer, with the result that termination of such contracts of employment must be regarded as resulting from the action of the employer.[135]

THE LEGISLATIVE RESPONSE TO THE COURT'S CASE-LAW ON ACQUIRED RIGHTS: DIRECTIVES 98/50 AND 2001/23

In a 1992 report on the implementation of Directive 77/187, the Commission was already showing signs of unhappiness with some of the aspects of the law governing acquired rights as developed by the Court of Justice.[136] A proposal to amend the 1977 Directive was adopted by the Commission in 1994, the legal basis of the original Directive having been maintained.[137] According to the

---

[132] *Ibid*, para 39.

[133] *Ibid*, para 50.

[134] *Ibid*, para 53.

[135] *Ibid*, para 56.

[136] See the Commission's Report to the Council, SEC (92) 857. For a synopsis of the report's findings in terms of the implementation of Directive 77/187 in the Member States see Eurobrief, 'The Acquired Rights Directive' (1995) *European Business Law Review* 82–85, 83.

[137] See Hunt (1999), above n 91, 218, for an account of the interest groups' (contractors' associations and trade unions) and governmental efforts in the United Kingdom to restrict or preserve the scope of the original Directive. See also Hardy and Painter, above n 118; and J. Nazerali and K. Plumbley-Jones, 'New Draft Acquired Rights Directive—A Step in the Dark?' (1995) *European Business Law Review* 31–36 on the amendment of Directive 77/187.

Commission in the explanatory memorandum attached to the proposal, Directive 77/187 had proved an invaluable instrument for protecting employees in cases of corporate reorganisation, ensuring peaceful and consensual economic and technological restructuring and laying down minimum standards for promoting fair competition with respect to such changes. However, the Directive had failed to provide for greater flexibility in the event of transfers of insolvent businesses or of undertakings facing major economic difficulties and did not, in the words of the Commission, 'cover explicitly the transnational dimension of corporate restructuring'. The Commission's fear was that these shortcomings might jeopardise or prejudice the very objectives which the Directive was intended to achieve.[138]

By amending the 1977 Directive the Commission sought to achieve the following: clarify the terms 'undertaking' and 'transfer' which had proved problematic and given rise to so many references; define employees so as to include part-time and temporary workers; permit flexibility in insolvency procedures; extend the Directive to public undertakings carrying out economic activities whether or not they operate for gain; and introduce joint employer liability.[139] In particular, it wanted to exclude from the scope of the Directive the transfer of an activity, as distinct from the transfer of an economic entity which retains its identity. Although the Commission claimed that the intention behind this amendment was simply to clarify the scope of application of the Directive to help in its interpretation and application, in fact the amendment called the case-law of the Court on contracting out directly into question, particularly its decision in *Schmidt*, decided the same year. Furthermore, what the Commission seemed to have in mind when excluding activities as distinct from economic entities from the revised Directive's scope were services such as catering and cleaning. Yet, no thought seemed to have been given in the memorandum accompanying the proposal to the potentially indirectly discriminatory effects on women of withdrawing the Directive's protection from service industries where they predominate.[140] The Commission's proposal contradicted the objec-

---

[138] See More in Shaw and More (eds), above n 32, p 138, who highlights the seeming contradiction in the Court's case-law requiring certain standards of employment protection in contracting out situations when such employment is actually designed to facilitate a high degree of labour flexibility: 'the Court's promotion of the aims of the Directive which originated in the very different circumstances of the 1970s is simply not compatible with today's economic environment.' Although she argues cogently thereafter that that is not the case.

[139] For a detailed discussion of the Commission's proposals see the House of Lords Select Committee report on transfers of undertakings (1995–96), above n 1.

[140] See the Opinion of ECOSOC of March 1995, CES 317/95. See, however, the Opinion of ECOSOC (OJ 1995 C133/13) and the evidence submitted by the Trade Unions Congress (TUC) to the House of Lords Select Committee for its report on transfers of undertakings, above n 1, p 48, where it provided a table comparing the number of male and female workers working in community, social and personal services—broadly the category most likely to be affected by the exclusion of subcontracting from the Directive's scope; and the report by K. Escott and D. Whitfield, *The Gender Impact of CCT in Local Government*, Centre for Public Services, UK Equal Opportunities Commission Research Discussion Series (EOC, 1995), No 12.

tive of the Directive, which is the protection of the rights of employees of transferred undertakings, not the protection of employers who transfer activities.[141]
Faced with opposition from the European Parliament, ECOSOC, trade unions,
some Member State governments and even contractors' associations, the
Commission withdrew its 1994 proposal, replacing it in 1997 with a version
which excluded the controversial distinction between activities and economic
entities as regards the scope of application of the Directive.[142] In a remarkable
volte face, many contractors' associations, which had previously supported the
Commission's restrictive definition of undertaking, had changed tune. It seems
that they were 'fearful of being landed with the costs of redundancy payments
on the occasion of losing previously held contracts to other contractors who
would not be bound by the Directive, and would therefore not have to take on
former employees.'[143]

The Commission's proposed amendments relating to insolvent transferors
sought to downgrade the level of protection available to the undertaking's
employees, however. On the one hand, it sought to codify the distinction to be
found in the Court's case-law between insolvency proceedings and pre or non-
liquidation proceedings, such as those at issue in *d'Urso* or *Spano*. On the other
hand, the Commission sought, with respect to pre-liquidation proceedings, to
exclude the transfer to the transferee of debts owed by the transferor to the
employees and to permit Member States to authorise competent judicial authorities to alter or terminate the contracts of employment of workers who would
otherwise be transferred compulsorily on their existing terms and conditions,
provided that this was done to ensure the survival of the undertaking.

Directive 98/50 was adopted in June 1998 and came into force in July 2001. It
was subsequently consolidated by Directive 2001/23, adopted in March 2001,
reference to whose provisions is made herein. Article 1 of Directive 2001/23
seeks to clarify its scope of application without, according to the preamble,
seeking to alter the scope of Directive 77/187 as interpreted by the Court. It does
so essentially by codifying various aspects of the Court's existing case-law. The
new Directive, like its predecessor, applies to any transfer of an undertaking,
business or part of an undertaking or business to another employer as a result
of a legal transfer or merger. Unlike the 1977 Directive, Article 1(1)(b) of the
amended Directive 98/50 expressly provides that: 'there is a transfer within the
meaning of this Directive where there is a transfer of an economic activity which
retains its identity, meaning an organised grouping of resources which has the

---

[141] See further B. Bercusson, *European Labour Law* (London, Butterworths, 1996), pp 243–44.

[142] COM(97) 60 final. See OJ 1997 C33/81 (European Parliament); OJ 1996 C100/25 (Committee
of the Regions); and OJ 1995 C133/13 (ECOSOC) for criticism of the Commission's original amendment of the scope of Directive 77/187.

[143] See Hunt (1999), above n 91, 219, who also provides an interesting account of the change in
the United Kingdom government's position on the exclusion of contracting out from the scope of
the revised Directive following the election of Labour; and Bramhall, above n 91, on the consequences for contractors of the *Süzen* approach.

objective of pursuing an economic activity, whether or not that activity is central or ancillary.' In other words, the Community legislature has taken the essence of the Court's decisions in cases such as *Spijkers* (transfer of an economic activity which retains its identity), *Süzen* (definition of an economic activity which retains its identity) and *Rask* (irrelevance of the ancillary nature of the activity) in an attempt to clarify what constitutes a transfer of an undertaking.[144] What the Community legislature did not do when revising Article 1 was to adopt the suggestion made by the House of Lords Select Committee, for example, that the revised provision contain a non-exhaustive list of matters to be taken into account in determining the applicability of the Directive, presumably with the *Spijkers* shopping list of factors in mind. It remains to be seen whether the new version of Article 1 brings greater certainty or provokes fewer references from national courts than its cryptic predecessor. As some commentators have pointed out, since the reason behind the revision was, to a certain extent, the confused state of the case-law and national courts' difficulties in applying that case-law, it seems strange that, presented with an opportunity to revise the situation and introduce greater clarity, the Community legislature simply turned to that very case-law.[145] Presumably the number and nature of future references will depend on the willingness of national courts to apply the newly codified criteria and to identify for themselves what constitutes an 'organized grouping of resources.' However, as Davies points out, the amended Directive suggests that the Council has endorsed the Court's interpretation of the Directive to date, while leaving the 'hot potato' of determining the scope of the Directive, firmly in its hands.[146]

The revised Directive also applies to public and private undertakings engaged in economic activities whether or not they are operating for gain (as the Court had established as far back as *Redmond Stichting*). However it states, in line with the Court's decision in *Henke*, that an administrative reorganisation of public administrative authorities, or the transfer of administrative functions between public administrative authorities, is not a transfer within the meaning of the Directive (Article (1)(c)). The alternative suggestions of Advocate General Lenz in the *Henke* case have been ignored, despite the fact that subsequent case-law involving the public sector vindicated much of what he said in terms of the likely pattern of privatisation and the need to protect both private and public sector employees in line with the Directive's original stated objective—the protection of employees in the event of a change in their employer.

---

[144] See, however, Hunt (1999), above n 91, 227, who argues that although Article 1 codifies existing case-law, it is questionable whether conditions trawled from case-law addressing primarily the complicated issue of contracting out should apply generally to transfer cases; and P. Davies, 'Amendments to the Acquired Rights Directive' (1998) 27 *Industrial Law Journal* 365–73, 366, who points out that the definition now incorporated in the Directive proved extremely malleable in the hands of the Court of Justice in the past.

[145] See Hardy and Painter, above n 118, 368.

[146] See Davies (1998), above n 144, 366.

The revised Directive's definitions of transferor and transferee remain, by and large, the same, but an employee within the meaning of Directive 98/50 is taken to mean any person who, in the Member State concerned, is protected as an employee under national employment law (Article 2(1)(d)), the Commission's attempts to introduce a Community definition having been abandoned. In the same vein, the Directive is not intended to disturb national definitions of contracts of employment or employment relationships. However, Member States cannot exclude from its scope contracts of employment or employment relationships solely because of the number of hours worked, because of the fact that the relationship is governed by a fixed-duration contract or because it is a temporary employment relationship (Article 2(2)).[147]

Unlike the original Directive, Directive 2001/23 provides Member States with options when it comes to its application in key areas such as the joint and several liability of the transferor and transferee, insolvency and analogous proceedings, old-age, invalidity or survivor's benefits and full disclosure by the transferor of the rights and obligations falling due under the transferred contract. This less prescriptive approach to EC social law has been seen as acceptance of the principles of subsidiarity and flexibility—two of Brussels' buzzwords throughout the 1990s. From a practical point of view, however, this less regulatory approach must have made the negotiation and adoption process less difficult. Article 3 of Directive 98/50 adds, to the existing provision on the transfer of the transferor's rights and obligations arising from contracts of employment, a further detailed provision on the joint liability of the transferor and transferee. Member States may provide that, after the date of transfer, they are jointly and severally liable in respect of obligations which arose before the date of the transfer from a contract of employment or an employment relationship existing on the date of the transfer (Article 3(1)). Member States may also adopt appropriate measures to ensure that the transferor notifies the transferee of all the rights and obligations which will be transferred, so far as they are known or ought to have been known by the transferor at the time of the transfer (Article 3(2)). It also contains a provision on the transferee being bound by the terms of collective agreements in identical terms to that previously found in Directive 77/187.

As regards benefits which fall outside statutory social security schemes—old-age, invalidity or survivors' benefits—Article 3(4)(a) provides that, unless Member States provide otherwise, the provisions of Article 3 concerning the transfer to the transferee of rights and obligations arising from employment contracts, relationships or collective agreements shall not be applicable. However, Member States shall in any event adopt the measures necessary to

---

[147] For the definition of fixed-duration contracts or temporary employment relationships within the meaning of Article 2(2) Directive 98/50 see Council Directive 91/383/EEC of 25 June 1991 supplementing the measures to encourage improvements in the safety and health at work of workers with a fixed-duration employment relationship or a temporary employment relationship, OJ 1991 L206/19.

protect the interests of employees and of persons no longer employed in the transferor's business at the time of the transfer in respect of rights conferring on them immediate or prospective entitlement to old age benefits, including survivors' benefits (Article 3(4)(b)). Article 4 of the revised Directive, which concerns protection against dismissal, provides identical guarantees to those afforded by Directive 77/187. Article 4(1), which provides that the transfer shall not in itself constitute grounds for dismissal, remains unchanged.

In line with the established case-law of the Court, Article 5 of Directive 2001/23 codifies the existing position on transfers the subject of bankruptcy or analogous insolvency proceedings. It establishes that, unless Member States provide otherwise, the protection afforded by Articles 3 and 4 (in terms of transfer rights and protection against dismissal on grounds of the transfer) shall not apply to any transfer where the transferor is the subject of such proceedings, which have been instituted with a view to the liquidation of the assets of the transferor and are under the supervision of a competent public authority. In the context of insolvency proceedings to which articles 3 and 4 do apply, Member States may nevertheless provide, for example, that the transferor's debts arising from any contracts of employment or employment relationships and payable before the transfer (in other words, unpaid wages, holiday pay, bonuses), or before the opening of the insolvency proceedings, shall not be transferred to the transferee. This is on condition that affected employees are provided with protection at least equivalent to that provided in situations covered by the Directive on the protection of employees in the event of insolvency. In other words some of the employees' claims will be paid out of a guarantee fund financed by taxpayers and employers in general.[148] In the alternative, Article 5(2)(b) of the amended Directive provides that the social partners may agree alterations to the employees' terms and conditions of employment designed to safeguard employment opportunities by ensuring the survival of the undertaking or business. In particular, a Member State may apply Article 5(2)(b) to any transfers where the transferor is in a situation of serious economic crisis, as defined by national law, provided that the situation is declared by a competent public authority and open to judicial supervision. Finally, Article 5(4) requires Member States to take appropriate measures with a view to preventing misuse of insolvency proceedings in such a way as to deprive employees of the rights provided for in this Directive.

What is remarkable about Article 5(2)(b), in particular, is the fact that the social partners can agree changes to the employees' terms and conditions of employment, despite the fact that this contradicts decisions of the Court of Justice in cases such as *Daddy's Dance Hall* and *Rask*, where it had held that employment relationships could be altered with regard to the transferee to the

---

[148] As Davies (1998), above n 144, remarks, however, the level of protection afforded by the Insolvency Directive is low, with Member States permitted to limit liability both in terms of time and levels of payment.

same extent as they could have been with regard to the transferor, provided that the transfer of the undertaking itself may never constitute the reason for that amendment. Furthermore, in *d'Urso*, the Court was not willing to countenance collectively agreed modification of the terms and conditions of employment in the event of a transfer. What is true is that this amendment bears much resemblance to the doomsday scenario that convinced the Court in *Abels* to exclude, at the present stage of economic development, application of the Directive to insolvent transferors. Employees' representatives and unions can now be put in the terrible position of having to accept changes to their members' terms and conditions of employment ostensibly in order to save the business. The employees have no guarantee, of course, that that will be the case. Previous drafts had even included a provision permitting the parties to agree to the dismissal of employees to ensure the survival of the undertaking. This proposal did not survive the adoption process but undertakings can of course still resort to the provision permitting dismissals in crisis situations.[149] Finally, Article 7(1) of the amended Directive requires the transferor and the transferee to inform, in good time, the representatives of their respective employees affected by the transfer of the date or proposed date of the transfer, the reasons for the transfer, the legal, economic and social implications for employees and the measures envisaged in respect of them. These obligations apply irrespective of whether the transfer decision is taken by an employer or an undertaking controlling the employer. However, Member States can limit the information and consultation obligations in the Directive to undertakings or businesses which, in terms of the number of employees, meet the conditions for the election or nomination of a collegiate body representing employees. The Commission had previously proposed that the application of these provisions of the Directive be limited to undertakings or businesses with fifty employees or more. In the United Kingdom alone, this would have meant that approximately 35 % of workers would have been excluded from the scope of application of the information and consultation provisions of the Directive.

RECONCILING EMPLOYMENT PROTECTION AND BUSINESS INTERESTS

Even before the adoption of Directive 98/50, More, commenting on the acquired rights case-law of the Court and, particularly, on the controversy surrounding the 1977 Directive's scope, remarked that the case-law demonstrated how the Court's teleological method of interpretation can encounter obstacles where the political climate that engendered a piece of secondary legislation has changed with the passage of time. In her view: 'Whilst employment protection was clearly the predominant aim of the Acquired Rights Directive as it emerged in the 1970s,

---

[149] For a discussion of the minor amendments to the information and consultation provisions see Hardy and Painter (1999), above n 118, 374–75.

the Court has to tread a difficult path in attempting to adapt the application of the Directive to the changed "flexible" business environment of the 1990s.'[150]

Her remarks certainly seem vindicated by the change of heart which the Court experienced in cases like *Rygaard* and *Süzen*, decided at a time of record-breaking, high unemployment in the European Union, when the sweet, cost-cutting promises of globalisation for European businesses were generally presumed to demand less labour market regulation and greater flexibility in the labour market. In the absence of dissenting opinions at the Court of Justice, little can be said about the effect which changes in the Court's composition and the choice of formation had on the outcome of cases like *Rygaard* or *Süzen*. Given the level of political, business and even academic opposition to *Schmidt*, the *Süzen* case had been earmarked as controversial from the outset and a plenary formation was chosen to deliberate it. Many previous contracting out decisions, including *Schmidt*, had been decided by Chambers of five and even three Judges. Decided in 1997, *Süzen* came hot on the heels of the introduction by the Amsterdam Treaty of a title devoted to employment, pursuant to which Member States were to develop a co-ordinated employment strategy aimed at promoting a skilled, trained and adaptable workforce and labour markets responsive to economic change.[151] With flexibility, adaptability and employability now the new leitmotifs of EC employment policy, it was likely that the paramount place previously afforded the objective of employment protection might be challenged.[152] Since the practice of contracting out is an employment form designed to facilitate a high degree of labour flexibility, the court's jurisprudence was regarded in some quarters as overtly protectionist and hence as being in conflict not only with national labour market policies, but also with the employment policy commitments articulated within the political institutions of the European Community.[153] The inflexibility of the EU's labour market has been increasingly criticised in recent years and is seen as responsible for high labour costs and for much of the EU's structural unemployment.[154] Signs of change at the EU level were already evident in the Commission's proposed exclusionary definition of what constitutes a transfer for the purposes of the revised Directive. What was perhaps more surprising was the Court's adoption, in the judicial context of *Süzen*, of the thrust of the Commission's controversial

---

[150] See More (1995), above n 5, 153; and Hunt (1999), above n 91, 223, who observes that the 1998 amendment of Directive 77/187 took place against the backdrop of the employability and adaptability objectives of the European Union's post-Amsterdam employment initiative. Unlike when the original Directive was adopted, the objective with the new amended version was to create the legislative environment in which transfers could be executed without challenging and, if anything, increasing the competitiveness of the undertakings involved.

[151] Article 125 EC. See further the discussion above in ch 3.

[152] For an excellent analysis of the contradictions between employment protection and labour market flexibility in the specific context of transfers of undertakings see More in Shaw and More (eds), above n 32; see also Hunt (1999), above n 91, 229.

[153] Hunt (1998), above n 43, 337-38.

[154] See in this respect EC Commission, *Growth, Competitiveness, Employment: the Challenges and Ways Forward into the 21st Century*, Bull. EC. Supp. 6/93, ch 8, and the discussion above in ch 3.

proposal on contracting out; a fact rendered even more surprising when the Commission was forced to drop its proposal due to opposition from other EU institutions and some Member States. The reasoning of the Court in *Süzen* may have been in purely legal terms, but it did not escape commentators that the supposed clarification in *Süzen* came at a time when unemployment was deemed by the Member States as being of prime concern and when public sector belts were being tightened all over the EU in preparation for EMU.[155]

Yet, although the Court had always chanted the mantra of the Directive's purpose being to protect the employees of a transferred undertaking, its case-law on insolvency, contracting out and the application of the Directive to the public sector all contain examples of it making very clear choices at one stage or another not to strain the objective of employment protection so far that business would be unduly prejudiced. Its extension of the Directive to the contracting out of services on the facts of *Schmidt* may have been extensive, but the Court was quick to indicate to the national court that its application did not in any case exclude the possibility of all dismissals, given the flexibility permitted employers by Article 4(1) of Directive 77/187. Similarly in *Abels*, it drew what many regard as an illogical distinction between transfers in the context of insolvency proceedings which are not covered by the Directive and pre-liquidation transfers which are. It did so not only with the interests of the employees of endangered enterprises in mind, but equally with those of business. The Court has also held that by harmonising the rules applicable to the safeguarding of employees' rights in the event of transfers of undertakings, the intention of the Community legislature was 'both to ensure comparable protection for workers' rights in the different Member States and to harmonize the costs which such protective rules entail for Community undertakings.'[156]

Something in the recent references received by the Court, however, belies the notion that contracting out is universally favoured by companies due to the lower costs and enhanced competitiveness which it affords. In the *Hernández Vidal* and *Sánchez Hidalgo* cases what was in fact at issue was the decision by undertakings to perform in-house services such as cleaning or surveillance which had previously been contracted out. Strikingly, in *G.C. Allen*, a case involving contracted out work in British coal-mines, it emerged that, following privitisation, mining companies which awarded contracts to outside contractors, following competitive invitations to tender, became concerned about the lack of motivation amongst contracted workers. They believed that the cause of this

---

[155] Case C–13/95 *Süzen* was decided during the course of the IGC negotiation of the employment title in the Amsterdam Treaty and some months later the Member States met at an extraordinary European Council meeting in Luxembourg on 20–21 November 1997 to launch a concerted effort to reduce unemployment in the EU. See Bourn (1998), above n 57, 64 and the discussion of the European employment strategy developed pursuant to the employment title in the EC Treaty above ch 3.

[156] See Case C–382/92 *Commission v United Kingdom*, para 15; see also, with reference to the Directive on collective redundancies C–383/92 *Commission v United Kingdom* [1994] ECR I–2479, para 16.

lack of motivation could have been the poor terms and conditions of employment being offered by some of the contractors and subcontractors and recommended to the latter that they provide employees with a minimum period of paid leave and improve other aspects of their conditions of employment. One particular colliery owner decided to switch its contracts to a particular contractor which, albeit engaging its workers on worse terms of employment than the colliery had itself done previously, still provided more favourable terms and conditions than its rivals.[157]

This type of case ties in with broader questions which the EU must confront, about whether at least some Member States' traditional style of labour market regulation and their commitment to a minimum floor of employment protection are compatible with today's globalised, competitive market.[158] Although the jury is still out on whether or not this is the case, an increasing number of commentators have begun to refute the simplistic arguments put forward by those in favour of greater deregulation to the effect that lower wages (and, by implication, less employment protection) necessarily means cheaper services and enhanced competitiveness. In the context of the posted workers Directive,[159] Davies points out that what matters to an employer is not the absolute level of wages and other employment costs, but their level in relation to the productivity of workers: 'In other words, it is the labour cost per unit of output which is the significant issue. Highly paid workers who are highly productive may generate cheaper goods or services than lower paid workers who are inefficient'.[160] Similarly, Deakin argues that the availability of undervalued labour is a cause of productive inefficiency in its own right and encourages low-wage compensation among employers which makes workers increasingly dependent on social security.[161] Ultimately the question whether or not contracting out should come within the scope of the Directive is a political one and in answering it the Community legislature and the Court are deciding whether or not business should be able to achieve lower labour costs by depriving workers of certain rights which they previously enjoyed.[162]

As we have seen, insolvency, like contracting out, has proved another headache for the Court of Justice when determining the scope of application of

---

[157] See further the Opinion of Advocate General Ruiz Jarabo in Case C–234/98 *G.C. Allen*, para 10.

[158] Discussed above ch 3. See, in particular, S. Deakin, 'Labour Law as Market Regulation: the Economic Foundations of European Social Policy' in P. Davies *et al.* (eds), *European Community Labour Law: Principles and Perspectives. Liber Amicorum Lord Wedderburn of Charlton* (Oxford, Clarendon, 1996), pp 63–93.

[159] Council Directive 96/71/EC of 16 December 1996 concerning the posting of workers in the framework of the provision of services, OJ 1997 L18/1.

[160] See P. Davies, 'Posted Workers: Single Market or Protection of National Labour Law Systems' (1997) 34 *Common Market Law Review* 571–602, 599. See also G. Majone, 'The European Community Between Social Policy and Social Regulation' (1993) 31 *Journal of Common Market Studies* 153–70, 160.

[161] Deakin in Davies *et al.* (eds), above n 158, p 85.

[162] See B. Hepple, evidence submitted to the House of Lords Select Committee report on transfers of undertakings (1995–1996), above n 1, p 15. See also More in Shaw and More (eds), above n 32, p 142, who questions to what extent it is legitimate to promote flexibility at the cost of employment protection.

Directive 77/187. In *Abels* and subsequent cases the Court seemed convinced by arguments to the effect that applying the Directive to insolvent transferors would actually detract from the protection of workers which the Directive sought. Yet in evidence submitted to the House of Lords Select Committee for its report on acquired rights, insolvency practitioners emphasised that their interests, in max-imising the recovery and realisation of assets for the benefit of creditors, may also be served by the adoption of practices and procedures which preserve, rather than destroy, jobs. The proceeds on sale of the business as a going concern, may be greater than those on realisation of the assets on a break-up basis.[163] Although this 'rescue culture' is not principally inspired by a desire to benefit employees or the public interest, the preservation of jobs is one of its consequences.[164]

THE PRELIMINARY REFERENCE PROCEDURE AND THE
ACQUIRED RIGHTS DIRECTIVES

A perusal of the Court's case-law on transfer of undertakings also highlights the dilemma it faces when, in the context of preliminary reference procedures, it is asked extremely detailed questions by national courts regarding, effectively, the application of the Directive to the case in hand. The Court and, moreover, its Advocates General, have often observed that there is a distinction between the Court's role under Article 234 EC and the role of the national courts. It is for the former to lay down in general terms the conditions for the transfer of an under-taking and list some of the criteria for assessing whether those conditions are satisfied; while the latter must implement those interpretative criteria by means of factual assessments needed in order to establish whether or not there is a transfer.[165] Advocate General Darmon was particularly clear in the *Bork* case about what he saw as the consequences of this division of functions. Essentially, it was not for the Court to examine in successive references the different possible varieties of, in that case, a temporary cessation of business, in order to distin-guish those which preclude the application of the Directive from those which demand it.[166]

Nevertheless, the constant flow of cases to the Court relating, in particular, to how national courts should determine whether the Directive applies, suggests that national courts, at least those from some jurisdictions, have been unhappy with the guidelines handed down by the Court,[167] find them unworkable, or are

---

[163] See the Report of the House of Lords Select Committee on transfers of undertakings, above n 1, p 20.

[164] *Ibid*, evidence submitted by P. Davies, p 3.

[165] See, for example, para 11 of the Opinion of Advocate General Darmon in Case 101/87 *Bork*.

[166] *Ibid*, para 13.

[167] V. Leccese, 'Italian Courts, the ECJ and Transfers of Undertakings: A Multi-Speed Dialogue?' (1999) 5 *European Law Journal* 311–30, 326 *et seq.* argues that the Italian courts, although expressly citing Court of Justice precedents on contracting out, have been loath to follow the Court's inclu-sive approach to contacting out (at least prior to what appears to be a partial rethinking in Case C–13/95 *Süzen*).

simply lacking in confidence when it comes to applying them to the complicated facts of the business transactions at the heart of the cases before them. Indeed, if one examines the case-law on insolvency or contracting out, it is precisely Darmon's dreaded scenario of case-by-case analysis of whether or not the Directive applies that the Court has been called upon to administer. Leccese remarks that in the *d'Urso* and *Spano* cases the Italian courts were not content to make use of the approach outlined by the Court of Justice in previous cases but instead felt the necessity to ask for the support of the Court in order to obtain confirmation of the applicability of the Court's previous decisions to the specific Italian situation: 'It is almost as though, given the delicacy of the interests at stake, it was particularly important to obtain a *specific* decision from the Court of Justice, which would serve as authoritative support for the proper interpretation of the Directive.'[168] Similarly, underlying Advocate General La Pergola's change of tack in *Süzen*, on the applicability of Directive 77/187 to the contracting out of services, seems to have been his dissatisfaction with the ability of the case-law of the Court to date to provide national courts with sufficiently clear answers.

There are of course exceptions to this reluctance on the part of national courts to get to grips with the application of the Directive. In the United Kingdom, for example, Davies points out that:

> All the decisions of the Employment Appeal Tribunals, the first level of appeal in employment cases, which have been reported in recent years contain both a full citation and consideration of the relevant decisions of the ECJ and an acceptance that that guidance must, wherever possible, be given full effect in domestic law. Indeed, those decisions sometimes display not just an acceptance of the supremacy of EC law but a positive enthusiasm for its principles and a more whole-hearted application of them in the domestic context than the ECJ's guidance perhaps requires.[169]

Although there had been considerable resistance in the United Kingdom prior to *Schmidt* to the idea that all contracting out operations could come within the scope of the Directive, the Court of Appeal, soon after that decision, accepted the Directive's application to public service contracting out.[170] Part of the reason for this appears to be that United Kingdom courts could apply EC principles without being blocked by prior, opposing, national law. Davies also points out that there is a heavy burden on the Court to give effective guidance to national courts and he questions whether the Court is able to construct a coherent and consistent theory of what constitutes a transfer in relation, in particular, to the contracting out of services.[171] The answer to his question seems, in the light of *Süzen*, to be no. Courts in the United Kingdom at least are now divided between

---

[168] V. Leccese, 'Italian Courts, the ECJ and Transfers of Undertakings: A Multi-Speed Dialogue?' (1999) 5 *European Law Journal* 314 and 319.

[169] Davies (1997) EUI WP, above n 46, p 29.

[170] *Dines v Initial Health Care Services* [1994] IRLR 336, discussed in More (1996), above n 5, 145.

[171] Davies (1997) EUI WP, above n 46, p 32.

those willing to apply the restrictive criteria established in *Süzen* and those who regard that decision as depriving employees who most need it of the protection which the Directive previously afforded them.[172] Ironically, in a Member State not renowned in recent years for the commitment of government or the business community to high levels of employment protection, it seems that the United Kingdom government is considering a more straight forward application of the *Schmidt* decision in its secondary legislation and certainly the inclusion of a provision preventing employers from escaping application of the Directive by simply refusing to take on the previous contractor's workforce.

It is submitted that there are a number of reasons for the constant flow of cases to the Court seeking guidance on the interpretation (and application) of Directive 77/187. In the first place, although conceived as a limited tool of employment protection, the 1977 Directive was soon being used to deal with increasingly complicated forms of corporate restructuring, many of which were not foreseen or widespread at the time the Directive was adopted. Take, for example, the extent to which services or activities previously carried out in the public sector have been privatised throughout the EU in the past ten years—some of this privatisation mandated by EC law itself. The text of the 1977 Directive has also been the source of some of the problems experienced by national courts and indeed the Court of Justice—being poorly thought out, incomplete and lacking in clear definitions of the key concepts with which national courts would have to deal. If the disappointed commentaries which greeted the adoption of the amended Directive prove correct, many references are likely to follow that Directive's entry into force for some similar reasons.[173] At least some of the blame for continued lack of certainty regarding the interpretation of the Directive's provisions must be laid at the door of the Community legislature and, hence, at that of the Member States. As before, they have left the Court to resolve some of the most difficult questions which transfers of undertakings may raise.

Secondly, frequent references may be an inevitable consequence of the criteria laid down by the Court in its case-law from *Spijkers* onwards to determine whether the conditions for the transfer of an economic entity within the scope of the Directive are met. If the importance to be attached to each criterion varies according to the activity carried on, or indeed the production or operating methods employed in the relevant undertaking,[174] some national courts will be tempted to call on the Court for assistance in carrying out the assessment which the case-law and the division of functions pursuant to Article 234 EC actually requires them to undertake. The Court itself confuses matters further by shying away in some cases from 'application' of the Directive to the facts of the reference before it, while not being at all shy in others when it comes to indicating to

---

[172] See the discussion of the case-law in Davies (2001), above n 88, 234–35.
[173] See, for example, Davies (1998), above n 144.
[174] See Cases C–51/00 *Temco Industries* and C–172/99 *Oy Likenne*, para 35.

national courts whether, for example, they are dealing with a stable economic entity and whether, in consequence, the Directive applies.[175]

Thirdly, reference has been made elsewhere in this book to a possible reticence on the part of some national courts to resolve cases themselves and engage fully in the application of EC law in accordance with their role as Community courts. Re-reading the case-law on acquired rights one has the clear feeling that certain cases could quite easily have been decided at national level without reference to the Court of Justice. A fourth factor—which recurs throughout the book—is the ambiguous and changing nature of the Court's role pursuant to Article 234 EC. In this as in other contexts the Court has found itself increasingly charged with the application and not merely interpretation of EC law to the cases referred to it. Sometimes this is the inevitable result of the detailed nature of the questions devised by national courts, at other times it seems to be of the Court's own choosing. Although it has used acquired rights cases to expound general principles regarding the interpretation of Directive 77/187[176]— what could be regarded as fulfilment of its public interest role in the reference procedure—the Court has also come perilously close to dispute resolution.[177] The increasing assumption of the latter role may actually incite more national courts to refer questions to the Court when, in reality, existing case-law provides them with sufficiently clear guidelines with reference to which they can resolve the case at national level. National courts may find it increasingly difficult to extract a clear *ratio* from the Court's previous rulings when the latter are closely bound up with the factual circumstances and specifics of the references that spawned them. A never-ending stream of references on acquired rights which places the Court increasingly in the role of dispute resolver is clearly at odds with the Court's understandable preoccupation about the over-loading of the Community's judicial system. But is it not the inevitable result of reliance on the preliminary reference procedure for the development of the law in such a fact specific context?

---

[175] See, for example, Case C–172/99 *Oy Likenne*, paras 32, 39–43. See also C. Engels and L. Salas, 'Cause and Consequence, What's the Difference in respect of the EC Transfer Directive?' in C. Engels and M. Weiss (eds), *Labour Law and Industrial Relations at the Turn of the Century. Liber Amicorum in honour of Roger Blanpain* (The Hague, Kluwer, 1998), pp 275–89, p 289, who point out that the answer to the question whether a certain transaction is a transfer of an entreprise within the meaning of the Directive is highly fact specific: 'it is not surprising therefore that the predictability of the outcome of the court cases is not very high.'

[176] See, for example, Case C–24/85 *Spijkers*.

[177] See, however, D. Wyatt, 'Procedure and Principles' in M. Andenas (ed), *Article 177 References to the European Court—Policy and Practice* (London, Butterworths, 1994) pp 77–81, p 81: who thinks that the Court has been surefooted in the field of transfers of undertakings in distinguishing between interpretation and application: 'While the question of principle whether a particular transaction is capable of constituting a transfer is clearly a 'referable' question, the assessment in a particular case of the significance to be attached to, say, the transfer or not of particular moveable or immovable property raises questions which the European Court will decline to answer, and will leave to the national court. . . .The transfer of undertakings example is a good example for the future. A workable delimitation of the relationship between the Court of Justice and national courts is the interpretation and application of Community law.'

Bibliography

Alexander, W., 'La recevabilité des renvois préjudiciels dans la perspective de la réforme institutionelle de 1996' (1995) *Cahiers de droit européen* 561–76.

Alter, K.J. and Vargas, J., 'Explaining Variation in the Use of European Litigation Strategies. European Community Law and British Gender Equality Policy'(2000) 33 *Comparative Political Studies* 452–82.

Andenas, M. (ed), *Article 177 References to the European Court—Policy and Practice* (London, Butterworths, 1994).

Anderman, S., 'Constitutional Law and Labour Law Dimensions of Article 119: The Case of Justification for Indirect Discrimination' in Dine, J. and Watt, B. (eds), *Discrimination Law: concepts, limitations and justifications* (London, Longman, 1996) pp 100–09.

Anderson, D., *References to the European Court* (London, Sweet & Maxwell, 1995).

Armstrong, K.A. and Bulmer, S.J., *The governance of the Single European Market* (Manchester, Manchester University Press, 1999).

Arnull, A., 'Owning up to fallability: precedent and the Court of Justice' (1993) 30 *Common Market Law Review* 247–66.

——, 'Judging the New Europe' (1994) 19 *European Law Review* 3–15.

——, 'Judicial architecture or judicial folly? The challenge facing the European Union' (1999) 24 *European Law Review* 516–24.

——, 'References to the European Court' (1990) 15 *European Law Review* 375–91.

——, 'Taming the Beast? The Treaty of Amsterdam and the Court of Justice' in O'Keeffe, D. and Twomey, P. (eds), *Legal Issues of the Amsterdam Treaty* (Oxford, Hart Publishing, 1999) pp 109–21.

——, 'When is pregnancy like an arthritic hip?' (1992) 17 *European Law Review* 265–73.

——, *The European Union and its Court of Justice* (Oxford, OUP, 1999).

Arrowsmith, S., 'Developments in Compulsory Competitive Tendering' (1994) 3 *Public Procurement Law Review* CS153–CS172.

Ashiagbor, D., 'EMU and the Shift in the European Labour Law Agenda: From 'Social Policy' to 'Employment Policy'' (2001) 7 *European Law Journal* 311–30.

Bailey, S., 'Equal Treatment/Special Treatment : The Dilemma of the Dismissed Pregnant Employee' (1989) *Journal of Social Welfare Law* 85–100.

Ball, S., 'The European Employment Strategy: The Will but not the Way?' (2001) 30 *Industrial Law Journal* 353–74.

Bamforth, N., 'The Treatment of Pregnancy Under European Community Sex Discrimination Law' (1995) 1 *European Public Law* 59–68.

Banks, K., 'Social Security—Objective Justification in the Context of Indirect Discrimination' (1991) *Industrial Law Journal* 220–23.

Barav, A., 'Le juge et le justiciable' in *Scritti in onore di Giuseppe Federico Mancini* (Milan, Giuffrè, 1998) pp 1–74.

——, 'Preliminary Censorship? The Judgment of the European Court in *Foglia v Novello* (1980) 5 *European Law Review* 443–68.

Barnard, C., 'EC 'Social' Policy' in Craig, P. and De Búrca, G. (eds), *The Evolution of EU Law* (Oxford, OUP, 1999) pp 479–516.

——, 'Flexibility and Social Policy' in De Búrca, G. and Scott, J. (eds), *Constitutional Change in the European Union. From Uniformity to Flexibility?* (Oxford, Hart Publishing, 2000) pp 197–217.

——, 'Gender Equality in the EU: A Balance Sheet' in Alston, P. (ed), *The EU and Human Rights* (Oxford, OUP, 1999) pp 215–79.

——, *EC Employment Law*, 2nd edn. (Oxford, OUP, 2000).

Barnard, C. and Hepple, B., 'Indirect Discrimination: Interpreting *Seymour-Smith*' (1999) *Cambridge Law Journal* 399–412.

Barnard, C. and Hervey, T., 'Softening the approach to quotas: positive action after *Marschall*' (1998) 20 *Journal of Social Welfare and Family Law* 333–52.

Barnard, C. and Sharpston, E., 'The Changing Face of Article 177 References' (1997) 34 *Common Market Law Review* 1113–71.

Basenach, K., 'How judgments are reached in the Court of Justice of the European Communities in Luxembourg – Legal Basis and Legal Practice' (1993) *European Food Law Review* 51–70.

Bator, P.M., Meltzer, D.J., Mishkin, P.J. and Shapiro, D.L., *Hart and Wechsler's Federal Courts and Federal System*, 3rd edn, (Westbury/New York, Foundation Press, 1988).

Bebr, G., 'The Possible Implications of *Foglia v Novello II*' (1982) 19 *Common Market Law Review* 421–41.

Bennett, J. and Belgrave, S.L., 'Taking Stock after *Rygaard*' (1996) 5 *Public Procurement Law Review* CS16–CS25.

Bercusson, B., *European Labour Law* (London, Butterworths, 1996).

Bernard, N., 'Legislating European Union Law: Is the Social Dialogue the Way Forward?' in Shaw, J. (ed), *Social Law and Policy in an Evolving European Union* (Oxford, Hart Publishing, 2001) pp 279–301.

——, 'What Are the Purposes of EC Discrimination Law' in Dine, J. and Watt, B. (eds), *Discrimination Law: concepts, limitations and justifications* (London, Longman, 1996) pp 77–99.

Bertola, G., Boeri, T. and Caves, S., 'La protection de l'emploi dans les pays industrialisés: repenser les indicateurs' (2000) 139 *Revue internationale du Travail* 61–78.

——, *Labour Markets in the European Union*, EUI Working Papers, RSC No 99/24.

Beveridge, F. and Nott, S., 'Gender Auditing—Making the Community Work for Women' in Hervey, T. and O'Keeffe, D. (eds), *Sex Equality Law in the European Union* (Chichester, John Wiley, 1996) pp 383–98.

Biagi, M., 'The Impact of European Employment Strategy on the Role of Labour Law and Industrial Relations' (2000) 16 *International Journal of Comparative Labour Law and Industrial Relations* 155–73.

——, 'The Implemention of the Amsterdam Treaty with Regard to Employment: Co–ordination or Convergence?' (1998) 14 *International Journal of Comparative Labour Law and Industrial Relations* 325–36.

Blanpain, R., *et al.* (eds), *Institutional Changes and European Social Policies after the Treaty of Amsterdam* (The Hague, Kluwer Law International, 1998).

Boch, C., 'Official: During Pregnancy, Females are Pregnant' (1998) 23 *European Law Review* 488–94.

——, 'Où s'arrête le principe de l'égalité ou de l'importance d'être bien-portante (à propos de l'arrêt *Larsson* de la Cour de justice)' (1998) *Cahiers de droit européen* 177–90.

Bourn, C., 'When Does the Transfer of a Service Contract Constitute the Transfer of an Undertaking?' (1998) 23 *European Law Review* 59–64.

Bourn, C. and Whitmore, J., *Discrimination and Equal Pay* (London, Sweet & Maxwell, 1989).

Bramhall, P., 'Application of the Acquired Rights Directive to Contracting Out of Services: The Decision of the European Court of Justice in the Case of *Süzen*' (1997) 6 *Public Procurement Law Review* 179–81.

British Institute for International and Comparative Law, *The Role and Future of the European Court of Justice* (London, BIICL, 1996).

Brown, N.L. and Kennedy, T., *Brown & Jacobs The Court of Justice of the European Communities*, 4th edn. (London, Sweet & Maxwell, 1994).

Burrows, N., 'Maternity Rights in Europe—An Embryonic Legal Regime' (1991) 11 *Yearbook of European Law* 273–93.

Busby, N., 'Divisions of Labour: maternity protection in Europe' (2000) 22 *Journal of Social Welfare and Family Law* 277–94.

Canor, I., *The Limits of Judicial Discretion in the European Court of Justice* (Baden Baden, Nomos).

Caracciolo di Torella, E., 'The 'Family-Friendly Workplace': the EC Position' (2001) 17 *International Journal of Comparative Labour Law and Industrial Relations* 325–44.

——, 'Recent Developments in Pregnancy and Maternity Rights' (1999) 28 *Industrial Law Journal* 276–82.

Caracciolo di Torella, E. and Masselot, A., 'Pregnancy, maternity and the organisation of family life: an attempt to classify the case law of the Court of Justice' (2001) 26 *European Law Review* 239–60.

Chalmers, D., 'Judicial Preferences and the Community Legal Order' (1997) 60 *Modern Law Review* 164–99.

Chayes, A., 'The Role of the Judge in Public Law Litigation' (1976) 89 *Harvard Law Review* 1281–316.

Claussen, C.L., 'Incorporating Women's Reality into Legal Neutrality in the European Community: The Sex Segregation of Labor and the Work-Family Nexus' (1991) 22 *Law & Policy in International Business* 787–811.

Colucci, M., 'Searching for a European Employment Strategic Initiative' in Blanpain, R. *et al.* (eds), *Institutional Changes and European Social Policies after the Treaty of Amsterdam* (The Hague, Kluwer Law International, 1998) pp 101–156.

Common Market Law Review Editorial Comments, 'Growth, competitiveness and employment: the challenges facing the Union' (1994) 31 *Common Market Law Review* 1–6.

Cousins, M., 'Equal Treatment and Social Security' (1994) 19 *European Law Review* 123–45.

Craig, P. and De Búrca, G., *EC Law. Texts, Cases & Materials* (Oxford, Clarendon Press, 1995).

Cromack, V., 'The E.C. Pregnancy Directive—Principle or Pragmatism' (1993) *Journal of Social Welfare and Family Law* 261–72.

Cullen, H., 'The Subsidiary Woman' (1994) *Journal of Social Welfare and Family Law* 407–21.

Davies, P. 'Transfers of Undertakings' in Sciarra, S. (ed), *Labour Law in the Courts: National Judges and the European Court of Justice* (Oxford, Hart Publishing, 2001) pp 131–44.

Davies, P., 'Acquired Rights, Creditors' Rights, Freedom of Contract, and Industrial Democracy' (1989) 9 *Yearbook of European Law* 21–53.

——, 'Amendments to the Acquired Rights Directive' (1998) 27 *Industrial Law Journal* 365–73.

——, 'Market Integration and Social Policy in the Court of Justice' (1995) 24 *Industrial Law Journal* 49–77.

——, 'Posted Workers: Single Market or Protection of National Labour Law Systems' (1997) 34 *Common Market Law Review* 571–602.

——, 'Transfers – the United Kingdom Will Have to Make Up its own Mind' (2001) 30 *Industrial Law Journal* 231–35.

——, *The Relationship between the European Court of Justice and the British Courts over the Interpretation of Directive 77/187/EC*, EUI WP Law No.97/2.

Davies, P. *et al.* (eds), *European Community Labour Law: Principles and Perspectives. Liber Amicorum Lord Wedderburn of Charlton* (Oxford, Clarendon Press, 1996).

De Búrca, G., 'The Principle of Subsidiarity and the Court of Justice as an Institutional Actor' (1998) 36 *Journal of Common Market Studies* 217–35.

De Groot, C., 'The Council Directive on the Safeguarding of Employees' Rights in the Event of Transfers of Undertakings: an Overview of Recent Case Law' (1998) 35 *Common Market Law Review* 707–29.

De la Mare, T., 'Article 177 in Social and Political Context' in Craig, P. and De Búrca, G. (eds), *The Evolution of EU Law* (Oxford, OUP, 1999).

Deakin, S., 'Labour Law as Market Regulation: the Economic Foundations of European Social Policy' in Davies, P. *et al.* (eds), *European Community Labour Law: Principles and Perspectives. Liber Amicorum Lord Wedderburn of Charlton* (Oxford, Clarendon Press, 1996) pp 63–93.

——, 'Equality Under a Market Order: The Employment Act 1989' (1990) *Industrial Law Journal* 1–18.

Deakin, S. and Morris, G., *Labour Law* (London, Butterworths, 1998).

Deakin, S. and Reed, H., 'The Contested Meaning of Labour Market Flexibility: Economic Theory and the Discourse of European Integration' in Shaw, J. (ed), *Social Law and Policy in an Evolving European Union* (Oxford, Hart Publishing, 2000) pp 71–99.

Deakin, S. and Wilkinson, F., 'Rights vs Efficiency? The Economic Case for Transnational Labour Standards' (1994) 23 *Industrial Law Journal* 289–310.

Dehousse, R., 'Integration Through Law Revisited: Some Thoughts on the Jurisdiction of the European Political Process' in Snyder, F. (ed), *The Europeanisation of Law: the Legal Effects of European Integration* (Oxford, Hart Publishing, 2000) pp 15–29.

Demaret, P., 'Le juge et le jugement dans l'Europe d'aujourd'hui: la Cour de justice des Communautés européennes' in Jacob, R. (ed), *Le juge et le jugement dans les traditions juridiques européennes: Études d'histoire comparée* (Paris, L.G.D.J., 1996) pp 303–77.

Docksey, C., 'The Principle of Equality Between Women and Men as a Fundamental Right Under EC Law' (1991) 20 *Industrial Law Journal* 258–80.

Easson, A. 'Legal Approaches to European Integration: The Role of Court and Legislator in the Completion of the European Common Market' (1989) XII *Revue d'Intégration européenne/Journal of European Integration* 100–19.

EC Commission, *Growth, Competitiveness, Employment: the Challenges and Ways Forward into the 21st Century*, Bull. EC. Supp. 6/93.

ECB, *Labour Market Mismatches in Euro Area Countries*, March 2002.

Edward, D.A.O., 'Advocacy Before the Court of Justice. Hints for the Uninitiated' in Barling, G. and Brealey, M. (eds), *Practitioners' Handbook of EC Law* (London, Trenton Publishing, 1998) pp 27–45.

——, 'How the Court of Justice Works' (1995) 20 *European Law Review* 539–58.

——, 'What Kind of Law Does Europe Need? The Role of Law, Lawyers and Judges in Contemporary European Integration' (1998/99) 5 *Columbia Journal of European Law* 1–14.

Eeckhout, P., 'The European Court of Justice and the Legislature' (1998) 18 *Yearbook of European Law* 1–28.

Ellis, E., 'The Definition of Discrimination in European Community Sex Equality Law' (1994) 19 *European Law Review* 563–80.

——, 'Gender Discrimination Law in the EC' in Dine, J. and Watt, B. (eds), *Discrimination Law: Concepts, Limitations and Justifications* (London, Longman, 1996) pp 14–30.

——, 'Protection of Pregnancy and Maternity' (1993) 22 *Industrial Law Journal* 63–7.

——, 'Recent Case Law of the Court of Justice on the Equal Treatment of Men and Women' (1994) 31 *European Law Review* 43–75.

——, 'Recent Developments in European Community Sex Equality Law' (1998) 35 *Common Market Law Review* 379–408, 379–81.

——, 'The Concept of Proportionality in European Community Sex Discrimination Law' in Ellis, E. (ed), *The Principle of Proportionality in the Laws of Europe* (Oxford, Hart Publishing, 1999) pp 165–81.

——, 'The Recent Jurisprudence of the Court of Justice in the Field of Sex Equality' (2000) 37 *Common Market Law Review* 1403–26.

——, *EC Sex Equality Law* (Oxford, Oxford University Press, 1991).

Engels, C. and Salas, L., 'Cause and Consequence, What's the Difference in respect of the EC Transfer Directive?' in Engels, C. and Weiss, M. (eds), *Labour Law and Industrial Relations at the Turn of the Century. Liber Amicorum in honour of Roger Blanpain* (The Hague, Kluwer, 1998), pp 275–89.

Escott, K. and Whitfield, D., *The Gender Impact of CCT in Local Government*, Centre for Public Services, UK Equal Opportunities Commission Research Discussion Series (EOC, 1995), No 12.

Eurobrief, 'The Acquired Rights Directive' (1995) *European Business Law Review* 82–5.

Everling, U., 'Reflections on the Reasoning in the Judgments of the Court of Justice of the European Communities' in *Festskrift til Ole Due* (Copenhagen, G.E.C. Gads Forlag, 1994) pp 55–74.

——, 'The Member States of the EC before their Court of Justice' (1984) 9 *European Law Review* 215–41.

Evju, S., 'Collective Agreements and Competition Law. The *Albany* Puzzle, and *van der Woude*' (2001) 17 *International Journal of Comparative Labour Law and Industrial Relations* 165–84.

Fairhurst, J., 'SIMAP—Interpreting the Working Time Directive' (2001) 30 *Industrial Law Journal* 236–43.

Fenwick, H., 'Indirect Discrimination in Equal Pay Claims: Backward Steps in the European Court of Justice' (1995) 1 *European Public Law* 331–8.

——, 'From Formal to Substantive Equality : the Place of Affirmative Action in EU Sex Equality Law' (1998) 4 *European Public Law* 507–16.

Fenwick, H. and Hervey, T., 'Sex Equality in the Single Market: New Directions for the European Court of Justice' (1995) 32 *Common Market Law Review* 443–70.

Fernández Martín, J.M. and O'Leary, S., 'Judicially-created exceptions to the free provision of services' (2000) 11 *European Business Law Review* 347–62.

——, *The EC Public Procurement Rules. A Critical Analysis* (Oxford, Clarendon Press, 1996).

Finlay, L., 'Transcending Equality Theory: A Way Out of the Maternity and Workplace Debate' (1986) 86 *Columbia Law Review* 1118–82.

Fiss, O.M., 'The Social and Political Foundations of Adjudication' (1982) 6 *Law and Human Behaviour* 121–8.

Fitzpatrick, B., 'Towards Strategic Litigation? Innovations in Sex Equality Litigation Procedures in the Member States of the European Community' (1992) 8 *International Journal of Comparative Labour Law and Industrial Relations* 208–31.

——, 'Converse Pyramids and the EU Social Constitution' in Shaw, J. (ed), *Social Law and Policy in an Evolving European Union* (Oxford, Hart Publishing, 2001) pp 303–24.

Flynn, L., 'Equality between Men and Women in the Court of Justice' (1998) 18 *Yearbook of European Law* 259–87.

Fredman, S., 'Affirmative Action and the Court of Justice: A Critical Analysis' in Shaw, J. (ed), *Social Law and Policy in an Evolving European Union* (Oxford, Hart Publishing, 2000) pp 171–95.

——, 'European Community Discrimination Law: A Critique' (1992) 21 *Industrial Law Journal* 119–34

——, 'Labour Law in Flux: the Changing Composition of the Workforce' (2000) 26 *Industrial Law Journal* 337–52.

——, 'Parenthood and the Right to Work' (1995) 111 *Law Quarterly Review* 220–3.

——, 'Social Law in the European Union: The impact of the lawmaking process' in Craig, P. and Harlow, C. (eds), *Lawmaking in the European Union* (London, Kluwer Law International, 1998) pp 386–411.

——, 'A Difference with Distinction : Pregnancy and Parenthood Reassessed' (1994) 110 *Law Quarterly Review* 106–23.

Freedland, M., 'Employment Policy' in Davies, P. *et al.* (eds), *European Community Labour Law: Principles and Perspectives. Liber Amicorum Lord Wedderburn of Charlton* (Oxford, Clarendon Press, 1996) pp 275–309.

Freestone, D., 'The European Court of Justice' in Lodge, J. (ed), *Institutions and Policies of the European Communities* (London, Frances Pinter (Publishers), 1983) pp 43–53.

Friedbacher, T., 'Motive Unmasked: The European Court of Justice, the Free Movement of Goods and the Search for Legitimacy' (1996) 2 *European Law Journal* 226–50.

Fuller, L.L., 'The Forms and Limits of Adjudication' (1978) 92 *Harvard Law Review* 353–409.

Geyer, R. and Springer, B., 'EU Social Policy After Maastricht: The Works Council Directive and the British Opt-Out' in Laurent and M. Maresceau, P.-H., (eds), *The State of the European Union. Deepening and Widening*, Vol.4 (Boulder and London, Lynne Rienner Publishers, 1998) pp 207–23.

Gormley, L., 'Assent and respect for judgments: uncommunautaire reasoning in the European Court of Justice' in Krämer, L. *et al.* (eds), *Law and Diffuse Interests in the*

European Legal Order. Liber Amicorum Norbert Reich (Baden-Baden, Nomos, 1997) pp 11–29.

Guild, E., 'How Can Social Protection Survive EMU? A United Kingdom Perspective' (1999) 24 *European Law Review* 22–37.

Guild, E. and Martin, D., *The Free Movement of Persons in the European Union* (London, Butterworths, 1996).

Handoll, J., *The Free Movement of Persons in the European Union* (Chichester, Wiley, 1995).

Hardy, S. and Painter, R.W., 'The New Acquired Rights Directive and its Implications for European Employee Relations in the Twenty-First Century' (1998) 6 *Maastricht Journal of International and Comparative Law* 366–79.

Harlow, C., *Citizens Access to Political Power in the European Union*, EUI WP RSC No.99/2.

Hartley, T., 'The European Court, Judicial Objectivity and the Constitution of the European Union' (1996) *Law Quarterly Review* 95–109.

Hattersley, R., 'In Search of the Third Way' (2000) 71 *Granta* 231–55.

Hepple, B., 'Equality and Discrimination' in Davies, P. *et al* (eds), *European Community Labour Law: Principles and Perspectives. Liber Amicorum Lord Wedderburn of Charlton* (Oxford, Clarendon Press, 1996) pp 237–59.

——, 'Social Values and European Law' (1995) 48 *Current Legal Problems* 39–61.

Hervey, T., 'Sex Equality in Social Protection: New Institutionalist Perspectives on Allocation of Competence' (1998) 4 *European Law Journal* 196–219.

——, 'Social Solidarity: A Buttress Against Internal Market Law?' in Shaw, J. (ed), *Social Law and Policy in an Evolving European Union* (Oxford, Hart Publishing, 2000) pp 31–47.

——, *European Social Law and Policy* (Harlow, Longman, 1998).

Hervey, T. and Shaw, J., 'Women, Work and Care: Women's Dual Role and Double Burden in EC Sex Equality Law' (1998) 8 *Journal of European Social Policy* 43–63.

Hix, S., *The Political System of the European Union* (Basingstoke, MacMillan, 1999).

Hocking, B., 'Indirect Discrimination: A Comparative Overview' (1992) *International Journal of Comparative Labour Law and Industrial Relations* 232–56.

Honeyball, S., 'Pregnancy and Sex Discrimination' (2000) 29 *Industrial Law Journal* 43–52.

House of Lords Select Committee on the European Communities, *Protection at work of pregnant women and women who have recently given birth and child care*, HOL Session 1991–92, 2nd report.

House of Lords Select Committee on the European Communities, *The EU Social Policy Agenda*, Session 1999–2000, 20th Report.

House of Lords Select Committee on the European Communities, *Transfer of Undertakings: Acquired Rights*, Session 1995–1996, 5th Report.

Hunt, J., 'Success at last? The amendment of the Acquired Rights Directive' (1999) 24 *European Law Review* 215–30.

——, 'The Court of Justice as a Policy Actor: the case of the acquired rights directive' (1998) *Legal Studies* 336–59.

Issacharoff, S. and Rosenblum, E., 'Women and the Workplace: Accommodating the Demands of Pregnancy' (1994) 94 *Columbia Law Review* 2154–221.

Issing, I., *Cuadernos de Información Económica*, No.112, Madrid, July 1996.

Jacobs, F., 'Advocates General and Judges in the European Court of Justice: some personal reflections' in O'Keeffe, D. (ed), *Liber Amicorum in Honour of Lord Slynn of Hadley. Judicial Review in European Law* (The Hague, Kluwer Law International, 2000) pp 17–28.

Jacobs, F.G. and Karst, K.L., 'The 'Federal' Legal Order: The U.S.A. and Europe Compared. A Juridical Perspective' in Cappelletti, M., Seccombe, M. and Weiler, J.H.H. (eds), *Integration Through Law*, Vol.1 Bk.1 (Berlin, de Gruyter, 1985) pp 169–243.

Jacqmain, J., 'Pregnancy as grounds for dismissal' (1994) 23 *Industrial Law Journal* 355–59.

Jolowicz, J.A., 'The role of the supreme court at the national and international level' in Yessiou-Faltsi (ed), *The role of the supreme courts at the national and international level* (Thessaloniki, Sakkoulas, 1998) pp 37–63.

Kapteyn, P.J.G. and VerLoren van Themaat, P., *Introduction to the Law of the European Communities*, 3rd edn. edited and further revised by Gormley, L.W. (The Hague, Kluwer Law International, 1999).

Keeling, D., 'In Praise of Judicial Activism. But What Does it Mean? And has the European Court of Justice Ever Practised it?' in *Scritti in onore di Giuseppe Federico Mancini*, Vol. II, Diritto dell'Unione Europea (Milano, Giuffrè, 1998) pp 505–36.

Kennedy, T., 'First Steps Towards European *Certiorari*?' (1993) 18 *European Law Review* 121–9.

——, 'Thirteen Russians! The Composition of the European Court of Justice' in Campbell, A.I.L. and Voyatzi, M. (eds), *Legal Reasoning and Judicial Interpretation of European Law. Essays in Honour of Lord Mackenzie-Stuart* (London, Trenton Publishing, 1996) pp 69–91.

Kenner, J., 'Employment and Macroeconomics in the EC Treaty: A Legal and Political Symbiosis?' (2000) 7 *Maastricht Journal of European and Comparative Law* 375–97.

——, 'The EC Employment Title and the 'Third Way': Making Soft Law Work?' (1999) 15 *International Journal of Comparative Labour Law and Industrial Relations* 33–60.

Kenney, S., 'Beyond Principals and Agents. Seeing Courts as Organisations by Comparing *Référendaires* at the European Court of Justice and Law Clerks at the U.S. Supreme Court' (2000) 33 *Comparative Political Studies* 593–625.

——, 'The Members of the Court of Justice of the European Communities' (1998) 5 *Columbia Journal of European Law* 101–33.

Kilpatrick, C., 'Community or Communities of Courts in European Integration? Sex Equality Dialogues Between UK Courts and the ECJ' (1998) 4 *European Law Journal* 121–47.

Koopmans, T., 'Judicial Decision-Making' in Campbell, A.I.L. and Voyatzi, M. (eds), *Legal Reasoning and Judicial Interpretation of European Law. Essays in Honour of Lord Mackenzie-Stuart* (London, Trenton Publishing, 1996) pp 93–104.

——, 'The Future of the Court of Justice of the European Communities' (1991) 11 *Yearbook of European Law* 15–32.

Körner, M., 'The Impact of Community Law on German Labour Law—the example of transfer of undertakings' EUI WP Law No 96/8.

Lagrange, M., 'The Theory of *Acte Clair*: A Bone of Contention or a Source of Unity?' (1971) 8 *Common Market Law Review* 313–24.

Lasok, P.E., *The European Court of Justice. Practice and Procedure* (London, Butterworths, 1994).

Leccese, V., 'Italian Courts, the ECJ and Transfers of Undertakings: A Multi-Speed Dialogue?' (1999) 5 *European Law Journal* 311–30.

Legnier, M.F.G.M., 'Transferts d'entreprises et protection des travailleurs dans le cadre communautaire' (1977) *Revue du Marché Commun* 473–82.

Leibfried, S. and Pierson, P., 'Social Policy' in H. Wallace and W. Wallace (eds), *Policy-making in the European Union* (Oxford, OUP, 1996) pp 185–207.

Lenaerts, K. and Foubert, P., 'Social Rights in the Case-law of the European Court of Justice' (2001) 28 *Legal Issues of Economic Integration* 267–96.

——, K., 'Form and Substance of the Preliminary Rulings Procedure' in Curtin, D. and Heukels, T. (eds), *Institutional Dynamics of European Integration. Essays in Honour of H.G. Schermers*, Vol. II (Dordrecht, Martinus Nijhoff, 1994) pp 355–80.

Lewis, P., 'Pregnant Workers and Sex Discrimination: the Limits of Purposive Non-comparative Methodology' (2000) *International Journal of Comparative Labour Law and Industrial Relations* 55–69.

Lourtie, P., *Solving Europe's Unemployment Problem. The Demystification of Flexibility*, College of Europe, WP No.10 (Brussels, European Interuniversity Press, 1995).

Luckhaus, L., 'Egalité de traitement, protection sociale et garantie de ressources pour les femmes' (2000) 139 *Revue internationale du Travail* 163–99.

MacKinnon, C.A., 'Reflections on Sex Equality Under Law' (1991) 100 *Yale Law Journal* 1281–328.

Maher, I., 'National Courts as European Community Courts' (1994) 14 *Legal Studies* 226–43.

Majone, G., 'The European Community Between Social Policy and Social Regulation' (1993) 31 *Journal of Common Market Studies* 153–70.

Mancini, G.F., 'The role of the supreme courts at the national and international level: a case study of the Court of Justice of the European Communities' in Yessiou-Faltsi, P. (ed), *The role of the supreme courts at the national and international level* (Thessaloniki, Sakkoulas, 1998) pp 421–52.

Mancini, G.F. and Keeling, D., 'Language, Culture and Politics in the Life of the European Court of Justice' (1995) 1 *Columbia Journal of European Law* 397–413.

——, 'From *CILFIT* to *ERT*: the constitutional challenge facing the European Court' (1991) 11 *Yearbook of European Law* 1–13.

Mancini, G.F. and O'Leary, S., 'The new frontiers of sex equality law in the European Union' (1999) 24 *European Law Review* 331–53.

Martin, A., *Social Pacts, Unemployment and EMU Macroeconomic Policy*, EUI WP RSC No 2000/32.

Masselot, A. and Berthou, K., 'La CJCE, le droit de la maternité et le principe de non discrimination—vers une clarification?' (2000) *Cahiers de droit européen* 637–56.

Mattli, W. and Slaughter, A.-M., *Constructing the European Community Legal System from the Ground Up: The Role of Individual Litigants and National Courts*, EUI WP RSC No 96/56.

Mazey, S., 'EC Action on Behalf of Women: The Limits of Legislation' (1988) 27 *Journal of Common Market Studies* 63–84.

Mazey, S. and Richardson, J., 'Agenda Setting, Lobbying and the 1996 IGC' in Edwards, G. and Pijpers, A. (eds), *The Politics of European Treaty Reform* (London, Pinter, 1997) pp 226–48.

McCaffrey, E.J., 'Slouching Towards Equality: Gender Discrimination, Market Efficiency and Social Change' (1993) 103 *Yale Law Journal* 595–675.

McColgan, A., 'Family Friendly Frolics? The Maternity and Parental Leave etc. Regulations 1999' (2000) 29 *Industrial Law Journal* 125–43.

——, *Just Wages for Women* (Oxford, Clarendon Press, 1997).

McCrudden, C. (ed), *Equality of Treatment Between Men and Women in Social Security* (London, Butterworths, 1994).

McGlynn, C., 'Equality, Maternity and Questions of Pay' (1996) 21 *European Law Review* 327–32.

——, 'Ideologies of Motherhood in EC Sex Equality Law' (2000) 6 *European Law Journal* 29–44.

——, 'Pregnancy, Parenthood and the Court of Justice in *Abdoulaye*' (2000) 25 *European Law Review* 654–62.

——, 'Women, representation and the legal academy' (1999) 19 *Legal Studies* 68–92.

McRae, S., *Maternity Rights in Britain. The Experience of Women and Employers* (London, Policy Studies Institute).

Meulders, D. and Plasman, R., 'European Economic Policies and Social Quality' in Beck, W., Van der Maesen, L. and Walker, A. (eds), *The Social Quality of Europe* (1997), pp 15–33.

Mills, J.K., 'Childcare Leave: Unequal Treatment in the European Economic Community' (1992) *The University of Chicago Legal Forum* 497–515.

Moravcsik, A. and Nicolaïdis, K., 'Explaining the Treaty of Amsterdam: Interests, Influence and Institutions' (1999) 37 *Journal of Common Market Studies* 59–85.

More, G., 'Reflections on pregnancy discrimination under European Community law' (1992) *Journal of Social Welfare and Family Law* 48–56.

——, 'The Acquired Rights Directive: frustrating or facilitating labour market flexibility?' in Shaw, J. and More, G. (eds), *New Legal Dynamics of European Union* (Oxford, Clarendon Press, 1995) pp 129–45.

——, 'The Concept of 'undertaking' in the Acquired Rights Directive: the Court of Justice under pressure (again)' (1995) 15 *Yearbook of European Law* 135–55.

——, 'The Principle of Equal Treatment: From Market Unifier to Fundamental Right?' in Craig, P. and De Búrca, G. (eds), *The Evolution of EU Law* (Oxford, OUP, 1999) pp 517–53.

Morris, A. and Nott, S., 'The legal response to pregnancy' (1992) 12 *Legal Studies* 54–73.

N. Bruun, 'The European Employment Strategy and the '*Acquis Communautaire*' of Labour Law' (2001) 17 *International Journal of Comparative Labour Law and Industrial Relations* 309–24.

Nazerali, J. and Plumbley-Jones, K., 'New Draft Acquired Rights Directive—A Step in the Dark?' (1995) *European Business Law Review* 31–6.

Neal, A.C. 'United Kingdom' in *The Harmonization of Working Life and Family Life* (1995) 30 *Bulletin of Comparative Labour Relations* 105–22.

Neill, P., *The European Court of Justice: a case study in judicial activism* (London, European Policy Forum, 1995).

Nicol, D., 'Disapplying with relish? The Industrial Tribunals and Acts of Parliament' (1996) *Public Law* 579–89.

Nielsen, R. and Szyszczak, E., *The Social Dimension of the European Union*, 3rd edn (Copenhagen, Handelshøjskolens Forlag, 1997).

Ó Móráin, S., 'The European Employment Strategy—a Consideration of Social Partnership and Related Matters in the Irish Context' (2000) 16 *International Journal of Comparative Labour Law and Industrial Relations* 85–101.

O'Keeffe, D., 'Is the Spirit of Article 177 under Attack? Preliminary References and Admissibility' (1998) 23 *European Law Review* 509–36.

O'Leary, S., 'The Free Movement of Persons and Services' in Craig, P. and De Búrca, G. (eds), *The Evolution of EU Law* (Oxford, OUP, 1999) pp 377–416.

——, *The Evolving Concept of Community Citizenship: From the Free Movement of Persons to Union Citizenship* (London, Kluwer, 1996).

O'Loan, N., 'Acquired Rights and the Contracting Out of Services in the United Kingdom' (1993) 2 *Public Procurement Law Review* CS74–CS78.

O'Neill, M., 'Article 177 and Limits to the Right to Refer: an End to the Confusion' (1996) 2 *European Public Law* 375–91.

OECD, 'Employment Protection and Labour Market Performance' in *Employment Outlook*, 1999, OECD.

OECD, *Labour market flexibility*, 1986.

Palmer, C. and Wade, J., *Maternity and Parental Rights*, 2nd edn. (London, Legal Action Group, 2001).

Parkman, A.M., 'Why Are Married Women Working So Hard?' (1998) 18 *International Review of Law and Economics* 41–9.

Pennera, C., 'The Beginnings of the Court of Justice and its Role as a Driving Force in European Integration' (1995) 1 *Journal of European Integration History* 111–27.

Pepy, A., 'La rôle de la Cour de justice des Communautés européennes dans l'application de l'article 177 du traité de Rome' (1966) *Cahiers de droit européen* 459–89.

Pescatore, P., *References for Preliminary Rulings Under Article 177 of the EEC Treaty and Co-operation Between the Court and National Courts* (Luxembourg, 1985).

Plender, R. (ed), *European Courts: Practice and Precedents* (London, Sweet & Maxwell, 1997).

Poiares Maduro, M., 'Europe's Social Self: "The Sickness Unto Death"' in J. Shaw (ed), *Social Law and Policy in an Evolving European Union* (Oxford, Hart Publishing, 2000) pp 325–49.

——, *We, the Court. The European Court of Justice and the European Economic Constitution* (Oxford, Hart Publishing, 1998).

Prechal, S., 'Combatting Indirect Discrimination in Community Law Context' (1993) *Legal Issues of European Integration* 81–97.

Rasmussen, H., 'The European Court's Acte Clair Strategy in *C.I.L.F.I.T.*' (1984) 9 *European Law Review* 242–59.

Ress, G., 'Fact-finding at the European Court of Justice' in Lillich, R.B., *Fact-finding Before International Tribunals*, Eleventh Sokol Colloquium (Ardsley-on-Hudson, New York, Transnational Publishers Inc., 1992) pp 177–203.

Ricci, G., 'BECTU: an unlimited right to annual paid leave' (2001) 30 *Industrial Law Journal* 401–08.

Roberts, P., 'Current Developments' (1997) 19 *Journal of Social Welfare and Family Law* 87–104.

Robinson, D., 'Les rémunérations comparées des hommes et des femmes au niveau des professions' (1998) 137 *Revue internationale du Travail* 3–36.

Rodríguez Ortiz, F., 'Las políticas de la convergencia, el espacio social europeo y el empleo' (1998) 18 *Cuadernos Europeos de Deusto* 143–71.

Rodríguez-Piñero Royo, M.C., 'Transmisión de empresas y derecho europeo' in *La transmisión de empresas en Europa*, Collana di diritto comparato e comunitario del lavoro e della sicurezza sociale (Cacucci Editor, 1999).

Ryan, B., 'Pay, trade union rights and European Community law' (1997) *International Journal of Comparative Labour Law and Industrial Relations* 305–25.

Sadat Wexler, L., 'The Role of the European Court of Justice on the Way to European Union' in Lützeler, P.M. (ed), *Europe After Maastricht. American and European Perspectives* (Providence/Oxford, Bergahn Books, 1994).

Sarfati, H., 'Negotiating Trade-offs Between Jobs and Labour Market Flexibility in the European Union' (1998) *International Journal of Comparative Labour Law and Industrial Relations* 307–23.

Schepel, H., 'Reconstructing Constitutionalisation: Law and Politics in the European Court of Justice' (2000) 20 *Oxford Journal of Legal Studies* 457–68.

Schepel, H. and Wesseling, R., 'The Legal Community: Judges, Lawyers, Officials and Clerks in the Writing of Europe' (1997) 3 *European Law Journal* 165–88.

Schermers, H.G. *et al.* (eds), *Article 177 EEC: Problems and Experiences* (Amsterdam, North Holland, 1987).

Schermers, H.G. and Waelbroeck, D., *Judicial Protection in the European Communities*, 5th edn (Deventer, Kluwer, 1992).

Schmidt, M., 'The EC Directive on Parental Leave' (1998) 32 *Labour Law and Industrial Relations in the European Union. Bulletin of Comparative Labour Relations* 181–92.

Schulte, B., 'The Welfare State and European Integration' (1999) 1 *European Journal of Social Security* 7–61.

Sciarra, S. (ed), *Labour Law in the Courts: National Judges and the European Court of Justice* (Oxford, Hart Publishing, 2001).

——, 'Building on European Social Values: an Analysis of the Multiple Sources of European Social Law' in Snyder, F. (ed), *Constitutional Dimensions of European Economic Integration* (London, Kluwer Law International, 1996) pp 175–206.

——, 'The Employment Title in the Amsterdam Treaty. A Multi-language Legal Discourse' in O'Keeffe, D. and Twomey, P. (eds), *Legal Issues of the Amsterdam Treaty* (Oxford, Hart Publishing, 1999) pp 157–70.

——, *How 'Global' is Labour Law? The Perspective of Social Rights in the European Union*, EUI WP LAW No.96/6.

Senden, L., 'Positive Action in the European Union Put to the Test. A Negative Score?' (1996) 3 *Maastricht Journal of International and Comparative Law* 146–64.

Sevón, L., 'Languages in the Court of Justice of the European Communities' in *Scritti in onore di Giuseppe Federico Mancini. Diritto dell'Unione europea*, Vol. II (Milan, Giuffrè Editore, 1998) pp 933–50.

Shanks, M., 'Introductory Article: The Social Policy of the European Communities' (1977) 14 *Common Market Law Review* 375–83.

——, *European Social Policy, Today and Tomorrow* (Oxford, Pergamon, 1977).

Shaw, J., 'Gender and the Court of Justice' in G. De Búrca and J.H.H. Weiler (eds), *The European Court of Justice* (Oxford, OUP, 2001) pp 87–142, p 106.

——, *Social Law and Policy in an Evolving European Union* (Oxford, Hart Publishing, 2001).

——, 'European Union Legal Studies in Crisis? Towards a New Dynamic' (1996) 16 *Oxford Journal of Legal Studies* 231–53.

Shaw, J. and Hervey, T., 'Women, Work and Care: Women's Dual Role and Double Burden in EC Sex Equality Law' (1998) 8 *Journal of European Social Policy* 43–63.

Shaw, J. and More, G. (eds), *New Legal Dynamics of European Union* (Oxford, Clarendon Press, 1995).

Shrubsall, V., 'Competitive Tendering, Out-sourcing and the Acquired Rights Directive' (1998) 61 *Modern Law Review* 85–92.

Simitis, S., 'Dismantling or Strengthening Labour Law: The Case of the European Court of Justice' (1996) 2 *European Law Journal* 156–76.

Simitis, S. and Lyon-Caen, A., 'Community Labour Law: A Critical Introduction to its History' in Davies, P. *et al.* (eds), *European Community Labour Law. Principles and Perspectives. Liber Amicorum Lord Wedderburn* (Oxford, Clarendon Press, 1996) pp 1–22.

Simon, S., 'Discrimination on the Ground of Pregnancy: Chaos or Consistency from the ECJ?' (1999) 3 *The Edinburgh Law Review* 217–28.

Slaughter Burley, A.-M., 'New Directions in Legal Research on the European Community' (1993) 31 *Journal of Common Market Studies* 391–400.

Slaughter, A.-M., Stone Sweet, A. and Weiler, J.H.H. (eds), *The European Court and National Courts—Doctrine and Jurisprudence. Legal Change in its Social Context* (Oxford, Hart Publishing, 1998).

Slotboom, M., 'State Aid in Community Law: A Broad or Narrow Definition?' (1995) 20 *European Law Review* 289–301.

Sohrab, J.A., 'Women and Social Security: the Limits of EEC Equality Law' (1994) *Journal of Social Welfare and Family Law* 5–17.

——, *Women, Social Security and Financial Independence in EC Equality Law* (Dartmouth, 1996).

Somek, A. 'A Constitution for Anti-Discrimination: Exploring the Vanguard Moment of Community Law' (1999) 5 *European Law Journal* 243–71.

Stein, E., 'Lawyers, Judges and the Making of a Transnational Constitution' (1981) 75 *American Journal of International Law* 1–27.

Steiner, J., 'The Principle of Equal Treatment for Men and Women in Social Security' in Hervey, T. and O'Keeffe, D. (eds), *Sex Equality Law in the European Union* (Chichester, John Wiley & Sons Ltd, 1996) pp 111–36.

Stone Sweet, A., *Governing with Judges. Constitutional Politics in Europe* (Oxford, OUP, 2000).

Strasser, S.E., 'Evolution and Effort: Docket Control & Preliminary References in the European Court of Justice' (1995/6) 2 *Columbia Journal of European Law* 49–105.

Szyszczak, E., 'Community Law on Pregnancy and Maternity' in Hervey, T. and O'Keeffe, D. (eds), *Sex Equality Law in the European Union* (Chichester, John Wiley & Sons Ltd, 1996) pp 51–62.

——, 'Future Directions in European Union Social Policy Law' (1995) 24 *Industrial Law Journal* 19–32.

——, 'The Evolving European Employment Strategy' in Shaw (ed), *Social Law and Policy in an Evolving European Union*, pp 197–220;

——, 'The New Parameters of European Labour Law' in O'Keeffe, D. and Twomey, P. (eds), *Legal Issues of the Amsterdam Treaty* (Oxford, Hart Publishing, 1999) pp 141–55.

——, 'Pregnancy and Sex Discrimination' (1996) 21 *European Law Review* 79–82.

Teague, P., 'New Keynesianism and active labour market policies in Europe' in *Economic Citizenship in the European Union. Employment relations in the new Europe* (London and New York, Routledge, 1999).

Ter Kuile, B.H., 'To Refer or not to Refer: About the Last Paragraph of Article 177 of the EC Treaty' in Curtin, D. and Heukels, T. (eds), *Essays in Honour of H.G. Schermers* (Dordrecht, Martinus Nijhoff, 1994) pp 381–89.

Timmermans, C.W.A., 'Judicial Protection Against the Member States: Articles 169 and 177 Revisited' in Curtin, D. and Heukels, T. (eds), *Essays in Honour of H.G. Schermers* (Dordrecht, Martinus Nijhoff, 1994) pp 391–407.

Tobler, C., 'Encore: 'Women's Clauses' in public procurement under Community law' (2000) 25 *European Law Review* 618–31.

Townshend-Smith, R., 'Economic Defences to Equal Pay Claims' in Hervey, T. and O'Keeffe, D. (eds), *Sex Equality Law in the European Union* (Chichester, John Wiley & Sons Ltd, 1996) pp 35–48.

——, *Sex Discrimination in Employment* (London, Sweet & Maxwell, 1989).

Tridimas, T., 'The Court of Justice and Judicial Activism' (1996) 21 *European Law Review* 199–210.

——, 'The role of the Advocate General in the development of Community law: some reflections' (1997) 34 *Common Market Law Review* 1349–87.

Tucker, C., 'The Luxembourg Process: the UK View' (2000) 16 *International Journal of Comparative Labour Law and Industrial Relations* 71–83.

Upex, R., 'The Acquired Rights Directive and its effect upon consensual variation of employees' contracts' (1999) 24 *European Law Review* 293–99.

Van Gerven, W., 'The role and structure of the European judiciary now and in the future' (1996) 21 *European Law Review* 211–23.

Van Peijpe, T., 'Employment Protection in Industrialised Market Economies' in Blanpain, R. (ed), *Employment Protection under Strain, Bulletin of Comparative Labour Relations* 33–1998, pp 33–65.

Vandamme, F., 'Concentrations d'entreprises et protection des travailleurs' (1977) 13 *Cahiers de droit européen* pp 25–48.

Volcansek, M.L., *Judicial Politics in Europe. An Impact Analysis* (New York, Peter Lang Publishing Inc., 1986).

Von Prondzynski, F. and Kewley, A., 'Social Law in the European Union: The Search for a Philosophy' (1995/96) 2 *Columbia Journal of European Law* 265–75.

Von Prondzynski, F. and Richards, W., 'Equal Opportunities in the Labour Market: Tackling Indirect Sex Discrimination' (1995) 1 *European Public Law* 117–35.

Voss, R., 'The National Perception of the Court of First Instance and the European Court of Justice' (1993) 30 *Common Market Law Review* 1119–34.

Vousden, S., '*Albany*, Market Law and Social Exclusion' (2000) 29 *Industrial Law Journal* 181–91.

——, 'Gender, exclusion and governance by guideline' (1998) 20 *Journal of Social Welfare and Family Law* 468–79.

Waddington, L., 'Towards a Healthier and More Secure European Social Policy?' (1997) 4 *Maastricht Journal of European and Comparative Law* 83–100.

Weatherill, S., 'The common market: mission accomplished?' in Heiskanen, V. and Kulovesi, K. (eds), *Function and Future of European Law* (Helsinki, Publications of the University of Helsinki, 1999) pp 33–57.

Weiler, J.H.H., 'Journey to an Unknown Destination: A Retrospective and Prospective of the European Court of Justice in the Arena of Political Integration' (1993) 31 *Journal of Common Market Studies* 417–46.

——, 'The European Union Belongs to its Citizens: three modest proposals' (1997) 22 *European Law Review* 150–6.

——, 'The Function and Future of European Law' in Heiskanen, V. and Kulovesi, K. (eds), *Function and Future of European Law* (Helsinki, Publications of the Faculty of Law University of Helsinki, 1999) pp 9–22.

——, 'The Reformation of European Constitutionalism' (1997) 35 *Journal of Common Market Studies* 95–131.

Weiler, J.H.H. and Jacqué, J.P., 'On the Road to European Union—A New Judicial Architecture: An Agenda for the Intergovernmental Conference' (1990) 27 *Common Market Law Review* 187–207.

White, E., 'W(h)ither Social Policy?' in Shaw, J. and More, G. (eds), *New Legal Dynamics of European Union* (Oxford, OUP, 1996) pp 111–28.

Wilkinson, F., 'Equality, efficiency and economic progress: The case for universally applied equitable standards for wages and conditions of work' in Sengenberger, W. and Campbell, D. (eds), *Creating economic opportunities. The role of labour standards in industrial restructuring* (Geneva, International Institute for Labour Studies) pp 61–86.

Winch, F., 'Maternity Rights Provisions—A New Approach' (1981) *Journal of Social Welfare* 321–8.

Wincott, D., 'The Court of Justice and the European policy process' in Richardson, J.J. (ed), *European Union. Power and Policy-making* (London and New York, Routledge, 1996) pp 170–84.

Wintemute, R., 'When is Pregnancy Discrimination Indirect Sex Discrimination?' (1998) 27 *Industrial Law Journal* 23–36.

Wynn, M., 'Pregnancy Discrimination: Equality Protection or Reconciliation?' (1999) 62 *Modern Law Review* 435–47.

Index